CONFLICT
AND
UNITY

CONFLICT AND UNITY

An Introduction to Canadian Political Life

Second Edition

Roger Gibbins
Department of Political Science
University of Calgary

Nelson Canada

© Nelson Canada,
A Division of Thomson Canada Limited

Published in 1990 by
Nelson Canada
A Division of Thomson Canada Limited
1120 Birchmount Road
Scarborough, Ontario
M1K 5G4

Canadian Cataloguing in Publication Data

Gibbins, Roger 1947–
    Conflict and unity

2nd ed.
For use in schools.
ISBN 0-17-603486-2

1. Canada—Politics and government.   I. Title.

JL65   1990.G5   1990   320.971   C89-095118-7

Printed and bound in Canada
    2   3   4   5   6   7   WB   92 91

Contents

Acknowledgments

Len Norris cartoons reproduced by permission of the artist and *The Vancouver Sun*.

Roy Peterson cartoons reproduced by permission of the artist.

Excerpt from the *The Public Philosophy*. Copyright © 1955 by Walter Lippman. Copyright renewed © 1983 by Walter Lippman. By permission of Little, Brown and Company in association with the Atlantic Monthly Press.

"How Big is Big?" and "The Costs of Democracy" reprinted by permission of The Canadian Press.

"Mending Wall," from *The Poetry of Robert Frost*, edited by Edward Connery Lathem. Copyright 1930, 1939, © 1969 by Holt, Rinehart and Winston. Copyright © 1958 by Robert Frost. Copyright © 1967 by Lesley Frost Ballantine. Reprinted by permission of Holt, Rinehart and Winston, Publishers.

Excerpt from James Eayrs, "Sharing a Continent: The Hard Issues," p. 93, *The United States and Canada*, James Sloan Dickey, ed. Englewood Cliffs, N.J.: Prentice-Hall, 1964. Reprinted by permission of The American Assembly, Columbia University, New York.

"W.L.M.K." from *Collected Poems of F.R. Scott* reprinted by permission of McClelland and Stewart Ltd., The Canadian Publishers.

Duncan Macpherson cartoons reprinted with permission of the Toronto Star Syndicate.

Phil Mallette cartoon reproduced by permission of the artist.

Andy Donato cartoons reproduced by permission of Canada Wide/ Toronto Sun and Key Porter Books.

All material from Canadian government sources reproduced by permission of the Minister of Supply and Services Canada.

Vance Rodewalt cartoon reproduced by permission of the artist and *The Calgary Herald*.

Brian Gable cartoons reproduced by permission of the *Regina Leader Post*.

Preface

The first edition of *Conflict and Unity* was completed shortly after the Progressive Conservatives' landslide victory in the 1984 federal election. At that time, it seemed that Canada was about to enter a prolonged period of political stability. The Progressive Conservatives not only had a massive parliamentary majority in Ottawa, but also held office in eight of the ten provinces. The new Prime Minister, not coincidentally, was committed to a less confrontational style of federal-provincial relations, and given that the Constitution Act had only been in place for two and a half years, it looked as if Canadians would be spared further constitutional turmoil, at least in the intermediate run. Canadians had a national government in which *all* regions, including Quebec and the West, enjoyed effective representation. In the United States, Ronald Reagan had been elected to a second term, and no changes in Canadian-American relations were on the horizon. Thus it seemed an opportune time to map the Canadian political landscape, as the terrain, I thought, was unlikely to change.

It is now five—surprisingly tumultuous—years later. Canada has signed the Free Trade Agreement with the United States, the country is embroiled in an intense constitutional debate over the Meech Lake Accord, linguistic conflict is flaring up across the land, and five provincial governments have gone down to defeat. Admittedly, the federal Progressive Conservatives were re-elected in 1988, but in broader terms the political environment has been more fluid than I would ever have imagined in 1985. Certainly the international political environment has become fluid in the extreme as socialist regimes fall across the board in Eastern Europe, and as the Soviet Union throws off seventy years of communist dogma.

And yet, I would argue that the changes that we have seen over the past five years in Canadian political life support the original design of *Conflict and Unity*. The axes of Canadian political life around which the first edition was built remain firmly in place. Language politics remain front and centre, and retain the same capacity to excite emotional responses. Regional conflict has not disappeared, and if anything has intensified over the past five years. Canadian-American relations remain central to national political life as Canadians begin to read the entrails of the Free Trade Agreement, sorting out the winners and losers. In an important sense, then, while a lot has changed, the underlying political dynamics have remained the same.

The completion of the second edition of *Conflict and Unity* was made possible only through the assistance of many people, including my colleagues at the University of Calgary and writers across the country from whose works I drew in piecing together my own analysis. I would particularly like to thank David Ward and Mary Lynn Mulroney at Nelson Canada, Judi Powell and Valerie Snowdon in Calgary, and my family for once again putting up with the inevitable strain and preoccupations. I have many people to thank, but only myself to blame for any mistakes or inadequacies.

1

Setting The Stage

"The political game is a great one to play. It is exciting even to watch; it brings with it disappointments and frustrations, but there are compensations in the acquaintances it brings, in the friendships formed, and in the knowledge acquired of humanity, sometimes at its worst, more often at its best."
—Chubby Powers's memoirs, *A Party Politician*

This text provides an introduction to the complex and often tumultuous world of Canadian politics. Its focus is on what might be termed the *dynamics* of politics, the issues and conflicts that drive the political process. Woven into this analysis is a discussion of the institutional arenas within which political conflict takes place and the parties, leaders, and groups through which conflicting interests are mobilized.

It is useful to compare Canadian politics to Canada's national game of hockey. We can think of hockey as a set of rules for playing a game; as a network of professional and community arenas (not to forget backyard rinks and frozen prairie ponds); and as a vast army of referees, league officials, timekeepers, scorekeepers, coaches, parent helpers, skate-tiers, and rink-cleaners who make the game possible. On a different level, we can think of the Canadian political system in an analogous fashion. It encompasses a set of rules and procedures that govern elections, the legislative process, and the conduct of public officials. It comprises a network of political arenas including Parliament, provincial legislatures, federal–provincial conferences, town councils, school boards, and community associations. In addition, it is a multitude of federal, provincial, and municipal public servants who staff the bureaucratic infrastructure of government.

Hockey, however, is much more than rules, arenas, and officials. It embraces competing teams, stars and villains, traditional rivalries, the emotion of parents and fans, bodychecks, penalties, and questionable calls. While one must know the rules to understand the game, it is the action—the teams, emotion, and conflict—that brings the sport alive. In this text, particular emphasis will be placed on the issues and conflicts that energize political life. The institutional arenas and rules of the game will not be neglected, but will be introduced through a study of the broader game of politics.

Like hockey, politics is a great spectator sport. We read political news as we might read the sports pages, looking at the Gallup polls to determine the partisan point-spread and following political columnists as parties fire coaches, trade players, and combat dissension within their ranks. Yet politics is much more than a spectator sport, for the political process moulds our lives and shapes our futures. It is thus imperative that we become active players and not merely interested spectators. However, if we are to leave the sidelines, wade into the fray, and become players, we must first understand the game.

CONFLICT AND POLITICS

A study of politics is first and foremost a study of conflict. Political systems are systems of conflict management for dividing up the spoils of public life among competing individuals, groups, and interests. In the words made famous by Harold Lasswell, the study of politics is the study of who gets what, when, where, and how. In democratic political systems, however, conflict is largely contained within well-established institutional arenas. The scope and intensity of conflict are limited by a general respect for the rules of the game, and by an overarching set of values or political culture that most, though not all, participants share. Democratic systems are characterized by their capacity to manage conflict without recourse to violence. In the words of American essayist H.L. Mencken, "voting is simply a way of determining which side is the stronger without putting it to the test of fighting."[1]

It is the conflictual character of politics that makes the political world not only so fascinating but also so difficult to understand. For every event that takes place, citizens are bombarded by competing and contradictory explanations. The heroes and villains of the piece are very much a function of who is speaking, of the partisan lenses through which we see the political world, and of the ideological predispositions we bring to our analysis. Like beauty, much of the truth in politics lies in the eye of the beholder. It may be for this reason that the public school system conveys so little information about politics; educators choose to neglect political life rather than to send students and teachers into a partisan and ideological morass. Although at the college and university level we have no choice but to plunge into this morass, the discipline of political science fortunately provides a set of survival skills that makes the enterprise less risky, more fruitful, and considerably more enjoyable.

Observations on Political Life

Democratic politics has been the source of a good deal of sardonic commentary, as the following examples illustrate:

"Political language ... is designed to make lies sound truthful and murder respectable, and to give an appearance of solidarity to pure wind."
—George Orwell, *Politics and the English Language* (1950)

"Politics and the fate of mankind are shaped by men without ideals and without greatness. Men who have greatness within them don't go in for politics."

—Albert Camus, French author and philosopher

"[Democratic politicians] advance politically only as they placate, appease, bribe, seduce, bamboozle, or otherwise manage to manipulate the demanding and threatening elements in their constituencies. The decisive consideration is not whether the proposition is good but whether it is popular—not whether it will work well and prove itself but whether the active talking constituents like it immediately. Politicians rationalize this servitude by saying that in a democracy public men are the servants of the people."

—Walter Lippman, *The Public Philosophy*, p. 28

"Government runs on two things; patronage and the hope of patronage."

—George Ferguson, Ontario premier during the 1920s

"Now I know what a statesman is; he's a dead politician. We need more statesmen."

—Bob Edwards, *The Calgary Eye Opener*

"You must learn that there are times when a man in public life is compelled to rise above his principles."

—Arizona's Senator Ashurst

"In the trackless wastes of politics, men lose their purpose, and the stars by which they once steered vanish in the bottomless sky of other men's aspirations. They wander like nomads, from oasis to oasis, quenching their thirst from the wells of power and warming themselves by the abandoned fires of those who have come and gone before."

—Dalton Camp, *Gentlemen, Players and Politicians*

"Democracy substitutes election by the incompetent many for appointment by the corrupt few."

—George Bernard Shaw, British playwright.

The conflictual nature of politics contributes to, even if it does not wholly explain, one of the more intriguing democratic paradoxes. Canadians are generally proud to be living in a democratic country. Our system of government sets us apart from less fortunate countries in other parts of the world, and in the past tens of thousands of Canadian servicemen gave their lives in defence of democracy. Yet at the same time, "politics" is considered a very derogatory term in common usage. We have often heard of something being dismissed as "mere politics"; and terms like "office politics" and "political connections" are used to refer to the shady underside of life. (Robert Thompson, former leader of the national Social Credit party, even complained that Parliament was being turned into "a political arena"!) In novels, movies, and television programs politicians are the villains, thwarting the more honest endeavours of police officials, community groups, and private detectives. The paradox inherent in this contempt for politics is that it extends to those very elements—election campaigns, political parties, interest groups, office-seeking politicians, and voting itself—that make democratic government possible.[2]

Given widespread cynicism towards things political, it is important to stress that there is a positive side to political life. Throughout history people have banded together in political communities in order to achieve goals that they could not achieve alone. Whether those goals are a collective security from external foes or internal disorder, economic expansion, cultural enlightenment, or a sense of group identity and mission, which transcends and thus elevates the individual, political organization has provided an indispensable vehicle for their pursuit. It is because those things that transcend the individual are so integral to the human spirit that politics is so important. As Aristotle observed in the 4th century B.C., it is for this reason that man is a "political animal." Yet because conflict is also so intrinsic to human existence, we need means of conflict resolution which stop short of clubbing each other over the head. Well-functioning democratic political systems do not eliminate conflict but reduce its intensity and effects to a level compatible with a civil society.

Observations on Political Life

Not surprisingly, practising politicians have a more positive view of their art than that possessed by the man in the street. It is a view, moreover, that captures an important element of the political experience.

"... politics is the science which teaches the people of a country to care for each other. If a mischievous individual were to attempt to cut off his neighbour's hand, would that neighbour's other hand and feet do well quietly to permit the amputation of the limb if they could hinder it? All will say, No. This then is politics. That part of our duty which teaches us to study the welfare of our whole country, and not to rest satisfied altho' our own household is well off when our neighbours are in difficulty and danger. The honest politician is he who gives all he can of his time and means to promote the public good, whose charity begins at home *but does not end there*. The man who says he is no politician, is either ignorant of what he is saying, or a contemptible selfish creature, unworthy of the country or community of which he is a part."

—William Lyon Mackenzie, *The Colonial Advocate*, June 27, 1833

"I am asked—and I am speaking to Young Canada now—are there any rewards in public life? There are—not monetary, but there is a tremendous satisfaction in being able to say, 'I tried, I stood.' "

—John G. Diefenbaker, 1967

"The political game is a great one to play. It is exciting even to watch; it brings with it disappointments and frustrations, but there are compensations in the

acquaintances it brings, in the friendships formed, and in the knowledge acquired of humanity, sometimes at its worst, more often at its best."
—Chubby Powers' memoirs, *A Party Politician*

It should also be stressed that conflict is not necessarily bad. As former Prime Minister Pierre Trudeau has urged, we should keep our differences; "creative tension, after all, gives society its very life and growth."[3] Thus, to describe the Canadian political system as conflictual is to recognize the human side of politics.

There are a number of important questions about political conflict that merit consideration. Is our political system reasonably effective in handling the sources of conflict with which it must contend, or are there features of the political system which exacerbate rather than moderate conflict? Are there some forms of conflict that the system handles well, and others that it handles poorly or even creates? Have we become so preoccupied with certain conflicts that other important issues are pushed from the political agenda? Is the level of conflict so high that collective goals, including national unity and our survival as an independent country on the North American continent, are imperilled?

Underlying such questions is a concern for the integrative capacity of the Canadian political system—its capacity to knit together often disparate regional and linguistic communities into a national whole. The conclusion advanced in the chapters that follow is generally positive. Although the Canadian political system has been confronted with an array of very difficult problems, the national community has endured and prospered. Perhaps of even greater importance, it has done so while maintaining the strength and vitality of sub-national linguistic and regional communities.

THE CANADIAN CONFLICT AGENDA

If you were to take a copy of a major Canadian newspaper and list all the political disputes and issues raised within its pages, the list would be formidable even if you excluded those occurring outside Canada. It is the sheer volume of political information and the complexity of so many issues that make the study of politics so daunting to students. How can one hope to make sense out of a political world that is so complex, and often so unfettered by logic or rationality? One answer is to go to, if not "back to," the basics, to address a relatively small handful of issues forming the bedrock of Canadian political life. In so doing, of course, many exciting and some important issues will be neglected. The pedagogical premise of this text, however, is that the "big issues" provide the

"What is in behind the little curtains . . . just in case anyone should ask me?"

Len Norris, *9th Annual.* Originally published in *The Vancouver Sun*, December 9, 1959.

essential backdrop against which one can place the welter of other issues forming the daily grist of politics.

What, then, are the big issues, the threads which must be followed if one is to untangle the Gordian knot of Canadian national politics? To a degree, the selection of any set of issues will be contentious and idiosyncratic; both writers and readers will differ as to what issues should be included. I would argue, however, that the four pursued in this text— language politics, regionalism, Canadian–American relations, and constitutional politics—are fundamentally important to the Canadian political experience. While their relative importance can be debated, and while a case can undoubtedly be made for a more expansive set of issues, these four are essential to an understanding of Canadian political life. All share deep historical roots, and none is likely to slip from the nation's political agenda in the near future. Moreover, the four in combination provide a useful setting within which a much wider array of institutional and constitutional matters can be addressed.

The format of the text follows directly from the selection of these central issues. Chapter 2 provides a historical backdrop by looking at the confederation agreement and at the early emergence of the major axes of Canadian political life. The four issues are then examined sequentially in

Chapters 3 through 6. Chapter 7 looks at the Canadian party system and the extent to which it has been shaped by and reflects the principal lines of cleavage that have been identified. The concluding chapter is followed by brief appendices covering the legislative process, the Government of Canada, the 1982 Constitution Act, excerpts from the 1867 Constitution Act, the 1987 Constitution Amendment (Meech Lake Accord), and some pointers on how to write a term paper. A glossary provides brief definitions for the more technical terms used in the text, with glossary entries in bold print when first encountered in the text. Each chapter provides study questions and suggested readings. The latter, it should be stressed, provide some modest acknowledgment of the parasitical nature of textbooks. A good text builds upon, and to a degree pillages, the wealth of facts, theories, and insights put together over time with great effort by the academic community. I am thus deeply indebted to my colleagues whose research cleared the land and broke the soil; this text is far more the fruit of their labours than my own.

By the time you reach the final chapter, there is little doubt that many questions will remain unanswered. For this I make no apologies; my hope is that your appetite for things political will have been whetted, not satiated. This text can do no more than create a portal upon the rich and fascinating vista of Canadian political life. As a student of politics, you must demand more. As a citizen, you must be prepared to use your increased understanding as a bridge to active political participation. Not to participate in the political process is to abandon your fate to those who do, people who may not share your goals, ambitions, and dreams. As Plato warned in *The Republic*, "the punishment which the wise suffer, who refuse to take part in the government, is to live under the government of worse men."

SUGGESTED READINGS

For an excellent overview of postwar Canadian politics, see Robert Bothwell, Ian Drummond, and John English, *Canada Since 1945: Power, Politics, and Provincialism* (Toronto: University of Toronto Press, 1981).

For a more general historical overview, see J.L. Granatstein, Irving M. Abella, David J. Bercuson, R. Craig Brown, and H. Blair Neatby, *Twentieth Century Canada* (Toronto: McGraw-Hill Ryerson, 1983).

NOTES

1. *Minority Report*, 1956. Cited in Jonathon Green, *The Book of Political Quotes* (New York: McGraw-Hill, 1982), p. 213.

2. In a 1979 survey of 840 students attending ten Ontario universities, respondents were given a list of thirty occupations and, for each, were asked if they contributed a great deal to the general good of society, whether they contributed more good than harm, or more harm than good. Overall, politicians ranked 24th, coming ahead of corporate executives, bank presidents, oil company presidents, public relations experts, advertising executives and bill collectors, but behind military generals, plumbers, musicians, actors, sports stars, lawyers, union leaders and even professors! Only 4 percent of the students felt that politicians contributed a great deal to the general good of society; another 4 percent felt that they contributed more good than harm while 92 percent felt they contributed more harm than good. *Saturday Night*, October 1979, pp. 35-40.

3. Speech to the Confederation Dinner, Toronto, October 27, 1982.

2

In the Beginning . . .

The objective of this text is to introduce the reader to contemporary Canadian politics. Why, then, you might ask, do we begin in the distant past? Why is it important to delve into the pre-confederation politics of the 1850s and 1860s, to dust off the Constitution Act of 1867?

Here it should be recognized that Canadians tend to be a very ahistorical people believing, as one of my students wrote, that "Canada has very little history." Our reluctance to grapple with the past goes beyond the widely shared delusion that we are a new country—we are in fact one of the oldest countries in the world—to embrace two common assumptions. The first is that the past has little relevance for what is happening today. The second is that Canadian history is boring, lacking the clash of armies and the fiery rhetoric of revolution. Neither assumption can withstand serious examination. One has only to look at the slogan *je me souviens* on Quebec licence plates to realize not only the relevance of the past but also the way in which history is woven into the texture of contemporary political life. In some cases, the weaving is done with deliberate intent to shade our appreciation of current events, to alter our perception of the political landscape. Thus our views of Canada, and of our province and its place in the national fabric, are in part historical artifacts that should be carefully inspected.

For those interested in contemporary Canadian politics, the past provides a useful guide, highlighting important landmarks and identifying the winners and losers in political combat. As Canadian historian Donald Creighton has written:

> The waves behind the vessel which is carrying humanity forward into the unknown . . . can teach us where the winds of change are blowing and on what course the chief currents of our age are set. They can reveal to us the main direction of our voyage through time.[1]

For the political scientist, the currents rather than the details of the past are of particular importance, for they provide a clarity of perspective that is difficult to find amidst the complexities of contemporary events. They allow us to identify the harmonies and conflicts which have shaped and continue to shape Canadian political life. If, as Creighton has written, there are no "tragic finalities" in Canadian politics but "only the endless repetitions of the same themes,"[2] then it is important to have some appreciation of the historical setting from which those themes have emerged.

The reader who is prepared to go beyond the brief synopsis of this chapter to a deeper exploration of the confederation era will find that Canadian political history is far from colourless. In Sir John A. Macdonald, the chief architect of Confederation and Canada's first prime minister, one finds a fascinating mix of political brilliance, statesmanship, chicanery, human frailty, and personal charm. Even if the personalities of the day are put aside, the confederation era presents an intriguing tangle of political conflict and opportunity. The way in which that tangle was addressed by the fathers of confederation provides as good an introduction to political craftsmanship and applied political science as one is likely to encounter.

The Wit and Wisdom of Sir John A. Macdonald

There is no better advice for the after-dinner speaker in search of a humorous opening, or the student in search of some adornment for a term paper, than to rummage through the sayings of Sir John A. Macdonald. *Colombo's Canadian Quotations* (Edmonton: Hurtig, 1974) offers the following gems:

- "The task of the politician is to climb the tree and shake down acorns for the pigs below."
- In an exchange with Senator A.R. Dickey, who had promised to support Macdonald whenever he thought Macdonald was right, Macdonald replied: "That is no satisfaction. Anybody may support me when I am right. What I want is a man who will support me when I am wrong."
- "Given a Government with a big surplus, and a big majority and a weak Opposition, you could debauch a committee of Archangels."
- "I will have no accord with the desire expressed in some quarters by any mode whatever that there should be an attempt made to oppress the one language or to render it inferior to the other; I believe that would be impossible if it were tried, and it would be foolish and wicked if it were possible."
- "As for myself, my course is clear. A British subject I was born. A British subject I will die."
- "Let us be English or let us be French, but above all let us be Canadians."
- "Would you move away please, your breath smells terrible . . . it smells like water."

The politicians who drafted the confederation agreement and, in so doing, laid the foundations for the modern Canadian state, faced a formidable task. At the very least they had to accomplish the following objectives:

- They had to dissolve the 1840 marriage between Canada East (now Quebec) and Canada West (now Ontario) while at the same time

Confederation was first proposed in 1858 by John A. Macdonald, left, and George-Etienne Cartier, one of the most famous teams of political leaders in Canada—Macdonald from Canada West and Cartier from Canada East.

Archives of Ontario.

reuniting the two in a larger political community. Thus the instrument of divorce had also to be the instrument of reconciliation.

• They had to hold at bay an American military threat and the threat of American territorial expansion in the West.

• They had to meet the demand from Canada West for representation by population while meeting the demand from Canada East that "rep by pop," and through it the domination of the Catholic francophone minority by the Protestant anglophone majority, not be imposed.

• While recognizing a strong commitment to local autonomy in the existing British North American colonies, they had to create a strong central government that would be able to take over colonial debt and attract the financing required for railway construction.

- They had to entice the Maritime colonies into a transcontinental union centred far from the Atlantic coast, a union in which Maritimers would, at best, play a supporting role.

Quite remarkably, the fathers of confederation were successful, and for this reason alone the confederation agreement warrants our attention as a fine example of political craftsmanship. We also find in the agreement the emergence in elementary form of what have become perennial features of Canadian political life: the tensions between anglophones and francophones, between the centre and the periphery, between Canada and the United States, between the provincial and federal governments, and between parliamentary institutions and federal principles. In short, for those readers trying to understand Canadian politics today, Confederation is a good place to start.

FACTORS LEADING TO CONFEDERATION

The road to Confederation can only be summarized here, with a more detailed account being left to the historians.[3] Our discussion focuses upon four factors commonly acknowledged to have played key roles in bringing about the confederation agreement: political stalemate in the Canadas, a two-pronged threat from the United States, economic imperatives and, for lack of a better phrase, what might be termed the "national dream."

Political Stalemate in the Canadas

The 1760 conquest of Quebec by British forces set in motion a complex colonial interplay between the French and English communities in British North America. In 1774 the British Parliament passed the Quebec Act, which provided protection for the French language, French institutions, and the French civil law in what had become *British* North America. Beyond recognizing what has been termed "the French fact," the Act also extended the boundaries of the Quebec colony westward to the Great Lakes. Then, in the face of growing English settlement around the Great Lakes, Parliament passed the Constitutional Act of 1791 which divided Quebec into Upper Canada—now Ontario—and Lower Canada—now Quebec. The 1791 Act also provided for elected assemblies in each colony but not for responsible government; the appointed political executive could not be turned out of office by a majority vote of the legislative assembly. Thus by 1791 the French-speaking inhabitants of British North America had received legislative recognition of their language and institutions along with an elected assembly in which they exercised majority control.

In 1837 political unrest in both Upper and Lower Canada led to an investigation of the colonial situation by Lord Durham. In his *Report on the Affairs of British North America*, Durham made his famous observation on Canadian political life:

> I expected to find a contest between a government and a people: I found two nations warring in the bosom of a single state: I found a struggle, not of principles, but of races. . . .

Lord Durham's solution was straightforward; the French Canadians should be assimilated into what was then a smaller English Canadian community. It was a solution reflecting not only Durham's commitment to Liberal principles,[4] but also his harsh assessment of French Canadians:

> There can hardly be conceived a nationality more destitute of all that can invigorate and elevate a people, than that which is exhibited by the descendants of the French in Lower Canada, owing to their retaining their peculiar language and manners. They are a people with no history, and no literature.

Durham's solution abandoned the political accommodation that had been put in place following the conquest of New France, an accommodation in which British colonial control and economic dominance co-existed in Lower Canada with the French language and the social dominance of the Catholic church.

In partial response to the political unrest of 1837, Durham recommended that responsible government be implemented, that the executive's term of office be contingent upon continued majority support in the elected assembly. However, in order to ensure that responsible government did not fall under the control of French Canadian nationalists, that it was not bounded by racial-linguistic identifications, and in order to promote the assimilation of French Canadians, Durham also recommended the colonial union of Upper and Lower Canada. This second recommendation was carried out through the 1840 Act of Union, which combined Upper and Lower Canada into a single British colony, the Province of Canada, with a single elected assembly. The Act further promoted the assimilation of French Canadians by making English the only official language of the new legislative assembly, and by giving Canada East and Canada West, as Lower Canada and Upper Canada were now called, equal representation in that assembly even though only 432,000 people lived in Canada West compared to 717,000 in Canada East. Here it should be noted that although the population of Canada East included a significant number of English Canadians, the French Canadian population alone in Canada East exceeded the total population of Canada West.

Had the assimilationist objectives of the Act been achieved, Canada today would be a unilingual state with a fully assimilated French Canadian minority. In fact, they were not achieved. Acting as a bloc on matters of religion and language, French Canadians were able to protect their interests within the new legislative arena. French was re-instated as a language of legislative debate following the 1842 speech in French by Louis-Hippolyte Lafontaine. When faced with the demand that he speak in English, Lafontaine replied:

> I am asked to pronounce in another language than my mother tongue the first speech that I have to make in this House. I distrust my ability to speak English. But I must inform the honourable members that even if my knowledge of English were as intimate as my knowledge of French, I should nevertheless make my first speech in the language of my French Canadian compatriots, if only to protest against the cruel injustice of the Union Act in trying to proscribe the mother tongue of half the population of Canada. I owe it to my compatriots; I owe it to myself.[5]

Thereafter, French was used in the House, although it was not made an official language of parliamentary debate and record until 1848.

Even though the two colonies had been formally merged into a single unit, in practice a form of linguistic and political duality emerged which foreshadowed the introduction of federalism in 1867. Indeed, as J.M.S. Careless argues, the continued existence of two Canadas, East and West, " . . . destroyed Durham's very idea of a complete blending of the two peoples."[6] Governmental coalitions were headed by leaders from both Canada East and Canada West, with the team of George-Etienne Cartier and John A. Macdonald being the most famous. Legislation impinging upon linguistic or cultural interests required a double majority—a majority among members from both Canadas—to pass. The administration of the colony was carried out on a dual basis, with separate ministries for Canada West and Canada East. Macdonald, for example, served as Attorney General for Canada West, and not for the colony as a whole.

Practical as these adaptations were, the colonial marriage of the two Canadas proved to be unworkable, or workable only within an atmosphere marked by cultural polarization, governmental instability, and a growing pettiness in public life. The introduction of responsible government in 1848 did little to improve the situation. Deadlock rather than accommodation set the tone of legislative politics, with eighteen different ministries holding office between 1841 and 1867. Double majorities were increasingly difficult to find as the linguistic and religious division between the two Canadas came to be further reinforced by economic rivalry between the transportation, banking, and manufacturing interests of Montreal (supported to a degree by Toronto, Kingston, Hamilton, and

London) and the agrarian interests of western Ontario championed with such force by George Brown, editor of *The Toronto Globe*.

Of all the factors eroding the Act of Union, the most important was the shifting demographic balance between Canada East and Canada West. By 1851 Canada East no longer had the larger population; approximately 952,000 people lived in Canada West compared to 890,000 in Canada East. By 1861 the imbalance was even greater; 1,396,000 lived in Canada West compared to 1,112,000 in Canada East. Not unreasonably, Canada West became increasingly restive with the equal representation embedded in the Act of Union. Agitation grew for the introduction of representation by population in order to give Canada West the legislative clout that its numbers seemed to warrant. In 1861, for example, George Brown wrote the following editorial in *The Toronto Globe*:

> THE GLOBE is the unflinching advocate of REPRESENTATION BY POPULA-TION. By the present iniquitous system, Lower Canada sends the same number of Representatives to Parliament as Upper Canada, although Upper Canada has THREE HUNDRED THOUSAND SOULS more than Lower Canada, and contributes SEVEN DOLLARS to the general revenue for every THREE DOLLARS contributed by Lower Canada. By this system of injustice and the unanimity with which the French Canadians act together, the Representatives of the Lower Section not only administer the affairs of their own Province, but control those of Upper Canada as well.[7]

Just as reasonably, the French Canadians rejected representation by population. Stuck with the equal representation of the two Canadas despite their majority in 1841, they were quite happy to be stuck with it even when Canada East no longer had the majority.

While the failure of the Act of Union was clearly apparent by the late 1850s, proposals for reform foundered on the issue of representation by population. Stalemated within the colony, Canadian politicians began to seek an escape through territorial expansion which would make possible a more workable federal structure than could be attained with only two provinces.[8] Such expansion was indeed to provide the solution, but only in the wake of civil war in the United States and growing economic distress north of the American border.

The American Threat

Throughout its history, Canada has been buffeted by events in the United States. Indeed, the landmarks of early American history such as the revolution of 1776, the War of 1812, and the Civil War were also landmarks in Canadian history, with the Civil War providing a major impetus for Confederation.

When the American Civil War broke out in 1861, Canadian attitudes could best be described as anti-northern and anti-southern.[9] If anything, the former prevailed, not because Canadians sided with the South on the slavery issue, which they did not, but because the secession of the South would break up a growing American hegemony on the North American continent. When General Lee surrendered the Confederate forces in 1865, Canadian hopes for some future balance of strength on the continent were also lost. In the meantime, Canada had come to be seen in the victorious northern states, where Britain's support of the South during the war had soured perceptions of the British North American colonies, as decidedly pro-southern and anti-northern. Also, in 1864 a small Confederate raiding party had crossed the border from the Canadian side and robbed the bank in St. Albans, Vermont. When the raiders fled back into Canada, they were only briefly detained before being released with the bank's money. It was an admittedly minor event, but one which the North had by no means forgotten when the war ended a year later.

Canadian–American tensions at the end of the Civil War were heightened on the Canadian side by the Fenian threat. The Fenians were Irish–American veterans of the Civil War who sought to free their native Ireland from British rule. As the Atlantic Ocean prevented any direct Fenian intervention in Ireland, an attack on the British presence in Canada was considered. As the *Song of the Fenian Brotherhood* proclaimed:

> We are the Fenian Brotherhood, skilled in the art of war, And we're going to fight for Ireland, the land that we adore. Many battles have we won along with the boys in blue, And we'll go and capture Canada, for we've nothing else to do.[10]

In retrospect, the Fenians had a comic opera character that belied the very serious threat perceived by Canadians at the time. An anticipated Fenian invasion on St. Patrick's day, 1866, led to the mobilization of 10,000 volunteers for the defence of Canada. A month later 1,500 Fenians did cross the border, to be repulsed in a brief battle in which nine Canadians were killed. The Fenians, it should be stressed, constituted only the tip of a threatening iceberg—the largest army in the world was being demobilized in the American North, releasing thousands of trained soldiers who quite literally might have nothing else to do than "go and capture Canada."

The American military threat was exacerbated by British indifference. It had always been assumed in Canada that any Canadian war with the United States would be an offshoot of a larger British–American conflict, and hence Britain would come to Canada's defence. In the wake of the Civil War, however, a purely North American conflict seemed all too possible. For its part, the British government was more concerned with reducing the financial burden of colonial defence and resuming war-disrupted trading relations with the United States than with the defence of Canada. As Benjamin Disraeli, Chancellor of the Exchequer, wrote to the British Prime Minister, Lord Derby, in 1866:

> It can never be our pretense or our policy to defend the Canadian frontier against the United States. . . . what is the use of these colonial deadweights which we do not govern?

If the British North American colonies were to defend themselves, they had little alternative but to band together in defence of a common foe. External threat has played a significant role in the formation of most of the world's federal unions,[11] and Canada was no exception.

As things turned out, the American military threat did not materialize. However, the resumption of American westward expansion across the continent following the end of the Civil War posed an equally serious threat to Canadian interests. The creation of new American states had been checked by political deadlock over whether they would be slave-holding or free states, with neither the North nor the South prepared to accept any increase in the ranks of the other side.[12] With the slavery issue settled by the Civil War, unbridled western expansion began to threaten the unoccupied prairie land lying to the north of the forty-ninth parallel. If American settlement were to pre-empt Canadian settlement on the prairies, Canadians would be boxed into the small northeastern corner of the continent, and their absorption into the United States would be only a matter of time.

Finally, it should be noted that quite apart from the specific threats of the Fenians, demobilization, and westward expansion, a more general fear of the United States lay behind Confederation. As S.F. Wise and Robert Craig Brown conclude, " . . . it is not too much to say that the large measure of agreement among provincial leaders on the nature of and dangers from political *Americanism* constituted one of the unifying intellectual forces in the Confederation movement."[13]

Economic Imperatives

In the 1840s British economic policy swung towards international free trade and away from the preferential imperial tariffs which had been designed to promote trade between Britain and her colonial possessions. On the positive side, the British liberalization of trade encouraged the establishment of responsible government in British North America. As J.M.S. Careless explains, " . . . now that the Old Colonial System was being abandoned, now that trade was freed and the colonies' economic life was not to be controlled, there seemed little reason to control their political life either."[14] Responsible government came to Nova Scotia and the Province of Canada in 1848, to Prince Edward Island in 1851, to New

Brunswick in 1854, and Newfoundland in 1855. On the negative side, the British abandonment of "imperial preferences" was a serious, almost devastating, economic blow. The repeal of the Corn Laws in 1846 ended a privileged British market for Canadian flour and grain, and preferential treatment for Canadian timber also ended. In 1849 economic conditions were so bad in Montreal that over 1,000 merchants signed a manifesto urging annexation to the United States. In related riots, the Quebec parliament buildings were burned and the British Governor of the colony was pelted with stones.

In order to replace lost British markets, Canadians sought reciprocal tariff reductions with the United States. Although Americans were initially cool to the idea, representations by the British government eventually brought them round to the Canadian side. The New England states were particularly enticed by the promised access to the entire North American fisheries.[15] The southern states were persuaded by the British Colonial Secretary, Lord Elgin, that rather than bringing about the annexation of Canada and thus upsetting the delicate free state/slave state balance, reciprocity would be the one thing that would allow the British North American colonies to resist the siren call of annexation. The eventual outcome was the 1854 Reciprocity Treaty which significantly increased north-south trade and revitalized the Canadian economy.

While the Reciprocity Treaty cushioned the young Canadian economy from the British drift towards free trade, it also made the Canadian economy more vulnerable than it had been to events in the United States. With the outbreak of the Civil War in 1861 and the character of Canadian sympathies in that war, the prospects for the Treaty's survival looked bleak. As a consequence, the expected economic impact of the Treaty's termination became a major consideration in the discussions leading towards Confederation. Almost wholly dependent upon trade with Britain and the United States, yet facing a hostile political climate in both countries, the British North American colonies were caught between a rock and a hard place. The creation, through Confederation, of a free trade zone on the northern half of the continent offered the only prospect of economic relief. When the Reciprocity Treaty was cancelled in 1866, the new Canadian economic community was largely in place.

Economic factors played a particularly important role in the Maritime colonies, where they helped offset popular opposition to Confederation. By opening up a lucrative trade with the United States, the Reciprocity Treaty had launched the golden age of "iron men and wooden ships" in the Maritimes, an age in which the colonies were oriented towards the sea, Britain, New England, and the West Indies. As G.A. Rawlyk and Doug Brown explain, "it is difficult to imagine a people less concerned in their enterprise or vision with the interior of North America than were the Maritimers at the mid-way point in the nineteenth century."[16] However, with the looming loss of reciprocity, the onset of technological change that was making wooden ships (if not iron men) obsolete, escalating debts associated with extensive railway construction, and the ever growing importance of a rail-fed continental economy, Confederation became an increasingly attractive economic, if not emotional, enterprise.

Maritime Opposition to Confederation

In 1865 the pro-Confederation Tilley government in New Brunswick fought an election on the issue of Confederation, and was soundly defeated. This lesson was not lost on the pro-Confederation government in Nova Scotia, which avoided any electoral confrontation until Confederation was a fait accompli. When provincial and federal elections were held in Nova Scotia during the fall of 1867, pro-Confederation candidates went down to massive defeat; anti-confederates captured 36 of the 38 provincial seats and 18 of the 19 federal seats. Yet while Confederation was far from popular, to many it seemed an economic necessity.

For many French Canadians, Confederation promised the economic growth which was essential if emigration from Quebec into the New England states was to be stemmed.[17] More generally, Confederation provided the political foundation for a dynamic and expansionist capitalist state. Intrinsic to this vision was the construction of new railways that would connect the Maritimes to the continental economy, open up new markets for central Canadian manufacturers, and fend off the northward expansion of Americans in the West. Confederation would also enable existing railway debts to be taken over by the new central government; W.T. Easterbrook and Hugh Aitken go so far as to argue that the assumption of railway debts by the central government was "a prerequisite for the formation of the dominion."[18] Thus as Eric Nicol and Peter Whalley note in their irreverent history, "in Canada as in no other country the ties that bind are five feet long and creosoted."[19] More important is Pierre Berton's reminder, in the title of his history of the CPR, that the railways were part and parcel of a more encompassing "national dream."[20]

The National Dream

It is easy to emphasize the negative in a discussion of Confederation, to conclude that Confederation came about because of external threat from the United States and anti-colonial sentiment in Great Britain; that English and French Canadians could not work together within a single colonial government; that the economy was distressed; and that no one was willing or able to shoulder the debts associated with railway construction. This negative tone figures prominently in the writings of Canadian political scientists and historians. French Canadian historian Jean-Charles Bonenfant, for example, writes:

> Confederation was achieved because English Canadians had to exist with French Canadians, and the latter could not then become independent. The great majority of nations have been formed, not by people who desired intensely to live together, but rather by people who could not live separately.[21]

Bonenfant's sentiment is echoed in historian Arthur Lower's now-famous comment on Confederation:

> Some peoples are born nations, some achieve nationhood and others have nationhood thrust upon them. Canadians seem to be among these latter.[22]

This tone is very different from that associated with the founding of the United States. It also places insufficient emphasis on the positive appeal of Confederation, on the "national dream" of a new transcontinental state stretching from sea to sea—*a mari usque ad mare*—across the northern half of the continent. Thomas D'Arcy McGee, who was particularly concerned with American expansion, gave expression to the national dream in the 1860 speech to the House of Assembly in Quebec City:

> I see in the not remote distance, one great nationality bound, like the shield of Achilles, by the blue rim of ocean—I see it quartered into many communities—each disposing of its internal affairs—but all bound together by free institutions, free intercourse, and free commerce; . . . I see a generation of industrious, contented, moral men, free in name and in fact, men capable of maintaining, in peace and in war, a constitution worthy of such a country.

It was a bold vision, given that the British North American colonies had just over 3,000,000 people and that the much larger nation to the South was pursuing its self-proclaimed manifest destiny of continental expansion.

Admittedly, the territorial expansion embodied in the national dream was championed primarily by the banking, transportation, and manufacturing interests of central Canada which stood to gain most from the creation of new hinterlands to the east and west, and which sought a firmer governmental base to support the massive debt engendered by territorial expansion. There was, however, a grander vision than commercial exploitation, a vision bordering on imperialism. Note, for example, an editorial on western expansion which appeared in *The Toronto Globe* on January 22, 1863:

> If Canada acquires this territory, it will rise in a few years from a position of a small and weak province to be the greatest colony any country has ever possessed, able to take its place among the empires of the earth. The wealth

of 400,000 square miles of territory will flow through our waters and be gathered by our merchants, manufacturers and agriculturalists. Our sons will occupy the chief places of this vast territory, we will form its institutions, supply its rulers, teach its schools, fill its stores, run its mills, navigate its streams. Every article of European manufacture, every pound of tropical produce will pass through our stores. Our seminaries of learning will be filled by its people. Our cities will be the centres of its business and education, its wealth and refinement. It will afford fields of enterprise for our youth....

While it may be difficult from our contemporary perspective to see Canadians as imperialists, the sentiment captured above played an important role in forging the Canadian state.

Those who sought to build a new transcontinental nation had to face some harsh practical realities. Across the British North American colonies, there was a strong parochial attachment to local autonomy. In the Maritimes, where Prince Edward Island struggled to avoid the clutches of "imperialistic" Nova Scotia, there was little enthusiasm for being swallowed by the new Canadian whale. For Catholic francophones in Canada East, cultural autonomy from the Canadian Protestant (and anglophone) majority was an essential condition for entry into Confederation. In Canada West "local control of local affairs"—or freeing the Protestant majority from the shackles imposed by the Act of Union—was a longstanding plank of the Liberal-Reform movement. The trick, then, was to maintain or, in the case of Canada East and West, enhance local autonomy while at the same time creating a new national government strong enough to deal with the awesome tasks of territorial expansion and defence, to create a new Canadian nationality without submerging any of the constituent cultural or regional parts. The solution was found in the marriage of British parliamentary institutions to the American innovation of federalism.

THE CONSTITUTION ACT OF 1867

On July 1, 1867, the British North America Act—now the Constitution Act, 1867—was proclaimed and the embryonic Canadian state came into being. While at the time it encompassed only Nova Scotia, New Brunswick, and the southern portions of what are now Quebec and Ontario, the Constitution Act established the basic constitutional framework for the larger Canadian state that was to come. As new territories and provinces were added, that framework remained intact. Indeed, it continues to provide the basic constitutional skeleton for the Canadian federal state, although that skeleton has been augmented by the Constitution Act of 1982, which brought into play the Charter of Rights and Freedoms, an amending formula for the constitution, and the constitutional recognition

Convention at Charlottetown, Prince Edward Island, to consider the union of the British North American Colonies, 1864. (John A. Macdonald seated, centre of photograph.)

Public Archives Canada/C733.

of aboriginal peoples. Paradoxically, however, to understand the 1867 Act it is best to begin with what it was not.

What Did *Not* Happen in 1867

The 1867 Constitution Act did not emerge suddenly as a dramatic or revolutionary document, but rather through an extended series of inter-colonial negotiations. The confederation proposal was first broached in 1858 by the Macdonald-Cartier administration in the hope that a broader community would end the Union government's political impasse. When its major opponent, George Brown, endorsed the proposal in 1864, Canadian politicians sought an opportunity to present it to the Maritime colonies. The opportunity came that year when the Nova Scotia legislature called for a conference to discuss Maritime union. When the governments of New Brunswick, Nova Scotia, and Prince Edward Island agreed to meet in Charlottetown in early September, the coalition government in Canada asked to send a delegation. Through the leadership of John A. Macdonald, the Canadian delegation was able to have discussion of a Maritime union shelved in favour of debate on the Canadian proposal for a broader union. After ten days of talks, the delegates agreed to continue the following month in Quebec City. From the Quebec conference emerged a series of resolutions which were to form the core of the Constitution Act. Following approval of the Quebec resolutions by the governments of Nova Scotia, New Brunswick, and Canada, a final conference was held in London in December 1866, to work out the details of the new legislation with the British government.

The Constitution Act, it must be stressed, was not a declaration of Canadian independence; it was a British law passed by the Parliament of the United Kingdom. Canadians at the time did not seriously consider any alternative to remaining a colony within the British Empire. The Constitution Act simply regrouped three British North American colonies into a single colony and provided means for the eventual absorption of other British colonial possessions in North America into the new Canadian colony. Independence was to evolve more slowly. While Canada's independence was acknowledged by the Balfour Declaration of 1926 and formally recognized by Britain in the 1931 Statute of Westminster, it was not until 1946 that the Canadian Citizenship Act was passed. In 1949 the Supreme Court of Canada became the final court of appeal; in 1950 the first Canadian Governor General was appointed; in 1965 Canada had its own flag; and in 1982 the country's constitution was patriated from Great Britain.

There was no ringing rhetoric in the Constitution Act, nothing analogous to the American Declaration of Independence—"We hold these truths to be self-evident, that all men are created equal, that they are endowed by their Creator with certain unalienable Rights, that among these are Life, Liberty and the pursuit of Happiness"—or the opening words of the American Constitution—"We the People of the United States, in order to form a more perfect Union, establish Justice, insure domestic Tranquility, provide for the common defence, promote the general Welfare, and secure the Blessings of Liberty to ourselves and our Posterity, do ordain and establish this Constitution for the United States of America." The Constitution Act began in a far more prosaic fashion: "Whereas the Provinces of Canada, Nova Scotia, and New Brunswick, have expressed their desire to be federally united into one Dominion under the Crown of the United Kingdom of Great Britain and Ireland, with a Constitution similar in principle to that of the United Kingdom:

And whereas such a Union would conduce to the welfare of the Provinces and promote the interests of the British Empire: And whereas.... " This is not the sort of phrase that one shouts from the barricades or that school children memorize to give them a sense of their constitutional heritage. As Eric Nicol and Peter Whalley note, "in the entire history of literate man, no people has ever found endearing a document that began with 'Whereas.' "[23]

Confederation was not wrested from the unwilling hands of the British government. At the time colonial sentiment was weak in Britain, the consensus being that colonies were costing more than they were worth and that they should be encouraged to carry their own weight. Indeed, the British government played an important role in bringing about Confederation by closing off any alternative solution to the economic problems faced by the Maritime colonies. Britain was unwilling to negotiate a reciprocity agreement with the United States that did not include Canada, and would not discuss Maritime union apart from some broader union with Canada. Thus Canadians were assuming responsibilities that Britain was only too willing to shed. The Canadian negotiators who came to London in December, 1866, met general indifference rather than opposition. On March 1, 1867 a *Times of London* editorial stated that "we look to Confederation as the means of relieving this country from much expense and much embarrassment."[24] The contrast with the American revolution in the 1770s could not be more complete.

Lastly, the Constitution Act did not provide a complete constitution for Canada. A large part of the constitution remained unwritten, covered only by the opening phrase, "with a Constitution similar in principle to that of the United Kingdom." In practice this meant that Canada adopted British parliamentary institutions and the conventions of responsible government, that the provinces other than Quebec adopted British common law, and that Canadians were able to draw upon centuries of British parliamentary tradition. As John Diefenbaker so nicely put it, "the warp and woof of our constitution are the golden threads of our British heritage."[25] The Act itself was primarily concerned with those aspects of Canadian government which were not similar to the United Kingdom, such as the definition of Canada's colonial relationship, the establishment of new federal and provincial governments, the federal division of powers, the fiscal relationship between the two levels of government, and the protection of language and educational rights.

What Did Happen in 1867

The Constitution Act of 1867 divided the former colony of Canada into Quebec and Ontario, and then combined Quebec, Ontario, Nova Scotia, and New Brunswick into a single British colony, the Dominion of Canada.

Section 146 also provided for the eventual entry of Newfoundland, Prince Edward Island, British Columbia, Rupert's Land, and the Northwest Territories into the Dominion. The Act spelled out Canada's colonial relationship in a detailed description of the powers of Britain's representative in Canada, the Governor General. New national legislative institutions—the House of Commons and the Senate—were created, and their method of election and appointment was described. A national judicial system was created, and the financial obligations of the federal government to the provinces were described. Section 145 called for an immediate start to the construction of the Intercolonial Railway linking the St. Lawrence Valley to Halifax.

In many respects the key sections of the Constitution Act were those which put into place a federal system of government by specifying the division of powers between the national and provincial governments. It is here that the Act drew from American constitutional innovations and, to a degree, from the bifurcated administrative experience of the Province of Canada. It is here also that we find the most dramatic departure from British constitutional principles. Those principles, however, were not fully rejected nor was federalism fully embraced. The Constitution Act was an awkward marriage of parliamentary institutions and federalism, a marriage that has survived, but not without difficulty.

FEDERALISM

Federal systems divide the powers of the state between two levels of government, both of which govern the same people and the same territory. The residents of Manitoba, for example, come under the jurisdiction of both the parliament of Canada and the Manitoba Legislative Assembly. The government at each level, moreover, is elected directly by the people. Thus, the federal government is chosen by the people of Canada, not by the provincial governments or legislatures, and its impact on the Canadian people is not mediated by the provincial governments. In theory, each level of government should have at least one area in which it is sovereign, in which the other level of government cannot legislate. There must also be a written contract specifying the federal division of powers, a contract which cannot be unilaterally altered by either level of government. In Canada's case, this contract is embedded within the Constitution Act of 1867. Finally, there must be some impartial means of settling disputes which might arise over the meaning of that contract. In Canada this was provided first by the **Judicial Committee of the Privy Council** and, after 1949, by the Supreme Court of Canada.

Municipal Government and Federalism

People often refer to the *three* levels or "orders" of Canadian federalism—the *national* or *federal* government in Ottawa, the *provincial* governments, and the *local* or *municipal* governments in the cities and towns of Canada. However, it should be pointed out that municipal governments are not part of the federal system per se; the federal division of powers embedded in the Constitution Act relates only to the federal and provincial governments. Municipal governments, and indeed the territorial governments in Northern Canada, are creatures of the provincial and federal governments respectively. The powers they exercise are not constitutionally entrenched or defined, but rather are delegated powers which could, at least hypothetically, be diminished or withdrawn at the whim of the provinces (in the case of municipal governments) or Ottawa (in the case of territorial governments in the North).

The federal division of powers was initially set forth in a number of sections within the 1867 Constitution Act, the most important of which were Section 91, which specified the powers of Parliament, and Section 92, which specified those of the provincial legislatures. In a very general sense, the two sections gave Parliament control over national economic management (public debt, regulation of trade and commerce, legal tender, banking) while giving the provincial legislatures control over matters "of a merely local or private Nature in the Province." This division was designed to free the new federal government from the sectarian conflict that had crippled the Union government, while at the same time providing it with the economic leverage thought to be essential for territorial expansion. It was hoped that by assigning the major areas of French–English conflict to the jurisdiction of the provinces, Ottawa would be free to meet the challenges of national economic development.

Areas of sectarian conflict included property and civil rights, which Section 92 assigned to the provinces, and education, which Section 93 also assigned to the provinces, albeit with important constraints imposed to protect the educational interests of the Protestant minority in Quebec. Section 95 gave Ottawa and the provinces concurrent jurisdiction—both could be legislatively active—over agriculture and immigration with the proviso that should provincial legislation be "repugnant to any Act of the Parliament of Canada," the federal legislation would be paramount. Section 109 assigned "all lands, mines, minerals and royalties belonging to the several provinces . . . " to the provinces. It is this section, along with article 5 in Section 92 ("the management and sale of the Public Lands belonging to the Province, and of the timber and wood thereon") which established the provincial ownership of natural resources, a constitutional principle that has played a critical role in the evolution of the Canadian federal state.

The federal division of powers reconciled Canada West's demand for representation-by-population with Canada East's opposition to rep-by-pop. The terms of that reconciliation can be illustrated by the constitutional treatment of education. By assigning education to provincial jurisdiction, the Constitution Act put Quebec's educational system beyond the legislative reach of a national majority that was both anglophone and Protestant. This in turn meant that rep-by-pop within Parliament was acceptable to French Canadians because Parliament, with its anglophone Protestant majority, was constitutionally prohibited from infringing upon the provincial control of education. Rep-by-pop within Quebec was also acceptable as Catholic francophones made up a clear majority of the Quebec population, and were thus assured of political control in Quebec's National Assembly. In a more general sense, and to the extent that minority concerns are assigned to provincial jurisdiction, federalism blunts the inherent danger that majority rule poses to minority interests.

It should be stressed, however, that the federal division of powers protects only certain kinds of minority interests, and only under certain conditions. It only works if *national minorities* are also *provincial majorities*, as was the case for francophones living within Quebec. The federal division of powers provides no *formal* protection for minority group members who live outside the province where their group is a majority, such as francophones living outside Quebec. The minority protections embedded in the Constitution Act, apart from the division of powers itself, applied to the English minority within Quebec rather than to the French minority outside Quebec. As noted above, Section 93 provided protection for Protestant schools in Quebec. Section 133 provided for the use of both French and English in the Quebec legislature and courts, and for the representation of the English minority in both the Canadian Senate and the Quebec National Assembly. At the time of Confederation, provincial autonomy for Quebec was seen as the key safeguard for French Canadian interests, with little attention being paid to francophone minorities in other provinces. It was only *after* Confederation that these minorities were brought to the attention of Quebec by "the harassment of the Metis in the North-West, the dismantling of Catholic separate school systems in New Brunswick, Prince Edward Island and the prairie provinces, the disestablishment of the French language on the prairies, [and] the attempt to eliminate French from Ontario schools."[26]

The protection of minority interests through the federal division of powers is limited in a second way: it does not extend to minorities which have sharply different interests from the majority in matters of *national jurisdiction*. For example, French Canadians during the First and Second World Wars opposed the introduction of military conscription for overseas service, a policy that their English Canadian compatriots strongly supported. In this case, however, jurisdiction resided with Parliament and thus the division of powers per se failed to provide any shelter for French Canadian interests. A second example stems from the "energy wars" of the late 1970s and early 1980s, when Ottawa pursued a package of energy programs and policies strongly opposed by the Alberta government. The point to be emphasized is that well-designed federal states cannot and indeed do not rely exclusively on the division of powers for the protection of minority interests; other forms of protection must be built into the representational character and procedural norms of national political institutions.

This discussion should not leave the impression that the federal division of powers is watertight, for it is not. Take, for example, the contemporary issue of jurisdictional control over post-secondary education, a matter of particular concern for students and professors. Initially, the issue may seem quite clear; Section 93 of the Constitution Act assigns education to the provinces. However, although the federal government cannot *legislate* in the educational field, there are no constitutional limitations on its *spending power*. (If the Meech Lake Accord is ratified, provinces will be able to opt out of new federal programs in areas of exclusive provincial jurisdiction and receive full financial compensation, provided that they initiate a provincial program "compatible with the national objectives" of the federal program.) We find, then, that since the early 1960s Ottawa has been paying approximately half the cost of post-secondary education provided through provincial institutions, a contribution that now amounts to nearly $5 billion. The research activities of Canadian academics are largely funded by Ottawa through such agencies as the Social Sciences and Humanities Research Council and the National Research Council, a contribution that amounts to approximately $500 million. To the extent that universities can be seen as providing *manpower training* rather than *education*, the constitutional door is potentially opened for direct involvement by the federal government. Finally, both levels of government provide financial support for students, although perhaps not to the degree that readers might wish. Thus the practice of federalism is far more complex than one would suspect from an inspection of constitutional documents. Indeed, there are few policy areas today which fall under the exclusive jurisdiction of either level of government.

Some matters are not explicitly assigned to either level of government. The 1867 Constitution Act, for example, did not mention telecommunications or the disposal of nuclear wastes, lapses for which the politicians of the day can surely be excused. In Canada it is often argued that the opening clause of Section 91 gives such **residual powers** to Parliament: "It shall be lawful for the Queen, by and with the advice and consent of the Senate and House of Commons, to make laws for the peace, order, and good government of Canada, in relation to all matters not coming within the classes of subjects by this Act assigned exclusively to the Legislatures of the Provinces. . . . " Over time, however, the courts have interpreted the peace, order, and good government clause some-what narrowly, restricting its application to emergency conditions or situations in which a clear *national interest* can be demonstrated. At the same time, the property and civil rights clause in Section 92 has been broadly interpreted so as to verge upon being a residual powers clause. Other clauses in sections 91 and 92 can also be used to lodge powers which were not specified in the original division of powers. Consumer protection, which did not weigh heavily in the confederation debates, can be seen as falling under Parliament's responsibility for trade and com-merce or under the responsibility of provincial legislatures for property and civil rights.

In drawing this discussion to a close, it should also be pointed out that federalism acts as a constraint on the supremacy of Parliament. In the British Westminster model, Parliament—which includes the House of Commons, the House of Lords, and the Crown—is supreme: "there is no higher legislative authority; no court can declare Acts of Parliament to be invalid; there is no limit to Parliament's sphere of legislation; and no Parliament can legally bind its successor, or be bound by its predeces-sor."[27] In Canada, however, parliamentary supremacy has been limited in a number of ways. Until the passage of the Statute of Westminster in 1931, Canada remained a British colony. Thus the supremacy of the Canadian Parliament was in theory limited by Britain, although in practice this limitation was of little consequence. More importantly, the doctrine of parliamentary supremacy does not enable the Parliament of Canada to encroach upon provincial fields of jurisdiction. Within those fields, parliamentary supremacy rests within the provincial legislative assem-blies. Finally, and more recently, the Charter of Rights and Freedoms further restricts the supremacy of both Parliament and the provincial legislatures. The Charter now permits court challenges to the constitu-tionality of Acts of Parliament (or Acts passed by provincial legislatures) on grounds other than an alleged transgression of the federal division of powers. With respect to rights specified within the Charter, Parliament and the provincial legislatures are not supreme. At the same time, Section 1 of the Charter guarantees the rights and freedoms set forth within it "subject only to such reasonable limits prescribed by law as can be demonstrably justified in a free and democratic society." This clause would appear to rehabilitate the principle of parliamentary supremacy in that legislative action is central to any such demonstrable justification. Moreover, the "notwithstanding" provision of Section 33 enables legisla-tures to override some Charter rights for up to a five-year (renewable) period: "Parliament or the legislature of a province may expressly declare in an Act of Parliament or of the legislature, as the case may be, that the Act or a provision thereof shall operate notwithstanding a provision included in Section 2 or Sections 7 to 15 of this Charter."

To conclude, it is useful to reiterate how federalism provided a solution to the perplexing problems which faced Canadian politicians in the 1860s. Many of the factors that led to Confederation—political deadlock, the American threat, economic distress, and the national dream—did not dictate a *federal* constitution. Federalism, however, was dictated by the conflict over representation by population, by a widespread desire to protect local autonomy, and by the need to create a strong national government without mangling the cultural and regional components of the new Canadian state. Federalism permitted rep-by-pop while giving the French Canadian minority, or at least those French Canadians living in Quebec, constitutional protection from the Anglo-Canadian majority. It created a strong federal government while maintaining local autonomy in a number of important jurisdictional domains, and it laid the foundations for a new Canadian nationality without doing violence to the regional and cultural roots of the Canadian population. This was all possible because of the federal division of powers, a division which constrains the majoritarian impulse of national parliamentary institutions. While the founding fathers adopted the Westminster parliamentary model from Great Britain, they tempered its application by also adopting and adapting federal principles originating in the United States.

RESPONSIBLE GOVERNMENT

The term "responsible government" defines the relationship of cabinet ministers to the House, the Crown, and to each other. Collectively, the cabinet is responsible to the House of Commons in that the government must maintain the support of a majority of MPs if it is to continue in office. If cabinet loses the "confidence" of the House through a specific "want of confidence" or non-confidence vote, or through the defeat of a major government bill, unwritten constitutional convention calls for the government to tender its resignation. In practice, the prime minister would usually ask the Governor General for the "dissolution" of Parliament, and would go to the people in a general election. This was the course followed in 1979 by Joe Clark when his minority Progressive Conservative government lost a budget vote in the House. Thus, while the House can defeat a government, it cannot choose a new one.

Parliamentary Defeat and Responsible Government

The convention requiring the resignation of the government following its defeat in the House is open to interpretation. In February 1968, the minority Liberal government of Lester Pearson was defeated in the House through carelessness. Prime Minister Pearson, who had announced his retirement, was on holidays, and many prominent Liberal MPs were out of Ottawa campaigning for the upcoming Liberal leadership convention. When a vote was called in the House, the remaining Liberal MPs were outnumbered, and the government was defeated. A strict application of the doctrine of responsible government would have dictated the resignation of the government and the dissolution of Parliament. This would have pitched the leaderless and ill-prepared Liberals into a national campaign against a rejuvenated Progressive Conservative party and its new leader, Robert Stanfield.

The Liberals, however, argued that the defeat in the House was a mistake, and did not constitute a true loss of confidence in the government. To prove this point, the government introduced a formal vote of confidence in the House the next day. By this time Pearson was back from holidays, all leadership candidates and other absent MPs were in the House and, with the support of the *Créditistes*, the confidence motion was passed.

If the opposition parties had boycotted the House when the vote of confidence was called, if they had insisted that the government had been defeated and that an election should be called, it is unlikely that the Pearson stratagem would have worked. However, the Conservative leader decided that an election should not be forced at that time. As a consequence, the House continued to sit, the Liberals chose a new leader less than two months later, and the new leader, Pierre Elliott Trudeau, promptly called a general election. The Liberals swept to victory, and the Conservatives were to wait eleven years before briefly winning power in June 1979. In politics, nice guys finish last.

This episode could have provided an important precedent that might have loosened the bonds of party discipline for the House. If governments were deemed to fall only on explicit votes of non-confidence, as has become the parliamentary convention in Great Britain, then government backbenchers would be less compelled to support government legislation come hell or high water. However, the precedent was not picked up and the importance of party discipline was not eroded.

Individually, cabinet ministers are responsible for the conduct of their departments, and must answer for their departments on the floor of the House. Although they are not held personally responsible for everything that happens within their departments, which after all might encompass thousands of employees, their resignation is expected in the event of major scandals or blunders. Cabinet ministers are also responsible to the Crown, which formally appoints them, and to the prime minister, who in reality appoints them. Finally, cabinet ministers are collectively responsible to one another. Like the Three Musketeers, cabinet ministers operate on the principle of one for all and all for one. Cabinet speaks with a single voice, and thus *once a decision has been made* all ministers are expected to endorse that decision publicly even though they may have strenuously opposed it behind cabinet doors. As a consequence, any one minister speaks with the full weight of cabinet.

Collective responsibility necessitates that cabinet proceedings be secret, and indeed ministers are bound to secrecy through their Privy

Council oath. Secrecy in turn facilitates both frank discussion within cabinet and a facade of government cohesion for the external political environment. Collective responsibility also means that the House cannot oust a single minister but can only defeat the government as a whole; the prime minister alone can dismiss individual ministers. Nor can government backbenchers publicly promote the sacking of a specific minister, for an attack on one minister is an attack on the full cabinet. From the perspective of opposition parties, collective responsibility allows them to tar the whole government with a bad ministerial brush.

In reality, responsible government is constrained by the inability of the House to change governments without an intervening election, and by the fact that party leaders and thus indirectly prime ministers are selected by national party conventions lying beyond the control of the House. It is also constrained by strong party discipline. If the governing party controls a majority of seats in the House, it will not be defeated on a vote of confidence. The government will remain in office until the prime minister decides to go to the people, or until its constitutional term expires. As Thomas Hockin concludes, "ever since the ascendancy of mass, disciplined political parties in Canada was confirmed in 1878, the . . . notion of responsible government, except for its legal accuracy, has grown increasingly unhelpful as a way to understand day-to-day parliamentary activity and its role in policy-making."[28]

REPRESENTATIVE DEMOCRACY

The Canadian political system provides citizens with few opportunities to vote directly on matters of public policy. The instruments of direct democracy—referenda and plebiscites—are seldom used in federal or provincial politics; the 1949 Newfoundland vote on whether to join Confederation and the 1980 sovereignty association referendum in Quebec, discussed in the next chapter, are very much exceptions to the rule. Canadians have opted instead for a system of *representative democracy* in which the policy preferences of citizens are filtered through elected assemblies. Rather than govern directly, we elect representatives who govern in our place. If we are unhappy with the way in which our representatives interpret our policy preferences, we can retaliate through the electoral process but we cannot directly assume legislative power. The Canadian electorate makes governments, not laws.

Plebiscites in Canada

Plebiscites have only been used twice in federal politics; in 1898 a national plebiscite was held on the prohibition of liquor, and in 1942 a plebiscite was held on military conscription for overseas service. At the provincial level over 40 plebiscites have been held on issues ranging from prohibition to the introduction of daylight saving time, with plebiscites on liquor-related issues being by far the most common. Prince Edward Island, for example, held plebiscites on prohibition in 1878, 1901, 1929, 1940, and 1948, while Ontario held prohibition plebiscites in 1902, 1919, and 1921. In January 1988, a plebiscite was held in Prince Edward Island to measure public support for a fixed link with the mainland. At the municipal level, plebiscites and even referenda are more routinely used to address a wide range of policy issues running from local prohibition to the insurance of bonds.

It should be stressed that plebiscites are not formally or legally binding on the sponsoring government or legislature. They are a way of measuring public sentiment on the issue at hand, and legislative action is still required if such sentiment is to find reflection in law. In this sense, plebiscites are not unlike massive public opinion polls. Referenda, which have yet to make an appearance in provincial or federal politics, are legally binding and thus are much more difficult to reconcile with the principle of parliamentary supremacy.

Data drawn from Patrick Boyer, MP, "Plebiscites in a Parliamentary Democracy," *Canadian Parliamentary Review*, Vol. 11, No. 4 (Winter 1988-89), pp. 2-4.

Representative democracy can also be taken to mean that political institutions should be broadly reflective of the electorate in their composition, that politicians should not only represent their constituents in the sense of a lawyer representing his or her clients but should also, in the aggregate, constitute a broad cross-section of Canadian society. To a degree, this form of representation is provided by the structure of parliamentary institutions. There is rough regional equality in the Senate; each province is assured of a proportionate number of seats in the House; and the francophone majority in most Quebec ridings ensures that francophones within Quebec are well represented in the House of Commons. In other respects, Parliament is much less representative, with MPs and Senators tending to have higher incomes, more formal education, and higher-status occupations than the citizens they represent. Provincially, the situation is no different: "in every province, provincial MLAs, like federal MPs, are a socioeconomic and demographic elite."[29]

Nowhere is the House of Commons less representative of the Canadian population than in its gender composition. Of the 3,371 MPs elected from 1867 through 1984, only 57, or 1.6 percent, were women. (Twenty-four women were appointed to the Senate during the same time.) While more women MPs have been elected in recent years, their share of the total House membership is still small. In the 1980 election only 15 (5 percent) of the elected MPs were women; 28 women (10 percent) were elected in 1984 and 40 (13.6 percent) were elected in 1988.

Apart from a growing concern over the under-representation of women in public life, the fact that elected politicians tend to come from a socioeconomic and demographic elite has been the source of little political controversy in Canada. This may reflect an understandable normative ambivalence on whether political institutions *should* encompass a cross-section of the general population. It is not clear, for example, that we are poorly served by legislators who are better educated than the norm, or who are more likely to come from professional or managerial than from manual or unskilled occupations. There is much less ambivalence, however, on the representative character of the cabinet. It is in cabinet building that we see the full flowering of this second form of representative democracy.

Prime ministers strive for cabinets which, if not *proportionally* representative, should contain at least some representation from the major sectors of the electorate. Ideally, all Canadians should be able to find their reflection somewhere within the ranks of the cabinet. More practically, prime ministers face the following representational demands:

- With the possible exception of Prince Edward Island, there must be a minister appointed from each province. If the governing party has only one MP from a given province, he or she will be appointed regardless of ability. If the governing party fails to elect any MPs in a given province, Senators from the missing provinces can be appointed to fill the void. Of the initial cabinet appointments made between 1945 and 1976, 35 percent came from Ontario, which contained approximately 34 percent of the national population. Quebec had 31 percent of the initial appointees and 28 percent of the national population, Atlantic Canada 14 percent of the appointees and 10 percent of the population, and the West 20 percent of the appointees with 28 percent of the national population.[30]
- Not only must each province be represented, but Ontario generally has more ministers than Quebec, Quebec more than any province other than Ontario, and so forth. However, in the cabinet formed after the 1988 election, Quebec had 13 ministers, Ontario 12, British Columbia 4, Alberta 3, Manitoba and New Brunswick 2 each, and Newfoundland, Nova Scotia, and Saskatchewan one each.
- Francophones must be adequately represented. If there is an insufficient number of francophone MPs in the government caucus, as was the case following the 1979 election, Quebec senators can be appointed.
- Since John Diefenbaker's appointment of Ellen Fairclough, Canada's first female cabinet minister, women must be represented in the cabinet. Six women were appointed to the federal cabinet formed after the 1988 election.
- Major regions within the larger provinces must be represented. For

example, Ottawa and the Niagara Peninsula–Hamilton area are both traditionally represented in the cabinet.

- The cabinet should include a representative of the English-speaking population of Quebec and a representative of the French-speaking population outside Quebec, the latter usually coming from Ontario.
- There must be some visible representation of the roughly 30 percent of the Canadian population which is of neither French nor English ancestry.

Quite apart from these considerations, the prime minister must provide cabinet representation for the major factions within his own party, as cabinet building is carried out with an eye to party unity as well as national unity.

These representational demands make cabinet building a daunting task. There is only limited room to consider the ability of potential ministers apart from their representational characteristics. The ideal choices are those individuals who can represent several segments of the Canadian population, such as a woman MP from Quebec with a non-French ethnic background. Even then, however, there is considerable pressure to expand the size of the cabinet to ensure that no major group is left out.

THE MEANING OF CONFEDERATION

In a country's history, there are certain "formative events" which have an importance reaching far beyond their time and place.[31] Confederation was such an event, setting in place institutions which to this day shape the unfolding of political life in Canada. Confederation also plays an important role in debates over the direction Canada should follow in the years ahead for, to an extent, we all try to anchor our claims and visions in the past, portraying them as the inevitable outcome of historical forces set in motion by older and, if our thinking concurs, wiser men.

It is therefore useful to examine the *meaning* of Confederation, to go beyond the terms of the 1867 Constitution Act to their intent. What vision guided the politicians of the 1860s? What aspirations were they trying to achieve through dry and convoluted constitutional phrases? Here we must recognize, however, that most political events are ambiguous, open to widely divergent interpretations, and Confederation is no exception. The search for meaning is handicapped by a lack of consensus among the founding fathers themselves, by a contentious historical record, and by a human tendency to bend the historical record to fit the political needs of today.

Evidence that the intent of Confederation was to create a federal system with a strong central government and relatively subordinate provincial governments is provided by the terms of the Constitution Act and the argumentation on their behalf by John A. Macdonald. Here it must be remembered that the confederation agreement was reached against the tragic backdrop of the American Civil War. Although Canadians were prepared to adopt a federal system, and indeed had little choice in the matter, they were not prepared to adopt the specifics of an American model which had failed to prevent the calamity of civil war. Thus we find, in the 1860s, repeated references to the failure of American federalism and the lessons to be learned from that failure. At the 1864 Quebec conference, Macdonald argued that "we must have a strong Central Government with all authority except what is given to the local governments in each Province, and avoid the errors of the American constitution."[32] The point where the American Constitution broke down, Macdonald argued, was in the assignment of residual powers to the states and to the people rather than to the national government. The "peace, order and good government" clause was the product of Macdonald's concern.

To Canadians like Macdonald, the principal weakness of the American federal system was that the states had been given too much power. The lesson for Canada was that the federal government should be strengthened vis-à-vis the provinces, and the founding fathers set out to achieve that end through a number of provisions in the Constitution Act:

- The Act assigned what were thought to be the "great subjects of legislation" to Parliament; the provincial legislatures were restricted primarily to matters of a "merely local or private nature."
- Parliament was given the power to raise money by "any Mode or System of Taxation" while the provincial legislatures were restricted to direct taxation and federal subsidies.
- The Act gave Parliament **paramountcy** in areas of concurrent jurisdiction.
- Parliament was given the declaratory power to make laws in relation to "such works as, although wholly situate within the province, are before or after their execution declared by the Parliament of Canada to be for the general advantage of Canada or for the advantage of two or more provinces."
- The Act gave Parliament the power to make criminal law, with a national criminal code being the consequence, and gave the federal government the power to appoint all superior court justices.
- The federal government was given the power to appoint Lieutenant Governors who were to serve as a national check on the provincial governments, just as the Governor General was to serve as an

imperial check on the government of Canada. The Lieutenant Governor had the power to withhold assent from provincial legislation, and to reserve such legislation for acceptance or rejection by the federal government.

- Senators were to be appointed by the federal government, and not by the provinces.
- The Act gave Parliament the power to disallow provincial legislation—to prevent it from coming into effect—even when such legislation was wholly within the provincial legislative domain.

As Donald Smiley explains, "in terms of both the provisions of the Act and the expectations of those who framed it, the provinces were to be in precisely the same constitutional relationship to the federal government as the individual colonies of British North America had been to the Imperial authorities."[33] Indeed, the federal government's power to intervene in the constitutional domain of the provincial legislatures was so extensive that some federal scholars have been reluctant to describe the Constitution Act of 1867 as a federal document, preferring instead the term "quasi-federal."[34]

This view of Confederation has not gone unchallenged. A. I. Silver presents rather persuasive evidence that French Canadians did not see Confederation "...as a national unification transforming a scattered collection of colonies into a single people under a strong national government."[35] Rather, Confederation was endorsed because it was seen to protect the autonomy and separateness of Quebec. Silver points out that the assignment of issues of a "merely local or private matter" to the provinces was interpreted in Quebec as a recognition of, and not a diminution of, provincial autonomy. The mid-1860s attitude of the French Canadian press towards Confederation can be encapsulated by the following editorial statement appearing in *Le Courier de St-Hyacinthe*: "We want a confederation in which the federal principle will be applied in its fullest sense—one which will give the central power control over only general questions in no way affecting the interests of each separate section, while leaving to the local legislatures everything which concerns our particular interests."[36] Confederation was supported, then, because it would free Quebec from Upper Canada, and give French Canadians autonomous control over their local affairs. As E.-P. Taché explained in 1864, the federal government would have enough power "to do away with some of the internal hindrances to trade, and to unite the Provinces for mutual defence," but it would be the provinces to which people would look for the protection of their liberty, rights and privileges.[37]

Silver argues that, at the time of Confederation, Macdonald's vision was not characteristic of French Canada. More recently, "compact theories" have emerged to provide historical support for bicultural and, even more recently, province-centred visions of the Canadian federal state. Bicultural compact theorists do not dispute the letter of the Constitution Act but focus instead on its spirit. Confederation, they argue, was the result of an implicit but nonetheless very real bicultural compact between the French and English communities. Without that compact Confederation would not have occurred, and thus the meaning of Confederation is revealed more by that compact than by the letter of the Constitution Act. While there may be little evidence for the compact theory in the Act itself, evidence can be found in subsequent legislation such as the 1869 Act for the Temporary Government of Rupert's Land, the Manitoba Act of 1870, and the North-West Territories Act of 1875.[38]

Bicultural compact theories emerged in Quebec during the 1930s, and came to play a significant role in debates on the place of Quebec in Canada, and on the status of the French language outside Quebec. They have also been highly contentious, with critics charging that they distort if not falsify the historical record. One of the most outspoken critics has been the historian Donald Creighton, who has concluded that the evidence against the two-nation theory of confederation is overwhelming:

> It is obvious that the last thing the Fathers of Confederation wanted to do was to perpetuate duality; they hoped, through confederation, to escape from it entirely.... There was nothing in ... the British North America Act which remotely approached a general declaration of principle that Canada was to be a bilingual or bicultural nation.[39]

Nor have critics of the bicultural compact been confined to English Canada. In its background paper for the 1980 sovereignty-association referendum, the Parti Québécois government declared:

> Under the terms of the British North America Act, Quebec is not the homeland of a nation, but merely a province among the others.... Nowhere in the Act is there a talk of an alliance between two founding peoples, or of a pact between two nations.... [40]

Compact theories have also been tied to classical models of federalism in which federal constitutions are seen as legal contracts. If the Constitution Act is seen as a contract, one can ask whom the contract was between or among. Since the federal government did not exist prior to 1867, it can be argued that the contract was among the provinces, and that the provincial governments are the legitimate custodians of the constitution. In this view there is no acknowledgment of a subordinate role for the provincial legislatures, as the letter of the Constitution Act might suggest. As Garth Stevenson points out, the lack of public ratification of the confederation agreement has strengthened compact interpretations. Confederation, after all, was a governmental rather than a popular product, portrayed at the time as a treaty among governments.[41] As the only governments in existence at the time were the provincial governments, the compact interpretation gains weight.

THE CONFEDERATION LEGACY

The boundaries of the Canadian state have greatly expanded since 1867. In 1870 Manitoba entered Confederation, and both the Northwest Territories and Rupert's Land were acquired by Canada. On the promise of a transcontinental railroad, British Columbia joined in 1871, as did Prince Edward Island two years later, in the wake of a poor harvest, economic recession, and railway debt. In 1880 Canada acquired the Arctic islands, and in 1905 Alberta and Saskatchewan became the eighth and ninth Canadian provinces. In 1912 Ontario and Quebec nearly doubled in size as their boundaries were expanded to the north, and in 1949 Newfoundland became Canada's tenth province.

Canada, of course, has changed in countless other ways as well. Our population has increased from just over 3,000,000 at the time of Confederation to more than 26,000,000 in 1990. No longer a frontier society, Canada has become a modern industrialized state. No longer rural and agrarian, Canadians live in a highly urbanized and technologically dependent society. Yet the massive changes that have occurred have not rendered Confederation irrelevant for an understanding of contemporary Canadian politics. The Constitution Act of 1867 continues to provide the *federal* skeleton for the Canadian state. The political institutions put into place by the confederation agreement continue to provide the arenas within which most of our political life occurs. While Confederation did not provide the script for the political evolution of the Canadian state, it set the stage, provided the institutional props, and supplied many of the dramatic themes.

The Fathers of Confederation grappled with very difficult political problems. To the extent these problems are still with us, to the extent, for example, that linguistic tension remains and that we enjoy only a precarious independence from the United States, one might be tempted to conclude that Confederation was a failure. Yet such a conclusion would be too harsh. One must remember that the confederation agreement created a political community that has experienced quite remarkable stability, domestic peace, and material prosperity. Moreover, the problems that Canadians confronted in the 1860s are not ones that can ever be eliminated; at best they can be moderated and contained, their burden on the community lightened but not removed. As British Prime Minister James Callaghan said in 1978, you can never reach the promised land, but only march towards it. The fact that we are still here as a country to grapple with the same problems that faced the Fathers of Confederation pays no small compliment to their work.

SUGGESTED READINGS

Janet Ajzenstat, *The Political Thought of Lord Durham* (Kingston and Montreal: McGill-Queen's University Press, 1988).

Michel Brunet, "The Historical Background of Quebec's Challenge to Canadian Unity" in Dale C. Thompson, ed., *Quebec Society and Politics* (Toronto: McClelland and Stewart, 1973), pp. 39-51.

For a discussion of the compact theory, see Ramsay Cook, *Canada and the French Canadian Question* (Toronto: Macmillan, 1976).

For an illustration of the historical debate on the compact theory, see Ralph Heintzman, "The Spirit of Confederation: Professor Creighton, Biculturalism, and the Use of History," *Canadian Historical Review*, September 1971, pp. 245-75; and D.J. Hall, "The Spirit of Confederation: Ralph Heintzman, Professor Creighton, and the Bicultural Compact Theory," *Journal of Canadian Studies*, November 1974, pp. 24-43.

For a discussion of Nova Scotia's opposition to Confederation, see Colin D. Howell, "Nova Scotia's Protest Tradition and the Search for a Meaningful Federalism" in David Jay Bercuson, ed., *Canada and the Burden of Unity* (Toronto: Macmillan, 1977), pp. 169-91.

Rod Preece, "The Political Wisdom of Sir John A. Macdonald," *Canadian Journal of Political Science*, xvii:3 (September 1984), pp. 459-86.

G.A. Rawlyk and Doug Brown, "The Historical Framework of the Maritimes and Confederation" in G.A. Rawlyk, ed., *The Atlantic Provinces and the Problems of Confederation* (St. John's: Breakwater Press, 1979), pp. 1-47.

A.I. Silver, *The French-Canadian Idea of Confederation, 1864-1900* (Toronto: University of Toronto Press, 1982).

Garth Stevenson, *Unfulfilled Union: Canadian Federalism and National Unity*, Third Edition (Toronto: Gage, 1989).

Peter B. Waite, *The Life and Times of Confederation* (Toronto: University of Toronto Press, 1962); and *The Confederation Debates in the Province of Canada, 1865* (Toronto: McClelland and Stewart, 1963).

STUDY QUESTIONS

1. In light of the limited defence provided by the division of powers for francophones living outside Quebec, how would you assess the protection provided by the division of powers for anglophones living

inside Quebec? In what ways are the two situations analogous? In what ways are they not?

2. If your province was entering Confederation today, would your provincial government seek a different division of powers? If so, what would be the difference? What about you personally? Would you favour a different division of powers and, if so, what would the difference be?

3. Take a careful look at the federal division of powers outlined in Sections 91 and 92 of the Constitution Act, 1867. Given that division, which level of government do you think would have primary responsibility in the following fields: acid rain, the control of nuclear wastes, the regulation of professional sports, consumer protection, lotteries, medicare, and pollution control for automobile exhausts? In each case, to what extent does the formal division of powers provide a useful practical guide?

4. What relevance, if any, does the federal division of powers have for aboriginal peoples? For women? For visible minorities? Is their political leverage enhanced, reduced, or unaffected by the federal character of the Canadian state?

5. What would be the advantages and disadvantages of using a national plebiscite or referendum to address such issues as abortion, capital punishment, or constitutional amendment?

NOTES

1. Donald Creighton, *The Passionate Observer: Selected Writings* (Toronto: McClelland and Stewart, 1980), p. 19.
2. *Ibid.*, p. 51.
3. For example, see W. L. Morton, *The Critical Years: The Union of British North America 1857-1873* (Toronto: McClelland and Stewart, 1964).
4. Janet Ajzenstat, *The Political Thought of Lord Durham* (Kingston and Montreal: McGill-Queen's University Press, 1988).
5. Cited in Sheila McLeod Arnopoulos and Dominique Clift, *The English Fact in Quebec* (Montreal: McGill-Queen's University Press, 1980), pp. 56-57.
6. J.M.S. Careless, *Canada: A Story of Challenge*, Revised Edition (Toronto: Macmillan, 1963), p. 198.
7. *The Toronto Globe*, December 27, 1861.

8. Garth Stevenson, *Unfulfilled Union: Canadian Federalism and National Unity*, Third Edition (Toronto: Gage, 1989), pp. 22-23.

9. R. W. Winks, *Canada and the United States: The Civil War Years* (Baltimore, 1960), pp. 210-11 and 220-29.

10. Cited in John Murray Gibbon, *Canadian Mosaic* (Toronto: McClelland & Stewart, 1938).

11. William H. Riker, *Federalism: Origin, Operation, Significance* (Boston: Little Brown, 1964), pp. 12-13.

12. Stevenson, *Unfulfilled Union*, p. 24.

13. S.F. Wise and Robert Craig Brown, *Canada Views the United States: Nineteenth-Century Political Attitudes* (Toronto: Macmillan, 1967), p. 94.

14. Careless, *Canada: A Story of Challenge*, p. 202.

15. John Bartlet Brebner, *North Atlantic Triangle*, reprinted (Toronto: McClelland & Stewart, 1966), p. 158.

16. G.A. Rawlyk and Doug Brown, "The Historical Framework of the Maritimes and Confederation" in G.A. Rawlyk, ed., *The Atlantic Provinces and the Problems of Confederation* (St. John's: Breakwater Press, 1979), pp. 7-8.

17. A.I. Silver, *The French-Canadian Idea of Confederation, 1864-1900* (Toronto: University of Toronto Press, 1982), pp. 47-48.

18. W.T. Easterbrook and Hugh G.J. Aitken, *Canadian Economic History* (Toronto: Macmillan, 1967), p. 376.

19. Eric Nicol and Peter Whalley, *100 Years of What?* (Toronto: Ryerson, 1966), p. 10.

20. Pierre Berton, *The National Dream: The Great Railway, 1871-1881* (Toronto: McClelland and Stewart, 1970). The "national dream" aspect of Canadian railroads played a significant role in the late 1980s political debate over VIA Rail.

21. Jean-Charles Bonenfant, "Quebec and Confederation: Then and Now" in Dale C. Thomson, ed., *Quebec Society and Politics: Views from the Inside* (Toronto: McClelland and Stewart, 1973), p. 55.

22. Cited in J. Bartlet Brebner, *Canada: A Modern History* (Ann Arbor: University of Michigan Press, 1960), p. 277.

23. Nicol and Whalley, *100 Years*, p. 6.

24. Cited in Brebner, *Canada: A Modern History*, p. 281.

25. John A. Munro, ed., *The Wit and Wisdom of John Diefenbaker* (Edmonton: Hurtig, 1982), p. 30.

26. Silver, *The French-Canadian Idea of Confederation*, p. 220.

27. R.M. Punnett, *British Government and Politics*, Fourth Edition (London: Heinemann, 1980), p. 173.

28. Thomas A. Hockin, "Adversary Politics and Some Functions of the Canadian House of Commons," in Richard Schultz, Orest M. Kruhlak,

and John C. Terry, eds., *The Canadian Political Process*, Third Edition (Toronto: Holt, Rinehart and Winston, 1979), p. 315.

29. Allan Kornberg, William Mishler, and Harold D. Clarke, *Representative Democracy in the Canadian Provinces* (Scarborough: Prentice-Hall, 1982), p. 175.

30. Colin Campbell, *Canadian Political Facts, 1945 to 1976* (Toronto: Methuen, 1977), p. 32.

31. The concept comes from Seymour Martin Lipset, *The First New Nation* (New York: Basic Books, 1963), p. 7.

32. Cited in Robert A. MacKay, *The Unreformed Senate of Canada* (Toronto: McClelland and Stewart, 1963), p. 35

33. Donald V. Smiley, *The Canadian Political Nationality* (Toronto: Methuen, 1967), pp. 4-5

34. K.C. Wheare, *Federal Government* (London: Oxford University Press, 1953), p. 19.

35. Silver, *The French Canadian Idea of Confederation*, p. 218.

36. *Ibid.*, p. 35.

37. *Ibid.*, pp. 48-49.

38. For an example of this line of thought, see Ralph Heintzman, "The Spirit of Confederation: Professor Creighton, Biculturalism, and the Use of History," *Canadian Historical Review*, September 1971, pp. 245-75.

39. Donald Creighton, "John A. Macdonald, Confederation, and the Canadian West" in Donald Swainson, ed., *Historical Essays on the Prairie Provinces* (Toronto: McClelland and Stewart, 1970), p. 62.

40. Government of Quebec, *Quebec-Canada: A New Deal* (Editeur officiel du Quebec, 1979), p. 9.

41. Stevenson, *Unfulfilled Union*, pp. 40-41.

3

Language Politics

Two features of Canadian society have been of unsurpassed importance in shaping the contours of political life. The first is the existence of a large *francophone minority* which, over the last hundred years, has constituted between a quarter and a third of the national population. The second is *the concentration of that minority within Quebec*, where a solid francophone majority controls the provincial government. In conjunction, these two features have generated a complex pattern of language politics, weaving together the tensions between the anglophone national majority and the francophone national minority; between the Quebec and federal governments; between the francophone majority and the anglophone minority within Quebec; and between francophone minorities and anglophone majorities within the other nine provinces. The resultant pattern, which is fascinating in its own right, provides a useful window through which to view the broader Canadian political process.

The examination of Canadian language politics can be compared to opening a set of carved Russian dolls; within the first doll is another, and within that another, and so forth until one is left with a table covered in doll parts but no doll. Because the components of language politics are nested within one another, we must consider not only each component in turn but also the interplay among them in coming to grips with the language policies pursued by the governments of Canada, Quebec, and the other nine provinces. However, the reader should be cautioned, in tackling this chapter, that language forms only part of the complex relationship between the French and English communities in Canada. Historically, that relationship was founded on the religious division between Catholics and Protestants; language per se was important largely as a carrier of religious and cultural values. Then, as both social and political life became more secular in tone and substance, language came increasingly to the fore. As René Lévesque wrote in 1968:

> At the core of the Québécois personality is the fact that we speak French. Everything else depends on this one essential element and follows from it or leads us infallibly back to it.[1]

While cultural, class, and religious differences between the two linguistic communities are by no means absent today, it is largely in terms of the

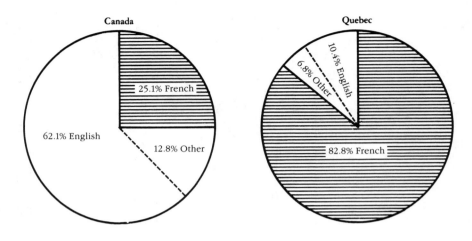

FIGURE 3.1

Linguistic Composition (Mother Tongue) of Canada and Quebec (1986)

status of the French language that one can define the place of Quebec and francophones within the broader fabric of Canadian life.

Although conflict tends to emerge as the dominant theme in any discussion of language politics, the two linguistic communities have co-existed without bloodshed and without the assimilation of the franco-phone minority. The survival of the "French Fact" in Canada speaks well not only for francophones' tenacious defence of their language and culture, but also for the political system's ability to maintain workable compromises in very contentious policy areas.

LINGUISTIC COMPOSITION OF CANADA

Over the years the linguistic composition of Canada has been reasonably stable. Figure 3.2 shows that since 1931 the percentage of Canada's population whose mother tongue (the language spoken most often at home when the individual was a child) is French has varied within a range of only four percent. (These data were not available prior to the 1931 census.) Figure 3.2 also shows that Quebec's share of the national popula-tion, a share roughly equivalent to the *combined* populations of Newfoundland, Prince Edward Island, Nova Scotia, New Brunswick, Manitoba, Saskatchewan, and Alberta, has been reasonably stable. How-ever, it is important to note that between 1966 and 1986 Quebec's share of the national population dropped by more than three percent.

In many ways it is remarkable that Quebec has retained a quarter of

FIGURE 3.2
Quebec and French Mother Tongue Shares of the National Population

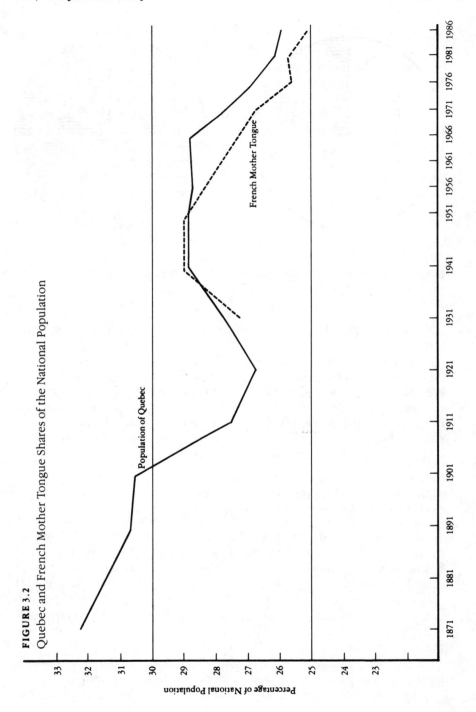

the national population, and that more than one Canadian in four is of French mother tongue. The present francophone population of over six million has evolved almost entirely from the 70,000 French settlers who remained in Canada after the "conquest" of New France in 1760.[2] Immigration from France virtually ceased in 1760, just as immigration into Canada from other countries was getting under way. Soon francophones became a minority within the British North American colonies, although they remained a majority in what is now Quebec. Immigrants from countries other than France tended to settle outside Quebec, in part because economic opportunities were better and land was more readily available; in part because of the closed nature of the French Canadian community; and in part because, if one had to acquire a new language, English was of greater economic currency in North America than was French. (For many immigrants, Canada was little more than a stopover on their way to the United States.) For every immigrant who settled in Quebec, three to four settled in Ontario.[3] Yet, regardless of where they settled, immigrants after 1760 were either anglophones to start with or overwhelmingly adopted English rather than French upon their arrival in North America. Richard Joy found that according to the 1961 census, 91 percent of the pre-war immigrants spoke English only, 7 percent spoke both French and English, and 1 percent spoke only French, the same proportion that spoke neither official language.[4] Between 1966 and 1976, 52.6 percent of the immigrants who settled in Canada were anglophones, only 6.7 percent were francophones, and 40.7 percent were neither.[5] Overall, then, immigration worked to erode the proportionate contribution of both Quebec and francophones to the national population.

Figure 3.3 provides a simplified illustration, drawn only roughly to scale, of the factors determining Quebec's share of the national population. In the past, Quebec, like other provinces, faced a steady loss of population through out-migration, a loss attesting to the geographical mobility that Canadians enjoy. In Quebec's case, however, out-migration was primarily to the United States rather than to other Canadian provinces. Quebec migrants therefore played a relatively minor role in the settlement of the Canadian West; for every one person who moved from Quebec to the West before 1931, six moved to the west from Ontario and eight moved from Quebec to the United States.[6] Thus most of those who left Quebec were lost not only to Quebec but to French Canada more broadly defined. Without the infusion of migration from Quebec, francophone communities outside Quebec were left exposed to the assimilationist pressure of the anglophone majority. As Joy concludes, "the great exodus of French Canadians toward the United States was one of the decisive factors contributing to the supremacy of the English language in Canada."[7]

Out-migration from Quebec was offset, not by immigration into the

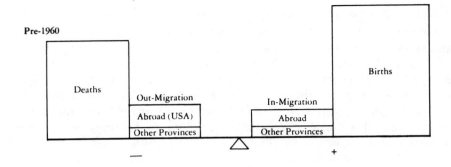

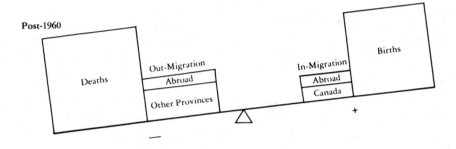

FIGURE 3.3

Factors Affecting Quebec's Share of Canada's Population

province from abroad or from other provinces, but by a high birth rate. This reflects not only the rural character of the Quebec population but also the dominance of the Catholic religion and a cultural ethos which linked a high birth rate to the very survival of French Canada. With respect to this last point, Joy cites the eulogy in a Beauce County newspaper for a Monsieur Philippon who, when he died at the age of 96, left 600 descendants: "the grandfather of Mr. Philippon met an honorable death at the Battle of the Plains of Abraham; his grandson has well revenged this death by adding, through his own efforts, an entire parish to French Canada."[8] This *revanche des berceaux*, or "revenge of the cradle," played a critical role in maintaining Quebec's share of the national population in the face of the "fatal hemorrhage" of French Canadians into the New England states, and the steady flow of overseas emigration into Ontario and the West.

By the 1960s, however, Quebec's demographic balance was upset by a number of changes, of which the most important was a decline in the birth rate. In 1931 Quebec's birth rate had been 40 percent greater than that for the country as a whole. This advantage declined to 35 percent in 1941, 26 percent in 1951, 9 percent in 1961, and 6 percent in 1966.[9] By 1971 Quebec's birth rate had fallen below the national average, and by the mid-1970s it was the lowest in Canada. By the late 1980s the provincial birth rate had fallen to 1.4 children per fertile woman, a rate well below the national rate of 1.8, and even further below the replacement rate of 2.1 required for a stable population. Indeed, Quebec's birth rate is now one of the lowest in the world, above only that for West Germany, and it has prompted the Quebec government to introduce special financial incentives designed to reduce the financial burden imposed by young children.[10]

At the same time that Quebec's birth rate was plummeting, provincial language legislation (discussed below) and intensified Québécois nationalism increased emigration from Quebec's anglophone community and reduced even further in-migration from other provinces and countries. Between 1976 and 1981, 106,000 more anglophones left Quebec for other provinces than moved to Quebec from other provinces, while from 1981 to 1986 there was a further net loss of 41,000 anglophones.[11] On balance, Quebec anglophones tend to leave the province and francophones from outside Quebec tend to be drawn to the province. Between 1966 and 1976, for example, 63 percent of those who left Quebec were of English mother tongue (another 8 percent were neither English nor French), while 42 percent of those who moved to Quebec were of French mother tongue.[12] This pattern of interprovincial migration works to strengthen, not weaken, the country's linguistic divide.

In combination, these demographic changes have begun to erode significantly Quebec's share of the national population, a process likely to accelerate in the years ahead. This erosion has in turn strengthened nationalist arguments in Quebec. In its 1979 proposal for sovereignty association, the Quebec government stated that it would be an illusion to believe that francophones could, in the future, play a determining role in the Government of Canada:

> On the contrary, they will be more and more a minority and English Canada will find it increasingly easy to govern without them. . . . Given these prospects . . . Quebecers feel it is urgent to take action before it is too late.[13]

From this perspective, the longer Quebec stays in Canada, the weaker her demographic and political position will be, and thus the more difficult it will be to negotiate favourable terms through which Confederation might be dissolved. More recently, Quebec's concern over the impact of immigration on the province's linguistic profile and future found expression in the immigration provisions of the Meech Lake Accord, discussed in Chapter 6.

Immigration into Canada has posed a dual linguistic problem for Quebec. First, it has reduced Quebec's share of the national population. Second, to the limited extent that immigrants have come to Quebec, they have threatened the province's francophone majority either by assimilating into the anglophone community or by assimilating into the francophone community, thus eroding the cultural homogeneity of that community. Historically, the proportion of immigrants adopting English rather than French was only slightly less in Quebec than in Canada as a whole; René Lévesque estimated that of the 620,000 immigrants who came to Quebec between 1945 and 1966, of whom only 8 percent came from France, 80 percent were absorbed into the anglophone population.[14] More recently, the majority of immigrants arriving in and deciding to stay in Quebec appears to be opting for the francophone community, although it should also be noted that 60 percent of the immigrants arriving in Quebec over the past twenty years have since left the province. Quebec's principal linguistic "battleground" has been Montreal where the west end of the island has been predominantly English, the east end predominantly French, and the middle the primary locale for immigrant settlement. It is in that middle community that the important choice between Canada's official languages has been made.

Yet, as Table 3.1 shows, the French language has more than held its own in Quebec, despite the problems associated with immigration. Anglophones are increasingly confined to the Montreal area, although significant enclaves still exist in the eastern townships, the upper Ottawa Valley, and Hull. Anglophones are also more likely than in the past to be recent immigrants to Canada. Between 1971 and 1986, the proportion of Quebecers with English as their mother tongue declined from 13.1 percent to 10.4 percent. The proportion of students attending French schools increased from 83.4 percent in 1976–77 to 87.5 percent in 1982–83, and is expected to reach between 91 percent and 92 percent by 1993–94.[15] Here it should be noted, however, that some of the very factors which are strengthening the French language in Quebec, such as the anglophone exodus, are undercutting the demographic strength of Quebec in Canada.

The Canadian population outside Quebec is often referred to as "English Canada," a term that neglects both anglophones within Quebec and francophones outside Quebec—groups which play critically important roles in Canadian language politics. It also distorts our perception of the non-French community which has become progressively less English, more ethnically diverse or multicultural, and more Canadian over time.[16] While 88 percent of the non-French population was of British descent in 1871, that proportion has fallen to less than 60 percent today.

Table 3.1
Percentage of Quebec Population with French Mother Tongue

1931	79.7%
1941	81.6
1951	82.5
1961	81.2
1971	80.7
1976	80.0
1981	82.4
1986	82.8

Yet, while English Canada is much more heterogeneous in its regional, ethnic, and religious composition than is "French Canada," this greater heterogeneity has not affected the supremacy of the English language outside Quebec. In the 1986 census, 80.0 percent of Canadians living in provinces other than Quebec reported English as their mother tongue.

Canadians of French mother tongue living outside Quebec at the time of the 1986 census constituted only 5.0 percent of the non-Quebec population, a decline from 7.8 percent in 1941 and 6.0 percent in 1971. In the past, Canada was sprinkled with French Canadian communities whose relatively self-contained educational, social, and religious institutions preserved the French language. Today, that insularity has disappeared in the face of social and technological change, and the linguistic assimilation of franchophones has been progressive and far-reaching. While francophones constitute one-third of New Brunswick's population, their proportion falls to approximately 5 percent in Ontario, Manitoba, and Prince Edward Island; 4 percent in Nova Scotia; 2 percent in the three western-most provinces; and less than 1 percent in Newfoundland.[17] Even the small proportion of non-Quebec residents whose mother tongue is French overstates the strength of the French language outside Quebec, since many such Canadians have been or are being assimilated into the anglophone community. When anglophones and francophones have come into contact anywhere across the country, linguistic assimilation has favoured anglophones, except in those cases where francophones make up more than 95 percent of the population.[18]

The linguistic trends inside and outside Quebec reveal that *linguistic segregation is increasing* in Canada. The francophone proportion of Quebec's population is increasing and will continue to increase, while the francophone proportion of the non-Quebec population is decreasing and will continue to decrease. As a consequence, Canada's francophone population is increasingly concentrated within Quebec. (In the 1986 census, 85.3 percent of those whose mother tongue was French, and 90.4 percent whose home language was French, resided in Quebec.) This

Table 3.2
Home Language, 1986 Census

	English[a]	French[b]	English and French[c]	Other
Canada	69.2%	23.3	1.6	5.9
Newfoundland	99.2	0.3	0.2	0.3
P.E.I.	96.3	2.3	1.0	0.4
Nova Scotia	95.8	2.4	0.9	0.9
New Brunswick	66.6	29.7	3.2	0.5
Quebec	11.2	81.5	3.0	4.3
Ontario	87.4	3.1	1.4	8.1
Manitoba	88.5	2.3	1.2	8.0
Saskatchewan	94.7	0.7	0.6	4.0
Alberta	93.0	0.8	0.7	5.5
B.C.	92.5	0.4	0.5	6.6
Northern Territories	76.9	1.0	0.7	21.4

[a]Includes those whose "home language" includes both English *and* a non-official language.
[b]Includes those whose "home language" includes both French *and* a non-official language.
[c]Includes those whose "home language" includes English, French, *and* a non-official language.

trend of linguistic segregation threatens francophone minorities outside Quebec and the anglophone minority inside that provide, and raises concerns about the long-term viability of national policies to promote bilingualism. As Donald Smiley notes,

> The ongoing territorial separation . . . means that a decreasing proportion of Canadians experience duality as an important circumstance of daily life. . . . Because of this, the resistance of most non-francophones to a view that the essential nature of their country is dualistic is understandable. . . . [19]

While the national linguistic split may be approximately three to one, anglophones to francophones, nobody lives in such a community. As Table 3.2 shows, we live in provincial communities where the linguistic balance is much more lopsided; only New Brunswick resembles the national average. Our local communities are likely to be even more homogeneous in their linguistic composition. Thus the national "average" has little resemblance to the linguistic reality that most Canadians experience.

Figure 3.4 presents a set diagram incorporating two overlapping segments of the Canadian population—those living in Quebec and those whose mother tongue is French. In combination, those segments identify the three linguistic groups around which the remainder of this chapter

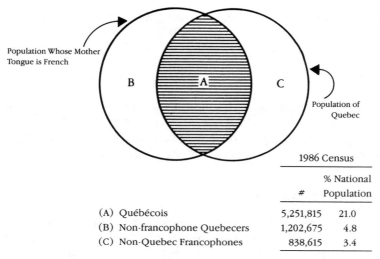

| | | 1986 Census | |
		#	% National Population
(A) Québécois		5,251,815	21.0
(B) Non-francophone Quebecers		1,202,675	4.8
(C) Non-Quebec Francophones		838,615	3.4

FIGURE 3.4

The Three Nodes of Linguistic Politics

will be structured. The largest group is the Québécois, defined here as the francophone residents of Quebec. This, of course, is a rather barren definition and the reader should be aware of the emotional baggage associated with the term. René Lévesque, for example, began his independence manifesto with the statement "We are *Québécois*," and then elaborated: "what that means first and foremost—and if need be, all that it means—is that we are attached to this one corner of the earth where we can be completely ourselves: this Quebec, the only place where we have the unmistakable feeling that 'here we can really be at home.' "[20] Anglo-Quebecers, a residual category composed of Quebec residents whose mother tongue is other than French, form the second group. This increasingly heterogeneous group encompasses the descendants of United Empire Loyalists whose roots in the province go back to the 1770s; more recent immigrants to Quebec who have assimilated into the anglophone rather than the francophone community; and anglophones who have moved to Quebec from other provinces. The third group is composed of those persons of French mother tongue living outside Quebec. With the emergence of Québécois as a group identity, the term "French Canadian" has come to be more specifically identified with these non-Quebec francophones. Interestingly, the federally funded organization for this group is called *Francophones hors Québec*, a label that describes the group by what it is not rather than by reference to a more positive, national affiliation such as is embodied in the term French Canadian. A fourth group not shown in Figure 3.4, composed of bilingual Canadians whose mother tongue is English rather than French, is now beginning to emerge as an important political constituency, and will be discussed in conclusion.

THE QUÉBÉCOIS

In order to set the stage for a discussion of contemporary language politics in Quebec, some historical background is required. This will be provided by a brief look at the Union nationale government of Maurice Duplessis, the Quiet Revolution, and the Parti Québécois.

Duplessis and the Union nationale

Revolutionary change must be measured against the benchmark of the past, the essence of the new being the negation of the old. For the Quiet Revolution of the 1960s, that benchmark became the Duplessis years, *la Grande Noirceur* (the "great darkness" or "dark ages"). Yet we also find in the Duplessis years one of the more enduring features of Quebec life— the use of the provincial state to protect Québécois interests and to hold at bay the national anglophone community and its perceived political agent, the Government of Canada.

The Duplessis years began with the victory of the Union nationale in the 1936 provincial election. The victory had been put together by a coalition of nationalist and Conservative elements, with control of the new party quickly coming to rest in the hands of Maurice Duplessis, who was to lead the party until his death in 1959. Although the Union nationale was defeated in 1939, it rebounded to win large majorities in 1944, 1948, 1952, and 1956 before narrowly losing to the Liberals in 1960. With a platform stressing Quebec nationalism, Catholic values, and strident anti-communism, the party's electoral appeal extended outward from its heartland in rural and small-town Quebec to encompass a majority of the francophone constituencies in Montreal and Quebec City.

The Union nationale's first defeat in 1939 helped establish its long-term success. Duplessis called the election three weeks after the outbreak of the Second World War, contending " . . . that the federal government was using the sweeping powers it possessed under the War Measures Act as a pretext for curtailing the rights of the province under the British North America Act."[21] (Here we have an example of the Canadian tendency to perceive the world through the narrow prism of federal–provincial relations!) Quite rightly, Duplessis's campaign was seen as a direct challenge to the national war effort, and Ottawa was quick to respond. The Quebec ministers in Mackenzie King's Liberal government took the unusual step of campaigning in the provincial election, stating that they were the only barrier to military conscription (see Chapter 7), and that they would resign from the federal cabinet if Duplessis won. Faced with this prospect and the certainty of conscription should the Conservatives form the national government, Quebec voters elected 69 Liberals and only 14 Union nationale candidates. However, it proved to be a Pyrrhic victory for the provincial Liberals when the King government was eventually forced to impose conscription despite intense opposition from Quebec. In the 1944 provincial election, the Union nationale became the nationalist vessel into which anti-conscription sentiment was poured, and the party captured 48 seats compared to 37 for the Liberals.

The Second World War and the postwar expansion of the federal government (see Chapter 6) threatened the constitutional autonomy of Quebec, the protection of which has been a primary objective for Quebec governments from Confederation through to the 1990s. Duplessis defended a classic vision of the federal state, albeit one garbed in the clothing of Quebec nationalism; the provinces, he argued, should be sovereign and autonomous within their own constitutional domain. At the 1950 federal–provincial conference, Duplessis stated: "I definitely and firmly believe that Canada is and should always be a federation of autonomous provinces,"[22] a stance he placed before the provincial electorate in the campaigns of 1948, 1952, and 1956.

Duplessis defended provincial autonomy in the face of a variety of federal incursions including unemployment insurance, family allowances, a national plan of hospital insurance, and the construction of the Trans-Canada Highway. Following the expiration of wartime tax agreements, Ottawa and Quebec clashed on the collection and share of personal and corporate income taxes. Duplessis also campaigned against federal immigration policy, postwar loans to the United Kingdom, and foreign aid to developing countries. In the 1948 provincial campaign, the Union nationale slogan was *Les liberaux donnent aux étrangers; Duplessis donne à sa province.* It should be stressed, though, that Duplessis's opposition to the expansion of government was not restricted to federal programs originating in Ottawa.

In step with most nationalist intellectuals in the Quebec of his time, Duplessis opposed the expansion of the provincial state on ideological grounds as much as he opposed the expansion of the federal state on constitutional grounds. Schools, hospitals, and social services remained almost entirely in private—mostly church—hands. The growth of the Quebec provincial state, a matter quite different from the constitutional defence of its legislative domain, was to await and characterize the Quiet Revolution.

Although Duplessis was vigilant to the point of extremism in warding off constitutional intrusions by Ottawa, his government actively encouraged the intrusion of anglo-Canadian and American capital into the Quebec economy. A combination of low taxes, minimal royalties on natural resources, and legislation which crippled provincial trade unions

Le Chef, Maurice Duplessis, leader of the Union Nationale from 1936 until his death in 1959.

Canapress Photo Service

created a receptive investment environment. The Duplessis government and the anglophone business elite enjoyed in turn a close and mutually beneficial working relationship. The business community gave Duplessis full authority within the political arena in return for freedom from state intervention and a restrained trade union movement.[23] The relationship was cemented by generous campaign contributions which fuelled the legendary Union Nationale patronage machine.[24] "Duplessism," which Clift describes as "the corruption of the social and personal bonds which people in traditional societies have towards one another," was part of the Union Nationale legacy.[25]

While a close relationship between the business community and provincial governments was not unusual in Canada, it had the effect in Quebec of reinforcing the linguistic segmentation of the provincial economy. This segmentation was captured by the expression, "capital speaks English and labour speaks French." Capital and labour were bridged by bilingual supervisors and foremen drawn almost exclusively from the francophone community. Thus the class division inherent in any industrialized society and the linguistic cleavage in Quebec were mutually reinforcing. Here it should be stressed, however, that Duplessis was not without supporters among the francophone elite, many of whom believed that distinctive French Canadian cultural values could only be preserved through insulation from the secular and anglophone world of commerce. Duplessis, in an explicit political alliance with the Catholic church, stuck to the tacit bargain that followed the Treaty of Paris: economic control would rest in English hands while control over social and cultural affairs would rest with the Catholic Church. As a consequence, the economic horizon for Quebec francophones was restricted.

For the many Quebec intellectuals and labour leaders radicalized during the **Asbestos Strike** in 1949, and for those Canadians outside the province who followed Quebec affairs, Duplessis symbolized an old, almost archaic Quebec. His death in 1959, followed by the defeat of the Union nationale government a year later, strengthened this symbolic role; he became the antithesis to, and thus helped define, the Quiet Revolution. The excesses of his administration—the authoritarianism, the patronage machine and electoral corruption, the political influence of the Catholic church, the antediluvian approach to trade unions—have been highlighted with the passage of time while the important threads of continuity in his constitutional stance, reaching back to the confederation agreement and forward to Quebec governments of the 1970s and 1980s, are often overlooked.

The Quiet Revolution

The 1960 election of Jean Lesage's Liberal government marks the onset of the "Quiet Revolution," an event of mythological proportions in Quebec. The "revolution" was not so much in the social and economic underpinnings of Quebec, which had been in a state of transition since the 1930s, as it was in the province's state of mind. It was in the "beliefs about the purpose and character of society and polity," as McRoberts describes it, that the change was "so profound and far-reaching that we can see how many would have found it 'revolutionary.' "[26] Yet even in this respect, the extent of change should not be exaggerated.[27] To call the Quiet Revolution the "springtime of Quebec," a phrase that has become commonplace, is to exaggerate the seasonal change and to understate the threads of continuity which link Quebec's past, present, and future.

The Quiet Revolution entailed an acceptance of the modern economic order and an enthusiasm for urban life. Gone was the cultural nostalgia for the values of a rural society long since departed. More importantly, the Quiet Revolution addressed the linguistic stratification of Quebec. In a province where 80 percent of the population was of French mother tongue, those who spoke only English earned substantially more on average than those who spoke only French or *those who were bilingual.* One could debate whether this reflected a host of cultural values and economic choices made by generations of francophone and anglophone Quebecers, whether it reflected economic reality on a continent where the vast majority of the population was anglophone, or whether it reflected the raw edge of corporate power. Yet, whatever the reason, it is clear that the injustice of a situation in which the language of the majority was an economic burden lay at the root of the language legislation that was to emerge from the Quiet Revolution.

Linguistic tension grew in step with the Quiet Revolution's secularization of Quebec society. In the past, the Catholic church had played a dominant role in the province. It controlled the educational system (apart from the Protestant schools) and most social services; it was a central actor in the trade union movement; and it had a pervasive influence in political affairs. By 1960 this influence was on the wane as the Church withdrew from an active role in political affairs, and many Quebecers withdrew from the Church. At the onset of the Quiet Revolution, more than 80 percent of the Catholic population of Quebec, which was more than 80 percent of the Quebec population, went to Mass every Sunday; by 1983 the attendance rate had fallen to only 25 percent.[28] With the drop in church attendance, the protection of the French language and cultural values passed from clerical hands to the secular hands of the provincial state.

The most important short-term impact of secularization came with the 1964 transfer of control over education from the Church to the Quebec Ministry of Education, a transfer associated with the modernization of the educational curriculum and a rapid growth in the proportion of students pursuing post-secondary education. No longer were post-secondary students channelled through the classical colleges into the three traditional francophone occupations—law, medicine, and the clergy— where they could work in French without getting entangled in the English business community. Graduates began to emerge with degrees in business administration, the social sciences, engineering, and communications. The modern economy was no longer rejected; it was embraced. English, however, was the language of work in that economy, at least at the levels to which the new graduates aspired. If one chose to or could work only in French, the limited employment opportunities in the private sector were not commensurate with the skills newly acquired from the secularized educational system. Immersion in the English work environment was equally unattractive given the personal cost of learning a second language, the handicap of operating in a second language, and the perceived danger of absorbing anglophone cultural values embedded in the workplace. From this dilemma came the pressure for legislation which would turn the ability to speak French into an economic asset, and which would shift the burden of bilingualism from the francophone majority in Quebec to the anglophone minority.

Another alternative for young francophone graduates was to pursue a career within the Quebec public service, where French was the language of work. In the face of limited employment prospects in the private sector, educational reform thus promoted a rapidly expanding public service staffed with young, aggressive, well-trained, and highly ambitious people. They were to spearhead Quebec's bureaucratic assault on the Canadian federal system, an assault designed to shift jurisdictional responsibilities *and the accompanying career opportunities* from Ottawa to Quebec City.[29] In a related move, René Lévesque, then Minister of Natural Resources in the Lesage government, created Hydro-Quebec in 1962, through the nationalization of the province's privately owned electric power companies. Upon nationalization, French replaced English as the language of work in the corporation, and Hydro-Quebec became both the showpiece for francophone managerial and technological competence, and an important employment pole for nationalistic francophones.[30]

It was the new Québécois middle class—the bureaucrats, writers, artists, intellectuals, teachers, musicians, technocrats, communications experts, and business managers—that derived the greatest personal benefits from the Quiet Revolution, and who stood to gain the most from independence.[31] (Not coincidentally, such individuals outside Quebec are the ones who stand to gain the most from Canadian policies of cultural nationalism vis-à-vis the United States.) The benefits of nationalism are rarely distributed evenly across social classes, and Quebec was to prove no exception. Within Quebec, trade union leaders have argued that the replacement of an anglophone managerial class with a francophone managerial class is not enough, that for a true revolution to occur there must also be a redistribution of wealth across social classes. To date, however, the primary income redistribution arising from the Quiet Revolution has been between anglophones and francophones rather than among social classes within the francophone community.

Before the Quiet Revolution, Quebec nationalism had been defensive in character, a bulwark for *la foi, la langue, la race* (faith, language, and race). Distinctive cultural values embedded in the Catholic religion and French language were to be protected by the federal division of powers, and by the insulation of francophones from the commercialism of the English world. By 1960 both forms of protection were breaking down. The federal government was encroaching upon Quebec's political autonomy, and the modern mass media had breached the cultural walls of "Fortress Quebec." In this environment, nationalism based on *la survivance* was not enough, and the theme of the Quiet Revolution became *la rattrapage*, the desire to catch up to the modern world, to make up for the winter of the Duplessis years. Here Jean Blain referred to the *déblocage* of the sixties, "the progress of Quebec at a more normal rate towards the ideals familiar to every modern society."[32] For some, particularly those associated with the Quebec Liberal party, the rejection of the Duplessis era led to the rejection of nationalism itself. For others, nationalism became more outward looking, expressing a new sense of confidence that Quebec could compete on equal terms in the modern social and economic order. For all, *la langue* rather than *la foi* or *la race* became the overarching concern.[33]

The Quiet Revolution initially had a positive reception outside Quebec, where it was assumed that *rattrapage* would strengthen national unity by moving Quebec into the Canadian and North American mainstreams, and that the language divide could be bridged by a national commitment to bilingualism. In fact, the Quiet Revolution exacerbated language conflict both inside and outside the province as francophones sought to establish French as one of the two national languages in Canada and as the dominant language in Quebec. Because of its *étatist* orientation, in which the provincial state was seen as the principal vehicle for *rattrapage*, the Quiet Revolution also posed a fundamental challenge to the Canadian federal system. As James Mallory explained in 1971, it was to the provincial state that Quebec leaders looked for economic development, social change, and career opportunities; "for them, these things must be done by their own French-Canadian state of Quebec, and not by Ottawa."[34]

The Liberal campaign slogan in the 1962 provincial election— *maîtres chez nous* or "masters in our own house"—became the slogan of the Quiet Revolution. For some, this meant the rollback of federal intrusions into the provincial legislative domain and the search for greater fiscal transfers to the Quebec government so that it could meet growing legislative commitments. Yet for many Québécois rollbacks were not enough, for the existing "house," as defined by the federal division of powers, was too small. If, they argued, the Quebec government was to meet its responsibilities as the "national" government for French Canada, Quebec needed, at the very least, a restructured federal system with expanded provincial powers. This would still mean, however, that some important decisions would continue to be made by the federal government, in which francophones were a minority, and a shrinking minority at that. For those who believed that national decisions should be made within the context of Quebec rather than Canada, any federal limitation on *maîtres chez nous* was unacceptable. In this sense, the independence movement can be seen as a logical although not a necessary extension of the Quiet Revolution.

Growing unrest with the federal status quo began to cause considerable unease outside Quebec. There were no comfortable answers to *the* political question of the late 1960s and 1970s: "what does Quebec want?"[35] Francophones who defended the federal system and who sought to exercise the power of French Canada through the government in Ottawa—people like Jean Chrétien, Marc Lalonde, Jean Marchand, Gérard Pelletier, and Pierre Trudeau—asked for a national commitment to bilingualism that many English Canadians were not prepared to make. Demands from the government of Quebec for a radically restructured federal system aided and abetted a broader assault by other provincial governments on the powers of the federal government. Of greatest concern was the growing support in Quebec for independence, for the dismantling of the Canadian state. Independence, it should be stressed, was seen not as a Quebec issue but as a direct threat to the very survival of Canada. As John Meisel wrote in 1973, "for many English Canadians the internal threat to the continuation of Canada is emotionally and in every other way the equivalent of the challenge to their own survival experienced by most French Canadian nationalists."[36]

Independence and the Parti Québécois

Although there had been sporadic agitation for Quebec's independence since the Rebellion of 1837, only in the 1960s did independence emerge as a serious option commanding a reasonable degree of popular support, a broad intellectual following, and the backing of organized political parties. Indeed, the 1960s witnessed a plethora of separatist groups, some of which sought Quebec's independence as a means to a fundamental transformation of the social and economic order. Here it should be noted that such groups, and indeed the Quiet Revolution itself, reflected in part a broader current of social and political unrest sweeping across North America and western Europe—a current that incorporated student radicalism, the American civil rights movement, opposition to the war in Vietnam, and early manifestations of the ecology and feminist movements.

The first and most important of the early independence groups, the *Rassemblement pour l'Independance nationale* (RIN), emerged only months after the Liberal victory in 1960. Other groups, while enjoying less popular support, achieved a high public profile through the use of terrorist tactics. Quebec politics during the 1960s were marked by bombs, politically motivated robberies, and extremist rhetoric borrowed heavily from radical movements in the United States, Cuba, and across the Third World.[37] Quebec was portrayed as a colony (or as a colony within a colony, depending upon one's perception of the Canadian–American relationship), destined like other colonies in the Third World for national liberation.[38] Repeated reference was made to the fact that the General

Assembly of the United Nations was rapidly filling up with countries that were smaller, less populous, and much poorer than Quebec.

While the colonial analogy continues to inform political debate on the place of Quebec in Canada, the radical stage of the independence movement was brought to a close by two events. The first was the founding of the Parti Québécois in 1967. Led by René Lévesque, the PQ grew out of the *Mouvement Souveraineté-Association* and retained sovereignty association as the foundation for its political platform. After the RIN was disbanded and largely absorbed by the PQ in 1968, the PQ dominated the independence movement although smaller, more radical groups remained. In Lévesque, a former broadcast journalist, the independence movement had found an inspired and inspiring leader. A seasoned politician and master communicator, Lévesque was able to orchestrate the ideologically diverse independence movement. He was the ideal foil for the province's most popular federalist spokesman, Pierre Trudeau. Lévesque was also effective in carrying the case for independence into English Canada. Unlike most of his contemporaries, Lévesque tried to show that Quebec's independence would be to the advantage of English Canada, that it would free the anglophone majority from continual compromise with the francophone minority. The rejection of independence, he argued, would mean perpetual wrangling "over everything and over nothing"; it would mean "the sterilization of two collective personalities which, having squandered the most precious part of their potential, would weaken each other so completely that they would have no other choice but to drown themselves in the ample bosom of 'America.' "[39]

The second event was the October 1970 kidnapping of James Cross, British Trade Commissioner in Montreal, and Pierre Laporte, Quebec's Minister of Labour, by the FLQ (*Front de Libération du Québec*). Cross was eventually freed but Laporte was killed; this was the first political murder in Canada since the 1868 assassination of MP Thomas D'Arcy McGee by an Irish nationalist. The kidnappings and associated political turmoil came to be known as the "**October Crisis**," in response to which the federal government imposed the War Measures Act. In conjunction with the Act, which gave law enforcement agencies extraordinary powers of search and arrest, the Canadian Armed Forces took on a highly visible role in guarding political leaders and public institutions. Membership in the FLQ was declared a post facto crime, and over 400 people were arrested in Quebec, none of whom were linked to the kidnappings. Although at the time the imposition of the War Measures Act enjoyed strong public support both inside and outside Quebec, it has subsequently been the topic of intense and generally critical debate.[40] Yet, regardless of the merits of the federal response, the October Crisis did mark the disappearance of terrorist factions within the Quebec independence movement. Whether violence was dropped for strategic reasons, given Ottawa's demonstrated willingness to counter force with superior force,[41] or out of a sense of revulsion towards the excesses of the FLQ is not clear. What is clear is that in the wake of the October Crisis the electoral aspirations of the Parti Québécois became virtually the exclusive concern of what had been an ideologically fragmented independence movement.

In the 1970 provincial election, the Parti Québécois captured 23 percent of the popular vote, but elected only seven members in the 110-seat National Assembly. In 1973 the PQ won only six seats, compared to 102 seats for the Liberals, although its share of the popular vote increased to 30 percent. On November 15, 1976, the PQ increased its vote to 41 percent and captured 71 seats; 26 seats were won by the Liberals, 11 by the Union nationale, and one each by the *Ralliement créditiste* and by the *Parti national populaire*. For the first time, a government had been elected which was committed to the withdrawal of Quebec from the federation. Ironically, however, the PQ's success stemmed as much from its promise *not* to secede, or at least not to interpret its election as an endorsation of independence, as it did from the party's support for independence.[42] In the 1976 campaign the PQ had promised that a referendum on sovereignty association would be held before any steps were taken towards independence. This strategy of *étapisme* (independence by stages) was based on public opinion polls which showed that support for the PQ and its leader ran consistently ahead of support for independence. The strategy, then, would enable voters to support the PQ while reserving judgment on independence. By postponing the decision on independence, the PQ assumed that time and demography were on its side, given that opposition to independence was most widespread among older voters and that support was strongest among the younger Québécois, many of whom were not yet in the electorate.

Sovereignty Association

The term "sovereignty association" binds together the goal of political independence (or sovereignty) for Quebec with both a recognition and acceptance of Quebec's economic integration with the rest of Canada. Its closest model comes from the European Community, wherein still-sovereign states pursue coordinated and integrated economic policies.

The proposal for sovereignty association called for Quebec and Canada-minus-Quebec to negotiate a series of agreements designed to preserve the existing benefits of economic association. Such agreements might yield a common tariff union, a common currency, the free flow of goods, people, and capital, and joint economic institutions such as a central bank. These agreements, however, would take the form of treaties between sovereign states, and hence would be flexible and adaptable rather than constitutional in character. The government of Quebec would be the only national government for Quebecers. Quebec residents would not elect representatives to Parliament, but instead would be represented in Ottawa by the Quebec government.

Sovereignty association would provide an equal partnership between Quebec and the rest of Canada, a partnership based on diplomatic norms of equality between sovereign states. Quebec would continue to enjoy the economic benefits of the larger Canadian union (as would other provinces) without being reduced to minority status within the Canadian state. In essence, then, sovereignty association would preserve economic linkages while creating a new form of political association.

For almost four years after the election of the PQ government, Canadians inside and outside Quebec waited for the referendum shoe to drop. In late 1979, Premier Lévesque set the stage with an emotional call to the people of Quebec, describing a yes-vote in the forthcoming referendum as " ... the only road that can open up the horizon and guarantee us a free, proud and adult national existence."[43] When the referendum was held on May 20, 1980, voters were not asked if they supported independence per se, but whether they supported the Quebec government entering into sovereignty association negotiations with Ottawa, with the final and at that point unknown pact being left for voter approval in a subsequent referendum. The intense referendum campaign, however, addressed the broader issue of independence rather than the specific question posed by the ballot.[44] The *oui* forces favoured independence in some fashion and at some time, although the immediate consequences of a yes vote were not at all clear. The *non* forces, united by the slogan *mon non est québécois*, favoured the retention of Canadian federalism, although not necessarily the federal arrangements in place at the time.[45] Indeed, the *non* campaign explicitly linked a no vote in the referendum to the promise of a "renewed federalism," an unspecified promise that was to ripple through subsequent national debates on the 1982 Constitution Act and the 1987 Meech Lake Accord. Speaking during the campaign, Trudeau declared:

> ... I can make the most solemn commitment that following a No, we will start immediately the mechanism of renewing the Constitution, and we will not stop until it is done. We are staking our heads, we Quebec MPs, because we are telling Quebecers to vote No. And we are saying to you in other provinces that we will not accept having a No interpreted as an indication that everything is fine, and everything can stay as it was before. We want change.... [46]

The campaign engaged all political forces within Quebec, including the seventy-four Quebec Liberal MPs led by Jean Chrétien and Prime Minister Trudeau. To an important degree the contest was personalized—Lévesque against Trudeau and, to a lesser extent, Quebec Liberal leader Claude Ryan—making it a battle not only between competing visions of

Quebec's future but also between leaders who had come to symbolize those competing visions.

In the end, 60 percent voted no and 40 percent voted yes; the sovereignty association proposal was defeated. (Although the *oui* camp captured close to 50 percent of the francophone vote, little attempt was made to claim a moral victory.) In the short term, however, the independence forces were not routed. In April 1981, the PQ government was re-elected with an *increased* majority and an 8 percent gain in its popular vote. In March 1982, an opinion poll conducted for *La Presse* found 28 percent of Quebecers supported sovereignty association and an additional 13 percent supported outright independence; among francophones alone, the total reached 48 percent.[47] Yet in the longer run the referendum decision emerged as a more decisive turning point. Regardless of the apparent contradiction of the 1981 election, the nationalist cause had been dealt a devastating blow; the PQ won despite its support for independence.[48] Then, in the 1985 provincial election following Lévesque's retirement, PQ support fell to 38 percent of the vote and only 24 seats in the National Assembly. The provincial Liberals, with former Premier Robert Bourassa at the helm, received 56 percent of the vote and 98 seats.

Quebec Language Legislation

Although, at the onset of the Quiet Revolution, francophones in Quebec made up 80 percent of the population and controlled the electoral process, they earned considerably less than anglophones in the province and shouldered virtually the entire burden of bilingualism. Initially, little was done to overcome the linguistic income gap, and anglophone domination of the provincial economy continued unabated.[49] Yet the discrepancy between the political power and the economic subservience of the Québécois was inherently unstable, and some legislative response was inevitable. In essence, that response would try to make French the language of work within the province and to make French more visible on signs, billboards, and advertisements; it would also try to ensure that immigrants to Quebec assimilated into the francophone majority. All of these objectives were seen as essential if francophones were to enjoy a full range of economic opportunities and if the French language and culture were to be kept afloat on the North American anglophone sea. The primary concern lay with the francophone majority in Quebec and not with francophone minorities in other provinces, minorities who in any event were beyond the legislative reach of the Quebec National Assembly.

The first major piece of language legislation was steered through the National Assembly by Robert Bourassa's Liberal government in 1974. Bill

Pierre Elliott Trudeau, elected in 1968 as the leader of the Liberal Party and the Prime Minister of Canada, was a strong advocate of a bilingual Canada and a forceful opponent of the independence movement in Quebec.

Canapress Photo Service.

René Lévesque, founder of the Parti Québécois, led his party to victory in the 1976 Quebec provincial election but failed to carry Quebec in the 1980 referendum on sovereignty association.

Canapress Photo Service.

22 declared French to be the "official language" of Quebec, and required students who wished to enroll in schools where English was the language of instruction to pass an English proficiency test, a measure designed to channel the children of immigrants into French schools. Although businesses were not required to adopt French as the language of work, Bill 22 encouraged the use of French in the workplace by stating that contracts with the provincial government might hinge upon francization. Bill 22 also required the use of French on all signs; other languages were permitted, but French had to predominate.

Bill 22 was strenuously attacked by Québécois nationalists who argued that it did not go far enough, and by the English and immigrant communities who argued that it went too far. The most contentious aspect of the legislation was the English proficiency requirement, limiting the freedom of parents to send their children to the school of their choice. As it turned out, Bill 22 had little impact on the pattern of school enrollments, in part because the English proficiency barrier could be overcome by immigrant parents and their children who made the effort, and in part because the legislation did not prevent francophone parents from enrolling their children in English schools. In the 1973/74 school year, before Bill 22 came into effect, 16 percent of pre-college students were enrolled in schools where the language of instruction was English; with the passage of Bill 22, this proportion marginally *increased* over the next three years.[50]

In 1977 the new Parti Québécois government passed Bill 101, Quebec's French Language Charter (*Charte de la langue francaise*). Bill 101 did not depart from the principles of Bill 22 so much as it strengthened both their application and their extension into Quebec society.[51] French was reaffirmed as the official language of Quebec; official bilingualism was rejected; and the only legislative reference to English was the passing mention of "other languages" in use in Quebec. Bill 101 abolished English as an official language of the legislature and courts, a provision overturned by the Supreme Court of Canada in 1979. English language schooling was restricted to children with at least one parent educated in English in Quebec, children who were attending an English school when Bill 101 came into effect, children who had a brother or sister already in an English school, and children whose parents were living in Quebec in 1977 but were educated in English elsewhere. Thus immigrants, people moving into Quebec from elsewhere in Canada, and Quebec francophones were denied educational freedom of choice. In order to strengthen the visibility of French, all public signs and advertisements were to be in French only. Municipalities, school boards, and hospitals, many of which were in English communities serving a largely anglophone clientele, were required to use French as the internal language of communication. The right to work in French was given legislative support, and firms employing more than 100 people were required to establish labour-management francization committees. (The legal requirements for francization, however, could be met by improving the French language skills of anglophone employees rather than by hiring or promoting francophones.) *L'Office de la langue française* was established to oversee the legislation, and its more zealous officials became known as the "tongue troopers."

In late 1983 the Quebec National Assembly moved to relax some of the provisions of Bill 101. Limited recognition was given to Quebec's English community by an addition to the Bill's preamble, stating that the Assembly pursues the objective of making French Quebec's official and working language "in a spirit of justice and openness, and showing respect for the institutions of the English Quebec community and of ethnic minorities, whose precious contribution to the development of Quebec it recognizes." English educational rights were extended to children from those provinces which offered French schooling similar to the level of English schooling provided in Quebec. Only New Brunswick qualified at the time but Ontario, the province from which Quebec employers would be most likely to recruit, could well qualify in the future. Students who had spent at least three years in an English-language high school in Quebec no longer had to pass a French proficiency test to practise as professionals in the province. Local institutions were no longer required to operate internally in French or to ensure that all employees spoke French, as long as French language services could be provided. Bilingual signs were allowed, but only for stores specializing in products "typical of a foreign country or particular ethnic group." Under the terms of the legislation, English Canadians did not qualify as a "particular ethnic group."

There is little question that Quebec's language policies have been successful in many respects, and that the French language in Quebec enjoys greater security in the early 1990s than it did in the 1960s and 1970s. Yet at the same time, those policies have become entangled in a series of conflicts with both the bilingualism policies of the Canadian government and the Charter of Rights. On July 26, 1984, a unanimous ruling of the Supreme Court struck down the "Quebec clause" in Bill 101 which required parents (or at least one parent) to have received their primary education *in English in Quebec* before their children could attend English schools in Quebec. In upholding the 1982 decision by the Quebec Court of Appeal, the Supreme Court ruled that the Bill 101 provision was inconsistent with Section 23 of the Charter, the "Canada clause" which guarantees the educational rights of linguistic minorities—whether French or English—across the country, where numbers warrant. In its case before the Supreme Court, the government of Quebec recognized the inconsistency but argued that the Bill 101 provision was consistent with

Demonstrators use their placards to beat an effigy of Quebec Premier Robert Bourassa at a 1986 demonstration against the Bourassa government in Montreal.

The Canadian Press.

Article One of the Charter, which states that the rights and freedoms guaranteed by the Charter are subject to "such reasonable limits prescribed by law as can be demonstrably justified in a free and democratic society." The Quebec submission concluded that the limitation placed on English education in Quebec "is reasonable because it is the expression of a collective right of the francophone majority—vulnerable because it is a minority in Canada and only constitutes 2.5 percent of the population of North America—to assure its rightful cultural security." The Supreme Court did not concur, ruling that Canadian citizens (and Quebec residents) who have themselves been educated in English elsewhere in Canada retained the right to have their children educated in English in Quebec, should numbers warrant.

The Supreme Court ruling will not have a dramatic impact on Quebec's linguistic profile or educational system. Bill 101's provisions have not been altered for immigrant children, nor has the educational situation been altered for francophone families in Quebec, as the Charter provisions do not extend to the children of francophone parents the right to an English education. Prior to the Supreme Court ruling, a study for the *Conseil de la langue française* by demographer Michel Paille predicted that the application of the Canada clause would increase the proportion of Quebec students attending English schools only from 13.1 to 13.5 percent.[52] As Liberal MNA Richard French said at the time of the ruling,

> The future of the French language is not going to be played out in the courtroom or in the classroom—but in front of a TV set and a computer screen. If you compare the importance of this decision with the importance of cablevision in Chicoutimi with American TV channels, or the impact of Boy George and Michael Jackson on the Quebec record industry, or the importance of English as the language of international technology, you are talking about another order of magnitude.[53]

Nevertheless, the Supreme Court ruling was of considerable symbolic importance. In a policy area of vital concern to the Quebec government, the Charter prevailed over legislation passed by the Quebec National Assembly.

This situation was repeated on December 15, 1988, when the Supreme Court of Canada overturned provisions of Bill 101 requiring that all signs, posters, and commercial advertising in the province be only in French. In upholding earlier decisions by the Quebec Superior Court in 1984 and the Quebec Court of Appeal in 1986, the Supreme Court ruled that such provisions violated freedom of expression guarantees in both the Quebec Charter of Rights and Freedoms and the Canadian Charter of Rights and Freedoms. The Court ruled that, while the province could require the use of French in public signage, it could not prohibit the use of other languages along with French:

> Whereas requiring the predominant display of French language, even its marked predominance, would be proportional to the goal of promoting and maintaining a French *visage linguistique* in Quebec and therefore justified under Section 9.1 of the Quebec Charter and Section 1 of the Canadian Charter, requiring the exclusive use of French has not been so justified.

In this case, however, Section 33 of the Constitution Act, 1982, enabled the Quebec government to override the Supreme Court decision. The Supreme Court's 1984 decision on minority education rights had been based on Section 23 of the Charter, a section to which the notwithstanding provisions of Section 33 do not apply. To the extent that the Canadian Charter applied in the 1988 case, the Court's decision was based on Charter protection for freedom of expression, to which the notwithstanding provisions can be applied. Therefore, the Quebec government responded with Bill 178 which, notwithstanding Charter guarantees with respect to freedom of expression, prohibits businesses from using bilingual signage or advertising outside their establishments while permitting limited bilingual signage inside. With respect to indoor signs, the regulations accompanying Bill 178 require that French letters be bigger than English letters, that the space around the French letters be larger, that the

French message be placed to the left of or above the English message, and that the colours of the French and English messages be the same. If they are not, the colour of the French message must be stronger.

Quebec's use of the notwithstanding clause was roundly condemned outside the province, while the inside–outside solution received a mixed reception at best inside Quebec. If nothing else, the episode demonstrates how difficult it can be to find a consensual middle ground in the emotionally charged arena of language politics.

SETBACK IN QUEBEC
Editorial in *The Globe and Mail*,
December 20, 1988

The signs issue carries heavy symbolic freight, and this thumping decision [to introduce Bill 178] sends a clear message to the anglophone minority in Quebec. It is the brutal message of Camille Laurin, father of Law 101, the man who actually wanted to raze the Quebec countryside of all English place names. The message says: you are intruders here, you don't belong and never did, you are illegitimate, your language pollutes the atmosphere and even to see it on a sign is an insult; pack up and go. Sadly, many of them will.

The consequences outside Quebec are equally grave. As of yesterday, Meech Lake was dead in the water, perhaps simply dead.

Worse, the generous vision of Canada that has transformed public policy in the last quarter century will come under renewed attack. From Lester Pearson through Pierre Trudeau to Joe Clark and Brian Mulroney, support for a bilingual country that respects its minorities has been painstakingly stitched together. Federal politics and institutions have been entirely transformed. Provincial governments have improved the lot of francophones outside Quebec. There have been setbacks, God knows, but overall progress has been tremendous.

What now? Almost certainly a hardening of hearts, a less generous attitude, an unwillingness to spend precious political capital on bilingualism and francophones, tougher questioning of the primordiality granted to Quebec's concerns; in sum, a quiet, unspectacular but undeniable backlash that will do us all no good.

ANGLO QUEBEC

Historically, Quebec's anglophones carried far greater weight than their numbers warranted. A minority within Quebec, albeit one with deep historical roots, they were able to draw upon the political power of the anglophone national majority, and upon the cultural and economic power of an overwhelming continental majority. Anglophones formed the economic elite in Quebec, although not all Quebec anglophones were part of that elite. They were the representatives of Anglo-Canadian and American capital and, in a crude sense, had the power and political protection that money can buy.[54] Anglophones also formed a sizable electoral constituency in Quebec that could be ignored only at considerable political risk. Anglophone or, more accurately, Protestant educational institutions were constitutionally protected through Sections 93.2 and 93.3 of the Constitution Act, 1867. Finally, Section 133 of the same Act stated that "either the English or the French language may be used by any Person in the Debates of the Houses of the Parliament of Canada and of the Houses of the Legislature of Quebec; and both those Languages shall be used in the respective Records and Journals of those Houses; and either of those Languages may be used by any Person or in any Pleading or Process in or issuing from any Court of Canada established under this Act, and in or from all or any of the Courts of Quebec."

In retrospect, two things are clear. First, the Quebec anglophone minority enjoyed a far more advantageous, even privileged position than that enjoyed by francophone minorities in other provinces. Second, the political position of the anglophone minority was precarious over the long run. It was inevitable that at some point the large francophone majority would use its democratic control of the provincial political system to redress the linguistic disparities in wealth and economic opportunity. What was needed before this could occur was a more positive outlook towards state intervention in the economic order, and an altered political perspective in which Anglo-Quebecers were seen less in a Canadian context (as part of the national *majority*) and more in a Québécois context (as a provincial *minority*). The Quiet Revolution provided both.

> In March 1988, Canada's Commissioner of Official Languages, D'Iberville Fortier, touched off a political furor when he rebuked the Quebec government for trying to "humiliate the adversary" (French version) or "humble the competition" (English version) in its treatment of the anglophone minority. The comment in the Commissioner's annual report provoked a heated response from the Quebec National Assembly, which unanimously denounced Mr. Fortier's intervention in Quebec affairs, and from Progressive Conservative MPs in Quebec.

In the wake of the Quiet Revolution and the coming to power of the Parti Québécois a decade later, Quebec anglophones underwent a dramatic transformation. They became strangers, if not imperialists, in their own land, *les autres* in a province vibrating to the themes of Québécois nationalism. Anglophones took up the uncomfortable garments of minority status being shed by Quebec francophones. Their relative wealth became a political stigma, and their contribution to the province was stripped of symbolic recognition as Quebec was recast as a Québécois and francophone society. Their grip on the province's business community was loosened, although not broken, by language legislation and educational reform. Many left Quebec to seek a more hospitable social and linguistic climate elsewhere in Canada. The remaining "allophone" community is no longer *English* Canadian, as it had largely been in the past. Somewhat ironically, its diverse ethnic population, composed of those whose mother tongue is not French, is cast together and bound together by the province's language legislation.

Here it is interesting to note parenthetically that Quebec's language legislation has also increased the heterogeneity of the francophone community. Such legislation has separated language and culture, with the French language becoming the primary language of communication for all cultures in Quebec. Whereas in the past francophones shared a common history, culture, and religious orientation, this will be less and less the case in the future as the francophone community expands to encompass the totality of Quebec society. Historical events like the Conquest may lose their integrative and symbolic force, as a growing proportion of the francophone community comes to find its roots in a quite different historical setting.

Quebec's language legislation has set in motion a modest redistribution of economic opportunities and social advantage in which middle-class francophones have been the principal winners, and Quebec anglophones the principal losers. To defend their linguistic interests, Quebec's anglophones must rely upon their declining economic and demographic power, their cultural identification with the North American mainstream, and the language policies of the national government. However, those policies, to which we now turn, are directed more to the protection of the French language outside Quebec than to the protection of either official language within Quebec.

FRENCH CANADIANS AND BILINGUALISM

Beyond the provincial jurisdiction of Quebec, language conflict has taken two forms. The first has occurred when the interests of French Canada, broadly conceived, have clashed with those of the English Canadian majority. Apart from the conscription crises, discussed in Chapter 7, and the 1885 execution of Louis Riel following the **North-West Rebellion**, this first form of conflict has been surprisingly rare.

In English Canada, Riel's execution was seen as just and deserved. Prime Minister Macdonald's statement that "he shall hang though every dog in Quebec bark in his favour" captured the more moderate reaction, while *The Toronto Star* (May 18, 1885) wrote: "Strangle Riel with the French flag! That is the only use that rag can have in the country." In Quebec, the reaction was dramatically different. Israel Tarte, a prominent Quebec Liberal, predicted that "at the moment when the corpse of Riel falls through the trap and twists in convulsions of agony, at that moment an abyss will be dug that will separate Quebec from English-speaking

Canada, especially Ontario."[55] Tarte's prediction was borne out as 40,000 people took to the streets of Quebec to burn Macdonald in effigy.

It is often assumed in Canadian political folklore that the French Canadian reaction to Riel's execution set in motion a political realignment that persisted into the 1980s. Honoré Mercier, who declared that "the murder of Riel was a declaration of war upon French-Canadian influence in Confederation," formed the Parti National and, in 1886, drove the provincial Conservatives from power in Quebec.[56] Wilfrid Laurier, who said "had I been born on the banks of the Saskatchewan I myself would have shouldered a musket," became leader of the national Liberal party and, in 1896, inaugurated a Quebec-based Liberal dynasty that was to dominate Canadian politics for most of the next 90 years.[57] While electoral statistics suggest that the role of Riel's execution has been exaggerated in explanations of both Liberal success and Conservative failure in Quebec,[58] the execution has nonetheless become an important symbol in the mythology of Canadian partisan politics.

The second form of conflict has centred on the language and educational rights of French Canadian minorities outside Quebec, with the "Manitoba Schools Question" providing an early example.[59] In 1890 the Manitoba legislature abolished the existing denominational school system, which included Catholic schools using French as the language of instruction, and replaced it with a non-sectarian public system in which English was the sole language of instruction. Franco-Manitobans, with ecclesiastical support from the Catholic Church in Quebec, urged the Conservative government in Ottawa to **disallow** the Manitoba legislation. The government demurred, pending an appeal to the Judicial Committee of the Privy Council. When that appeal upheld the provincial legislation, Ottawa was urged to pass **remedial legislation** restoring the dual school system. This demand was deflected onto the Canadian Supreme Court, which ruled that Parliament could not pass such legislation, and then onto the Judicial Committee, which ruled that it could. All this set the stage for the 1896 general election campaign in which the Conservatives promised remedial legislation, believing that the consequent losses in English Canada (21 Conservative seats were in fact lost) could be offset by gains in Quebec, where remedial legislation was strongly supported. However, although the Liberals opposed remedial legislation and incurred the wrath of the Catholic church by so doing, Wilfrid Laurier's appeal to his fellow French Canadians was too great. The Liberals captured 49 Quebec seats, a gain of 14 from 1891, and won the election.

In the Manitoba Schools Question, Laurier charted a constitutional course similar in principle to that followed by Quebec governments over the next 90 years. Because Laurier attached great importance to the federal division of powers in the protection of French Canada, he opposed remedial legislation, portraying it as a threat to provincial autonomy. If remedial legislation was used in the short term to protect Franco-Manitobans by breaching the federal–provincial division of powers, in the longer term it could lead to the intrusion of the English Canadian national majority into the internal affairs of Quebec. Thus, on constitutional grounds, Franco-Manitobans had to be sacrificed to the greater good of provincial autonomy. Laurier, however, did work out a practical compromise with the Manitoba government which met many, albeit not all, of the educational concerns of Franco-Manitobans.

Conflict over minority education rights brings us back to a basic limitation in the federal protection of minority interests. In the specific case of French Canada, federalism provides protection *to the extent that* French Canadian interests fall within the provincial domain, and *because* francophones form a majority in Quebec. The federal division of powers per se provides protection to national minorities which can be recast as provincial majorities; it provides no protection within the domain of the national government, and no protection for provincial linguistic minorities, be they French or English. Given these limitations, it is not surprising that many French Canadians have sought protection within "Fortress Quebec," defending and where possible expanding the powers of *their* government. Nor should it be surprising that this strategy is rejected by French Canadians living in other parts of Canada, for whom Quebec has been a fickle ally at best. However, it has also been rejected by a significant number of francophones within Quebec who see the fulfillment of French Canada taking place within the Dominion rather than the more narrow confines of Quebec. It is this perspective that is closely associated with the writings and political leadership of Pierre Elliott Trudeau.

In reaction to the claustrophobic Duplessis years, many French Canadians sought an expanded national vision in which French and English Canada would co-exist in an equal partnership rather than as the "two solitudes" so vividly portrayed by novelist Hugh MacLennan in 1945. This vision was captured by the Royal Commission on Bilingualism and Biculturalism, which had been established in 1963 by Prime Minister Lester Pearson "to inquire into and report upon the existing state of bilingualism and biculturalism in Canada and to recommend what steps should be taken to develop the Canadian Confederation on the basis of an equal partnership between the two founding races...." Chaired by André Laurendeau and Davidson Dunton, the B & B Commission laid the foundations for national bilingualism. However, while its call for the equality of the English and French language—for a *bilingual* Canada— was accepted, its call for the equality of the English and French societies—for a *bicultural* Canada—was not. In its response to the Commission, the federal government separated the threads of language and culture which the Commissioners had woven into a single strand; the federal government argued that *multiculturalism within a bilingual framework* was a vision which better captured the demographic and political realities of modern Canada.

Prime Minister Pearson started the federal public service down the long, rocky road towards full bilingualism in 1966. Then, in July 1969, Parliament passed the Official Languages Act which declared English and French to be Canada's official languages; granted all citizens the right to communicate with the federal government in the official language of their choice; enabled employees of the federal government to work in the official language of their choice; and provided funds for second language education across Canada. Official bilingualism had arrived. In 1982 the principal features of the Official Languages Act were "constitutionalized" in Sections 16 through 23 of the Charter. The most recent development came with the passage of Bill C-72 in the summer of 1988. Bill C-72 amended the Official Languages Act by formally establishing English and French as the official languages of the federal courts (but not of provincial courts presided over by federally appointed judges), extending the bilingual provision of federal government services where a "significant demand" exists, committing the government to ensuring that French and English Canadians have equal access to appointment and promotion in the federal public service, and increasing the powers of the Commissioner of Official Languages. As a consequence, there has been some expansion, particularly in western Canada, in the number of public service jobs designated as "bilingual-imperative" positions. When the Bill was initially introduced, it provoked considerable opposition, particularly in western Canada and even among western Canadian Progressive Conservative MPs. Opposition to the Bill formed a major plank in the 1988 campaign platform of the nascent and western Canada-based Reform Party of Canada. However, after relatively minor amendments in committee, the Bill was passed by the House of Commons with only nine MPs, all Conservatives, voting against it.

Language Provisions in the Canadian Charter of Rights and Freedoms

The 1969 Official Languages Act has now been "constitutionalized" in Sections 16 to 20 of the Charter of Rights and Freedoms.

Section 16(1) of the Charter states that "English and French are the official languages of Canada and have equality of status and equal rights and privileges as to their use in all institutions of the Parliament and government of Canada." Section 16(2) extends this provision to the legislature and government of New Brunswick.

Sections 17 and 18 establish the equality of English and French in the proceedings of Parliament and the New Brunswick legislature (debate, statutes, records, journals), while Sections 19(1) and 19(2) state that "either English or French may be used by any person in, or in any pleading in or process issuing from" any court established by Parliament or any court of New Brunswick."

Section 20(1) states that "any member of the public in Canada has the right to communicate with, and to receive available services from, any head or central office of an institution of the Parliament or government in English or French, and has the same right with respect to any other office of any such institution where (a) there is a significant demand for communications with and services from that office in such language; or (b) due to the nature of the office, it is reasonable that communications with and services from that office be available in both English and French."

Section 23 of the Charter goes beyond the Official Languages Act to state that, where numbers warrant, "citizens of Canada (a) whose first language learned and still understood is that of the English or French linguistic minority population of the province in which they reside, or (b) who have received their primary school instruction in Canada in English or French and reside in a province where the language in which they received that instruction is the language of the English or French linguistic minority population of the province, have the right to have their children receive primary and secondary school instruction in that language in that province." Section 23(2) states that "citizens of Canada of whom any child has received or is receiving primary or secondary school instruction in English or French in Canada, have the right to have all their children receive primary and secondary school instruction in the same language."

Although national bilingualism was set in motion by Lester Pearson, it has been more closely identified with the personality and career of Pierre Trudeau, whose government introduced the 1969 Official Languages Act. His flawless command of both languages epitomized the bilingual ideal, and bilingualism was a central concern, at times even a preoccupation, of the governments he led. In *Grits*, Christina McCall-Newman captures the Trudeau image, if not mythology, in the following passage: "above all he was perfectly bilingual, with his French father and his English mother, his Jesuit education at home and his post-graduate education abroad, the pan-Canadian the country had been looking for, who fused the French and English into one, a kind of racial hermaphrodite, the unmatchable bicultural man."[60] Bilingualism was to Trudeau " . . . as the CPR was to John A. Macdonald, his instrument for building a continent-wide country out of a huddled group of provinces."[61]

Bilingualism was well received initially in English Canada; it was seen as a necessary and appropriate response to the Quiet Revolution and to the growing independence movement in Quebec. Given the role that young francophones were beginning to play as nationalist pointmen within the Quebec public service, it seemed essential that countervailing career opportunities be opened up for francophones in Ottawa. More generally, if French Canadians were to be bottled up in Quebec by their language, the appeal of independence would be difficult to counter.

Bilingualism thus appeared to be an acceptable price for national unity. It might also be speculated that national bilingualism played a significant role in the resurgent Canadian nationalism of the period. At a time when the British connection no longer played a useful role in setting Canada apart from the United States, Canada's bilingual character came to satisfy the same nationalistic need.

For many English Canadians growing uneasy about the independence movement in Quebec, Trudeau was the champion they sought, the leader who would stand up to the separatists and defend Canada in a way that no anglophone of the times could do, at least in Quebec. This role was dramatically illustrated on the eve of the 1968 federal election when Trudeau reviewed Montreal's St. Jean Baptiste Day parade. As separatist demonstrators threw bottles at the reviewing stand, and as other dignitaries fled, Trudeau stood alone, unmoved and defiant. It was a moment of personal courage and dramatic political symbolism that anointed the new prime minister as Canada's champion against the *indépendantistes*. Yet this role was easily misunderstood, for although Trudeau opposed the *indépendantistes* and the more extreme constitutional demands of Quebec governments, he vigorously promoted the extension of the French presence throughout the institutional fabric of the Canadian society. In its own way, Trudeau's vision of Canada was no less sweeping in the demands that it would make upon English Canadians than was the vision held by René Lévesque. As Richard Gwyn argues, although "Trudeau and Lévesque are the heroes of opposing armies . . . each has fought for his people, the French Canadians, even though Lévesque's francophones are limited to those within Quebec while Trudeau's vision encompasses all in Canada whose mother tongue is French."[62] As Gwyn goes on to argue, Trudeau sought to extend the French fact across Canada while Lévesque sought to consolidate and defend it within Quebec. In either case, English Canadians faced the linguistic transformation of their society.

Official bilingualism was not new in Canada. As noted above, Section 133 of the 1867 Constitution Act provided for the use of both English and French in Parliament, in federal courts created through the Act, and in the legislature and courts of Quebec. Thus on Parliament Hill both languages were used in debate and Hansard. All Acts of Parliament were printed in both languages; even the prayer beginning each sitting day was read by the Speaker in English and French on alternate days. Bilingual stamps appeared in 1927; bilingual currency in 1936; and in 1962 Prime Minister John Diefenbaker introduced bilingual federal cheques and simultaneous translation in Parliament. Such forms of bilingualism were virtually cost-free to English Canadians. The effect of the Official Languages Act, however, was to extend the parliamentary equality of the two languages into the wider society, to broaden the scope of state intervention in the language field, and thus to intrude in a more direct and visible fashion into the lives of Canadians. All federal government signs and publications began to appear in both languages. Consumer products were required to carry bilingual labels, and airline passengers were told to buckle up in English and French. In short, Ottawa was increasing the visibility of French across Canada, albeit in a bilingual context, in a manner analogous to the Quebec government's efforts to increase the visibility of French in Quebec, albeit in a unilingual context.

When Trudeau worked in the Privy Council Office in the early 1950s, during the time when Louis St. Laurent was serving as Canada's second French Canadian prime minister, he witnessed what Christina McCall-Newman has described as an "unbelievable fight" to have a sign put up in the East Block reading *Bureau du Premier Ministre* as well as *Prime Minister's Office*.[63] In retrospect, and given the extent to which the Official Languages Act has transformed the linguistic face of Canada, opposition to such an innocuous proposal, particularly during the tenure of a French Canadian prime minister, almost defies comprehension.

Bilingualism had its most immediate impact on the federal public service. The *institutional* bilingualism embodied in the Official Languages Act was designed so that *individuals* would not have to be bilingual—Canadians would be able to communicate with the federal government in the official language of their choice. However, bilingual institutions necessitated a bilingual public service. Before the reforms launched by Prime Minister Pearson, English had been *the* language of work in the federal public service. Francophones were proportionately under-represented in Ottawa, with under-representation increasing as one moved up through the ranks. Virtually the only bilingual public servants were those of French mother tongue. As senior positions demanded a skilled and even artful use of language, francophones were placed at a double disadvantage. Not only did they have to absorb the costs of learning a second language but, in having to function in their second language, they often appeared less subtle, less sensitive, and thus less competent than their anglophone compatriots.

Official Languages Programs

In the 1987–88 fiscal year, the government of Canada allocated $542 million to official languages programs. This total included $217 million transferred to the provinces and territories for language programs, $20 million for official language minority groups, $33 million for language training within the Public Service Commission, $84 million for official languages services offered through the Secretary of State, $50 million for the Armed Services, $27 million for programs in crown corporations, and almost $11 million for the Commissioner of Official Languages.

Source: *1987 Annual Report of the Commissioner of Official Languages* (Ottawa: Minister of Supply and Services, 1988), p.218.

"Darling, I am just a poor civil servant . . . cheri, je ne suis qu'un pauvre fonction-naire . . . but I love you . . . mais je vous aime beaucoup . . . will you . . . voulez-vous . . . "

Len Norris, *15th Annual*. Originally in *The Vancouver Sun*. April 15, 1966.

With the introduction of bilingualism, knowledge of French became a career asset rather than a liability; anglophones now faced limited career mobility unless they learned French. Although the majority of public service positions were not designated as bilingual, the senior positions and thus, implicitly, the middle-rank positions from which senior managers were drawn, were so designated. To ease the transition to bilingualism, French language training was made available in 1973 for anglophones holding positions which had been designated as bilingual. For thousands of anglophones, many of whom were senior officials at the peak of their careers, this meant months of struggling with the acquisition of a new language. By the early 1980s French language training began to be phased out, with greater reliance being placed on an adequate knowledge of both official languages prior to initial recruitment. Nonetheless, as late as 1987 more than 20,000 civil servants, at a cost of more than $20 million, were still receiving second-language training provided through the Public Service Commission.[64]

Bilingualism has resulted in an increase in the number of francophones employed within the federal public service. The 1987 report of Canada's Official Languages Commissioner shows that the proportion of francophones has risen to almost 28 percent from 21 percent in 1965, and that the proportion in senior positions has risen from 17 percent to almost 26 percent over the same period. Not coincidentally, bilingualism is now a requirement for over 28 percent of positions within the federal public service. This increase reflects the fact that, during the Trudeau governments, bilingualism was associated with the growth of "French Power" in Ottawa, a phenomenon marked by the emergence of highly visible and influential French Canadian ministers, deputy ministers, heads of crown corporations, and senior advisors. At the same time, a knowledge of both official languages became increasingly useful outside the government for the leaders of professional organizations, interest groups, and cultural associations claiming to be national in character. In short, bilingualism became almost a prerequisite for individuals hoping to scale the peaks of Canadian political life.

Bilingualism was also associated with the widespread symbolic transformation of Canadian public life that began in the mid-1960s with the creation of a Canadian flag to replace the Union Jack and Red Ensign. Symbols grounded in only one of the two linguistic communities, such as the coat-of-arms on mail boxes, were replaced by symbols which might include not only French Canadians but also Canadians of neither British nor French descent. The names of government departments and agencies were changed to names that could be easily expressed in either official language, and thus we had Transport Canada/Transports Canada, Canada Post/Postes Canada, Lotto Canada, and so forth. The national anthem was increasingly sung in its bilingual version, to the initial accompaniment of boos from some sports fans in English Canada. During the same period Canada began to convert to the metric system of measurement, a system described by both its opponents and opponents of bilingualism as the "French system of measurement."

The Official Languages Act captured an important if contentious tenet of Canadian life. If French Canadians were to be *Canadians*, then not only Quebec but also Canada would have to be the home of the French language. As Henri Bourassa wrote in 1912:

Rodney the Redneck at full voice and prepared to make one of his typical arrangements for René Lévesque.

"I know what I'd tell Quebec . . . the Plains of Abraham are still there and I'll even make it best two out of three."

we deserve better than to be considered like the savages of the old reservations and to be told: "Remain in Quebec, continue to stagnate in ignorance, you are at home there; but elsewhere you must become English. No, we have the right to be French in language; we have the right to be Catholics in faith; we have the right to be free by the constitution. We are Canadians before all; and we have the right to be as British as anyone. And we have the right to enjoy these rights throughout the whole expanse of Confederation."[65]

Bourassa's logic is persuasive, but it did not prevent the development of significant opposition to bilingualism outside Quebec. As Raymond Breton has argued more recently, "individuals expect to recognize themselves in public institutions."[66] Unfortunately, while the symbolic transformations noted above made it easier for French Canadians to find their reflection, it had the opposite impact on segments, and particularly

older segments, of the English Canadian population. The national majority was being asked to accept extensive symbolic change for the sake of
the national minority, change that included a significant redistribution of
status between the English and French communities. To many, bilingualism was seen not as the foundation for a stronger pan-Canadian nationalism but as an assault on the country's British heritage. Opposition was
particularly intense in the more multicultural West, where the French
Canadian minority tended to be seen in a regional rather than national
context. While in the latter context French Canadians made up almost a
third of the national population, in a regional context they were outnumbered by many of the ethnic groups who had settled in the West and had
adopted the English language in the process.

Regional Differences in Support for Bilingualism

An April 1988 survey for Southam News by Angus Reid Associates found
strong national support for official bilingualism. Across the country, 67
percent of the respondents supported official bilingualism, with 32 percent
offering strong support and 35 percent more moderate support. Only 31
percent opposed official bilingualism, 17 percent strongly and 14 percent
moderately.

There were, however, sharp regional variations in this national pattern.
Support for official bilingualism, be it strong or moderate, ranged from 88
percent in Quebec to 67 percent in Atlantic Canada, 63 percent in Ontario, 58
percent in British Columbia, and only 47 percent on the prairies. Conversely,
opposition ranged from 49 percent on the prairies to 40 percent in British
Columbia, 34 percent in Ontario, 30 percent in Atlantic Canada, and only 9
percent in Quebec. Of those respondents whose mother tongue was French,
87 percent supported official bilingualism compared to 62 percent of those
whose mother tongue was English.

Although bilingualism affected career opportunities for a substantial
number of anglophones, it may have been the perception of a threat to
"status" that best explained the intensity of opposition among individuals
who were untouched in any practical or objective sense by the introduction of bilingualism. For others, opposition was not to bilingualism per se
but to what they saw as Ottawa's excessive preoccupation with bilingualism and the consequent neglect of economic and regional concerns.
In this respect Dalton Camp argues that the politics of bilingualism
intensifies regional and intergovernmental strains within the national
community:

The persistence and growing pervasiveness of bilingualism had alienated
English Canadians from their federal government, turning them inwards to
more familiar, compatible and nearer political jurisdictions in the provinces. ... The government of Canada had lost its constituency.[67]

The surprising thing about opposition to bilingualism is that it failed to find a champion within the party system. Apart from a few dissenting voices among Progressive Conservative MPs, the major parties locked arms on the original Official Languages Act and, with the exception of the Reform Party and another handful of Conservative MPs, on the 1988 Bill C-72 amendments. In elections subsequent to 1969, voters were not given a choice between parties supporting and opposing bilingualism. Conservative leaders Robert Stanfield and Joe Clark, whose party potentially had the most to gain from catering to anti-French sentiment, given its then bleak electoral prospects in Quebec, were adamant in their support of bilingualism. Outside the party system, opponents of bilingualism who found their way into the media encountered a consistently hostile reception. They tended to be treated as bigots and political Neanderthals rather than as citizens with legitimate concerns about the direction of national policy.

Within the political science literature, the deliberate exclusion of potentially divisive issues from public debate and electoral competition by political and social elites is termed "consociationalism." A consociational democracy can be defined as one " . . . with subcultural cleavages tending towards immobilism and instability but which is deliberately turned into a stable system by the leaders of the major subcultures."[68] In the case of French–English relations, consociationalism has shaped an asymmetrical national debate over Quebec's place within the Canadian federal state. Although the debate in Quebec has ranged freely over the full range of alternatives, from support for the federal status quo to the advocacy of complete independence, the debate in English Canada has been far more restricted. Rarely has it encompassed the creation of a unilingual anglophone state including Quebec, the use of force to suppress Quebec's independence, or the welcomed departure of Quebec. Persons holding such views have not been encouraged to join in the debate over Quebec's place in Canada; they confront an elite consensus that national unity must be maintained, and that bilingualism is essential for this.

Bilingualism in Canada

In the 1986 census, more than four million Canadians stated that they could conduct a conversation in both English and French. This figure represents 16.2 percent of the national population, up from 15.3 percent in 1981 and 13.4 percent in 1971. (Between 1981 and 1986 bilingualism increased in every province except Alberta, where the proportion was unchanged.) However, it should be noted that the prevalence of bilingualism varies dramatically across Canada's linguistic communities. More than half of the bilingual population lives in Quebec, where 54 percent of anglophones and 30 percent of francophones declared themselves bilingual in the 1986 census. Outside Quebec,

79 percent of francophones but only 6 percent of anglophones were bilingual. Rates of bilingualism ranged from 29 percent in New Brunswick to 12 percent in Ontario and less than 3 percent in Newfoundland.[69]

The national policy of bilingualism has created a new linguistic constituency which, in turn, provides important political support for that policy. Historically, only a small fraction of the Canadian population—12.7 percent between 1931 and 1971—has been bilingual, and of those 60 percent lived in Quebec, with only 8 percent of the non-Quebec population being bilingual.[70] The vast majority of bilinguals were those of French mother tongue who had learned English for reasons of employment, or who were in the process of being assimilated into the English Canadian community. English mother tongue bilinguals were a rare breed until the passage of the Official Languages Act, when knowledge of French became an economic asset for anglophones and unilingualism could eventually mean "a life sentence to job immobility."[71] As a result, an explosive growth in French immersion programs occurred across the country—programs which cater largely to an English mother tongue clientele. By the end of the 1980s, over 200,000 Canadian students were in French immersion programs. In the lower grades outside Quebec, anglophone immersion students now outnumber French mother tongue students who are receiving their education in French. It is interesting to note, however, that at the same time immersion enrollments have been increasing, the overall proportion of students outside Quebec who are taking French has been decreasing. *Thus French language education has become a more intensive experience for a smaller proportion of the student body.*[72] As a consequence we may be developing, for the first time in our history, " . . . a distinct social elite of young, upper middle-class, bilingual graduates."[73] This elite will form a powerful lobby for the national bilingualism policies from which it derives its elite status. It may also reinforce class cleavages within the Canadian body politic. As Donald Smiley explains, " . . . because in anglophone Canada it is the more prosperous parents who are most insistent about their children's becoming bilingual, the issue has the potentiality of dividing English-speaking Canadians along class lines."[74]

Bilingualism Pays!

A study for the Economic Council of Canada has shown that in 1980 bilingual individuals earned more. Across Canada, bilingual men earned 11 percent more than unilingual men, and bilingual women earned 12 percent more than unilingual women. The gap was greatest in Quebec, but still averaged 6 percent for both sexes outside Quebec. The gap has been growing over time. (Cited in Jeffrey Simpson, "The Bilingual Edge," *The Globe and Mail*, National Edition, February 24, 1984, p. 6.)

Political tensions stemming from a bilingual elite have also manifested themselves in other ways. When Newfoundland MP John Crosbie ran for the leadership of the national Progressive Conservative party in 1983, his lack of French proved to be an insurmountable problem. Crosbie's reaction on the campaign trail is worthy of note:

> There are over 20 million of us who are unilingual English or French . . . I don't think that the 3.7 million who are bilingual should suddenly think themselves some kind of aristocracy and leaders can come only from their small group.[75]

Don Braid of the *Edmonton Journal* called Crosbie's comments a "burst of insight." For this "self-satisfied ruling elite," Braid charged,

> Bilingualism has become a ritual chant . . . they demand it of national leaders, thus guaranteeing their continued membership in the club. They dismiss dissenters as red-necked bigots and intellectual lightweights, while exercising a powerful bigotry of their own.[76]

Perhaps the most acute political tensions stemming from official bilingualism have arisen within the provincial arenas, as minority language groups and governments have wrestled with the provincial implications of the federal policy. There is no question that the existence of national language legislation has increased pressure from francophone minorities for bilingual access to provincial programs and, in some cases, recognition of French as an official language. In New Brunswick, English and French are now constitutionally entrenched as official languages. In Ontario, where francophones make up less than five percent of the population, most government services are provided in both English and French, and every French-speaking student has been guaranteed the right to an education in French. French-language rights, however, are enshrined in provincial statutes only and not in the constitution. The Ontario government has resisted calls for constitutional entrenchment, arguing that the backlash which might result could jeopardize francophone interests within the province.

In 1979 the Supreme Court of Canada ruled that Manitoba legislation making English the province's only official language was unconstitutional; the 1890 provincial legislation violated the terms of the 1870 Manitoba Act, passed by the Parliament of Canada, which had brought Manitoba into Confederation and which now forms part of the Canadian constitution. This ruling threw into question the constitutionality of 14,000 pages of laws passed since 1890 and written only in English. Thus the Supreme Court ruling forced Manitoba to translate its provincial statutes and to restore French as an official language in the legislative assembly and courts. For its part, the provincial government designated

500 public service positions to be filled eventually by bilingual employees.

In February 1988, the Supreme Court ruled that the language provisions in Section 110 of the North-West Territories Act, added to the Act in 1877 at a time when there was a substantial francophone population in the prairie west, remained in effect in Saskatchewan. Those provisions held that either English or French could be used in the legislature and in the courts, and that the records, journals, and ordinances of the legislature were to be in both languages. As the settlement of Saskatchewan proceeded, the francophone population shrank proportionately; today Saskatchewan's approximately 25,000 francophones constitute less than three percent of the provincial population. Not coincidentally, the government and legislature of Saskatchewan have functioned in English only since the province was created in 1905. Then, in 1988, the Supreme Court ruled that the Saskatchewan Act of 1905, which established the province, provided for the "continuation of all laws governing the Legislature," and therefore that Section 110 remained in force until it was replaced by another law. Thus the ruling potentially voided all provincial statutes passed since 1905, although the Court also decreed that, to prevent a legal vacuum, the statutes would temporarily remain in effect until the provincial government had a chance to respond to the Court's ruling. Here the Court presented two options. First, the province could comply with the existing law (Section 110) by translating, re-enacting and printing all statutes in both French and English. Alternatively, the province could pass new legislation declaring that all existing statutes were valid even though they had been enacted and printed in English only. This option was possible because the Court ruled that Section 110 was not constitutionally entrenched, and therefore that the Saskatchewan legislative assembly was free to repeal or amend the existing legislation.

The provincial Progressive Conservative government, led by Premier Grant Devine, chose the second, minimalist option, and introduced legislation reducing the legal status of French within the province. At the same time, the provincial government stated that some of the more important existing statutes would be translated, at the discretion of the provincial government; that some future legislation might be translated; that translation facilities would be provided to francophones in court; and that the use of French would be permitted within the provincial legislature, although there would be no translation provided. For its part, the federal government agreed to provide Saskatchewan with $60 million to cover the costs of translation and to enrich educational programs for francophones in the province. Ottawa also agreed to give Saskatchewan's francophone community an additional $17 million to help them protect and encourage the use of French.

Although the Supreme Court ruling applied directly only to Saskatchewan, it had clear and inevitable consequences for Alberta, given that the North-West Territories Act also applied to Alberta prior to the province's creation in 1905. Thus in June 1988 Premier Don Getty's Progressive Conservative government moved to pre-empt similar Supreme Court intervention in Alberta. The provincial legislative assembly passed legislation, ironically written in both English and French, which retroactively validated English-only legislation. Unlike the case in Saskatchewan, the Alberta legislation did not provide for the selective translation of provincial statutes nor for the translation of future legislation, although it did remove restrictions on the use of French in the provincial legislative assembly. Alberta's 60,000 francophones, constituting less than three percent of the provincial population, expressed anger and dismay at the government's very limited recognition of linguistic rights dating back to 1887.

Provincial language policies in the western provinces are inextricably linked to language policies in Quebec. On the one hand, if the rights and interests of the anglophone minority of Quebec are to be protected, then it is imperative that the rights and interests of francophone minorities in the other provinces also be protected. On the other hand, the drift of Quebec towards a more unilingual society, a drift inherent in Bills 101 and 178, weakens political incentives for protecting linguistic minorities elsewhere in the country. Here it should also be stressed that provincial language policies in Quebec and the other provinces do not directly interact; it is the federal government which plays a critically important mediative role, trying at the same time to offer political support for francophones outside Quebec and anglophones inside Quebec. In most such cases, Ottawa can rely upon only moral suasion and financial incentives rather than legislative authority. As the recent experiences in Saskatchewan and Alberta have shown, there are very real limits to Ottawa's influence, even when the federal and provincial governments are of the same partisan stripe.[77]

BILINGUALISM IN CANADA
Editorial from *The Globe and Mail*,
January 12, 1989

The line heard from some people outside Quebec runs this way: why bother providing French-language services for francophone Canadians in other parts of the country when Quebec won't even let merchants post bilingual signs? Why go forward when Quebec is going backward?

There are a few quick responses: that Quebec has moved slightly forward from the existing law by permitting bilingual signs inside shops; that anglophone Quebeckers enjoy a wide range of services in their mother tongue; that Mr. Bourassa's Liberals brought in laws in 1987 to give English-speaking Quebeckers social services and health care in their own language, and amnesty to students illegally registered in English schools; that Quebec remains bound by constitutional obligations which cannot be overridden by the Charter's "notwithstanding" clause, including the right of parents educated in English in Canada to have their children educated in English.

But the broader response is that two official languages are not some artificial construct imposed on the country by the Pearson/Trudeau Liberals, to be endured only as long as everything goes smoothly. They are a reflection of the social contract between English and French which gave birth to this country, a bond maintained not because it is easy—heaven knows it's not—but because to a significant extent it defines the Canadian national identity. That remains so despite the many other linguistic groups who have helped build this country and remain prominent in many parts of it.

D'Iberville Fortier, Canada's Official Languages Commissioner, put the point eloquently in his report last March. Most Canadians, he wrote, "remain firmly opposed to a straight territorial solution to Canada's special linguistic dilemma, as being, in the end, a recipe for national suicide. With all its imperfections, some form of official bilingualism is the only answer that does not point toward a progressive dismemberment of Canada."

Historically, English Canadian provincial governments have been far less sympathetic towards provincial francophone minorities than Ottawa has been towards the national francophone minority. This is not surprising, given that the provincial minorities have been proportionately much smaller than the national minority. Perhaps more surprising, and more lamentable, has been the reluctance of the federal government to defend the interests of francophone minorities against anglophone and Protestant provincial majorities.[78] Historian W.L. Morton has argued that this reluctance has forced French Canadians to turn to the Quebec provincial state for protection, and has thus made an important contribution to the ongoing constitutional tension between the Quebec and federal governments.[79]

National bilingualism draws its political support from a diverse constituency that includes French Canadians living outside Quebec, anglo-Quebecers, a substantial proportion of French Canadians living inside Quebec, new anglophone bilinguals who have invested heavily in their own bilingualism or that of their children, and those English Canadians who believe that bilingualism, like it or not, is essential to the survival of Canada. It is a powerful coalition that commands support from all three major parties, and from the social, economic, and cultural elites from which those parties in turn draw their support. There are, however, two critically important political facts that remain. The first is that the bilingual coalition and its supportive legislation address linguistic and electoral *minorities*—francophones in Canada and the provinces, and anglophones in Quebec. The relevant linguistic and electoral *majorities*—anglophones in Canada and nine provinces, and francophones in Quebec—often constitute a tough sell for the proponents of bilingualism.

Juggling minority language rights as defined by federal and provincial legislation has been a formidable political task, as this cartoon, featuring Prime Minister Mulroney and Premiers Robert Bourassa and Grant Devine, illustrates.

Globe and Mail, April 21, 1988, p. A6.

The second fact is that the bilingualism coalition finds itself confronting the Quebec government. While it might be thought that Ottawa's legislation to protect the francophone national minority and, to a lesser degree, francophone provincial minorities outside Quebec would complement Quebec's legislation to protect the francophone majority in Quebec, this has not been the case.

To understand why the language policies of Ottawa and Quebec collide, we must go back to basic policy objectives. The Official Languages Act was designed to create a sense of security for francophones within Canada comparable to their sense of security within Quebec. This was to be achieved by strengthening the French language within national institutions and by increasing the visibility of French in the society at large. The Act and the entrenchment of language rights within the Charter protect the language rights of *individuals*; all Canadians, inside or outside Quebec, anglophone or francophone, have the *same* language rights based on their common Canadian citizenship. In practice, however, the language guarantees are of greatest relevance for linguistic *minorities*, be they francophones outside Quebec or anglophones inside. They are of much less relevance for the francophone *majority* in Quebec, to whom

"Two Solitudes"

Globe and Mail, October 17, 1988, p. D6.

Bills 101 and 178 are addressed. Indeed, by protecting the anglophone minority in Quebec, they may even threaten the linguistic interests of the francophone majority.

The language policies of Ottawa and Quebec rest on different philosophical foundations. Ottawa's policies assert language rights as individual rights, indeed as fundamental human rights; the primary concern is with the protection of linguistic *minorities* across the country. As a political and constitutional corollary, it is the federal government that should have ultimate responsibility for linguistic minorities. Quebec's policies, on the other hand, promote collective interests even to the point of restricting the linguistic choices of individuals; the primary concern is with the protection of the province's linguistic *majority*. The constitutional corollary is that provincial governments, and not Ottawa, should be vested with ultimate responsibility. While Ottawa's policies promote a bilingual Canada, and respect for individual rights, those of Quebec promote a unilingual Quebec and the collective security of the province's francophone majority. In so doing, Quebec's language policies may erode public support in English Canada for bilingualism. Unfortunately, any backlash would further support the rationale of Bill 101, compounding the vicious circle that bedevils language politics in Canada.

The Future of Language Politics

In January 1989, during the wake of the sign controversy in Quebec, Angus Reid Associates conducted a survey of 1,509 Canadian respondents for Southam News. Across the country, 43 percent of respondents expected that English–French relations would "get worse" in the future, 31 percent expected that they would remain the same, and only 22 percent expected that relations would improve. The prognosis was particularly pessimistic among anglophone respondents; 47 percent expected relations to get worse, a view shared by only 32 percent of the francophone respondents.

The survey also found that: (1) 42 percent of Canadians approved, and 32 percent disapproved, of Manitoba Premier Filmon's decision to withdraw support for the Meech Lake Accord in response to Quebec's French-only sign laws; (2) 58 percent of Canadians stated that they were unhappy with the notwithstanding clause and 30 percent approved of the clause, with the latter proportion rising to 58 percent among Quebec respondents; and (3) among francophone respondents in Quebec, 32 percent supported independence for Quebec, a proportion close to the 28 percent of Prairie respondents who also said that Quebec should leave Canada.

FRENCH CANADA, QUEBEC, AND THE CANADIAN FEDERAL STATE

Two linguistic features of Canada are of vital importance to an understanding of Canadian federalism: that in the country at large, one Canadian in four is of French mother tongue, and that francophones constitute a clear majority in the second-largest province. Hence the ongoing conflict between the linguistic majorities of Canada and Quebec. The basic question is this: which government best speaks for French Canada? Is it the Government of Canada, which represents all French Canadians, but does so through institutions within which French Canadians are a minority, albeit a large and influential minority? Or is it the government of Quebec, which represents only 80 percent of the French Canadian population, along with a significant non-French element, but does so through institutions within which French Canadians form a majority?

In many respects, of course, both governments do and must speak for French Canada. The problem is that they speak for overlapping but nonetheless quite distinct linguistic communities. The linguistic concerns of *French Canadians* (primarily the protection of minority interests in the face of an anglophone national majority and nine provincial anglophone majorities) are quite different from the linguistic concerns of the *Québécois* (primarily the promotion of majority interests which may run counter to those of the linguistic minority in Quebec). Yet, it must be stressed, the latter constitutes 80 percent of the former. It is perhaps surprising, then, that the governments of Canada and Quebec often articulate conflicting visions of French Canada. When the two visions differ as dramatically as they did under the governments of Pierre Trudeau and René Lévesque, the question inevitably arises: who speaks for Quebec? Here it is useful to note that within the space of little more than a year, in 1980/81, the Quebec electorate elected Liberals in 74 of the 75 federal ridings, defeated the sovereignty association proposal in a referendum, and re-elected the Parti Québécois government with an increased majority. During this period Trudeau and Lévesque both enjoyed strong personal and political support in Quebec, as did their competing visions of French Canada.

A number of factors have combined to create chronic uncertainty over the place of French Canada within the broader Canadian community. Quebec's declining share of the national population has raised fears that, over the long run, Quebec's and therefore French Canada's power within the national political community will be eroded. The demolinguistic transformation of Canada, in which Quebec is becoming progressively francophone and the rest of Canada is becoming progressively anglophone, raises concerns about the long-term survival of Anglo-Quebecers, French Canada outside Quebec, and the bilingual policies of the federal government. Finally, there is ongoing constitutional tension arising from the conflicting demands for a strong federal government that can protect linguistic minorities outside Quebec, and a strong provincial government that can more fully protect and promote the francophone majority inside Quebec.

SUGGESTED READINGS

Sheila McLeod Arnopoulous and Dominique Clift, *The English Fact in Quebec* (Montreal: McGill-Queen's University Press, 1980).

Conrad Black, *Duplessis* (Toronto: McClelland and Stewart, 1976).

For excellent overviews of much of the material covered in this chapter, see David R. Cameron, "Dualism and the Concept of National Unity," in John H. Redekop, ed., *Approaches to Canadian Politics*, Second Edition (Scarborough: Prentice-Hall, 1983), pp. 233-50; and Kenneth McRoberts, "Quebec: Province, Nation, or 'Distinct Society,' " in Michael S. Whittington and Glen Williams, eds., *Canadian Politics in the 1990s*, Third Edition (Toronto: Nelson, 1989), pp. 98-118.

Donald G. Cartwright, *Official Language Populations in Canada: Patterns and Contacts*, Occasional Paper No. 16, The Institute for Research on Public Policy, July 1980.

Lowell Clark, ed., *The Manitoba School Question: Majority Rule or Minority Rights?* (Toronto: Copp Clark, 1968).

Dominique Clift, *Quebec Nationalism in Crisis* (Montreal: McGill-Queen's University Press, 1982).

For a chronology and analysis of Quebec language policy, see William D. Coleman, "From Bill 22 to Bill 101: The Politics of Language Under the Parti Québécois," *Canadian Journal of Political Science*, XIV:3 (September 1981), pp. 459-86.

Susan Crean and Marcel Rioux, *Two Nations: An Essay on the Culture and Politics of Canada and Quebec in a World of American Pre-eminence* (Toronto: James Lorimer, 1983).

Russell Doern, *The Battle Over Bilingualism: The Manitoba Language Question, 1983-85* (Winnipeg: Cambridge Publishers, 1989).

Alain-G. Gagnon, ed., *Quebec State and Society* (Toronto: Methuen, 1984).

Alain-G. Gagnon and Mary Beth Montcalm, *Quebec: Beyond the Quiet Revolution* (Scarborough: Nelson, 1990).

Richard Gwyn, *The Northern Magus: Pierre Trudeau and Canadians* (Toronto: McClelland and Stewart, 1980).

For an excellent overview of Quebec politics and society, see Kenneth McRoberts, *Quebec: Social Change and Political Crisis*, Third Edition (Toronto: McClelland and Stewart, 1980).

Denis Moniere, *Ideologies in Quebec: The Historical Development*, Richard Howard, translator (Toronto: University of Toronto Press, 1981).

Maurice Pinard and Richard Hamilton, "The Parti Québécois Comes to Power: An Analysis of the 1976 Quebec Election," *Canadian Journal of Political Science*, xi:4 (December 1978), pp. 739-76.

Jean Provencher, *René Lévesque: Portrait of a Québécois*, translated by David Ellis (Toronto: Gage, 1975).

Herbert F. Quinn, *The Union Nationale: A Study in Quebec Nationalism* (Toronto: University of Toronto Press, 1963).

For a vigorous Québécois nationalist perspective on the material covered in this chapter, see Marcel Rioux, *Quebec in Question*, translated by James Boake (Toronto: James Lorimer, 1978).

Susan Mann Trofimenkoff, *The Dream of Nation: A Social and Intellectual History of Quebec* (Toronto: Macmillan, 1982)

STUDY QUESTIONS

1. The last twenty years have witnessed extensive discussion of the

federal division of powers. Are there powers which the people of Quebec would like to see transferred to the provincial governments, and residents of other provinces would like to see remain with the federal government in Ottawa? If so, how would you explain such different perspectives on the division of powers?

2. In the late 1970s, David R. Cameron described dualism as "the view which holds that the most significant cleavage in Canadian society is the line dividing English from French, and which identifies as the major challenge to domestic statecraft the establishment of harmonious and just relations between the English-speaking and French-speaking communities of Canada." ("Dualism and the Concept of National Unity" in John H. Redekop, ed., *Approaches to Canadian Politics* (Scarborough: Prentice-Hall, 1978), p. 237. As we enter the 1990s, do you feel that a dualist view is still appropriate? If so, why? If not, what other cleavages rival that between the English and French communities?

NOTES

1. René Lévesque, *An Option for Quebec* (Toronto: McClelland and Stewart, 1968), p.14.
2. The capture of Quebec by British forces was one of many military campaigns during prolonged hostilities between Britain and France. Hostilities were brought to a close by the Treaty of Paris, which ceded New France to Great Britain. The treaty also contained guarantees for the freedom of religious worship in the ceded territory.
3. Richard Joy, *Languages in Conflict* (Toronto: Macmillan, 1972), p.86.
4. *Ibid.*, p. 58.
5. Rejean Lachapelle and Jacques Henripin, *The Demolinguistic Situation in Canada* (Montreal: Institute for Research on Public Policy, 1982), p.233.
6. *Ibid.*, p. 123.
7. *Ibid.*, p. 69.
8. *Ibid.*, p. 51.
9. Daniel Kubat and David Thornton, *A Statistical Profile of Canadian Society* (Toronto: McGraw-Hill Ryerson, 1974), p. 38.
10. As of May 1989, the Quebec government paid a special allowance of $500 for the first child, $1,000 for the second, and $4,500 for the third child and subsequent children. The allowance is paid in installments ending at age three.
11. Luc Albert, "Language in Canada," *Canadian Social Trends* (Spring 1989), p. 11.
12. Lachapelle and Henripin, *The Demolinguistic Situation in Canada*, p. 196.

13. Government of Quebec, *Quebec–Canada: A New Deal* (Editeur Officiel du Québec, 1979), p. 30.
14. Lévesque, *An Option*, p. 93.
15. *The Globe and Mail*, National Edition, October 20, 1983, p. 8.
16. The changing ethnic and racial composition of the Canadian population is addressed in *Equality Now*, The Report of the Special Committee on Visible Minorities in Canadian Society, Bob Daudlin, MP, Chairman (Ottawa: Queen's Printer, March 1984).
17. Albert, "Language in Canada," p. 9.
18. Lachapelle and Henripin, *The Demolinguistic Situation*, p. 174.
19. Donald V. Smiley, "Reflections on Cultural Nationhood and Political Community in Canada," in R. Kenneth Carty and W. Peter Wards, eds., *Entering the Eighties: Canada in Crisis* (Toronto: Oxford University Press, 1980), p. 33.
20. Lévesque, *An Option*, p. 14.
21. Herbert F. Quinn, *The Union Nationale: A Study in Quebec Nationalism* (Toronto: University of Toronto Press, 1963), p. 105.
22. Cited in C. Nish, *Quebec in the Duplessis Era* (Toronto: Copp Clark, 1970), p. 36.
23. Kenneth McRoberts and Dale Posgate, *Quebec: Social Change and Political Crisis*, Revised Edition (Toronto: McClelland and Stewart, 1980), p. 74.
24. For a fascinating discussion of U.N. patronage and the electoral manipulation with which it was associated, see Quinn, *The Union Nationale*, chapter VII.
25. Dominique Clift, *Quebec Nationalism in Crisis* (Kingston: McGill-Queen's University Press, 1982), p. 15.
26. Kenneth McRoberts, *Quebec: Social Change and Political Crisis*, Third Edition (Toronto: McClelland and Stewart, 1988), p. 128.
27. Both trade union and intellectual discontent had been brewing since the early 1950s, with the latter finding expression in the small but politically influential magazine *Cité libre*, to which Pierre Trudeau was a frequent contributor.
28. Report by the Quebec Assembly of Bishops to the Pope, *The Globe and Mail*, National Edition, November 28, 1983.
29. For a discussion of this point, see Albert Breton, "The Economics of Nationalism," *Journal of Political Economy* (August 1964), p. 385.
30. McRoberts, *Quebec*, pp. 132-33.
31. For a discussion of the new middle class and the consequent restructuring of class politics in Quebec, see Herbert Guidon, "The Modernization of Quebec and the Legitimacy of the Canadian State" in D. Glenday, H. Guidon, and A. Turowetz, eds., *Modernization and the Canadian State* (Toronto: Macmillan, 1978). See also Henry Milner, *Politics in the New Quebec* (Toronto: McClelland and Stewart, 1977).

32. Cited in Lévesque, *An Option*, p. 9.
33. Sheila McLeod Arnopoulous and Dominique Clift, *The English Fact in Quebec* (Montreal: McGill-Queen's University Press, 1980), p. 61.
34. J. R. Mallory, *The Structure of Canadian Government* (Toronto: Macmillan, 1971), p. 397.
35. For a discussion, see André Bernard, *What Does Quebec Want?* (Toronto: James Lorimer, 1978).
36. John Meisel, *Working Papers on Canadian Politics* (Montreal: McGill-Queen's University Press, 1973), p. 205.
37. The most influential American analogy was drawn by Pierre Vallières in *White Niggers of America*, Joan Pinkham, translator (Toronto: McClelland and Stewart, 1971).
38. For an English-language expansion of this theme, see Sheilagh Hodgins Milner and Henry Milner, *The Decolonization of Quebec* (Toronto: McClelland and Stewart, 1973).
39. Lévesque, *An Option*, p. 26. Writing in *Le Devoir* (September 19, 1967), Lévesque argued that Quebec's independence "would allow our two majorities to extricate themselves from an archaic federal framework in which our two very distinct 'personalities' paralyze each other by dint of pretending to have a third personality common to both."
40. See Ron Haggart and Aubrey E. Golden, *Rumors of War* (Toronto: New Press, 1971); and Denis Smith, *Bleeding Hearts—Bleeding Country: Canada and the Quebec Crisis* (Edmonton: M.G. Hurtig, 1971).
41. For a discussion of this point, see Pierre Vallières, *Choose!*, Penelope Williams, translator (Toronto: New Press, 1972).
42. See Maurice Pinard and Richard Hamilton, "The Parti Québécois Comes to Power: The 1976 Election" *Canadian Journal of Political Science*, 11 (December 1978), pp. 739-75.
43. Government of Quebec, *Quebec-Canada*, p. 109.
44. For a discussion of the campaign, see McRoberts, *Quebec*, Chapter Nine.
45. As Louis Balthazar points out, "paradoxically, people had to be brought to vote for Canada in the name of Quebec." "Quebec at the Hour of Choice," in Carty and Ward, *Entering the Eighties*, p. 73.
46. Cited in McRoberts, *Quebec*, p. 326.
47. *The Globe and Mail*, National Edition, May 20, 1983, p. 8.
48. McRoberts, *Quebec*, p. 342.
49. McRoberts and Posgate, *Quebec*, p. 107.
50. William D. Coleman, "From Bill 22 to Bill 101: The Politics of Language Under the Parti Québécois," *Canadian Journal of Political Science*, XIV:3 (September 1981), p. 468.
51. *Ibid.*, p. 459.

52. *The Globe and Mail*, National Edition, July 27, 1984, p. 2.

53. *Ibid.*

54. See Pierre Fournier, *The Quebec Establishment: The Ruling Class and the State* (Montreal: Black Rose, 1976).

55. Cited in Raymond Reid, *The Canadian Style* (Toronto: Fitzhenry and Whiteside, 1973), p. 93.

56. J.W. Dafoe, *Laurier: A Study in Canadian Politics* (Toronto: McClelland and Stewart, reprinted 1963 (first printed 1922)), p. 26.

57. *Ibid.*

58. In the general election of 1882, the Conservatives captured 51 seats in Quebec with 52.3 percent of the popular vote. In 1887, two years after Riel's execution, they won only 33 seats after a very modest erosion of their popular vote to 49.6 percent. In the 1891 general election, the Conservative vote marginally increased to 50.8 percent while the number of Conservative seats fell to 28. The major drop did not occur until 1896 when the party won only 16 seats with 45.8 percent of the vote.

59. Another example is provided by Ontario during the early years of the First World War, when conflict over the educational rights of Franco-Ontarians intensified French Canadian opposition to conscription.

60. Christina McCall-Newman, *Grits: An Intimate Portrait of the Liberal Party* (Toronto: Macmillan, 1982), p. 62.

61. Richard Gwyn, *The Northern Magus* (Toronto: McClelland and Stewart, 1980), p. 220.

62. *Ibid.*, p. 236.

63. McCall-Newman, *Grits*, p. 79.

64. *1987 Annual Report of the Commissioner of Official Languages* (Ottawa: Minister of Supply and Services, 1988), p. 39.

65. Cited in Mason Wade, *The French Canadians, 1860-1967*, Volume II (Toronto: Macmillan, 1968), pp. 618-19.

66. Raymond Breton, "Multiculturalism and Canadian Nation-Building," in Alan Cairns and Cynthia Williams, eds., *The Politics of Gender, Ethnicity and Language in Canada* (Toronto: University of Toronto Press, 1986), p. 31.

67. Dalton Camp, *Points of Departure* (Toronto: McClelland and Stewart, 1979).

68. W.A. Matheson, *The Prime Minister and the Cabinet* (Toronto: Methuen, 1976), p. 22. Matheson uses consociationalism as a conceptual framework in this insightful look at cabinet government in Canada. For a more extended conceptual treatment, see K.D. McRae, ed., *Consociational Democracy: Political Accommodation in Segmented Societies* (Toronto: McClelland and Stewart, 1974).

69. Albert, "Language in Canada," p. 12.

70. Lachapelle and Henripin, *The Demolinguistic Situation*, pp. 32 and 39.
71. Gwyn, *The Northern Magus*, p. 223.
72. This decline is in part attributable to the disappearance of French language entrance and exit requirements in most English Canadian universities. Gwyn, *The Northern Magus*, p. 230.
73. *Ibid.*, p. 225.
74. Donald V. Smiley, *The Federal Condition in Canada* (Toronto: McGraw-Hill Ryerson, 1987), p. 146.
75. Patrick Martin, Allan Gregg and George Perlin, *Contenders: The Tory Quest for Power* (Scarborough: Prentice-Hall, 1983), p. 120.
76. *Toronto Star*, June 5, 1983, p. F3.
77. The Supreme Court case began with a speeding ticket issued in 1980 to a Saskatchewan priest, Father Andre Mercure. Father Mercure insisted that he had the right to enter a plea in French, to have his trial in French, and to have the proceedings delayed until the province could produce the relevant statutes in French. Father Mercure died in 1986.
78. Smiley, *The Federal Condition*, p. 29.
79. W. L. Morton, "Confederation, 1870-1896: The End of the Macdonaldian Constitution and the Return to Duality," in Bruce Hodgins and Robert Page, eds., *Canadian History Since 1867: Essays and Interpretations* (Georgetown: 1972), pp. 195-200.

4

Regional Politics

> To many foreign observers, the fact that Confederation is widely evaluated from the particular point of view of how given provinces have fared over the years is a remarkable feature of Canadian life. In other countries, cleavages such as social class, religion, race or creed have been of decisive importance to the collective lives of citizens. In Canada, how much the people of any given province have participated in the benefits of the federation, or shared its losses, has been at the forefront of our politics.[1]

It is not surprising that Canadians have an acute sense of territory and geography. Many of the symbols used to convey a sense of the country to non-Canadians and Canadians alike are rooted in geography. Peggy's Cove, Niagara Falls, the Great Lakes, the solitary splendour of the Canadian Shield captured in the paintings of the Group of Seven, the sweep of the prairies, the majestic Rocky Mountains, the blending of sea and air along the rain forest of the West Coast, and the vast silence of the Canadian North are intrinsic to the Canadian identity. Other symbols such as the maple leaf, the Canada goose, and the beaver are drawn from the land itself rather than from its human population. Yet many of the geographical features which give Canada definition—the Rockies, the Shield, the Atlantic Ocean, the Gulf of St. Lawrence—also carve up the country into territorially defined subnational communities and contribute to the strength of regional attachments. Geographical barriers make it difficult for Canadians to come to grips with the country as a whole. It is difficult, for example, for residents of the east coast to have an emotional handle on the "miles and miles of miles and miles" that make up the prairie West.

Given all this, we might well expect regional identities and regional conflict to play major political roles. It seems only reasonable to assume that, in the vast, transcontinental Canadian society, with its federal constitution designed to give political expression to territorial communities, regionalism will be a persistent feature of political life. Regionalism is thus attributable to the simple facts of size and diversity, and to the not so simple fact of federalism, even though in the equally vast, diverse, and *federal* society to the south, regional conflict is both less prevalent and less disruptive.[2] As former Prime Minister William Lyon Mackenzie King observed, "if some countries have too much history, we have too much geography."[3]

On closer inspection, however, this line of argument is less convincing. It does not explain why regional conflict in Canada appears to be increasing over time,[4] while in other western, industrialized countries there has been a marked and progressive decline in territorially based political conflict.[5] A further complication is that regional differences within the Canadian *society* appear to be waning at the same time that they are waxing within the political system. While lifestyles in Toronto, Halifax, Charlottetown, and Brandon are by no means identical, the differences are less acute today than they were in the past. With very few exceptions, Canadians can watch "The Journal," shop at Canadian Tire, eat at McDonald's, subscribe to the same pay-TV channels, drink the same beer, and read *The Globe and Mail* no matter where they might happen to live. As a consequence, the argument that political regionalism reflects regional divisions within the underlying society has become progressively less tenable over time.

Just as the Quiet Revolution led Quebec into the mainstream of Canadian life while at the same time increasing political conflict between Quebec and the broader Canadian community, so too the regional homogenization of Canada in the wake of technological and industrial change has been associated with increased regional conflict. By implication, then, the primary roots of regional conflict are to be found in the nature of the political system itself; regional variations in social characteristics are of secondary importance. While there are pronounced regional variations in the distribution of natural resources and the nature of economic activity, even here it can be argued that the study of regional conflict is primarily a study of *political* cause and effect.

Provincial Variation in Social Indicators

The argument that Canadian provinces are coming more and more to resemble one another in their social characteristics should not be carried to extremes. As the following data show, significant and indeed substantial provincial variation can still be found.

	1987 Drug Offence Rate per 100,000	1986 Divorce Rate per 100,000	1986 Suicide Rate per 100,000
	pop.	married women	pop.
Nfld.	180	467	4
P.E.I.	140	633	12
N.S.	210	1,200	11
N.B.	220	983	14
Que.	130	1,183	19
Ont.	250	1,200	13
Man.	280	1,100	15
Sask.	310	950	14
Alta.	250	1,616	18
B.C.	450	1,483	16

Source: Statistics Canada, Catalogues 85-205 (Drug Offences), 84-205 (Divorce), and 84-206 (Suicide).

Before exploring this thesis further, some guidelines must be established. First, our principal focus will be upon the intrusion of territorial interests, identifications, and conflicts into *national* political life. Thus little attention will be paid to intraprovincial territorial conflicts such as those between Vancouver and the interior communities of British Columbia; between northern Ontario and the "golden horseshoe" stretching along the shore of Lake Ontario; between St. John's and the outports of Newfoundland. While these conflicts can be of critical importance in shaping the contours of provincial politics, their national impact is less pronounced. Second, Quebec will not be brought into the regional analysis even though in many respects Quebec is a region analogous to other regions in Canada. Indeed, it can be argued that the province of Quebec, by facilitating the spatial organization of linguistic conflict, thereby enhances the salience of other forms of territorial conflict. At the same time, however, the differences that set Quebec apart and make it a "distinct society" tend to be of greater magnitude than those which set the other provinces apart from one another. Given that Quebec has been discussed in Chapter 3, and given the analytical distortions that arise in trying to pack Quebec into a regional framework, the focus of this chapter will be upon regional divisions *within English Canada*, with particular attention being paid to the regional peripheries lying to the east of Quebec and to the west of Ontario. Third, the chapter will not address Canada's northern territories, which, despite their great size, contain only 0.3 percent of the national population.

A troublesome conceptual problem in the discussion of regionalism comes from the unavoidable confusion between "provinces" and "regions." Although terms such as "western Canada," "Atlantic Canada," and "the Maritimes" imply the existence of transprovincial communities sharing at the very least common territorial interests, political perspectives, or economic orientations, the reality of such regional communities is a matter of contentious debate. As the former premier of Prince Edward Island, Alex Campbell, stressed in a 1977 address, the regional community is in many ways an artifact:

> The only people who consider Atlantic Canada as a region are those who live outside Atlantic Canada, the planners and bureaucrats in Ottawa, the newscasters in Toronto, and the airline executives in Montreal. We in Atlantic Canada have not yet made the decision to develop as a region. We are four separate, competitive, jealous, and parochial provinces.... I suggest to you that we do not have a regional identity; we do not have regional bonds; we do not have regional strategies....

With respect to western Canada, British Columbia is often portrayed, particularly by its residents, as a region quite apart from the prairie West, a region with a very different physical terrain, economic base, settlement pattern, and political history.

The complexities and some of the pitfalls of a regional analysis can be illustrated by the three prairie provinces.[6] Initially, the three were bound together as a regional community by a common wheat economy, and by the shared experiences, characteristics, and frustrations of an agrarian frontier. They constituted a distinctive and relatively well-integrated region because of what they had in common, and because what they shared clearly set them apart from other areas in Canada. Then, in the decades following the Depression and the Second World War, the prairie region began to come unstitched as the importance of the wheat economy declined and as the regional economy diversified. Heterogeneity among the three prairie provinces increased while at the same time regional differences between the prairies and other parts of Canada decreased. Yet, while Alberta and Manitoba may have less in common today than in the past, and while life in Edmonton, Saskatoon, or Winnipeg may be more like life in Toronto, Hamilton, or Halifax than in the past, regional commonalities have not totally disappeared. The prairie provinces continue to share a sense of alienation from the federal government, an economic reliance on the exploitation of natural resources, and a marked dependency on unstable foreign markets for those resources. In a similar fashion, one can identify points of commonality across the Atlantic provinces including, but not limited to, a concern with out-migration, a fragile and often depressed economic base, a coastal environment and, to a degree, an economic reliance on an ocean that is not shared by other Canadians, even those on the West Coast.

A regional analysis, therefore, must be alert to shared characteristics among provinces and, in particular, to shared characteristics that set one region off from another. Yet it must also be alert to provincial variations within commonly used regional units of analysis such as "the West" or "the Maritimes," variations that may seem quite pronounced to people living within the region. Although at some times and in some circumstances regional themes may dominate the territorial dimension of Canadian political life, at other times and in other circumstances disparate provincial interests may do so.

DEMOGRAPHIC PROFILE

Figure 4.1 plots the regional composition of the Canadian population from 1871 to 1986. The most dramatic change came with the settlement of the Canadian West when, between 1901 and 1931, the region's share of the national population rose from 12.1 percent to 29.5 percent. Then, with the onset of the Great Depression, accompanied on the prairies by drought, grasshoppers, and the collapse of foreign grain markets, the West's share

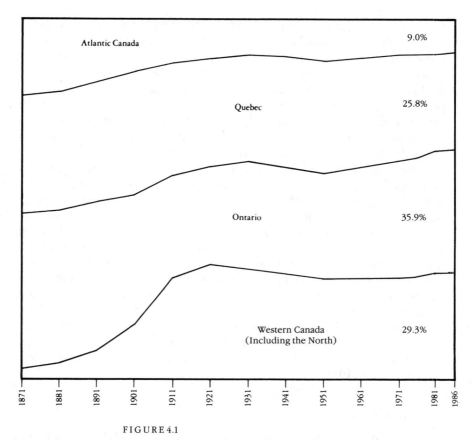

Atlantic Canada   9.0%

Quebec   25.8%

Ontario   35.9%

Western Canada   29.3%
(Including the North)

FIGURE 4.1

Regional Distribution of the Canadian Population

of the national population began a slide that was not arrested until the mid-1960s. Although the region's share of the national population increased between 1971 and 1986, it has yet to reach the 1931 peak. The westward shift in population at the turn of the century was reflected in part by the *relative* decline in population along Canada's East Coast, with the proportion of the national population living in the three Maritime provinces falling from 16.7 percent to 9.6 percent between 1901 and 1931. The addition of Newfoundland in 1949 proved only a temporary respite in the progressive, albeit modest, demographic decline of Atlantic Canada. In the twenty-year period from 1966 to 1986, Atlantic Canada's share of the national population fell from 9.9 percent to 9.0 percent.

Perhaps the most striking feature about Figure 4.1 is the demographic strength and resiliency of the centre. While Quebec's share of the national population has declined somewhat in recent years, dropping from 28.9 percent in 1966 to 25.8 percent in 1986, and while Ontario's share was eroded by the growth of the West in the early part of the twentieth century, the centre has held. Ontario's share of the national population has rebounded from a low of 32.8 percent in 1951 to almost 36 percent in 1986. Quebec and Ontario's combined share reached its lowest point—60.3 percent—in 1921. Since that time it has fluctuated between 61 and 63 percent. At the time of the 1986 census, 61.7 percent of Canadians lived in either Ontario or Quebec. Overall, then, Canada's demographic structure has been surprisingly stable, particularly since the Depression brought the agricultural settlement of the prairie West to a close.

Such stability has been less evident within Atlantic Canada and the West. As Figure 4.2 illustrates, a major change in the Atlantic region came with the addition of Newfoundland in 1949. The other shifts, including the gradual erosion of P.E.I.'s share of the regional population, have been more modest. Within the West there has been a steady westward shift in population since the onset of the Depression. Provincial differences in growth rates have been dramatic. From 1931 to 1986, British Columbia's population increased by 316 percent and Alberta's by 225 percent, while Manitoba's population grew by only 53 percent and Saskatchewan's by a minuscule 10 percent. (This translates into a net increase of 88,000 people in Saskatchewan compared to 2,195,000 in British Columbia!) As a consequence of this westward shift, 71.6 percent of the regional population resided in the two western-most provinces in 1986, compared to only 46.8 percent in 1931.

THE REGIONS

Before turning to a more general discussion of regional dynamics within Canadian political life, it is useful to look in some detail at the major regional communities within English Canada.

Atlantic Canada

At the time of Confederation, "Atlantic Canada" did not exist. It would be another six years before Prince Edward Island joined the Dominion, and 82 years before Newfoundland would expand "the Maritimes" to "Atlantic Canada." In the early years after Confederation, the region was marked by strong local and provincial loyalties which precluded any regional sense of community. As Ernest Forbes has noted, " . . . there was relatively little in the long history of the Maritimes to provide a truly collective historical experience, either actual or mythological, through which the people might develop a strong regional consciousness."[7] In the short run, Forbes argues, Confederation was an alternative to regional unity or consciousness; "the identification with the nation at the higher level and with the cultural group, economic interest, province, or local community

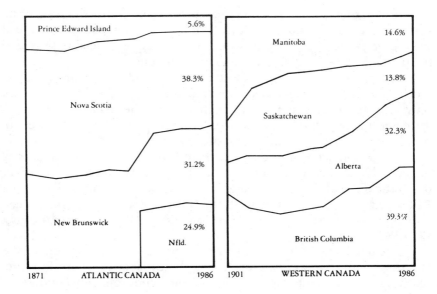

FIGURE 4.2

Provincial Distributions of Regional Populations

at the lower seemed to leave little reason for interest in or loyalty to a Maritime region."[8] Over the longer run, Confederation and the ongoing struggle over "**better terms**" for the Maritimes were to provide just such a regional bond.

1. The Maritimes in Historical Perspective

Confederation was greeted with a general lack of enthusiasm in Nova Scotia and New Brunswick. Opposition was particularly pronounced in the former colony, where a government pledged to repeal Nova Scotia's entry almost before the ink was dry on the 1867 Constitution Act. However, the repeal movement was short-lived. Joseph Howe, the leading spokesman for repeal, joined Macdonald's national cabinet after failing to win British support for repeal, and by 1870 the movement had collapsed.

The entry of Prince Edward Island into the Dominion in 1873 was also accompanied by little enthusiasm: "most Islanders met the end of their independent history with bitter resignation and, as was the case in the other two Maritime Provinces, the legacy of resentment against those responsible remained."[9] The end came in the wake of British pressure, an economic recession coupled with a poor harvest, an impending financial crisis precipitated by overly ambitious plans for a provincial railway, and the patient courtship of the Canadian government.

The years between P.E.I.'s entry into Confederation and the First World War saw the progressive "Canadianization" of the Maritime economy. On balance, regional integration into the national economy appeared to yield substantial regional benefits, even though that economy's centre of gravity came increasingly to rest in Ontario and Quebec. Maritime manufacturing industries shared in the economic prosperity generated by the settlement of the Canadian West. The protective tariffs of the **National Policy** and favourable freight rates on the Intercolonial Railway gave particular impetus to the Nova Scotia coal and steel industries, an impetus that was sustained by the industrial demands of the First World War.

Canadianization, however, was not complete. Other sectors of the Maritime economy—agriculture, forestry, and fisheries—were less successfully integrated into the national economy; they relied on continental and international markets and benefited less from the protective tariffs of the National Policy. Partly as a consequence, tensions developed between indigenous entrepreneurs and industries, on the one hand, and the increased presence of national economic interests, based in Ontario and Montreal, on the other. It should also be noted that the region was not bound together by a dominant economic interest, as the prairie West was to be bound together by the grain trade. When common economic interests did exist, they frequently resulted in intense intraregional rivalry and jealousy. Here the conflicts between the ports of Halifax, Nova Scotia, and Saint John, New Brunswick, took on legendary proportions. In combination, the diversity of economic interests and intraregional competition reduced the leverage of the Maritimes on national economy policy and hampered efforts to achieve better economic terms within Confederation. As Forbes explains:

> In trying to represent the diverse interests of their constituents Maritime politicians were often found quarrelling among themselves and attempting to influence national policy in different directions. This left them at a definite disadvantage in competing with regions having more clearly defined communities of interest.[10]

Such regions included both Ontario, with its manufacturing sector, and the emerging agricultural West.

The early years of Confederation also witnessed the political integration of the Maritimes into the broader Canadian party system, with the Conservative and Liberal parties sinking deep roots into the region. The major exception to this integration, although not to the dominance of the national parties, came with a flare-up of the Nova Scotia Repeal Movement in 1886-87. Faced with economic distress and federal reluctance to endorse better terms for the province, W.S. Fielding's Liberal government introduced and passed a resolution proposing that "the financial and commercial interests of the people of Nova Scotia, New Brunswick and Prince Edward Island would be advanced by these provinces withdrawing from the Canadian federation and uniting under one government." While the repeal agitation reflected the Maritime provinces' "deep and widespread, though not perhaps overwhelming, sense of grievance with their place in the new nation,"[11] the call for secession was more a matter of rhetoric and ritual, born out of frustration rather than serious intent. Certainly, regional unification had very limited appeal in Nova Scotia, or elsewhere for that matter.

Although the Fielding government was re-elected shortly after the legislative resolution was passed, its re-election was not widely interpreted as a mandate for secession. Nor was secession taken up by Nova Scotia's MPs and, within the year, it had fallen from the political agenda. The lack of support from the province's federal representatives is of particular importance. G.A. Rawlyk and Doug Brown argue that "in the only arena where regional grievances could be effectively redressed, the House of Commons in Ottawa, Nova Scotians as well as other Maritime Members of Parliament willingly sacrificed their regional interests on the altar of party loyalty."[12] This clash between party loyalty in the House, on the one hand, and effective regional representation, on the other, was to become a focal point of western Canadian political discontent in the years ahead. It was to result in a major challenge to, and transformation of, the national party system and indeed still finds reflection in contemporary support for Senate reform. However, no such challenge to the party system emerged in the Maritimes as a legacy of the repeal movement.

The first two decades of the twentieth century were prosperous ones for the Maritimes as the explosive rate of settlement in the prairie West created a strong demand for the industrial products of Ontario and the Maritimes. Yet the settlement of the West also opened up interregional conflict between the West and the Maritimes. This is conflict, incidentally, that western Canadians have all but ignored, focusing their attention instead on regional conflict between the West and central Canada, conflict in which the West could be unambiguously portrayed as the victim. These facts have not received adequate attention: the growth of the West came in part at the expense of the Maritimes and the interests of the western regional periphery were at times at odds with those of the eastern periphery.

Interregional conflict between the Maritimes and the West was fed from several sources. First, population growth in the West led to a regional redistribution of seats in the House of Commons which had the

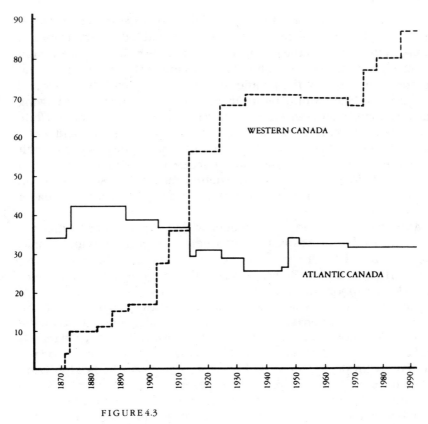

FIGURE 4.3

Number of Seats in the House of Commons

appearance, and to a degree the reality, of *taking* seats from the Maritimes and *giving* them to the West. Here Figure 4.3 shows the growth of western representation in the House and the corresponding decline in Maritime representation, a decline that was not only proportionate but also absolute. As Maritime seats disappeared, regional residents were provided with dramatic evidence of their declining role in the national political community, and of their eclipse by the ascendant West.

The two regions were also at loggerheads over the 1905 transfer of federal **Crown lands** in the Northwest Territories, which took place when Saskatchewan and Alberta were created and when the provincial boundaries of Manitoba were greatly expanded. As Ernest Forbes explains, the West and the Maritimes lodged mutually exclusive claims: "the prairie case rested on the contention that the public lands had always belonged legally to the provinces, the Maritime one on the assumption that they belonged to the Dominion."[13] Maritimers argued that the original members of the Dominion were entitled to compensation for the "loss" of public lands, a *national* resource, to the prairie provinces. This argument was linked to a broader sense of regional grievance, for it was not only the prairie provinces which benefited from the transfer of Crown lands; so too did Quebec and Ontario in 1912 when their provincial boundaries were expanded. For their part, the Maritime provinces were left without new land, because there was none available on the East Coast, and with a diminished share of a diminished national resource. In addition, Maritimers felt that the federal government had provided unreasonably generous financial subsidies to the new western provinces. For example, and quite apart from land transfers, the federal subsidy to the Saskatchewan government was set at approximately three times that of the Nova Scotia subsidy even though at the time Nova Scotia had twice Saskatchewan's population.[14]

There was, then, a not unfounded feeling that the settlement of the West was occurring at the expense of the Maritimes, and that its long-term consequence would be a diminished role for the Maritimes in the Canadian community. This concern apparently aroused little interest or empathy in the West. When disputes arose over freight rates, western politicians vigorously pursued their own regional interests with little regard to the potentially negative impact on Maritime industries. In a more general sense, the mythology that grew up around western settlement grated upon the people of the Maritimes. As Forbes explains, "the thesis which was then becoming widely accepted, that independence, economic and social progress, and even democracy itself were the products of a new and dynamic agrarian frontier, implied an unflattering role for the Maritimes."[15]

Regional unease with the ascendancy of the West and the consequent decline of the Maritimes was combined with other sources of political discontent in the *Maritime Rights Movement,* a broad-gauged movement of regional protest which swept across the Maritimes between 1919 and 1927. (Other sources included labour unrest and widespread interest in social reform, interest which in the West was expressed through the **Social Gospel Movement**. While regional discontent was accentuated by the onset of an economic recession in 1920, its roots were " ... firmly grounded among the deepest concerns and aspirations of the people— aspirations of a political, economic, social, and cultural nature which were seriously threatened by the relative decline of the Maritime provinces in the Canadian Dominion."[16] It was hoped that the political strength that would come through regional unity could correct the injustices being inflicted upon the Maritimes by the federal government and, through the federal government, by other regions. The Maritime Rights Movement was a continuation of the quest for better terms within Confederation, and for the protection of a region being eroded by both the growth of the West and the increased concentration of economic activity in the central Canadian provinces.

The regional plight of the Maritimes came to be symbolized by the Intercolonial Railway. The ICR, which linked the Maritimes to central Canadian markets and trade, was a direct legacy of Confederation. Based in the Maritimes, it was well attuned to the special economic and political interests of the region, and its rate structure was designed to further those interests. As a consequence, however, the ICR was dependent upon federal subsidies which in turn were attacked by competing regional interests outside the Maritimes. In 1919 the federal government was instrumental in moving the Intercolonial headquarters from Moncton to Toronto, and in 1923 the ICR was absorbed into the new Canadian National Railway system. The transfer of the ICR headquarters was a stunning blow, not only because of the loss of employment, but because of the more important loss of regional control. The operation of the railway and its freight rate structure would now be determined by external management remote from the myriad regional interests clustered around the ICR. Rawlyk and Brown conclude that "the integration of the Intercolonial into a national railway system, in which management was neither sympathetic nor knowledgeable concerning Maritime problems, spelled disaster for Maritime business."[17]

The Maritime Rights Movement culminated in the 1925 appointment of a federal Royal Commission to provide a full hearing on regional grievances. The Commission, chaired by Sir Andrew Rae Duncan, was successful in venting regional discontent. In 1926 it released a generally sympathetic report which, together with promises by the federal government to act on its recommendations and the economic recovery of 1927, brought the Maritime Rights Movement to a close. At a Federal–Provincial Conference held that year, interregional tensions were also eased as the Maritime provinces supported the West's demand for the provincial ownership of natural resources,[18] and the western provinces supported the Maritime quest for enhanced freight rate subsidies and intergovernmental fiscal transfers. While the Movement had not resulted in any significant progress towards the political unification of the Maritimes, it had helped foster a regional consciousness and identity that were to persist.

2. Newfoundland

Whether this regional consciousness and identity extended to include Newfoundland is a matter of ongoing and contentious debate. In the 1860s Newfoundlanders, faced with a vulnerable economy and widespread poverty, came up against the Canadian drive for Confederation. Although Newfoundland delegates did not attend the 1864 Charlottetown conference, they did attend the subsequent conference in Quebec City. At that time Newfoundland was offered generally favourable financial terms of entry, although Canadian politicians were not as insistent in their courtship of Newfoundland as they were in their courtship of Nova Scotia and New Brunswick. Given opposition to Confederation by economic elites in St. John's, and given the fact that little of Newfoundland's trade was with the Canadian mainland, Newfoundlanders rejected Confederation despite considerable British pressure. In 1869 an election was fought on the issue, with Confederation supporters winning nine seats and their opponents twenty-one. The island's sentiment was nicely captured by a song popularized during the campaign:

> Hurrah for our own native isle, Newfoundland!
> Not a stranger shall hold one inch of its strand!
> Her face turns to Britain, her back to the gulf.
> Come near at your peril, Canadian wolf![19]

The Canadian wolf took heed, and union was not considered again until 1895 when a severe recession led to unsuccessful talks with the Canadian government on financial terms of entry. When responsible government in Newfoundland came to an end in 1934 in the wake of near economic collapse, union with Canada, at the time in the throes of the Great Depression, was not considered. Instead, the reins of government were passed to an appointed six-man commission, with three of the commissioners coming from Newfoundland and three from Great Britain. The commission remained in place to steer Newfoundland through the wartime prosperity brought by American and Canadian airfields. The war years, as Terry Campbell and G.A. Rawlyk conclude, "...forced Newfoundland into the mainstream of North American life and... resulted in both a dramatic rise in the existing standard of living and also in the benchmark of expectations."[20]

With the end of the war and the departure of Allied airmen, the British government took a major step on the road to the island's union with Canada. The decision was made to hold a referendum on Newfoundland's future, and a convention was called to set the terms of the referendum. Initially, union with Canada was not to be one of the options. However, in the face of protest mobilized by broadcaster Joey Smallwood and sympathetically received by the British government, union was included along with retention of commission government and a return to responsible government under the British crown. The first round of the referendum narrowed the choice to union with Canada or a return to responsible government. On July 22, 1948, 52.4 percent of those voting opted for confederation with Canada, and on March 31, 1949, Newfoundland became Canada's tenth province. Eighty-five years after the Charlottetown conference, Confederation was complete.

Smallwood went on to dominate Newfoundland politics for the next twenty years. His passionate support for Canada and his success in entrenching the Liberal party on the island were to cement the relationship between Newfoundland and the broader Canadian community. Yet that relationship was not without difficulties as Newfoundland came to represent, albeit in exaggerated form, the pattern of dependency that was increasingly characteristic of Atlantic Canada. Fiscal transfers from the federal government accounted for roughly half the provincial budget, while individual Newfoundlanders were the net beneficiaries of federal government social support programs such as unemployment insurance. Intergovernmental and interpersonal transfers to Newfoundland and to the Atlantic region in general could be borne by the national community because of the region's small and declining share of the national population. At the same time, such transfers stopped well short of providing economic prosperity. Newfoundland, for example, still chronically suffers from the country's highest unemployment rates.

The end of dependency has been a persistent but elusive goal for Newfoundland's political leaders. Prospects brightened considerably in the 1970s with the discovery of the Hibernia oil field off the east coast of Newfoundland, although the discovery also touched off a bitter jurisdictional battle between the Newfoundland and Canadian governments which stretched through to the mid-1980s. In essence, Premier Brian Peckford's Progressive Conservative government claimed the same ownership, and thus control of offshore resources, that other provinces, and most particularly Alberta, exercised over continental resources. It was hoped that the revenues which would eventually flow from Hibernia could be used to lift Newfoundland from the ranks of the have-not provinces and transform Newfoundland as oil had transformed Alberta. For its part, the Liberal government in Ottawa claimed that offshore resources fell under federal jurisdiction, that oil revenues should replace rather than build upon equalization payments, and that once Newfoundland's provincial revenues reached the national average, the federal share of natural resource revenue should be greatly increased. Also at issue was the pace of Hibernia's development; should it be set by the needs of the provincial or national community?

The offshore dispute bounced around in the political arena for some time. Prior to his victory in the 1979 federal election, Progressive Conservative leader Joe Clark stated that, if elected, a Conservative government would transfer ownership of offshore resources to the provinces. However, no action was taken before the Clark government was replaced by a less sympathetic Liberal government in the 1980 general election. At that point the offshore dispute became thoroughly entangled with the broader constitutional debate set in motion by the sovereignty association referendum in Quebec. With the resolution of that debate in 1981/82, a resolution which did not address jurisdictional control over offshore resources, the Newfoundland government referred the offshore dispute to the provincial Supreme Court. When the Newfoundland court ruled in favour of Ottawa, the ruling was appealed to the Supreme Court of Canada. In February 1984, the Supreme Court ruled that jurisdiction over offshore resources lay with the federal government. Newfoundland's claim that it had retained ownership of the continental shelf upon entering Canada in 1949 was rejected.

The Court's decision put the dispute back into the federal-provincial arena, and into the 1984 federal election campaign. Shortly after the Progressive Conservative victory in September, Ottawa and Newfoundland endorsed the Atlantic Accord which largely met Newfoundland Premier Brian Peckford's conditions for provincial control over, and benefit from, offshore development. Once the Accord was in place, however, falling world oil prices threw Hibernia's development into further doubt. For development to proceed in the face of low oil prices, massive federal subsidies will be necessary. The extent and timing of such subsidies remain very contentious issues between the federal and provincial governments, issues that contributed to the defeat of the provincial Conservative government in the spring of 1989.

3. *The Atlantic Region*

Table 4.1 demonstrates a very high level of support for Confederation among Atlantic Canadians surveyed in 1978. While a significant number agreed that "the way Confederation was set gives all the advantages to Ontario," they were outnumbered more than two to one by those who disagreed. Fewer than 30 percent agreed that they belonged to "a group that hasn't got a fair deal out of federal government policy," even though 61 percent felt that people in Ontario were better off than were people in their own province. A majority of respondents also supported the federal status quo, with only 32 percent supporting a more decentralized federal system in which more power would be given to the provincial governments. Finally, it is interesting to note the very limited intraregional variation in the table. Opinion varied little from one province to the next, suggesting a regional perspective on political life transcending a respondent's provincial residence.

Yet the fact remains that, since the end of the Second World War, Atlantic Canada has become increasingly marginal to the national economy.[21] Interlocking economic and demographic decline has in turn eroded the region's position within the national political community. While the development of offshore resources, if it takes place, may forestall any further erosion, the prospects for a dramatic reversal in the region's fortunes are not bright. To date, though, the national fabric has

Table 4.1
Regional Sentiment in Atlantic Canada

In the fall of 1978 the Task Force on National Unity commissioned a comprehensive public opinion survey of the Atlantic region. Directed by Professors George Perlin and George Rawlyk, both from Queen's University, the survey encompassed 1,939 respondents. Although a number of years have since passed, it still stands as the most detailed snapshot available of political opinion in the region. While there has undoubtedly been some change in opinion since 1978, there is little reason to expect that the broad parameters sketched in by the questions below have been altered to any substantial degree.

	Atlantic Canada	Nfld.	P.E.I.	N.S.	N.B.
1. "Overall, would you say that Confederation has been a good thing or a bad thing for this province?"					
Good thing	84%	90%	80%	80%	84%
Bad thing	7	4	10	8	6
Both	1	1	1	1	1
D.K./N.O.	9	4	10	12	9
2. "Some people say that the way Confederation was set up gives all the advantages to Ontario. Other people say that is not true. What do you think?"					
True	24%	17%	21%	25%	27%
Not true	59	60	60	59	58
D.K./N.O.	17	22	19	16	15
3. "Do you feel you belong to a group that hasn't got a fair deal out of federal government policy?"					
Yes	28%	29%	22%	29%	27%
No	67	65	74	65	68
D.K./N.O.	6	6	4	6	5
4. "In terms of their incomes and standard of living, on average, do you think people in Ontario are better off, about the same or worse off than people here in (name of province)?"					
Better off	62%	61%	73%	63%	59%
About the same	27	23	22	28	30
Worse off	5	7	1	4	6
D.K./N.O.	6	9	4	4	5
5. "Some people think that more of the power to make decisions should be taken from the federal government and given to the provincial governments. Other people would rather keep things as they are. What do you think?"					
Decentralize	38%	32%	38%	41%	39%
Status quo	50	55	47	50	49
D.K./N.O.	11	14	14	9	12

not been seriously strained by regional discontent. As G.A. Rawlyk and Doug Brown conclude, "in a fascinating twist of a complex relationship, the region of Canada which was once most vociferously opposed to Confederation has become one of its most ardent and committed supporters."[22] Atlantic Canadians have not challenged the basic institutional or constitutional structure of the Canadian federal state, and have not allowed regional discontent to dampen their electoral support for the two mainline national parties. Economic competition among the Atlantic provinces,[23] a declining share of the national population, widespread dependency on transfer payments from the federal government, and powerful regional spokesmen within the federal cabinet have all served to contain regional discontent and set Atlantic Canada apart from the Canadian West. It should also be stressed, however, that the region's political agenda is now heavily laden with issues which pit specific provincial governments, and at times the region as a whole, against the federal government. Conflict over issues such as federal subsidies for offshore resource development, the closure of military bases, changes in the unemployment insurance system, fish quotas and foreign fishing fleets, and the Meech Lake Accord portend intensified regional discord in the years ahead.

Western Canada

In a narrow sense, Confederation was the amalgamation of existing British North American colonies into the single colonial unit of Canada. In a broader sense, it was also the vehicle through which a new and unsettled region could be developed, a region whose resources were believed to be immense. This region was the prairie West, stretching over 1,600 kilometres from the western edge of the Canadian Shield to the Rocky Mountains.

Even before Confederation, the prairie West assumed an important place in the Canadian national vision. Note, for instance, an editorial that appeared in *The Toronto Globe* on March 6, 1862:[24]

> When the territory [the West] belongs to Canada, when its navigable waters are traversed for a few years by vessels, and lines of travel are permanently established, when settlements are formed in favourable locations throughout the territory, it will not be difficult by grants of land to secure the construction of a railway across the plains and through the mountains.... If we set about the work of opening the territory at once, we shall win the race [against the United States, which was pushing steadily westward].... It is an empire we have in view, and its whole export and import trade will be concentrated in the hands of Canadian merchants and manufacturers if we strike for it now.

To a large degree, the West has fulfilled even the most optimistic visions of early Canadians. Yet it has done so through prolonged and often acrimonious regional conflict, the seeds of which are to be found in the above quotation. The conflict between national interests and the more narrow economic interests of central Canada, on the one hand, and the regional aspirations of those who settled the prairie West, on the other, has not been easily resolved. Indeed, contemporary western alienation provides ample testimony that a resolution still eludes Canadians, over a hundred years after settlement began to spread across the prairies.

To explain the contemporary nature of political life in western Canada, we must first sketch, with very broad strokes indeed, the region's historical evolution. In doing so we must also recognize that there have been two quite different Wests—the prairie West encompassing Manitoba, Saskatchewan, and Alberta, and, across the mountain divide, British Columbia. The settlement pattern, economic foundations, and political history of British Columbia have been very different from those of the prairie provinces. For this reason, our initial discussion focuses on the prairie West alone and its incorporation into the Canadian union.

1. The Prairie West in Historical Perspective

For many Canadians, Confederation was the key that would unlock the riches of the North-West and, in so doing, stimulate economic growth and prosperity in central Canada. However, for almost the first thirty years after Confederation, settlement was slow and prosperity elusive. A world-wide economic depression in the 1870s and 1880s stemmed the tide of immigration to the New World and, for those who did come, open land was still available in the United States. There was also considerable scepticism as to whether the prairie climate and terrain would even support agricultural settlement. Nevertheless, the rail system that was to transport western resources to world markets and settlers to the West was put in place, while incremental settlement spread across Manitoba and westward along the CPR tracks and the North Saskatchewan valley.

The long-anticipated settlement boom began in the late 1890s as the depression lifted, large-scale immigration resumed, and free land in the United States all but disappeared. The success of early settlers, and the introduction of new and hardier strains of wheat, put the earlier scepticism about prairie agriculture to rest. In the single decade from 1901 to 1911 the prairie population rose from 419,000 to 1,328,000, an increase of over 216 percent in only ten years. When Prime Minister Wilfrid Laurier declared in 1904 that the twentieth century belonged to Canada, his optimism fully reflected the spirit of the "last, best West," as the prairies were described in promotional literature put out by the Canadian Pacific Railway and the federal government.

While the settlement of the West is a saga that cannot be recounted in any detail here, a number of features should be noted, given their impact on Canadian political life. Although the West was settled in large part by the westward migration of Canadians, and in particular by those from Ontario, many settlers came from Europe and the United States. These latter settlers had spent little, if any, time in other parts of Canada, and had limited exposure to the political values, institutions, and parties of the central Canadian heartland. A substantial portion of the prairie population, therefore, had *relatively* shallow roots in Canadian political soil and, more particularly, in the mainstream Conservative and Liberal parties. In the economic crises to come, western Canadians, as a consequence, were open to new political ideas and were quite prepared to abandon the traditional parties for more radical, regional parties.

The prairie population was also set apart by its ethnic composition. In the 1931 census, which marked the ethnic crystallization of the prairie community, only 56.5 percent of the residents were of British or French descent, compared to 80.1 percent for Canada as a whole and 82.7 percent for Ontario. The prairie population was marked by large numbers of German, Scandinavian, Ukrainian, Dutch, Polish, Russian, and American settlers. With that diversity came a multiplicity of religions, languages, and cultures, all giving the prairies a uniquely multicultural cast. French Canadians made up only 5.8 percent of the prairie population in 1931, a proportion surpassed by those of German, Ukrainian, and Scandinavian descent. This demographic feature has been of long-lasting political importance, helping to explain why French Canadians have often been seen as simply another ethnic minority, and a relatively small one at that, and why the *regional* rather than *national* size of the francophone population has dominated prairie reactions to bilingualism and biculturalism. Moreover, in the historical process of assimilating a linguistically diverse immigrant population, the protection of the French language was often seen as an unwelcome shield behind which other ethnic groups might seek protection from assimilationist pressures. In combination, these demographic features help account for widespread opposition in the West to bilingualism, and to more broadly conceived dualistic interpretations of Canadian political life.

Although the prairie population was demographically diverse, it was pulled together by the wheat economy, which touched the lives of virtually every prairie resident. Unlike the Maritime provinces, the prairie provinces shared a common and overriding set of economic interests. The wheat economy bound the prairie provinces into a single economic unit within which individuals shared essentially the same environment, interests, and problems. The wheat economy forged a "regional way of life,"[25] facilitated the political integration of the prairie West and set the region apart from central Canada to the east and British Columbia to the west.

Prairie agriculture was a precarious undertaking at the best of times. Farmers were dependent upon an uncertain and often harsh climate, and upon volatile foreign markets lying beyond their control. (While the Canadian economy at large was dependent upon unpredictable foreign markets, no other region exported as much or was dependent on such a narrow market base.) Wheat was not a crop that could be sold to any great extent on the local or even Canadian market. It had to be sold—through the middlemen in the grain trade—on distant foreign markets, and then shipped across Canada and the Atlantic Ocean on a monopolistic transportation system. The wheat economy was also afflicted by cycles of boom and bust, determined in the first place by weather conditions in Europe and western Canada, which in turn determined the demand from European markets and the size of the Canadian crop. Thus grain farmers rode an erratic, unpredictable roller coaster over which they had little control, and which destabilized both economic and political life on the prairies.

The nature of prairie agriculture led to a litany of economic grievances. At the top of the list came tariff protection for central Canadian manufacturers, protection which increased the price western Canadians had to pay for consumer goods and farm machinery while their own crops sold on the unprotected international market. Other grievances included transportation bottlenecks; freight rates which were seen to be excessive; inequities in the grading and marketing of grain; and the frustrations of a debtor frontier towards the central Canadian financial institutions which loaned badly needed capital, collected the interest and, when times were tough, foreclosed on the family farm.

Economic Alienation

It is a long-standing tenet of western alienation that the federal government has been at best indifferent to the economic woes of the West, and at worst a major contributor to those woes through national tariff and freight rate policies.

As economist Kenneth Norrie has pointed out, however, the West is a relatively sparsely populated economic hinterland within both the Canadian and North American market economies. As many of its economic grievances, such as the lack of secondary manufacturing and economic diversification, arise from the region's location in these market economies, they " . . . must be interpreted as dissatisfaction with a market economy rather than with discriminatory policies of the federal government."[26] Norrie goes on to argue that the negative effects of federal policies have been exaggerated, and to question whether even the most supportive national policies would be able to overcome market forces and encourage any substantial increase in manufacturing and secondary industry in the prairie West. While extensive government intervention in the market economy would be a necessary condition, it may not prove to be a sufficient condition.

Here it should be noted that the Free Trade Agreement should enhance the impact of market forces in western Canada. If Norrie is correct, there is little prospect that the freer play of continental markets will promote economic diversification in western Canada, although it may prompt further development in the resource sector.

These economic grievances generated, in turn, a regional set of political grievances embodied in the term "western alienation."[27] Apart from the specific economic grievances mentioned above, western alienation reflected the belief that the West's contribution to the national economy was not being sufficiently acknowledged. Wheat was a mainstay of the national as well as the regional economy in the early part of this century. As James Mallory has pointed out, "almost the whole Canadian economy was vitally affected by, and organized around, the movement of the annual grain crop into world markets."[28] Although that movement supported the national railway system, which in turn bound the new country together and provided essential western Canadian markets for central Canadian industries, the West received few compensations from national policies on tariffs and freight rates. At the heart of the matter lay the belief, and essentially the reality, that western Canadians lacked political muscle commensurate with their contribution to the national economy. The region found itself in a quasi-colonial position vis-à-vis central Canada and the federal government, with the specific economic problems confronting the West being attributed to the region's political impotence. Thus, their solution required a regional assault on the political and institutional status quo.

The quest for political reform followed a number of paths, including support for national opposition parties; the creation of new, regionally based parties that would hopefully be more attuned to western Canadian interests; the rejection of the party system altogether and the advocacy of non-partisan forms of government; and the advocacy of changes in the rules of the House of Commons which would weaken party discipline and make MPs the agents of their constituents rather than of their parties. The quest, therefore, lacked a clear focus or target. Westerners were divided among those who sought simply a change in government; those who sought new, regionally based parties; and those who rejected the party system altogether. The regional critique of parliamentary institutions was hesitant and inconsistent; although party discipline was assailed, Parliament itself was venerated without a clear recognition that party discipline was an essential feature of parliamentary democracy. The desire to weaken party discipline was not coupled with practical proposals for alternate institutional arrangements to sustain parliamentary democracy once the prop of party discipline had been removed.[29]

Perhaps the most significant thing about western agrarian protest is that it failed to have any substantive impact on the *institutional* fabric of the Canadian federal state before western Canada was transformed by the calamitous events of the 1930s. The **Great Depression** began in 1929, reached its peak in the early 1930s, and lingered on until the start of the Second World War. Although the Depression was a major economic shock for the country at large, its impact on the prairies was catastrophic. The collapse of world trade devastated the export-based prairie grain economy. Accompanying the collapse in markets came drought, grasshoppers, and high winds which stripped the topsoil from the land, creating the immense duststorms of the "dirty thirties." Debts incurred in the good years, when farmers expanded their holdings and improved their equipment, became a crushing burden in the 1930s. Often crops could not be sold, or could be sold only at a price insufficient to cover the costs of production and transportation. Farmers frequently had no choice but to plough their crops under and hope for better times "next year." For many others in "next year country" the only alternative was to leave both the land and the region as debts mounted and the banks foreclosed.

The Depression redefined the place of the prairie West in Canada. Prior to the 1930s, the prairies had been the magnet drawing immigration into Canada. With the onset of the Depression and the Second World War, immigration into Canada slowed to a trickle. When it resumed after 1945, the prairie West was bypassed. Unsettled agricultural land had all but disappeared, and grain prices were low. The grain economy had become more capital-intensive, offered fewer employment opportunities, and was costly to enter for new farmers. Most postwar immigrants, moreover, came primarily from urban backgrounds and lacked the skills needed for prairie agriculture. In addition, the prairie West, struggling to recover from the devastation of the Depression, was no longer seen as a region of promise and new beginnings. Even a passing familiarity with the Depression was sufficient to deter all but the most masochistic immigrants from settling on the prairies.

The end of in-migration to the region, the out-migration of hundreds of thousands of prairie residents during the Depression, and the increasing mechanization of prairie agriculture all combined to undercut the region's population base and political power. Western agriculture also became less central to the Canadian economy; even though more grain than ever was being produced, the grain economy's proportionate contribution to the national economy steadily declined. As fewer people produced more and more with less and less economic impact, the prairie West drifted towards the margins of Canadian life.

The Mulroney Grain Elevator

Donato's cartoon shows that perceptions of regional exploitation can cut both ways.

Andy Donato, *Gucci Blues: Political Cartoons* (Toronto: Key Porter Books, 1988). Originally published in *The Toronto Sun*.

2. The "New West"

As the "old," agrarian West declined, a "new West" was beginning to emerge, its birth marked by the discovery and commercial development of the Leduc oil field in Alberta during the late 1940s and early 1950s. The new West, like the old, was based on natural resources, but these now included oil, natural gas, potash, coal, and uranium. The *relative*, but not *absolute*, decline of agriculture and the broadened resource base brought the prairie economy more into line with that of British Columbia, and laid the foundation for a broader political region than had existed in the past. (The resource base of the British Columbia economy encompassed not only forestry and the Pacific fisheries but also coal, natural gas, hydro-electric power and a variety of minerals including copper, lead, molybdenum, and zinc.) Although resting on a broader base, the new regional economy was similar to the old in that it was heavily dependent upon foreign markets and highly variable world prices. The "boom and bust" problems of the wheat economy were inherited, moderated to a degree by diversification *within* the resource sector, but not surmounted.

The new West developed slowly at first, with British Columbia being the primary growth pole and population magnet. Then, after 1973, escalating world prices for oil fuelled rapid growth in the Alberta and, to a lesser degree, Saskatchewan economies. The face of the new West was urban rather than rural, its features coming from the skylines of Vancouver, Calgary, and Edmonton rather than from the silhouettes of grain elevators against the prairie sky. The spirit of the region was marked by the aggressive boosterism of communities on the move and on the make. Migration into the region accelerated as thousands of Canadians packed their belongings into U-haul trailers and moved to the West in search of a slice of the natural resource pie. Once again the West seemed to be at the cutting edge of Canadian society, and the smouldering coals of political discontent burst into flame.

During the 1970s and early 1980s, western alienation was fuelled from a number of sources. Provincial governments in the West, growing rapidly in size and bureaucratic expertise, challenged the federal government's management of national economic policy and sought to roll back federal intrusions into provincial fields of jurisdiction. In this respect, political developments in the West closely paralleled those occurring simultaneously in Quebec. At the same time, national bilingualism policies found an unsympathetic and at times hostile audience in the multicultural West. This reaction was symptomatic of more general frustration stemming from Ottawa's apparent preoccupation with national unity problems originating in Quebec, a preoccupation that pushed western concerns off the nation's political agenda. Note a 1979 speech by Stan Roberts, then president of the **Canada West Foundation**:

The new fury of the Westerner demonstrates itself when it strikes home that Quebec's six million plus citizens have turned the country on its collective ear and created an enormous attention to their problems by the election of a pequiste government, while the West's six million plus citizens (still) can't be heard over the rush and scramble to accommodate Quebec. Sometimes the West's frustration and rage is misconstrued as antiQuebec in nature. It is not. It is, in most cases, envy of Quebec's political prowess combined with fury at the West's own impotence on the national scene.[30]

Of perhaps greatest importance was the lack of elected western representation within the federal government, and thus the inability of westerners to see their own regional reflection in national institutions. As Figure 4.4 illustrates, there have been dramatic swings in western Canadian representation on the government side of the House of Commons, dramatic in comparison with the more stable pattern in Atlantic Canada. The high water mark came in 1958 when the West moved overwhelmingly into the Progressive Conservative camp, and when John Diefenbaker swept the region and the country in the largest Canadian electoral landslide ever. While Diefenbaker's appeal in 1958 was undeniably national in scope, it was particularly strong in the prairie West. As Denis Smith explains,

> He gave to the Prairies for the first time in their history the same sense of dynamic and central participation in nation-building that his predecessor, John A. Macdonald, had given to central Canada after 1867.... [his policies] were policies of national integration that typified the prairie conception of Canada.[31]

When other regions swung back to the Liberals in the early 1960s, the West stood pat, and with Diefenbaker's defeat in 1963 western representation on the government side of the House fell to precariously low levels. The situation was particularly bleak on the prairies. Of the 65 western Liberal MPs elected in the 1963, 1965, 1968, 1972, and 1974 general elections combined, only 23 came from the three prairie provinces. In 1979 the Progressive Conservatives formed a minority government in which the West enjoyed strong representation. The Conservative leader, Joe Clark, was the first Canadian prime minister born in the West. Only nine months later, however, the Conservatives were defeated and replaced by a majority Liberal government. In that election only two Liberal MPs were elected west of Ontario, both in Manitoba. The West had been all but shut out.

The lack of elected representation in the federal government was at odds with the growing economic muscle of the West and the region's increasing share of the national population. It was irksome to westerners that a majority government could be elected before a single ballot was counted west of Ontario, as had happened in 1980. (When this happened

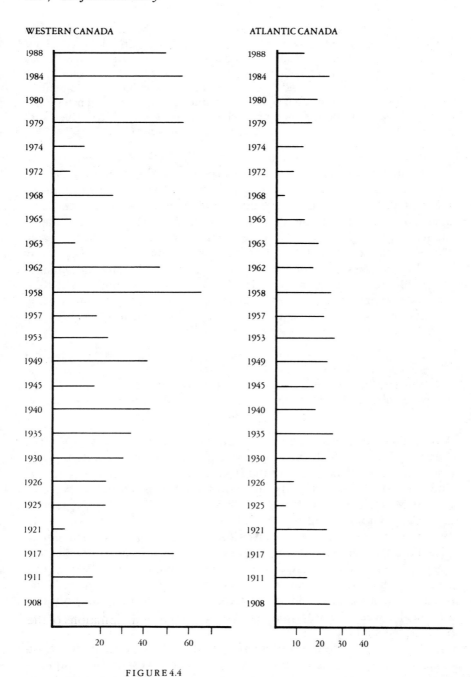

FIGURE 4.4

MPs Elected to the Government Side of the House

again in 1984, but with the West on the winning side, it provoked little comment!) The practical cost of regional exclusion from the federal government was driven home, at least to Albertans, by the federal response to rising world oil prices in 1973-74, by the introduction of the National Energy Program in the fall of 1980, and the related and acrimonious conflict between the federal and Alberta governments over the price structure for Canadian oil and natural gas. As Figure 4.5 shows, at the peak of western alienation nearly a third of western Canadians agreed with the statement that "western Canadians get so little out of Confederation that they might as well go it on their own." Throughout this period, levels of western alienation tended to be higher in Alberta and British Columbia than they were in Saskatchewan and Manitoba, although the sentiment was far from absent in the eastern half of the region. Alienation was also much more pronounced among Conservatives than among Liberals, with New Democrats occupying an intermediate position.

Western alienation, it should be stressed, cannot be equated with support for western separatism. Although in the early 1980s separatist parties did emerge for the first time in western Canada, they attracted only marginal support. In the absence of a federal election, separatist candidates ran provincially, where they played a minor role at best in the provincial elections held in Saskatchewan and Manitoba, and no role whatsoever in the British Columbia election. Only in Alberta did the Western Canada Concept party make a mark by electing an MLA in a provincial by-election, and by capturing 11 percent of the popular vote in the subsequent provincial election. In that election, however, the sitting WCC member was defeated as the governing Progressive Conservatives picked up 75 of the 79 seats. In ten surveys tracked by the Canada West Foundation between mid-1979 and mid-1980, support for separatism averaged only 6.6 percent across the region. Even this figure may overstate the true level of separatist support, as some respondents used the question to express the intensity of their frustration rather than to endorse an independent West.

Western Canadians sometimes drew a tactical parallel between their own situation and that faced by the residents of Quebec who, the argument went, had used the threat of separatism to extract political and economic concessions from the federal government. Only if western Canadians were prepared to play the same game, the argument continued, would Ottawa pay attention to the complaints and aspirations of the West. The Quebec analogy failed to recognize that many Québécois had more than a tactical commitment to independence—that for many independence was a positive goal and not simply a club with which to beat concessions out of Ottawa. More importantly, the analogy failed to recognize the essential core of western alienation. Unlike the Québécois, who have sought to ward off assimilation, western Canadians have sought

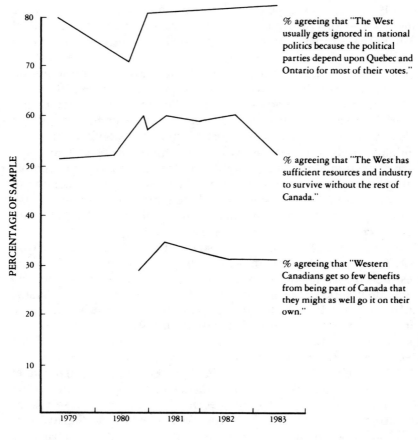

% agreeing that "The West usually gets ignored in national politics because the political parties depend upon Quebec and Ontario for most of their votes."

% agreeing that "The West has sufficient resources and industry to survive without the rest of Canada."

% agreeing that "Western Canadians get so few benefits from being part of Canada that they might as well go it on their own."

FIGURE 4.5

Western Alienation

These data are taken from a series of public opinion polls conducted for the Canada West Foundation, Calgary, Alberta. For details, see the Foundation's *Opinion Update* series.

integration into the Canadian political, economic, and social mainstreams. In the words of the late W.L. Morton:

> the West has been defined as a colonial society seeking equality in Confederation. That equality was sought in order that the West should be like, not different from the rest of Canada.[32]

Western alienation captures the frustration that comes from incomplete integration, from the belief that western Canada has failed to play a role in the nation's life commensurate with the region's resources, potential, and aspirations. Western Canadians have wanted in, not out. Even among separatists, the cry has been: "we are not separating, it is Canada that is abandoning the West." Thus western alienation has been not so much a vociferous expression of a regional or provincial identity as the expression of a frustrated Canadian identity.

At its peak, western alienation represented a demand by the "new West" for greater recognition within the nation's political and economic fabric. This demand came to a head in the political struggle over the patriation of Canada's constitution, a struggle that took place when the federal government had but two elected representatives from western Canada. It was also at a time when the West's economy was strong, its population was growing relative to the nation as a whole, and its provincial governments were led by popular and articulate leaders. Yet, when the dust had settled on the patriation battle and the Constitution Act of 1982 had been proclaimed, little had been done to redress long-standing western grievances.[33] Admittedly, provincial control over natural resources had been strengthened through the addition of Section 92A—"Non-Renewable Natural Resources, Forestry Resources and Electrical Energy"—to the Constitution Act, and the new amending formula was modelled after western proposals. However, parliamentary institutions had not been reformed so as to provide more visible and more effective regional representation in Ottawa. More generally, the West had not been able to impose its own political and institutional vision upon the Canadian federal state despite a nearly unbroken tradition of regional political discontent reaching back a hundred years.

There is an important lesson to be learned from the western Canadian experience over the late 1970s and early 1980s. When all was said and done, once the price of oil had gone up and down again, once thousands had moved into the region and left again, *the centre held*. The West remained on the national periphery, a region rich in resources and territory but with a relatively small and widely dispersed population. The lesson is that regional discontent will not be overcome by dramatic shifts in the regional location of people and industry. In the short and intermediate run, the Canadian economic and demographic landscapes are immutable. Marked differences in the regional distribution of natural resources, population, and industry will remain, and will continue to generate tension within the national political system. Therefore, if we concede that regional discontent is a problem and seek solutions, we must look to the way in which we conduct our political affairs. More specifically, we must examine the role played by political institutions in both moderating and exacerbating regional conflict. New leaders and intraparty reform may help,[34] as may more regionally attuned development policies.[35] However, it is not clear that either solution will be sufficient, or even likely, without complementary institutional reform.

The Political Economy of Regionalism

The argument that regionalism has institutional rather than geographical roots is one that is developed at length within the political economy literature. Note, for example, the following discussion by Wallace Clement:

> Regionalism is but one expression of more deeply rooted inequalities and social problems in Canada. Any dominant class creates problems through its very existence and actions; one such problem is regionalism. To suggest that regional inequalities are "natural" ignores the realities of power and the control some men have over the lives of others. Thus a detailed analysis of the current structure of regionalism would show that it is not the product of some natural phenomenon like geography or resources or even historical accident; rather, it is the product of a series of actions and institutions created and alterable by man.[36]

Clement goes on to argue that primary importance should be attached to economic institutions and the impact of class. Thus it is not "Ontario" that dominates Canada: "it is the capitalist class and its operating arm in the economy, the economic elite, which has always performed and continues to perform this task."[37] Political factors, such as the federal structure of the Canadian state, take on a somewhat secondary role:

> But do ... political boundaries really explain regionalism in Canada? Are the real regional splits not based more on economics than politics? ... While political fragmentation aggravates regionalism, it is not itself the cause of regionalism. That cause must be found in the uneven economic development of the country and the branch-plant structure of corporate capitalism.[38]

During the 1970s and early 1980s, Pierre Trudeau served as the lightning rod for western Canadian political discontent. It is thus appropriate that, in one of his last speeches as prime minister, Trudeau should capture the essence of western Canadian discontent. Speaking before the Quebec wing of the federal Liberal party on March 31, 1984, Trudeau said:

> No Canada can exist without the support of this province. Remind yourselves of that during the leadership race to elect my successor, during the coming election. Quebec is strong. Quebec can decide who will govern this country, but more importantly how this country will be governed.

Western Canadians would not challenge that statement. Their frustration stems from the fact that Canadian leaders could not make a similar statement about the West even though more people live in the four western provinces than in Quebec. (At the time of the 1986 census, 6,540,300 people lived in Quebec compared to 7,345,900 in the four western provinces.) The result is not discontent with Canada per se but with the Canadian political system—discontent which in the past bound four rather disparate provinces into a single regional community and which helped to make regionalism a pervasive and enduring feature of Canadian political life.

Federal Government Treatment of Quebec and the West

In a national survey conducted by Angus Reid Associates for Southam News in late August 1988, 1,506 respondents were asked if they thought Brian Mulroney's Progressive Conservative government was doing too much, too little, or about the right amount for Quebec (*Calgary Herald*, September 3, 1988, p. A1). Including Quebec respondents, 47 percent of the national sample felt that the federal government was doing too much for Quebec, 13 percent too little, and 34 percent about the right amount. Among English Canadians alone, 60 percent felt that too much was being done for Quebec compared to only 29 percent who felt that the federal government was doing about the right amount.

In western Canada, 71 percent of the respondents thought that the federal government was doing too much for Quebec while 73 percent felt that too little was being done for the West. Nationally, 46 percent of the respondents said that too little was being done for the West, 37 percent said that the West was being treated about right, and 7 percent said Ottawa was doing too much for the West.

Within the context of western alienation, the results of the 1984 federal election provided an important test for Canadian parliamentary institutions. Following that election, western Canadian representation on the government side of the House of Commons surged from two to fifty-eight MPs, and the West had a strong voice in the federal cabinet through such ministers as Joe Clark, Jake Epp, Ray Hnatyshyn, and Don Mazankowski. Thus western Canadians would be able to see how parliamentary institutions worked in the best of times rather than in the worst of times when, under the Liberal governments of Pierre Trudeau, the region had been all but shut out of the federal government. There is little question that the new Progressive Conservative government initially met the admittedly high expectations of western Canadians. The Western Energy Accord, signed by Ottawa and the three oil producing provinces on March 27, 1985, brought an end to the protracted energy wars between the federal and western provincial governments. The Accord removed or began to phase out most of the contentious tax provisions imposed by the National Energy Program, deregulated the price and sale of oil, eliminated the Petroleum Incentive Program, and created a better atmosphere for foreign investment. Through the Western Grain Stabilization Fund and a variety of other measures, $10 billion was spent over the first four years of the Mulroney government to protect western farmers facing drought, falling world grain prices, and a crushing debt load.[39] In August 1987, the federal government created the Department of Western Economic Diversification in order to help diversify the western economy.

It might have seemed, therefore, that parliamentary institutions did in fact perform well under the "right conditions." And yet western alienation not only persisted, but flared up in potentially virulent forms. In the 1988 election, the Progressive Conservatives lost substantial ground in the West, dropping from 58 of 77 seats (75 percent) in 1984 to 48 of 86 seats (56 percent) in 1988. Perhaps more importantly, the new Reform Party of Canada fought an energetic campaign across the West. (In Alberta, Reform candidates picked up 15.3 percent of the popular vote and finished second in nine of the province's twenty-six constituencies.) Reform candidates, led by Preston Manning, provided a forceful and at times articulate expression of both traditional western grievances, including any expansion of official bilingualism, and more contemporary concerns including Senate reform and opposition to the Meech Lake Accord. Although the Reform Party had some trouble getting its concerns onto a campaign agenda dominated by the debate over the Free Trade Agreement, and although no Reform candidates were elected until a March 1989 by-election in the Alberta riding of Beaver River, the party nonetheless made a significant mark on western Canadian politics. At the very least, the 1988 campaign demonstrated that the ghost of western alienation had not been laid to rest by four years of Conservative government in Ottawa, a government within which the West had been well represented and through which economic policies favourable to the West had been pursued.

Ontario

Embodied within western alienation lies a polarity which is fundamental to an understanding of both political life in western Canada and the dynamics of regionalism more broadly conceived. The polarity pits the region against "central Canada," against the "East" or "Upper Canada," the latter term being more common in political discourse in Atlantic Canada than in the West. While central Canada and the East are often used to include Quebec, it is Ontario that forms the regional pivot for Canadian political life.

By any measure other than geographical size, Ontario is Canada's largest "region." Moreover, we find within Ontario a concentration of people, wealth, industry, and cultural activity that sets Canada apart from the more geographically dispersed American federal system to the south. Ontario contains 36 percent of the national population whereas California, the largest state in the United States, contains less than 10 percent of the American population. Ontario not only forms the economic heartland of Canada, but its domination of the national economy far surpasses that exercised by any single state in the United States. For its part, Toronto dominates English Canadian cultural life to a far greater extent than any one city is able to do in the United States; there is no ready Canadian equivalent to the cultural competition among New York, Boston, Los Angeles, San Francisco, and Washington, to name but a few. Ontario, furthermore, is the site not only of Canada's largest city but also of the national capital. While the American capital is located in the District of Columbia, outside the boundaries of any state, Ottawa's location reinforces Ontario's position at the centre of Canadian life.

It may seem odd, then, that the analysis of regionalism in Canada largely neglects Ontario. When the term "regionalism" is used in reference to Ontario, the focus is usually upon territorial divisions within the province—on conflict, for example, between northern Ontario and the "golden triangle"—rather than upon Ontario's position in and impact upon national political life. Conventional political discourse rarely treats Ontario as one of the many Canadian regions. In this respect, Joe Clark is considered to have made a major strategic blunder in his 1983 bid to retain the leadership of the national Progressive Conservative party when he declared that, should Ontario Premier Bill Davis run for the leadership, Davis would be seen as "a regional candidate." Ron Graham concluded, in a retrospective look at the leadership campaign, that "however true that observation was, the heart of Ontario is not won by treating it as less than the centre of the universe."[40] Certainly the study of regionalism in Canada has been primarily the study of the regional peripheries, with the central Canadian linchpin placed aside.

How do we explain a regional analysis which all but ignores Canada's largest and most influential region? Why is Ontario little more than a residual term in the regional analysis of Canadian political life? In part, the answers have to do with the manner in which regionalism is conceived. The analytical focus is not on the relationship *among* the various regions that make up the Canadian community, but rather the relationship *between* the centre and the periphery. In this context, the centre ceases to be a region like other regions and instead takes on the colouration of the whole. It is the *metropolis* to the regional *hinterlands*.[41] Given Ontario's size and weight within the national community, and its central location, the identification of the regional part—Ontario—with the national whole—Canada—is understandable. To illustrate the point simply, it is conceivable to imagine Quebec, Newfoundland, or the West separating from Canada, but it is inconceivable to imagine Ontario separating; Ontario *is Canada* to a degree that no other region can claim.

To cast the argument in more political terms, Ontario's share of the national electorate is sufficient to ensure at least adequate representation within the federal government. Since the end of the Second World War, there has not been a federal government with fewer than 35 Ontario MPs, and the average has been close to fifty. (In the 1984 and 1988 federal elections respectively, 67 and 47 Progressive Conservative MPs from Ontario were elected.) Ontario traditionally has more representatives in the federal cabinet than any other province, and the majority of Canadian prime ministers, including Macdonald, Mackenzie, Borden, King, Meighen, and Pearson, have held seats in Ontario. There is, then, a ready identification of Ontario with the federal government, an identification reinforced by the location of the national capital. This does not mean a lack of intergovernmental conflict between Ottawa and the Ontario provincial government in Queen's Park, nor does it mean that the direction of the federal government always follows the wishes of the Ontario electorate. What it does mean is that Ontario cannot be shut out of the federal government in the way in which both Quebec and the West have been in the past. It means, furthermore, that the "national interest" as articulated by Ottawa will reflect in large part the national interest as perceived by the voters of Ontario. In this vitally important respect, Ontario is not a region like the others, and the difference tends to place the province outside the framework of regional analysis.

> Resentment towards Ontario and/or Toronto has played an important role in tying together Canada's regional communities. As the following cartoons illustrate, this resentment was very apparent during the late 1980s when the Ontario economy was booming, and when other regions were trying to cope with the adverse inflationary and interest-rate spin-offs of the Ontario boom.

REGIONAL AND NATIONAL IDENTIFICATIONS

Lodged within the above discussion of Ontario is the assumption that regional and national identifications overlap in the province, that there is no conflict between being an "Ontarian" and being a Canadian, that one is simply the expression of the other. In other parts of the country, however, we cannot assume an harmonious relationship between regional and national identities.

Conflicting Expectations

There is little reason to doubt that the great majority of Canadians are strongly attached to their country. While it might be argued that nationalism in Canada is less intense than in some other countries, this is not to question the existence of a strong emotional bond between Canadians and their country. There is also little reason to doubt that Canadians are characterized by strong regional attachments, that where we live *within*

Andy Donato, *Gucci Blues: Political Cartoons* (Toronto: Key Porter Books, 1988). Originally appeared in *The Calgary Herald*, February 19, 1989, p. C4.

Canada shapes our personal identity, our sense of who and what we are. What is less clear is how national and regional identifications interrelate.

For many observers of the national scene, regional identities form the building blocks of the Canadian identity. Historian J.M.S. Careless, for example, writes that "what has been sought and to some degree achieved [in Canada] is not really unification or consolidation, but the articulation of regional patterns in one transcontinental state."[42] Regional identities, in other words, are found at the core of the Canadian *national* identity. This line of thought has been given political expression by former Prime

Globe and Mail (National Edition), September 23, 1988, p. A6.

Minister Joe Clark's description of Canada as a "community of communities." It also found expression, to cite but one of many possible examples, in speeches by former Alberta Premier Peter Lougheed in the political debate leading up to the patriation of the Canadian constitution. Rankled by the charge that his vigorous defence of Alberta was in some sense "un-Canadian," Lougheed asserted that to defend Alberta was to defend Canada, that one's Canadian identity could be legitimately expressed through a strong provincial identity. To the Premier there was no intrinsic conflict between regional and national identities; they were more appropriately seen as different but complementary modes of expressing one's attachment to Canada.

   This conclusion is not universally accepted. The counterargument has been made that regional identities, or at the very least *strong* regional identities, constitute a corrosive influence on the strength and vitality of Canadian nationalism. It is if individuals have only so much loyalty to give, that there is a "zero-sum" relationship between national and regional identifications in which a gain by one entails a corresponding loss by the other. While one can, from this perspective, be both a British Columbian and a Canadian, one can only be strongly attached to British Columbia at the expense of one's sense of attachment to the country as a whole. Therefore, those who perceive, and are concerned about, a relatively weak sense of Canadian nationalism often finger regionalism as the cause; Canadians are accused of putting the regional cart before the Canadian horse, of being preoccupied with narrow regional interests while the larger interests of Canada are ignored. For still others, the strength of regional identifications is seen as the consequence rather than the cause of a weak sense of Canadian nationalism; regional identifications fill the vacuum left by the absence of a more dynamic Canadian nationalism.

The Evidence

By far the clearest finding from survey research explorations into citizen identifications is that *regional* identities, as opposed to *provincial* or *national* identities, are very weak. In the Perlin and Rawlyk study of opinion in Atlantic Canada, respondents were asked the following question: "Do you think of yourself first as a Canadian, as a Maritimer or as a (Newfoundlander, Prince Edward Islander, Nova Scotian, New Brunswicker)?" Across the region, only 6 percent of the respondents first chose a Maritime identity. When a similar question was posed to western Canadian respondents in 1982, less than 8 percent identified themselves as "western Canadians."[43] Although neither finding demonstrates that respondents lack regional identities, the evidence suggests that regional identities pale in importance compared to the identifications citizens have with their province and country. It also suggests that pan-provincial regional identities may come into full blossom only within the political environment, that the terms "western Canada" and "Atlantic Canada" have a political resonance that they lack in other spheres of life.

It is not coincidental that identifications lacking a corresponding governmental structure are also the weakest. As Alan Cairns has argued, governments are not passive reflectors of their social environment.[44] They are actively involved in shaping that environment, in moulding the contours of citizen identifications as they seek to maximize political support. Thus one's sense of being a Canadian, and of being a resident of a specific province, is nurtured by our federal and provincial governments respectively. No government exists, however, to nurture one's sense of being a western Canadian or an Atlantic Canadian. There are no regional flags, holidays, ceremonies, capitals, licence plates, or symbols. It is not surprising, then, that few western Canadians or Atlantic Canadians see themselves *first* in regional terms.

Repeated surveys have found that when respondents are asked to choose between national and provincial identifications, the former prevail by a wide margin. In the Perlin and Rawlyk study, 62 percent of those selecting either a national or a provincial identification selected the former, while 38 percent said that they thought of themselves first in provincial terms. In a 1980 national telephone survey, the Carleton School of Journalism asked 1,275 respondents the following question: "Where does your first loyalty lie—with Canada or with the province in which you live?" Nationally, 74 percent chose Canada and 26 percent their province. The ratio was 66 percent to 34 percent in the Atlantic provinces, 53 percent to 47 percent in Quebec, 90 percent to 10 percent in Ontario, and 80 percent to 20 percent in the West.

A final illustration of this point is provided by Table 4.2. The data in the table are derived from a national survey conducted by the author in April 1983. Overall, 73 percent of the respondents said that they thought of themselves first as Canadians, 17 percent first as provincial residents, 8 percent refused to choose or stated an equal preference, and 2 percent did not have an opinion. The interesting aspect of Table 4.2 is the marked provincial variation. Thus we find, for example, that while 93 percent of the Ontario respondents identified themselves as Canadians first, a plurality of Newfoundland respondents identified themselves as Newfoundlanders first. Although Table 4.2 should not suggest that provincial identities are absent in Ontario, it does support the conclusion that provincial and national identifications overlap to a greater extent in Ontario than they do elsewhere in the country. At the same time, national identities elsewhere are far from weak. In the West, 74 percent of the respondents identified themselves as Canadians first, even though western alienation was very pronounced at the time of the survey.

The finding that national rather than provincial identifications tend to prevail in most parts of the country is an important one, but it does not address the relationship between the two identifications. Although hard information on the nature of that relationship is neither abundant nor clear-cut, what there is suggests that national and provincial identifications are not in conflict and may even be mutually reinforcing to a modest degree. In an analysis of the 1974 national election survey, the "feeling thermometer" scores assigned by respondents to Canada and the various provinces were *positively* correlated; relatively positive assessments of one's country and province tended to hang together, as did relatively negative assessments of the two.[45] As the relationship was weak and, under some statistical conditions, inconsistent, the authors stopped short of concluding that national and provincial identifications were mutually reinforcing. However, they did conclude that "in simple affective terms, liking one's own region does not seem to be a deterrent to liking Canada as a whole."[46]

Table 4.2
Provincial Variation in Citizen Identifications, April 1983

"Do you think of yourself *first* as a Canadian or as a Newfoundlander/
Nova Scotian/New Brunswicker/Prince Edward Islander/Quebecer/Ontarian/
Manitoban/Saskatchewanian/Albertan/British Columbian?

	Canadian	Provincial Identification	Both Equally
Newfoundland	42%	47%	11%
Prince Edward Island	57	38	5
Nova Scotia	65	30	5
New Brunswick	78	18	3
Quebec	50	34	15
Ontario	93	5	1
Manitoba	85	11	2
Saskatchewan	73	14	12
Alberta	71	12	16
British Columbia	72	14	14

(Table excludes the 0.7% of the sample who failed to answer the question, and the 1.2% who cited identifications other than national or provincial.)

This conclusion was supported in a subsequent analysis of the 1974 data by David Elkins. While Elkins notes that Canadians have a "deep and abiding" sense of place extending to their local area, province, and country at large, and that this sense of place has heightened over time, the various identities are not competitive.[47] Indeed, respondents in the 1974 survey who were the most sensitive to regional considerations had the strongest sense of themselves as Canadians. Thus Elkins concludes that the assumption that provincial identities override a sense of nationalism or national identity "is totally unwarranted, except in the case of a minority of Quebec French respondents with separatist sentiments."[48] Far from precluding a sense of national identity, a regional identification is best seen as a partial identification within a grander, more diverse whole. Here it is also interesting to note that in the 1974 survey, regional sensitivity was positively correlated with generally high levels of knowledge about Canada, a familiarity with several parts of Canada, and a preference for the federal government over provincial governments.

This discussion should conclude with a number of methodological points. The first is that research to date may distort reality by asking the wrong questions. When, for example, respondents are asked if they "first think of themselves as Canadians or New Brunswickers," they are being placed in a forced-choice situation. Yet, if national and provincial identifications are not competitive, the forced choice does not square with the psychological reality of respondents. For many and perhaps most Canadians, national and regional identities may be two sides of the same coin. This point was captured in the slogan of those Quebecers opposed to the 1980 Quebec referendum on sovereignty association; *mon non est Québécois* emphatically rejects the proposition that one must or can choose between Canadian and provincial identities. In the words of John Holmes, "it is in the Canadian tradition for citizens to want to preserve the Canadian framework in order to live more securely as Quebeckers or Nova Scotians or British Columbians."[49]

Secondly, regional identities take on a poetic, almost mythical character that makes empirical measurement difficult. Richard Allen, for example, has described the Canadian West as "a region of the mind," an evocative and in many ways compelling phrase which nevertheless provides little guidance for empirical research.[50] Historian Douglas Francis invokes the same imagery, arguing that there is an aspect of the West's history

> ... which transcends the decisions of politicians, the intricate workings of the economy, and the daily activities of its peoples; it exists in the mind. The history of the West has often been governed as much by what people imagined the region to be as the "reality" itself.[51]

Survey researchers have yet to design instruments of sufficient sensitivity to capture the richness of regional imagery and identification implied in this passage. Until they do, a firm understanding of the relationship between national and regional identifications will have to wait.

Thirdly, it should be noted that regional and/or provincial variations in public opinion are often not very pronounced. Admittedly, the empirical evidence here can be contentious for, within the mountain of public opinion data generated every year, one can select particular surveys, and particular questions within particular surveys, to support virtually any argument. Nonetheless, there are many issues for which regional differences in policy preference are either small, or for which significant variation is limited to single provinces or regions. Put somewhat differently, in many and perhaps even most cases, knowing where a person lives provides little indication of his or her policy preferences.

By way of example, Table 4.3 shows that in the late fall of 1988, Albertans and Quebecers were considerably more supportive of the proposed Free Trade Agreement than were other Canadians. At the same time, differences among respondents living in Atlantic Canada, Ontario, Manitoba, Saskatchewan, and British Columbia were much more modest. Here it should also be kept in mind that the Free Trade Agreement was an intensely politicized issue, one that was thoroughly entangled in partisan loyalties during the run-up to the November federal election. In short, it was precisely the sort of issue for which one would expect to find regional differences. Table 4.4, on the other hand, presents some illustra-

Table 4.3
Regional Support for Free Trade

In a national survey conducted by the Environics Research Group between November 3 and November 8, 1988, 1,275 respondents were asked if they favoured or opposed the Free Trade Agreement with the United States. The national and regional results were as follows:

	% Favour	% Opposed	D.K.	Margin of Error
Canada	39	51	10	± 2.7%
Atlantic	38	45	17	± 8.8%
Quebec	47	42	11	± 5.5%
Ontario	32	60	8	± 4.6%
Manitoba	38	48	14	±12.5%
Saskatchewan	39	58	13	±13.5%
Alberta	56	32	12	± 8.9%
B.C.	31	59	10	± 8.2%

Source: *The Globe and Mail*, November 11, 1988, p. A1.

tive data drawn from a survey conducted between federal election campaigns, and addressing issues somewhat less entangled with partisan allegiances. As the reader will note, some regional variation is still apparent in the table. Quebecers, for example, were less supportive of traditional values and more resistant to defence spending, while prairie residents were less supportive of gender equality. Nonetheless, the table does not suggest an electorate sharply divided along regional lines. To the contrary, it suggests an electorate for which, in many important areas of public policy, an individual's regional location plays little role.

What, then, do we conclude from all of this? First, public opinion data offer greater support for dualistic conceptions of Canada than they do for regional fragmentation. In general, differences between respondents inside and outside Quebec, or between anglophones and francophones, tend to be greater than regional differences within English Canada. If, in the murky realm of public opinion data, there is a "distinct society" within Canada, it is Quebec and quite likely Quebec alone. A second and perhaps more speculative conclusion is that regional disputes within the political arena need not and often do not reflect regional differences in policy preferences within the general electorate. Canada's regional communities are not sharply divided in terms of their basic political values or policy preferences, and thus intergovernmental conflict may well stem from the electoral, bureaucratic, and constitutional self-interest of political elites as much as it does from differences in policy preferences across provincial electorates.

Table 4.4
Regional Variation in Public Opinion

Percent of Respondents:	Atlan.	Que.	Ont.	Prairies	B.C.
Saying it is very important to preserve traditional ideas of right and wrong.	66	47	62	69	62
Saying it is very important to guarantee equality between men and women in all aspects of life.	75	73	74	64	69
Who agree that people who come to live in Canada should try harder to be more like other Canadians.	54	73	60	66	63
Who feel we are spending too much money on military armaments and defence.	22	56	23	23	26
Who feel we are spending too much on welfare.	51	50	45	53	38
Who agree that people in the various provinces should put less emphasis on their regional identities and more emphasis on their Canadian identity.	71	58	83	81	79
Who agree that government regulation of business usually does more harm than good.	31	28	34	33	38

Source: Civil Liberties and the Charter of Rights in Canada, a national survey of over 2,000 respondents conducted in 1987 by Paul M. Sniderman, Joseph F. Fletcher, Peter H. Russell, and Philip E. Tetlock.

THE REDISTRIBUTION OF WEALTH ACROSS REGIONS

The regions of Canada differ significantly in their natural and human resources. Not surprisingly, such differences are reflected in marked variations both in personal income, as Figure 4.6 illustrates, and in the fiscal resources available to provincial governments. In the absence of government intervention, the mobility of people and capital would be the natural consequence of such regional variations. Other things being equal, people would tend to move to those locations where employment prospects were the most promising, where government programs were the most richly endowed, and where tax rates were the lowest. In regions where resources were limited, both wages and the level of government services would fall, encouraging further out-migration until some equilibrium was established, with low wages drawing in new investment capital. In this manner the United States has experienced pronounced internal shifts in the regional distribution of its population. These have included not only the westward shift involved in the initial settlement of the continent, but also shifts from the rural South to the industrial cities of the Northeast and then, in more recent years, the shift from the Northeast and "frost-belt" states to the "sun-belt" states of the American South and Southwest. The mobility of both people and capital has been an acknowledged feature of the American experience, and an accepted response to changing economic circumstances across the United States.

Canada has also experienced substantial interregional migration. As Chapter 3 noted, out-migration, albeit mostly to the United States rather than to other parts of Canada, has played an important role in the demographic evolution of Quebec, and regional migrations have been of great importance in the histories of both Atlantic Canada and the West. However, there has been less acceptance in Canada than in the United States of individual mobility as the appropriate response to regional differences in economic potential. Federal and provincial governments have intervened in a variety of ways to shore up regional communities and thus reduce the need for mobility. Here, three broad strategies have been employed: fiscal transfers from the national treasury to provincial governments in relatively depressed regions; redistributive programs run through the departments of the federal government; and "province-building" strategies pursued by provincial governments. Each of these will be examined in turn.

Intergovernmental Transfers and Equalization

Intergovernmental transfers have been an integral part of the Canadian federal system since the passage of the Constitution Act in 1867. Initially, they resulted from a fundamental imbalance between the federal division of legislative powers, on the one hand, and the division of fiscal resources, on the other. Ottawa's power to raise monies by "any Mode or System of Taxation" gave the federal government access to revenues well in excess of its expenditure obligations under the legislative division of powers, while the provincial governments had access to less revenue than their expenditure obligations required. Thus Sections 118 and 119 of the 1867 Constitution Act provided for federal subsidies to provincial governments, subsidies which were constantly under review and which served as a permanent source of contention between the two levels of government.[52] The "subsidy question" was of particular importance in the Maritimes, where the search for "better terms" played a major role in the Nova Scotia Repeal Movement of 1886-87 and the Maritime Rights Move-

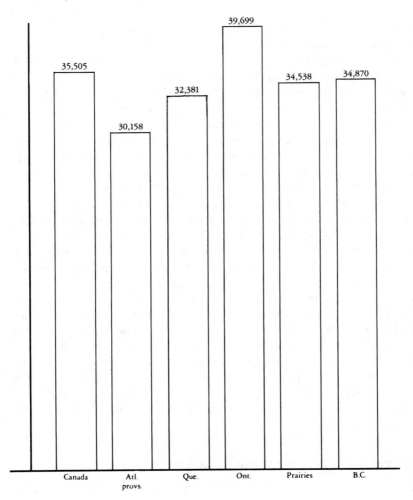

Figure 4.6

Regional Variations in Family Income (after tax), 1987

Source: Statistics Canada, *Income After Tax. Distributions by Size in Canada, 1987* (Ottawa: Supply and Services, 1989).

ment of the 1920s. It should be stressed, however, that the initial provincial subsidies were intended to correct the fiscal imbalance stemming from the federal division of powers, rather than to redistribute wealth from the "have" to the "have not" regions of Canada, although the latter aspect came into play when subsidies began to assume much greater importance in the Maritime provinces than elsewhere in the country.

Interregional redistribution came more to the fore in an array of **conditional grant programs** launched by the federal government in the 1950s and early 1960s.

As conditional grant programs are discussed in Chapter 6, suffice it to say here that they involved shared-cost programs in which Ottawa picked up half the cost of provincially administered programs in provincial fields of jurisdiction, provided that minimum national standards were observed. Through such assistance Ottawa made a very substantial contribution to provincial programs in health care, post-secondary education, and social assistance. Conditional grant programs enabled "have-not" provinces to supply a level of social services roughly equivalent to that provided by the "have" provinces *in those program areas covered by conditional grants*. There was, as a consequence, some significant redistributive effect as basic social services were provided at a roughly equivalent level to all Canadians, regardless of where they happened to live. The redistributive effect was blunted, however, by the fact that the provinces received *matching* grants. By spending more, the wealthier provinces were able to receive more from Ottawa. They were also able to use the federal funds to free up previously committed provincial funds, and thus launch new program initiatives.[53]

The emergence of unconditional equalization payments, which were specifically directed towards the have-not provinces rather than towards all provinces, began with the 1940 *Report of the Royal Commission on Dominion-Provincial Relations*. In its report, the Rowell-Sirois Commission recognized that the regional structure of the Canadian economy, with its concentration of corporate head offices in Montreal and Toronto, gave Ontario and Quebec disproportionate access to corporate taxes. The Commission therefore recommended a system of National Adjustment Grants paid by the federal government so as "to enable each province (including its municipalities) without resort to heavier taxation than the Canadian average to provide adequate social, educational and developmental services."[54] Although this recommendation was not implemented at the time, the principle of equalization endured. The governments of Canada began to move towards a system of fiscal transfers which would ensure that citizens of similar economic status would have equal access to government services and face equal tax loads no matter where they happened to live. This principle is now constitutionally entrenched in Section 36 of the Constitution Act, 1982.

Section 36: Equalization

Section 36 of the 1982 Constitution Act captures the national commitment to equalization that began with the 1940 Rowell-Sirois recommendations:

36 (1) Without altering the legislative authority of Parliament or of the provincial legislatures, or the rights of any of them with respect to the exercise of their legislative authority, Parliament and the legislatures, together with the government of Canada and the provincial governments, are committed to (a) promoting equal opportunity for the well-being of Canadians; (b) furthering economic development to reduce disparity in opportunities; and (c) providing essential public services of reasonable quality to all Canadians.

36 (2) Parliament and the government of Canada are committed to the principle of making equalization payments to ensure that provincial governments have sufficient revenues to provide reasonably comparable levels of public services at reasonably comparable levels of taxation.

The equalization principle was first put into practice through the Federal–Provincial Tax Sharing Arrangements, 1957-62. Provincial governments were provided with unconditional grants[55] from the national treasury totalling $139 million in the first year, and designed to bring their yield from individual taxes, corporate taxes, and succession duties up to the average per capita yield for the two wealthiest provinces, British Columbia and Ontario. In the 1962–67 fiscal agreement, the equalization formula was extended to include provincial revenues from natural resources, and the British Columbia/Ontario average was replaced by the national average. In 1967 the formula was expanded to include 16 provincial revenue sources, and in the Federal–Provincial Fiscal Arrangement and Established Program Funding Act of 1977 this was further expanded to include 29 revenue sources, or virtually all the revenue sources available to provincial governments. At that time the formula was also amended to include only 50 percent of the revenue accruing to provincial governments from nonrenewable natural resources, a modification to which we shall return shortly.

Table 4.5 provides one snapshot showing how **equalization payments** are distributed across the provinces. There you will note that Quebec receives the largest total payment, whereas the largest per capita payments are received by Prince Edward Island and Newfoundland. As can be seen from the table, the general purpose transfers to the smaller Atlantic provinces are, on a per capita basis, very substantial. Table 4.5 also records specific purpose transfers from Ottawa to the provincial governments, transfers that cover the federal contribution to medicare, hospital care, advanced education, and social assistance. Again on a per capita basis, these payments are not equal across the ten provinces. The northern territories constitute a special case in that there are no provincial governments in the North, and thus the total transfers from the federal government are much greater than in the case of the provinces.

The application of the equalization formula is a complex undertaking. For each province, the per capita revenue yield is calculated for each

Table 4.5

Fiscal Transfers from the Federal Government to Provincial Government (1985)

	Total $ (000,000)			Per Capita $ (1986 Population)		
	General Purpose Transfers	Specific Purpose Transfers[1]	Total Transfers	General Purpose Transfers	Specific Purpose Transfers	Total Transfers
Nfld.	574	384	958	962	675	1,638
P.E.I.	159	102	261	1,256	806	2,062
N.S.	639	502	1,141	732	575	1,307
N.B.	553	481	1,034	778	677	1,455
Que.	3,184	3,315	6,499	487	994	1,481
Ont.	129	4,300	4,429	14	486	500
Man.	499	654	1,153	466	1,076	1,542
Sask.	2	933	935	–	924	926
Alta.	197	2,834	3,031	83	1,276	1,359
B.C.	123	1,834	1,957	43	677	720
Yuk./N.W.T.	497	88	585	6,565	1,162	7,727
Canada	6,556	15,427	21,983	259	608	867

[1]Specific purpose transfers include federal contributions toward hospital care and medicare, advanced education and social assistance.

[2]Equalization payments constituted approximately 70 percent of all general purpose transfers from the federal government to the provinces. Thus the total transfers column also entails other general purpose transfers such as statutory subsidies, tax revenue guarantee payments, and federal corporate income tax rebates for privately owned utility companies.

Source: Statistics Canada, *Canada Year Book 1986-87*, pp. 829-32.

"During the course of this election campaign, it has not been my intention to give anyone the impression that Easterners are a festering horde of greedy-eyed, furry little demons and fat, pompous robber-barons who would like nothing better than to sneak into my beloved Alberta in the dead of night and rob me blind. If this impression has inadvertently been presented, it is, indeed, truly unfortunate."

Phil Mallette, *Globe and Mail*, March 13, 1979

of the 29 revenue sources. If, across the 29 sources, the provincial yield is less than the average yield of Ontario, Quebec, Manitoba, Saskatchewan, and British Columbia, the federal government makes up the difference. If the provincial yield is more than this average, no equalization payments are made. The point to be stressed is that equalization payments are made from the federal treasury. The equalization formula does *not* take money from the richer *provincial governments* and redistribute it to the poorer ones. Provincial revenues per se are not redistributed; they are used only in the calculation of equalization payments to be made by Ottawa to the have-not provincial governments. Thus the "burden" of equalization is carried by all Canadian taxpayers, including those in the have-not provinces.

One of the reasons for equalization payments is that the Constitution gives provincial governments primary access to revenues derived from natural resources, revenues which are not evenly dispersed across the provinces. In the 1970s the concentration of oil reserves in Alberta and, to a much lesser extent, Saskatchewan severely disrupted the equalization formula. When the price of oil escalated after 1973, and the Alberta government imposed higher royalties, the revenues accruing to Alberta grew enormously. When this increase was fed into the equalization formula, the national treasury faced a significant leap in equalization payments. Yet Ottawa had no access to the oil revenues which were generating the increased equalization payments. Although Alberta's revenues were driving equalization payments upwards, it was not those revenues which were being redistributed.[56]

A number of important consequences flowed from the resulting fiscal crisis. The Alberta government diverted a substantial portion of its oil revenues into the Alberta Heritage Savings and Trust Fund. This portion was not included in the equalization formula, and thus reduced the strain on the federal treasury. The formula itself was amended so that no province could receive equalization payments if its per capita income was above the national average. This amendment pre-empted equalization payments to Ontario which, under the old rules, would have qualified as a have-not province from 1977 to 1982. As noted above, the formula was changed to include only 50 percent of nonrenewable natural resource revenues. The federal government also moved to keep Canadian oil prices below world levels. Finally, in 1980 Ottawa introduced the National Energy Program, which was designed in part to give the federal government access to oil revenues, and thus to finance the increased equalization payments that the increase in oil prices had brought about.

The redistribution of resource revenues poses a very thorny problem for the Canadian political system. If revenues were to go primarily to individuals or to corporations, as is the case with oil revenues in the United States, redistribution would be relatively easy as the federal government would have access to such revenues through personal and corporate income taxes. However, to the extent that revenues go to provincial governments in the form of royalties, they are not accessible to Ottawa through personal or corporate taxes, even though Ottawa is still faced with the bill for equalization. This leads in turn to attempts by the federal government to capture a share of resource revenues, attempts that were incorporated in the controversial National Energy Program. In this narrow sense, the equalization program can promote federal raids on provincial treasuries even though, more generally, equalization does not entail any expropriation or redistribution of provincial government revenues.

Equalization payments alter the dynamics of individual mobility by reducing the costs of staying in relatively depressed regions: they both reduce the tax load and improve the quality of public services in the have-not provinces. At the same time, equalization payments have altered the dynamics of federalism in the have-not provinces. In conjunction with other federal subsidies, they have transformed the Atlantic provinces into virtual client states of the federal government.[57] The extreme case is Prince Edward Island, where nearly 60 percent of the provincial budget comes from federal transfer payments of one kind or another, and where the provincial treasury has become little more than an agent for the distribution of federal funds.[58] Somewhat ironically, equalization payments may also contribute to intergovernmental conflict. Hugh Thorburn maintains that they have enabled the have-not provinces to strengthen their bureaucracies and thus challenge the federal government across a broader front: "in short, the improved financial capacity of the provinces may well have served to accentuate the rivalries between provinces, and between federal and provincial authorities, because it has made possible a level of provincial intervention that could not have occurred without such improved financial capacity."[59] In a crude sense, equalization payments enable the have-not provinces to bite the federal hand that feeds them.

Redistributive Effects of Federal Programs

Although equalization payments provide the centrepiece for federal efforts to redistribute wealth across the provincial communities of Canada, there are a host of other federal programs with significant redistributive effects. In 1961 Parliament passed the Agricultural Rehabilitation and Development Act which was designed to address rural poverty. The Act provided for joint federal–provincial funding of rural development projects and the coordination of federal and provincial programs in the policy field. In 1965 the terms of the Act were expanded by the passage of the Agricultural and Rural Development Act (ARDA), followed by the creation of the Fund for Rural Economic Development in 1966. ARDA was later expanded to include development programs in tourism and fisheries. In 1962 Ottawa also established the Atlantic Development Board to coordinate the developmental activities of federal departments and the four provincial governments in the region. While these legislative initiatives were not designed to redirect economic activity from one region to another, they were designed to promote economic development in rural as opposed to urban Canada.

The major federal initiative came with the creation of the Department of Regional Economic Expansion (DREE) in 1969.[60] DREE's mandate was to ensure that economic growth was widely dispersed across Canada, and that employment and income prospects in slow-growth regions were brought up to the national average.[61] Building on the precedents of the Area Development Agency (1963) and the Area Development Incentives Act (1965), DREE was designed to give Ottawa a direct and high-profile role in regional economic development, a role well beyond the provision of equalization payments which were then spent solely at the discretion of provincial governments. In 1982 DREE was merged with the Department of Industry, Trade and Commerce to form DRIE, the Department of Regional Industrial Expansion. On the one hand, DRIE was to maximize industrial competitiveness and efficiency, while on the other hand it was to reduce regional disparities brought about in part by the operation of market forces. In 1987 DRIE was merged with the Ministry of State for Science and Technology to form the Department of Industry, Science and Technology (DIST). Much of DRIE's former involvement in regional economic development was taken up by new agencies (discussed below) with specific mandates for Atlantic Canada, western Canada and northern Ontario.

The DREE-DRIE-DIST initiative represents only one of many strategies the federal government has taken or could take to alleviate regional disparities. The drilling incentives in the National Energy Program, for example, were designed to shift drilling activity onto federal Crown lands in the Canadian North and off the east coast of the Atlantic provinces, much to the outrage of the Alberta government. Federal support for energy mega-projects on the East Coast and in western Canada is designed to promote development which the market alone would not support. The federal government may pick up infrastructure costs in the hope that improved ports, roads, and airports will promote private economic development. Ottawa may also move federal agencies to specific areas in the hope that the agencies will bring business development in their wake. An example here is provided by Ottawa's decision to locate the new Space Agency in Montreal. Finally, the government may intervene in countless ad hoc ways to provide financial support for existing firms or new development.

All such programs are designed to influence the locational decisions of private firms. The starting assumption is that market-determined locational decisions may not be optimal from a social or political perspective. Thus an array of public incentives is brought into play to affect locational decisions. These incentives can include tax breaks, the public provision of infrastructure support, subsidized land, and preferential government services. Unfortunately, their impact on regional economic development is very difficult to assess. In some cases, grants go to firms that may have located in the region anyway. In other cases new firms may not survive, or may displace existing firms in the region. New firms may discourage additional investment by driving up the costs of wages and services. Finally, Ingrid Bryan argues, "firms that need to be 'bribed' to invest in an area may be less likely than other firms to reinvest, and therefore the long-term benefits of subsidized investments may be small."[62] Thus, while public expenditures may be clearly redistributive, flowing from the national treasury to disadvantaged regions within the country or from the provincial treasury to disadvantaged regions within the province, it is less clear that such expenditures significantly alter the regional distribution of investment and employment opportunities.

When the Progressive Conservatives came to power in 1984, the emphasis of the new Mulroney government was on a market-driven economy, and on improving Canada's international competitiveness. Regional development incentives were difficult to square with this commitment, given that they constituted direct intervention in the market, and thus the Conservative government displayed little initial enthusiasm for regional economic development. In 1987, however, Ottawa introduced a series of new initiatives. On June 6, the federal government announced the creation of the Atlantic Canada Opportunities Agency (ACOA) with a staff of 300 and an annual budget of $200 million for each of the next five years. (In 1989, Ottawa announced that the same amount of money would be spread over seven and not five years.) With headquarters in Moncton, ACOA was to assume responsibility for the bulk of existing regional economic development programs in the Atlantic provinces. On July 13, Ottawa announced the creation of FED-NOR, a development program for northern Ontario with an initial budget of $55 million. Then, on August 4, the picture was rounded out with the creation of the Western Diversification Office (WDO), a parallel agency to ACOA. WDO has headquarters in Edmonton, with sub-offices in Vancouver, Saskatoon, and Winnipeg, and a budget of $1.2 billion spread over five years. In the first eighteen months it provided grants and loans to 765 diversification projects across the West, including a special $45 million fund to promote the sale of low-sulphur coal. Per capita expenditures amounted to $37 in Manitoba, $35 in Saskatchewan, $26 in Alberta, and $22 in British Columbia.[63]

Other federal programs, including transfers to individuals, have redistributive regional effects even though they have not been designed with any redistributive intent. If the need that a program is designed to address is more prevalent in one region than another, or if the clientele of a particular program is disproportionately located in one region rather than another, some regional redistribution will occur. For example, if the birth rate in one region is higher than in others, as it was in Quebec prior to the Quiet Revolution, then a universal program such as the Family Allowance Program will benefit that region more than others. The beneficiaries of the Canada Assistance Plan are not evenly dispersed across the country, and thus some modest regional redistribution occurs to the benefit of the Atlantic provinces. Canada's Unemployment Insurance program also results in a net transfer of resources into Atlantic Canada.

Ottawa's procurement of goods and services; the location of military bases, research centres, mints, and head offices of Crown corporations; and, in the rare instance, the location of government departments, all have potential redistributive effects.[64] As Herman Bakvis points out in a more general sense, it is rarely the case that the effects of *any* government policy or development program are distributed evenly across geographical space.[65]

While expenditure patterns often provide unequal regional benefits, and while specific programs exist to encourage the regional dispersion of economic activity, the net effect on the regional distribution of wealth and employment opportunities is difficult to determine. It is not clear whether the distributional objectives of public policy are being met and, if they are, at what cost to the growth objectives of public policy, assuming that some tension between the two is inevitable.[66] What is clear is that the effective management of regional economic development is dependent upon extensive intergovernmental coordination and cooperation. This is not easily achieved given the zero-sum character of locational decisions, where the gain of any one province may be the loss of its provincial competitors.

Province-Building and Redistributive Politics

Within the context of the national economy, it is of little concern if individuals in depressed regions "go down the road" to seek employment in other regions. Indeed, such mobility may be a useful form of adjustment to changing economic conditions. It may alleviate unemployment in depressed regions, raise wages for those left behind, and reduce the costs of social assistance. From the perspective of provincial governments, however, out-migration is a matter of considerable concern. In part, the concern stems from the fact that it is the young and the best educated who are most likely to migrate, leaving behind an impoverished pool of human resources.[67] Out-migration can further depress the local economy by decreasing the size of local markets, and can erode the local tax base to the point where the quality of public services will deteriorate.[68] Thus, while out-migration may not be damaging to the national economy, it is resisted by provincial governments who seek to convince voters that their sons and daughters will be able to live and work within their home province no matter what career they may wish to pursue.

Provincial governments seek to ward off out-migration by province-building strategies designed to strengthen the provincial economy. Provincial businesses are shored up through tax breaks, infrastructure support, and preferential purchasing and contracting policies. Extensive efforts are made to attract investment from outside the province and the country, efforts that may entail a "beggar-thy-neighbour" policy of luring investors away from neighbouring provinces. Economic strength alone, however, is not sufficient to prevent out-migration if that strength rests on a capital-intensive rather than labour-intensive base, and if the provincial economy lacks sufficient economic diversification. In the latter case, out-migration can still be forced upon those who choose to pursue careers falling beyond the parameters of the provincial economy. In western Canada, economic diversification has been the primary focus of province-building strategies, given the somewhat narrow natural resource base of the regional economy, the concentration of labour-intensive industries in central Canada, and the historical lure of a more complex labour market outside the region.

Province-building strategies can have a somewhat contradictory effect in that provincial economic strength may weaken the national economy. As Hugh Thorburn explains, the understandable effort by provincial governments to curtail out-migration

> has counteracted the natural adjustment process by which movements of people and capital would take place in response to variation in wages, job opportunities, production costs, and so forth. The result was the creation of ten provincial economies rather than one Canadian economy.[69]

This suggests in turn that economic management can be a very complex task in a federal state when one level of government tries to ensure a healthy and vital national economy while the second level tries to ensure healthy provincial economies, even to the extent of inhibiting the mobility of capital and labour within the national economic community. The management task is not only complex from the standpoint of intergovernmental relations; it is also complex for the federal government alone when it tries to ensure both national economic growth and an equitable regional distribution of economic activity.

POLITICAL ROOTS OF REGIONAL DISCONTENT

National communities such as Canada are made up of countless competing groups and interests, only some of which are territorially based. To a degree, the political system provides an arena within which group competition is played out. In other respects, however, the political system is more than the arena or a passive reflection of social conflict, for it actually shapes the pattern of conflict by moderating some of its forms and exaggerating others. The specific manner in which the political system shapes social conflict depends upon the nature of political institutions. As the American political scientist E.E. Schattschneider observed,

> all forms of political organization have a bias in favour of the exploitation of some kinds of conflict and the suppression of others because organization is

the mobilization of bias. Some issues are organized into politics while others are organized out.[70]

We might ask, then, whether there is an institutional bias to the way in which the Canadian political system handles regional conflict. Is regionalism organized into or out of Canadian political life? Do Canadian political institutions moderate regional conflict, building bridges across regional divisions and thereby integrating a large and regionally diverse national community, or do they exacerbate regional conflict? Is regional conflict more intense and more pervasive within the political system than within the society itself? To address such questions, we must begin with a look at federalism and federal institutions.

Federalism is an institutional device through which the potentially conflicting interests of national majorities and territorially bounded minorities can be reconciled. It provides a check on the national majority in some instances while permitting reasonably unfettered majority rule in others. To understand just how this is accomplished, it is useful to draw a distinction between "interstate" and "intrastate" federalism.

Interstate federalism refers initially to the federal division of powers. Minority interests, or at least the interests of those minorities which can be reconstituted as provincial majorities, can be protected from the national majority through the federal division of powers. To the extent that provincial governments have jurisdiction over matters of minority concern, the weight of the national majority cannot be brought into play. In practice, however, a clear division of powers has been impossible and even inconvenient to maintain. Thus, interstate federalism has been extended to encompass the protection of minority interests by provincial governments in the intergovernmental arena. The distinctive characteristic of contemporary interstate federalism in Canada is the representation of regional interests *to* the federal government by provincial governments, rather than the representation of such interests *within* the institutions of the federal government by MPs and Senators.

This latter form of representation is referred to as intrastate federalism, which in part can be seen as an alternative to interstate federalism. The need for provincial governments to represent regional interests to the federal government, as opposed to their more narrow governmental interests, is reduced if such interests receive full expression within national institutions. Intrastate federalism can also be seen as an essential complement to interstate federalism. While the federal division of powers provides significant protection for minority interests, communities may still have important regional stakes in those fields falling within the jurisdiction of the federal government. An example here might be a decision by the federal government to alter the eligibility requirements for Unemployment Insurance, or to close military bases. If effective means of intrastate representation are not built into national institutions, regional conflict can be intensified by national policies which fail to take full account of regional concerns, sensitivities, and peculiarities.

Intrastate and interstate federalisms shape political conflict in quite different ways. Intrastate federalism emphasizes the national dimension of conflict by channelling it through the institutions of the central government, whereas interstate federalism emphasizes the regional dimension of conflict by channelling it through intergovernmental relations. As a general rule of thumb, there are more incentives for the conflict resolution in the intragovernmental arenas of intrastate federalism than exist within the intergovernmental arenas of interstate federalism.

The Constitution Act of 1867 tried to marry British parliamentary institutions, which had evolved within a small and relatively homogeneous country, to the American innovation of federalism, which had evolved to meet the political demands of a large and territorially segmented society. The marriage was not fully consummated. While the federal division of powers—interstate federalism—was put into place, national parliamentary institutions were not adequately modified to accommodate the needs of intrastate federalism—to provide for the representation of regional interests by national politicians within national institutions. The cost has been a political system that does not handle regional conflict as well as it might.

Canadian parliamentary institutions frustrate intrastate federalism in a variety of ways, with the nature of the Senate heading the list. All federal systems have a bicameral or two-chamber legislature, with one chamber based on representation by population and the other based on territorial representation in which disproportionate weight is given to territorial units with relatively small populations. In the Canadian case, the House of Commons is based on representation by population while the Senate incorporates representation by territory. The Senate does so, however, in a rather peculiar and increasingly inappropriate way. Initially, the Senate provided equal *regional* representation: 24 seats each were assigned to Ontario, Quebec, and the Maritimes, and when the West was recognized as a Senatorial district, it too was given 24 seats. While premised on a certain rationality, this system has produced, over time, a pattern of *provincial* representation that is almost haphazard. Although, in general, smaller provinces are over-represented in the Senate relative to their population, the pattern is not consistent. As Table 4.6 shows, the populations of British Columbia and Alberta are under-represented, not over-represented, relative to the population of Ontario.

A far more serious flaw comes from the fact that the Senate is an appointed, not an elected, institution. Unfortunately, but perhaps inevitably, the appointment process, and hence the Senate, have fallen into disrepute. Appointment to the Senate is seen primarily as a reward for

Table 4.6
Provincial Senate Representation

Province	1986 Population	No. of Senators	Population per Senator
Ontario	9,113,500	24	380,000
Quebec	6,540,300	24	273,000
British Columbia	2,889,200	6	482,000
Alberta	2,375,300	6	396,000
Manitoba	1,071,200	6	179,000
Saskatchewan	1,010,200	6	168,000
Nova Scotia	873,200	10	87,000
New Brunswick	710,400	10	71,000
Newfoundland	568,300	6	95,000
Prince Edward Island	126,600	4	32,000
Northwest Territories	52,200	1	52,000
Yukon	23,500	1	23,000

party service, as a means of paying off political debts, and as a way of removing deadwood from active political life. While this perception is not always justified, it is correct often enough to tarnish even most worthy Senate appointment. More importantly, an appointed Senate lacks political legitimacy within a democratic system. As a consequence it is unable, except on rare occasions, to challenge the House of Commons. There is, then, no effective balancing of majority interests, expressed through the House of Commons, and regional interests, expressed through the Senate. Although the Senate may at times harass the government by delaying the passage of government legislation and supply bills, the House dominates the national legislative process. While this should not imply that the Senate fails to perform useful legislative functions, those functions do not include providing effective regional representation. Given the role that second chambers are assumed to play in federal states, it is not surprising that the Canadian Senate has become an habitual target of reform for those promoting more effective forms of regional representation. To date, however, Senate reform has not progressed beyond the modest initiatives linked to the Meech Lake Accord, discussed in Chapter 6.

The institutional characteristics of the House also tend to close off rather than facilitate regional representation. Here the principal culprit is party discipline, one of the most striking and important features of modern parliamentary government. In the early decades following Confederation, party discipline was much looser, a reasonable number of MPs were elected as independents, and many MPs behaved as such within the House. Today, as the national parties and their leaders dominate election campaigns, the prospects of an independent candidate being elected are little better than those of the proverbial snowball in hell.[71] Within the House, opportunities for independent action are rare. The House is organized along party lines, the MP is elected in large part as a party symbol, and both the MP's career within the House and fate in the next election are yoked to the electoral fate of the party. As C.E.S. Franks explains:

> To party leaders, the function of the MP, like the function of the party outside, is to support. Though MPs find their party a source of strength and influence, they also submerge their identity within party. Party and party discipline have moulded the structure and process of parliament. . . . It is the most dominant and pervasive force in parliament and the work world of MPs.[72]

In a classic commentary written shortly before the Second World War, Richard Crossman characterized the British House in the following terms: "one can say that the scale of ethics in parliamentary democracy today is roughly that your conscience comes last, your constituency second, and your party requirements come first."[73] There would be little quarrel in applying Crossman's characterization to the contemporary Canadian House. As Robert Jackson and Michael Atkinson maintain, ". . . the overriding fact of parliamentary life is the existence of persistent and powerful political parties, and members of parliament are encouraged to regard party cohesion as more important than freedom of action in the House."[74]

Party discipline on the government side of the House is essential given the conventions of responsible government. If backbenchers—government MPs who are not members of the cabinet—were to vote against the government, more than the specific bill would be at stake: the very survival of the government would hang in the balance. The price of defeat in the House, followed by dissolution and an uncertain general election, is so high that government MPs have no choice but to follow the cabinet through hell or high water. For opposition parties, the conventions of responsible government per se do not impose rigid party discipline. Opposition MPs can break party ranks without immediate impact on the composition of the government, although to do so in a minority government situation might deny one's party the opportunity to defeat the government. It is nevertheless important for opposition parties to maintain a united front in the House. If the Leader of the Opposition wages a spirited attack against a government bill, it is awkward if some members of his party then support the bill in the House. To the extent that opposition parties try to present themselves to the electorate as alternative governments, disunity within the House can tarnish this image. Thus, both opposition and government MPs who break party ranks do so at considerable risk to their political careers.

The individual responsible for making sure that MPs are in the House to vote when needed, and that they vote correctly, is the party Whip. The name is unfortunate in that it draws too much attention to the coercive enforcement of party discipline. While coercion is not entirely absent, party cohesion is maintained by a variety of other factors. In writing about his experiences as a Liberal backbencher, Mark MacGuigan, former Justice Minister in the Trudeau government, dismissed heavy-handed pressure as a factor in maintaining party discipline, arguing that a more compelling factor was

> ... the desire to get along with and to be well thought of by one's closest associates. It is, in other words, an in-group feeling that is generated by constant association, a common philosophy, and the desire to keep the party strong.[75]

Party discipline follows from the conventions of responsible govern-ment, from a very human desire to be a good team player, from the rewards that party loyalty provides (including possible cabinet appoint-ment), from peer pressure, from a willingness to follow the leader of one's party despite disagreement on particular policies, and from an understandable belief among long-time partisans that what is best for their party is also best for their country. It is hard to imagine a government member who would feel so strongly about a specific piece of legislation that he or she would be prepared to attack it even at the risk of the country falling into the hands of the opposition.

The point be stressed, then, is not that party discipline is a malignant growth within Parliament that should be removed, nor that MPs are little more than robots with little effective freedom of action. Private channels of protest do exist, including the weekly caucus meeting where dissen-sion can be safely and at times effectively vented behind closed doors. To a limited degree, public dissension is also possible in speeches outside the House, and MPs can lobby members of the cabinet on behalf of constituency interests. "Free votes," where MPs are not bound by party discipline and where the fate of the government is not held to be at stake, do occur, although they are generally restricted to issues with a heavy moral content, such as capital punishment and abortion, where party discipline would be difficult to maintain even if imposed. The committee system also provides an opportunity for backbenchers to question at least the details of government legislation.

Nevertheless, in the final analysis, MPs cannot place the interests of their region above the interests of their party. Thus, if the two should clash, the MP may be perceived by his or her constituents as having sold out, of having forsaken constituency and region. Unfortunately, much of the representational work that MPs may do, such as speaking out in caucus meetings and bending the ears of parliamentary colleagues and cabinet ministers, takes place in private, out of the sight of constituents. Although the public image of the MP may be that of a slave to party discipline at the expense of regional interests, the private reality may be that of a spirited and indefatigable champion of regional interests. Thus it is not that party discipline prevents regional representation, but rather that it inhibits dramatic public displays of regional representation in action. The MP cannot stand on the floor of the House and demand that regional interests prevail. For such histrionics, voters must look to their provincial premier.

The manner in which parliamentary conventions inhibit public forms of regional representation takes us to the issue of regional representation within the federal cabinet. From the time of the Confederation debates in the 1860s, cabinet has been seen as the first line of regional defence in Ottawa.[76] Ideally, the cabinet contains representatives not only from the ten provinces but also from the major regions within the larger provinces. It should be noted, however, that while the appearance of the cabinet conveys an overriding concern with regional representation, the reality of regional representation takes place far from the public eye. Cabinet ministers are bound not only by party discipline but also by the cabinet conventions of secrecy and collective responsibility. Thus, while vigorous regional representation may take place behind the closed doors of cabinet, in public all ministers support cabinet policy. This places regional residents in a difficult position should the cabinet announce policies at odds with their perceived regional interest. In public, their "representative" in cabinet has no alternative but to endorse and defend the government. In private, any number of things could have happened: the minister may have fought hard for his region but lost; he may have traded a regional loss on one policy for a regional gain on another; he may have been convinced that on this particular issue the national interest or the interest of some other region should prevail; he may have been asleep at the switch; or he may have sold his region and constituents down the river. Voters have no way of determining what in fact took place. Thus, with respect to the public defence of regional interests, voters are likely to receive more satisfaction from their provincial premier, who is unhampered by party discipline, collective responsibility, or cabinet secrecy.

Cabinet Representation

In 1978, when the Liberal government of Pierre Trudeau had been in power for over ten years with largely the same cast of ministers, a Gallup survey asked a national sample of Canadians the following question: "Apart from Prime Minister Trudeau, do you happen to recall the name of a cabinet minister in Ottawa?"

Only 33 percent of the respondents could name a minister and correctly identify his or her portfolio. A further 14 percent were able to name a minister, but could not correctly identify the portfolio. Nineteen percent mentioned the name of an individual who was not in the cabinet, and 34 percent would not even venture a guess! (*The Gallup Report*, October 28, 1978.)

These findings raise some doubt as to the importance Canadians attach to regional representation within the federal cabinet. If many Canadians are unaware as to who is even in the cabinet, it is doubtful that they think of a particular minister as "their spokesperson in Ottawa." This suggests, in turn, that the much higher profile of provincial premiers, relative to that of cabinet ministers, greatly enhances the representative role of premiers within the national political process.

When the problems attendant upon regional representation in the Senate, House, and cabinet are taken together, and when they are considered in conjunction with the frequent inability of parties to elect candidates from all regions of the country, it seems fair to conclude that intrastate federalism in Canada is, at best, impaired. Partly—although not entirely—as a consequence, there has been a growing emphasis on the interstate representation and protection of regional interests. More and more, the provincial premiers and their governments have come to be seen as the primary line of regional defence *within the national political process*. However, this emphasis on interstate federalism is not cost-free. It inflates the role of provincial premiers, giving them a national prominence not envisioned in the original federal design. The resolution of regional conflict is removed from the parliamentary arena and placed in the more abrasive intergovernmental arena. An over-reliance on interstate federalism undermines the role of MPs, stripping them of an important function which is then transferred to the premiers. It can inflame intergovernmental conflict, allowing governments to present what may be a governmental struggle over resources, programs, and prestige as a regional conflict.

The preceding paragraph should not suggest that provincial governments and premiers do not have the responsibility to speak out for their provinces. The problem arises from the lack of an effective counterbalance from national politicians. Instead of a multiplicity of regional voices articulating a variety of regional perspectives, the stage is dominated by the premiers. The regional voices of Senators and MPs have been muted by the institutional constraints within which they must work. Thus, parliamentary institutions, despite their other virtues, often fail to provide an effective forum for the resolution of regional conflict, conflict which consequently has been deflected into the intergovernmental arena.

Frustration with both impaired intrastate channels of regional representation and resultant intergovernmental conflict lay behind the search for institutional reform which preoccupied governments, task forces, policy institutes, and political scientists for much of the late 1970s and

"This year,
in the spirit of national equalization,
Reggie and I feel we should spend
our vacation in the have-not provinces . . . "

Len Norris, *23rd Annual.* Originally published in *The Vancouver Sun*, January 25, 1974.

early 1980s. Given the regional role that second chambers play in other federal systems, it is not surprising that much of the search focused upon Senate reform,[77] although other institutions were not neglected. Procedural reform of the House of Commons has been pursued on a periodic basis and electoral reform has been frequently proposed.[78] About the only reform that has been definitely ruled out is the amalgamation of the existing provinces in the eastern and western peripheries into larger and, in theory, more powerful provincial units.[79] It is evident that any serious proposal for institutional reform will have to accept the existing provincial boundaries as given; the smaller provinces are no more likely to join together than the larger ones are to subdivide.

The quest for institutional reform has not been hobbled by a lack of alternatives. If anything, more of a problem has been posed by the very multiplicity of reform options. If significant institutional reform on the scale of an elected Senate is to be attained, two conditions will have to be met. The first is that the costs of regional conflict must come to be seen as intolerable, or at least sufficiently onerous as to impair seriously the performance of the federal government and to threaten the stability of the political community. Second, Canadians must come to believe that only institutional reform offers a solution to regional discontent—that a solution is not to be found in a new leader, a new party, or a new government. Although the first condition was approached during the later Trudeau governments, the election of the Mulroney Conservatives in 1984 appeared to provide an appropriate, non-institutional response. The 1984 and 1988 elections have given Canadians the opportunity to assess whether a new leader and a new party constitute a sufficient response.

To describe regional conflict as something akin to a cancer in the Canadian body politic, a cancer that should be removed by institutional surgery, would be to overstate the problem that most Canadians perceive. Yet to describe it as a mere wart or mole would be to understate the problem. Perhaps, then, an analogy might be found in arthritis. The condition can be painful and limiting but, even with no satisfactory cure in sight, we can get by.

THE NATIONAL INTEREST

While it is important to understand the political roots of regional conflict in Canada, the impression should not be given that such conflict is entirely the product of flawed institutions and flawed political leadership. The regions of Canada are different in their resources, in their population base, and in their industrial organization. These differences produce conflicting regional interests and aspirations, which percolate in turn within the political system.[80] Many features of the Canadian landscape, furthermore, lie beyond the reach of political institutions, reformed or otherwise. Institutional reform will not move oil from the prairie sedimentary basin to the Canadian shield, or the pulp forests of Ontario and

Quebec to Prince Edward Island. Nor will it dramatically affect the regional location of the Canadian population, the rate of unemployment in Newfoundland, or the concentration of industrial activity in central Canada.[81]

As Paul Phillips notes, "for most of the country outside of the industrial heartland, economic fortunes rest directly on the fortuitous distribution of climate, geography and natural wealth, and on the state of foreign markets, none of which respond much to Canadian policies."[82] The dependency on volatile foreign markets exposes the Canadian economy to sharp and unpredictable dislocations which are often regionally specific in their effects, both positive and negative. For example, the impact of the Depression was more catastrophic on the prairies than it was elsewhere, just as escalating world prices for oil in the 1970s conveyed widely divergent benefits and costs on the Canadian provinces. As Richard Simeon explains,

> exogenous economic factors like the energy crisis have a highly differential regional impact. Because the domestic economy is so regionalized, this impact sharpens internal divisions; it is disintegrative rather than unifying . . . the territorially specific location of resources combines with their allocation to the provinces to maximize regional conflict.[83]

Although governments cannot move resources and can do little to control foreign markets, they can, at least in the abstract, transfer the revenues that come from resource development and cushion the impact of foreign markets. Within the context of a national economy, regional dislocations need not be as severe as they might otherwise be nor economic specialization as risky. Regions whose markets have gone soft can ride out the storm, sheltered by those sectors of the national economy that remain strong. However, the redistributive mechanisms that are required are complex and politically contentious. They also bring us up against conflicting visions of the national interest.

Discussions of regionalism often boil down to arguments over which should prevail: regional interests or the national interest? When the question is put in this form, the answer in a democratic country seems obvious. The national interest should prevail, given that it reflects the aspirations of a larger number of citizens. However, the simple juxtaposition of regional and national interests obscures an interesting and difficult problem.

There are essentially three issues at stake in discussions of the national interest. The first is the extent to which the national majority should prevail, an issue that arose in last chapter's discussion of English–French relations. On this point, Pierre Trudeau has been an emphatic spokesman for the supremacy of the national will:

Globe and Mail, January 7, 1989, p. D7.

> If Canada is indeed to be a nation, there must be a national will which is something more than the lowest common denominator among the desires of the provincial governments. And when there is a conflict . . . between the national will and the provincial will, the national will must prevail. Otherwise, we are not a nation.[84]

Yet when Canadians adopted a federal system of government, they rejected the assumption that the national majority should always prevail. The essence of federalism is that, for at least some issues in some circumstances, the will of the national majority should be *constitutionally frustrated*. A political system is not federal if it is predetermined that national majorities will prevail over provincial majorities, should the two collide. As the Canadian political system is thoroughly federal in principle and design, it cannot be assumed that the national majority *should* prevail. The perception that the national majority *will* prevail, notwithstanding the principles of federalism, lies close to the heart of regional discontent. Note, for example, Dalton Camp's distillation of the political sentiment he found in British Columbia:

> Where the wealth is found, the numbers are still few; where the numbers are found, so too are the looters, carpetbaggers and welfare indolents. And since democracy is the rule of numbers, the pillage of the West seems certain.[85]

In federal systems, numbers alone should not rule.

The second issue is who should articulate the national interest or, if there are several articulations, which one should prevail. The House of Commons, with representatives elected from every nook and cranny of the country through a system that ensures the equal weighting of individuals and the proportionate weighting of provincial populations, is certainly a claimant. Yet how do we deal with the facts that Ontario and Quebec jointly determine the composition of the national government, that the House is organized along party lines, that when the House speaks it is actually the governing party speaking, that important groups may lack adequate representation on the government side of the House, and that francophones constitute a permanent minority? Should provincial governments be involved in the articulation of the national interest? Should the national interest be articulated by the governments of Canada, rather than by the federal government alone? If so, what would be the appropriate institutional mechanism for orchestrating the voices of eleven governments? How would we handle conflicts between governments, such as those which arose during the early 1980s when the Alberta government argued that higher oil prices were in the national interest and the federal government argued just the reverse?

The third issue has to do with the way in which we conceptualize the "national interest." Is it something that transcends regional interests, or is it best seen as something that faithfully reflects regional interests? Is the whole greater than the sum of its parts, or is the whole equal to the sum of its parts? Ironically, one of the most colourful statements in support of a transcendent national interest came from the West's most successful politician, John Diefenbaker:

> We shall never build the nation which our potential resources make possible by dividing ourselves into anglophones, francophones, multicultural phones, or whatever kind of phoneys you choose. I say Canadians, first, last and always.[86]

This issue takes us back to the nature of Canadian society. Is Canada best seen as a community of communities, or is there a national community that in some meaningful way transcends its regional components? These are not easy questions to answer. They do show, however, that the articulation of the national interest in a regionally diverse federal state is never straightforward and seldom non-contentious. To appeal to the national interest in the resolution of regional conflict is to avoid a set of issues which adds much of the flavour and spice to Canadian political life.

SUGGESTED READINGS

David G. Alexander, *Atlantic Canada and Confederation: Essays in Canadian Political Economy*, compiled by Eric W. Sager, Lewis R. Fischer, and Stuart O. Pierson (Toronto: University of Toronto Press, 1983).

Herman Bakvis, *Federalism and The Organization of Political Life: Canada in Comparative Perspective* (Kingston: Institute of Intergovernmental Relations, Queen's University, 1981).

Herman Bakvis, "Regional Politics and Policy in the Mulroney Cabinet, 1984-88: Towards a Theory of the Regional Minister System in Canada," *Canadian Public Policy* XV, No. 2 (June 1989), pp. 121-34.

J.F. Conway, *The West: A History of a Region in Confederation* (Toronto: James Lorimer, 1983).

David J. Elkins and Richard Simeon, eds., *Small Worlds: Provinces and Parties in Canadian Political Life* (Toronto: Methuen, 1980).

Ernest R. Forbes, *The Maritime Rights Movement, 1919-1927: A Study in Canadian Regionalism* (Montreal: McGill-Queen's University Press, 1979).

C.E.S. Franks, *The Parliament of Canada* (Toronto: University of Toronto Press, 1987).

Roger Gibbins, *Regionalism: Territorial Politics in Canada and the United States* (Toronto: Butterworths, 1982); and *Prairie Politics and Society: Regionalism in Decline* (Toronto: Butterworths, 1980).

Donald S. MacDonald, ed., *Government and Politics of Ontario* (Toronto: Macmillan, 1975).

Ralph Matthews, *The Creation of Regional Dependency* (Toronto: University of Toronto Press, 1983).

Paul Phillips, *Regional Disparities*, Revised Edition (Toronto: James Lorimer, 1982).

G.A. Rawlyk, ed., *The Atlantic Provinces and the Problems of Confederation* (St. John's: Breakwater Press, 1979).

John Richards and Larry Pratt, *Prairie Capitalism: Power and Influence in the New West* (Toronto: McClelland and Stewart, 1979).

STUDY QUESTIONS

1. How would *you* answer the survey question discussed in this chapter:

"Do you think of yourself first as a Canadian or as a Manitoban, Ontarian, Nova Scotian or whatever?" In your own case, how would you describe the relationship between national and provincial identifications?

2. How would you characterize your own province in terms of the costs and benefits of Confederation? Compared to other provinces, has your own province done relatively well or relatively poorly? Do you find the cost-benefit approach to be a useful one, or do you find it difficult to apply to your own or other provinces?

3. Trace the history of your province's representation on the government side of the House of Commons and within the federal cabinet. How has your province fared compared to others?

4. Have there been occasions in the past when the national interest, as articulated by Parliament, has been clearly at odds with the majority interest within your province? If so, how was the conflict resolved? Are there such conflicts at present, or can such conflicts be seen on the political horizon?

5. What would you propose as the best method of articulating the national interest? How would you defend this choice?

NOTES

1. Task Force on National Unity, *A Future Together* (Hull: Supply and Services Canada, 1979), p. 29.
2. For an expansion of this contrast, see Gibbins, *Regionalism: Territorial Politics in Canada and the United States* (Toronto: Butterworths, 1982).
3. June 1936. Cited in Warner Troyer, *The Sound and the Fury* (Toronto: John Wiley and Sons, 1980), p. 11.
4. See Robert W. Jackman, "Political Parties, Voting and National Integration: The Canadian Case," in Richard Schultz, Orest M. Kruhlak, and John C. Terry, eds., *The Canadian Political Process*, Third Edition (Toronto: Holt, Rinehart and Winston, 1979), pp. 130-44; and Richard Johnston, "Federal and Provincial Voting: Contemporary Patterns and Historical Evolution," in David J. Elkins and Richard Simeon, eds., *Small Worlds: Provinces and Parties in Canadian Political Life* (Toronto: Methuen, 1980), pp. 131-78.
5. See Seymour Martin Lipset and Stein Rokkan, "Cleavage Structures, Party Systems, and Voter Alignments: An Introduction," in Lipset and Rokkan, eds., *Party Systems and Voter Alignments: Cross-National Perspectives* (New York: The Free Press, 1967), pp. 1-64; and Herman Bakvis, *Federalism and the Organization of Political Life: Canada in*

Comparative Perspective (Kingston: Institute of Intergovernmental Relations, Queen's University, 1981), pp. 40-48.

6. For an expansion of this discussion, see Gibbins, *Prairie Politics and Society: Regionalism in Decline* (Toronto: Butterworths, 1980).

7. Ernest R. Forbes, *The Maritime Rights Movement, 1919-1927: A Study in Canadian Regionalism* (Montreal: McGill-Queen's University Press, 1979), p. 2.

8. *Ibid.*, p. 2.

9. G.A. Rawlyk and Doug Brown, "The Historical Framework of the Maritimes and Confederation," in G.A. Rawlyk, ed., *The Atlantic Provinces and the Problems of Confederation* (St. John's: Breakwater Press, 1979), p. 14.

10. Forbes, *Maritime Rights Movement*, p. 8.

11. Rawlyk and Brown, "The Historical Framework," p. 18.

12. *Ibid.*

13. Forbes, *Maritime Rights Movement*, pp. 20-21.

14. *Ibid.*

15. *Ibid.*

16. *Ibid.*

17. Rawlyk and Brown, "The Historical Framework," p. 26.

18. When Alberta and Saskatchewan were created in 1905, the ownership of natural resources was retained by the federal government. Ownership was not transferred to the western provinces until 1931.

19. Raymond Reid, *The Canadian Style* (Toronto: Fitzhenry & Whiteside, 1973), p. 105.

20. Terry Campbell and G.A. Rawlyk, "The Historical Framework of Newfoundland and Confederation," in Rawlyk, ed., *The Atlantic Provinces*, p. 70.

21. Rawlyk and Brown, "The Historical Framework," p. 31.

22. *Ibid.*

23. See Anthony Careless, *Initiative and Response: The Adaptation of Canadian Federalism to Regional Economic Development* (Montreal: McGill-Queen's University Press, 1977).

24. Cited in Frank H. Underhill, *In Search of Canadian Liberalism* (Toronto: Macmillan, 1960), p. 55.

25. Vernon C. Fowke, *The National Policy and the Wheat Economy* (Toronto: University of Toronto Press, 1957), p. 282.

26. Kenneth H. Norrie, "Some Comments on Prairie Economic Alienation," in J. Peter Meekison, ed., *Canadian Federalism: Myth or Reality*, Third Edition (Toronto: Methuen, 1977), p. 325.

27. For an expanded discussion of western alienation, see Gibbins, *Prairie Politics and Society: Regionalism in Decline* (Toronto: Butterworths, 1980), Chapter Five.

28. J.R. Mallory, *Social Credit and the Federal Power in Canada* (Toronto: University of Toronto Press, 1953), p. 39.

29. See W.L. Morton, *The Progressive Party of Canada* (Toronto: University of Toronto Press, 1950).

30. Stanley C. Roberts, "Canadian Federalism and the Constitution: What is at Stake in the West," Alan B. Plaunt Memorial Lecture, Carleton University, April 6, 1979, p. 2. For empirical data on the relationship between western alienation and antipathy to Quebec, see Gibbins, "Models of Nationalism: A Case Study of Political Ideologies in the Canadian West," *Canadian Journal of Political Science* (June 1977), pp. 341-73.

31. Denis Smith, "Liberals and Conservatives on the Prairies, 1917-1968," in David P. Gagan, ed., *Prairie Perspectives* (Toronto: Holt, Rinehart and Winston, 1970), p. 41.

32. W.L. Morton, "The Bias of Prairie Politics," *Transactions of the Royal Society of Canada*, Series III, Vol. XLIX, June 1955, Section II, p. 66.

33. For an elaboration of this point, see Gibbins, "Constitutional Politics and the West," in Keith Banting and Richard Simeon, eds., *And No One Cheered: Federalism, Democracy and the Constitution Act* (Toronto: Methuen, 1983), pp. 119-32.

34. For an interesting look at the negative impact of reform within the Liberal party on the regional sensitivities, see David E. Smith, *The Regional Decline of a National Party: Liberals on the Prairies* (Toronto: University of Toronto Press, 1981), Chapter Six.

35. For a discussion, see Ralph Matthews, *The Creation of Regional Dependency* (Toronto: University of Toronto Press, 1983); and Paul Phillips, *Regional Disparities*, Revised Edition (Toronto: James Lorimer, 1982).

36. Wallace Clement, "A Political Economy of Regionalism in Canada," in Daniel Glenday, Hubert Guindon, and Allan Turowetz, eds., *Modernization and the Canadian State* (Toronto: Macmillan, 1978), p. 89.

37. *Ibid.*, p. 94.

38. *Ibid.*, p. 99.

39. "Painting the Farm Tory Blue," *Alberta Report*, October 17, 1988, p. 49.

40. Ron Graham, "The Legacy of Joe Clark," *Saturday Night*, September 1983, p. 19.

41. The metropolis–hinterland model dates from the work of economic historian Harold Innis. See *Empire and Communications* (Toronto: University of Toronto Press, 1950).

42. J.M.S. Careless, " 'Limited Identities' in Canada," *Canadian Historical Review*, Vol. 50, 1969, p. 9.

43. This survey, conducted by the author in June 1982, encompassed

1,402 randomly selected respondents from the four western provinces.

44. Alan C. Cairns, "The Governments and Societies of Canadian Federalism," *Canadian Journal of Political Science*, Vol. 10, 1977, pp. 695-726.

45. Harold D. Clarke, Lawrence LeDuc, Jane Jenson, and Jon Pammett, *Political Choice in Canada* (Toronto: McGraw-Hill Ryerson, 1979). In feeling thermometer questions, respondents are handed a cardboard thermometer with values ranging from 0 (very negative) through 50 (indifferent) to 100 (very positive). They are then asked to locate various objects, such as Canada, their province, or political leaders, on this scale. Although the thermometer may seem somewhat crude, it has proved to be a valuable tool in measuring the degree of respondent affect or emotional predisposition towards a wide range of political objects.

46. *Ibid.*, p. 64.

47. David J. Elkins, "The Sense of Place," in David J. Elkins and Richard Simeon, eds., *Small Worlds: Provinces and Parties in Canadian Political Life* (Toronto: Methuen, 1980), p. 16.

48. *Ibid.*, p. 21.

49. John W. Holmes, "Impact of Domestic Political Factors on Canadian-American Relations: Canada," in Annette Baker Fox, Alfred D. Herd, Jr., and Joseph S. Nye, eds., *Canada and the United States: Transnational and Transgovernmental Relations* (New York: Columbia University Press, 1976), p. 32.

50. Richard Allen, ed., *A Region of the Mind* (Regina: Canadian Plains Study Centre, University of Saskatchewan, 1973).

51. R. Douglas Francis, "Changing Images of the West," *Journal of Canadian Studies*, Vol. 17, No. 3 (Fall 1982), p. 5.

52. Donald V. Smiley, *Canada in Question: Federalism in the Eighties*, Third Edition (Toronto: McGraw-Hill Ryerson, 1980).

53. Careless, *Initiative and Response*, p. 169.

54. See *Ibid.*, p. 166 for a discussion.

55. Unconditional grants have no federal "strings" attached. The money can be spent as the provinces see fit, without the necessity of meeting federal program conditions or spending priorities.

56. For a discussion of the impact of higher oil revenues on equalization, see I.A. McDougall, *Marketing Canada's Energy* (Toronto: J. Lorimer, 1983), pp. 66ff.

57. T.W. Acheson, "The Maritimes and 'Empire Canada,' " in David Jay Bercuson, ed., *Canada and the Burden of Unity* (Toronto: Macmillan, 1977), p. 103. See also Donald V. Smiley, *Canada in Question: Federalism in the Seventies*, Second Edition (Toronto: McGraw-Hill Ryerson, 1976), p. 192.

58. Frank MacKinnon, "Prince Edward Island: Big Engine, Little Body," in Martin Robin, ed., *Canadian Provincial Politics* (Scarborough: Prentice-Hall, 1972), p. 256.

59. H.G. Thorburn, *Planning and the Economy: Building Federal-Provincial Consensus* (Toronto: James Lorimer, 1984), p. 150.

60. For a discussion of DREE, see Careless, *Initiative and Response.*

61. Ingrid Bryan, *Economic Policies in Canada* (Toronto: Butterworths, 1982), p. 210.

62. *Ibid.*, p.211.

63. *Calgary Sun*, December 6, 1988, p. 4.

64. In 1976 the Department of Veterans Affairs was moved from Ottawa to a new $50 million headquarters in Charlottetown.

65. Bakvis, *Federalism and the Organization of Political Life*, p. 44.

66. Richard W. Phidd and G. Bruce Doern, *The Politics and Management of Canadian Economic Policy* (Toronto: Macmillan, 1978), p. 317.

67. T.J. Courchene, "Interprovincial Migration and Economic Adjustment," *Canadian Journal of Economics*, III, 1970, pp. 550-76; and Economic Council of Canada, *Living Together: A Study of Regional Disparities* (Ottawa: Supply and Services, 1977).

68. Bryan, *Economic Policies*, p. 207.

69. Thorburn, *Planning and the Economy*, p. 120.

70. E.E. Schattschneider, *The Semi-Sovereign People* (New York: Holt, Rinehart and Winston, 1959).

71. In the 1984 federal election Tony Roman was elected as an independent in the Ontario riding of York North. Roman had earlier run for the Conservative nomination in the riding, and his campaign was openly supported by Conservatives opposed to their party's official candidate, incumbent John Gamble.

72. C.E.S. Franks, *The Parliament of Canada* (Toronto: University of Toronto Press, 1987), p. 115.

73. Richard Crossman, *Government and the Governed* (London: Christophers, 1939), p. 5.

74. Robert J. Jackson and Michael M. Atkinson, *The Canadian Legislative System*, Second Edition (Toronto: Macmillan, 1980), p. 113.

75. Mark MacGuigan, "Impediments to an Enlarged Role for the Backbencher," in Paul Fox, ed., *Politics: Canada*, Fifth Edition (Toronto: McGraw-Hill Ryerson, 1982), p. 496.

76. Robert A. MacKay, *The Unreformed Senate of Canada* (Toronto: McClelland and Stewart, 1963), p. 44.

77. For examples only, see Gibbins, *Senate Reform: Moving Towards the Slippery Slope* (Kingston: Institute of Intergovernmental Relations, Queen's University, 1983); Peter McCormick, Ernest C. Manning, and Gordon Gibson, *Regional Representation: The Canadian Partnership*, A Task Force Report prepared for the Canada West Foundation

(Calgary: 1981); *Senate Reform,* The Report of the Special Joint Committee of the Senate and the House of Commons on Senate Reform (Ottawa: January 1984); and William J. Yurko, MP, *Renewed Federalism: Structural Reform of the Canadian Senate* (Ottawa: December 1982).

78. For an informative discussion, see William P. Irvine, *Does Canada Need a New Electoral System?* (Kingston: Institute of Intergovernmental Relations, Queen's University, 1979).

79. David K. Elton, ed., *One Prairie Province?* (Lethbridge: Lethbridge Herald, 1970).

80. For an overview of this line of argument, see Phillips, *Regional Disparities.*

81. For a discussion of this last point, see N.H. Lithwick, *Regional Economic Policy: The Canadian Experience* (Toronto: McGraw-Hill Ryerson, 1978), p. 144.

82. Phillips, *Regional Disparities,* p. 130.

83. Richard Simeon, "Natural Resource Revenues and Canadian Federalism: A Survey of the Issues," paper presented to the Conference on the Alberta Heritage Savings and Trust Fund, Edmonton, October 18-19, 1979, p. 2.

84. Speech at the Liberal Party of Canada Fund Raising Dinner, Vancouver, November 24, 1981.

85. Dalton Camp, *An Eclectic Eel* (Ottawa: Deneau, 1981), p. 84.

86. June 4, 1973. Cited in John A. Munro, ed., *The Wit and Wisdom of John Diefenbaker* (Edmonton: Hurtig, 1982), pp. 80-81.

5

Canadian–American Relations

> Perhaps the most striking thing about Canada is that it is not part of the United States. Somehow more than half of North America has escaped being engulfed by its immensely more powerful neighbor although that neighbor has expanded fairly continuously in North America and elsewhere from 1776 to the present day.[1]

Canadian-American relations have been symbolized by "the world's longest *undefended* border," a phrase which brings to mind a poem by one of America's foremost poets, Robert Frost. The narrator of "Mending Wall," who is helping his neighbour repair the stone wall separating their properties, questions the very need for such a wall. The neighbour, however, insists that "good fences make good neighbours," and against this insistence Frost's narrator makes no headway:

> Before I built a wall I'd ask to know
> What I was walling in or walling out,
> And to whom I was like to give offence.
> Something there is that doesn't love a wall,
> That wants it down. I could say 'Elves' to him,
> But it's not elves exactly, and I'd rather
> He said it for himself. I see him there
> Bringing a stone grasped firmly by the top
> In each hand, like an old-stone savage armed.
> He moves in darkness as it seems to me,
> Not of woods only and the shade of trees.
> He will not go behind his father's saying,
> And he likes having thought of it so well
> He says again, 'Good fences make good neighbours.'[2]

In "Mending Wall," Frost has captured a fundamental tension in the Canadian-American relationship. The walls between the two countries are cumbersome and to some extent anachronistic; they are continually under attack by the combined forces of a continental economy, technological innovations such as cable and satellite delivery of television signals, and a continental approach to military defence. *As a consequence*, the building of "good fences" in order to maintain some independent national existence from the United States has been a major preoccupation of Canadian public policy-makers. Maintaining those fences in a continental environment has proved to be an ongoing and daunting task.

Canadians, and English Canadians in particular, have not been sheltered from the American society by differences in language, race, or religion. Even the physical features that cross the continent have done more to separate Canadians from one another than from Americans. The international border has been breached by countless corporations, trade unions, service clubs, professional societies, sports leagues, and cultural organizations. With three out of four Canadians living within 150 kilometres of the border, and a majority living farther south than the 49th parallel, the United States is readily accessible. Canadians and Americans by the millions cross the border each year to visit friends, vacation, and pursue business interests. Kinship ties, fostered by extensive migration between the two countries, span the international border as readily as they do provincial borders within Canada. And yet *because* the border is so permeable, its defence has taken on great importance within the Canadian political system. Given the lack of cultural, linguistic, geographical, religious, or racial defences, political defences have come to the fore.

The focus upon political boundary maintenance adopted for the present chapter runs a risk of painting Canadian-American relations in overly conflictual hues. Thus, it should be stressed at the outset that the political preoccupation with "good fences" does not arise because the Canadian-American relationship is predominantly ill-spirited or conflictual. It is precisely because the relationship has generally been so harmonious that boundary maintenance presents such a difficult challenge. It should also be stressed that boundary maintenance is more complex than simply building fences; it may take the form of active cooperation in order to ward off more damaging alternatives. In this respect, for example, supporters of the Free Trade Agreement have argued for closer economic integration in order to strengthen the Canadian economy, and thereby to shore up other distinctive features of Canadian culture, public policy, and social orientation. In the Canadian-American case, therefore, boundary maintenance is concerned with controlling rather than preventing American access to the Canadian society—with regulating access so as to maximize Canadian gains and minimize Canadian losses across the countless interchanges which take place between the two countries.

If Americans were not so much like Canadians and if there were not such a broad range of common values and interests, boundary maintenance would be far easier. It is precisely because the two countries are good neighbours that the maintenance of good fences is such a problematic and interesting aspect of Canadian public policy.

HISTORICAL BACKGROUND

Over the past two centuries the United States has had a great impact on Canada, while Canada has had a much more modest, although not insignificant, impact on the United States. This asymmetry reflects the basic demographic fact underlying Canadian–American relations—Americans outnumber Canadians by approximately ten to one.

The American War of Independence in 1776 helped lay the foundations for the Canadian society. Of the approximately 100,000 United Empire Loyalists who fled the American revolution, over 40,000 came north. More than 30,000 settled in Nova Scotia, tripling the colony's population and spilling into New Brunswick, which was consequently established as a separate colony in 1784. Others formed the bedrock of what is now Ontario, where their settlement led to the Constitutional Act of 1791, dividing what had been the single territory of Quebec into Upper and Lower Canada. In what is now Quebec, "the influx of Anglophone loyalists, pushed by expropriation or drawn by good farmland, changed Quebec once and for all from a homogeneous French-Canadian society to one with a prosperous and vocal English minority."[3] It is in this sense, then, that historian A.R.M. Lower has described Canada as a "by-product" of the American revolution.[4]

The United Empire Loyalists—anti-American Americans—helped put in place the cornerstone of Canadian nationalism. As J.M.S. Careless explains, they

> represented a declaration of independence against the United States, a determination to live apart from that country in North America. As a result, they helped to create not only a new province [Ontario], but a new nation.[5]

By rejecting Britain, the Americans allowed Canadians to carve out a distinctive niche on the North American continent. Canadians stood apart by virtue of their attachment to things British, and in particular their attachment to parliamentary institutions.

The American Revolution raised fears of military conquest that were to remain with Canadians until Confederation. In 1776 John Adams, who was to become the second president of the United States, declared that "the Unanimous Voice of the Continent is Canada must be ours; Quebec must be taken."[6] In 1775 American forces had in fact captured Montreal and, over the winter, had beseiged Quebec until that garrison was relieved by the British fleet in the spring of 1776. Even with the subsequent withdrawal of American forces, the fear persisted that the Americans would not rest until the British had been expelled from the continent. The invitation in Article IV of the American Articles of Confederation, that Canada "join us in Congress and complete the American Union," was seen by Canadians more as a threat than as an act of generosity.

Thirty-seven years after the American Revolution, Canadians again found themselves at war with the United States. Although Britain and the United States were the principal players in the War of 1812, some of the fighting took place on Canadian soil, as Americans invaded the Niagara Peninsula and burned the city of York (now Toronto), for which Washington was burnt in retaliation by the British. At the start of the conflict, former president Thomas Jefferson declared that "the annexation of Canada this year as far as the neighbourhood of Quebec will only be a mere matter of marching, and this will give us experience for the assault on Halifax next, and the final expulsion of England from the American continent."[7] As events turned out, it was not merely a matter of marching, and the American forces were repelled. The war nonetheless left a strong mark on Canada. Despite the Rush–Bagot Convention of 1817 which demilitarized the Great Lakes, subsequent years saw the construction of the Rideau canal and an impressive string of military fortifications including Kingston's Fort Henry, the Quebec Citadel and its companion forts on the south shore of Lévis, and the Halifax Citadel. More importantly, the invading American forces had destroyed more than homes, barns, and crops: they had also destroyed any lingering sense among the United Empire Loyalists that the Loyalists were exiled Americans rather than British subjects and, in a nascent sense, Canadians.

The military threat from the United States remained dormant until the aftermath of the American Civil War when, as discussed in Chapter 2, it reappeared to play a significant role in Confederation. After 1867 the military threat subsided and then disappeared, to be replaced by new forms of American expansionism. The most immediate threat came in the largely unoccupied Canadian West, as Americans spread westward and then, as free land disappeared, northward. The more general threat came from the American assertion of a "manifest destiny" which appeared to preclude sharing the continent with an independent Canada. In 1871 the *Globe* warned its readers that "we are divided only by an imaginary border . . . from a people . . . [who] have before now proved themselves aggressive—a people who believe in 'manifest destiny', 'universal sovereignty', and other ideas not very reassuring to their neighbours."[8] French Canadian assessments were even harsher. Olivar Asselin declared that "the amiable Nation of Pirates which stole Texas, Cuba, Porto Rico and the Philippines cannot be depended upon to act justly towards a weaker nation,"[9] while Henri Bourassa maintained that the United States was "waiting to gobble us up."[10]

Manifest Destiny

The phrase "manifest destiny" was coined in 1845 by John L. O'Sullivan, an American journalist and diplomat. Writing in the *US Magazine and Democratic Review*, O'Sullivan described America's "manifest destiny to overspread the continent allotted by providence for the free development of our yearly multiplying millions."[11] The theme came to be applied with special force to the northern half of the continent:

- In 1867, the same year in which he acquired Alaska for the United States, Secretary of State W.H. Seward declared that "nature designs that this whole continent, not merely these thirty-six states, shall be, sooner or later, within the magic circle of the American Union."
- In 1889 James G. Blaine, U.S. Secretary of State, said that Canada was like "an apple on a tree just beyond reach. We may strive to grasp it, but the bough recedes from our hold just in proportion to our effort to catch it. Yet let it alone, and in due time it will fall into our hands."
- Champ Clark, Speaker of the U.S. House of Representatives, declared in 1911 that "We are preparing to annex Canada . . . I hope to see the day when the American flag will float on every square foot of British North American possessions clear to the North Pole."

Such American aspirations did not end with Speaker Clark. In 1952 Timothy Sheehan of Illinois proposed in the House of Representatives that the United States buy Canada from Great Britain! However, despite the American belief in a manifest destiny, the 10-to-1 American edge in population, and the far greater economic and military power of the United States, Canadians ended up with more than half of the continent, albeit the colder part.

As the twentieth century unfolded, Canadian fears of absorption were replaced by anxieties over the growing American presence *within* Canada. Whereas in the past Britain had served as a counterweight to American influence in Canada, that role was now weakened as Britain's position in the international order declined, as Canada shed its colonial ties, and as the English Canadian community diversified and drew away from its British roots. British investment in Canada was supplanted by American investment, trade with the United States far surpassed trade with Britain, and American cultural patterns began to prevail over those from the United Kingdom. In short, by the end of the Second World War, the North Atlantic triangle formed by the United States, Britain, and Canada had been transformed. At least from the Canadian perspective, the Canadian–American side of the triangle was now dominant. The relationship between Canada and Great Britain had not only declined in relative importance, but had become increasingly irrelevant to the Canadian–American relationship. To an extent unknown in the past, Canada now faced the United States alone.

This new *continental* relationship was highlighted in a speech to the Canadian Parliament by President John F. Kennedy on May 17, 1962:

> Geography has made us neighbours. History has made us partners. And necessity has made us allies. Those whom nature hath so joined together let no man put asunder.

If anything, however, history made the two countries antagonists rather than friends. As James Eayrs wrote in response to Kennedy's speech, "if they are friends today, it is in spite of history, not because of it."[12]

THE ECONOMIC RELATIONSHIP

In 1891, at a time when Canadians were grappling with proposals for greater free trade between Canada and the United States, Goldwin Smith wrote what has become a classic statement of support for continental integration:

> Let any one scan the economical map of the North American continent with its adjacent waters, mark its northern zone abounding in minerals, in bituminous coal, in lumber, in fish, as well as in special farm products, brought in the north to hardier perfection, all of which the southern people have need: let him then look to its southern regions, the natural products of which as well as the manufactures produced in its wealthy centres of industry are needed by the people of the northern zone: he will see that the continent is an economic whole, and that to run a Customs line athwart it and try to sever its members from each other is to wage a desperate war against nature.[13]

Smith's description of continentalism as a "force of nature" has become common currency in discussions of Canadian–American relations. John Holmes, for example, argues that "the threat of continentalization comes not from governments but from forces beyond the control of governments."[14] James Eayrs asserts that the border between Canada and the United States is political rather than geographic, that "what nature joined together, Canadians have sought to sunder."[15] From wherever the pressures of continentalism spring, they have been readily acknowledged as a fact of Canadian life; the only matter of contention has been whether they should be resisted or embraced. However, to address this question requires that the "force of nature" be expressed in the more prosaic language of trade flows, tariff barriers, and foreign investment.

Continental Trade Flows

In the early decades after Confederation, Britain was Canada's most important trading partner and primary source of the non-resident investment capital needed to build the Canadian economy. By the turn of the century, however, Britain was being rapidly replaced by the United States as Canada's principal trading partner. Trade between the two countries was facilitated by a complex and growing web of corporations spanning the border. Today, Canada and the United States are each other's largest trading partners, with Canadian exports to the United States exceeding $100 billion per annum and American exports to Canada running close to that figure. The United States accounts for approximately 70 percent of Canadian exports, with approximately the same proportion of Canadian imports originating in the United States. These massive trade flows should be even further enhanced by the Free Trade Agreement, which went into effect on January 1, 1989.

Trading Perceptions

In early 1989, Decima Research conducted a survey of 1,000 Canadian and 1,000 American respondents for *Maclean's* (July 3, 1989). Not unexpectedly, the survey showed that Canadians were more aware of the Canadian–American trading relationship than were Americans. For example, 97 percent of the Canadian respondents were "aware that Canada and the United States had recently signed a Free Trade Agreement," an awareness shared by only 57 percent of the American respondents. When Canadians were asked to identify Canada's largest trading partner, 83 percent correctly named the United States, 9 percent named Japan, and 1 percent each named China and Europe. When American respondents were asked to identify the United States' largest trading partner, only 12 percent correctly identified Canada; 69 percent named Japan, 3 percent named China, and 2 percent each named Britain, the Soviet Union, and Europe.

In proportionate terms, foreign trade is more important to the Canadian economy than it is to the American economy. Canada exports approximately 28 percent of its Gross National Product, compared to approximately 13 percent for Japan and only 7 percent for the United States. Even in absolute terms, Canada is a major player in world trade; in 1987 Canadian exports amounted to 43 percent of Japan's exports and 39 percent of America's exports. This heavy reliance on trade means that the Canadian economy is very dependent upon the condition of foreign markets in general, and the condition of American markets in particular. If the American economy and therefore the demand for Canadian imports softens, the impact on Canada can be severe. Hence the expression, "when the American economy catches cold, the Canadian economy catches pneumonia."

One of the chronic problems in Canadian–American trade has arisen from the imbalance between natural resources and semi-processed goods, on the one hand, and manufactured products, on the other. While the former have constituted the bulk of Canadian exports to the United

States, the latter constitute the great bulk of Canadian imports. This imbalance was addressed by the Canada–United States Automotive Products Trade Agreement, or Auto Pact, of 1965. Prior to the Auto Pact, the Canadian automobile industry was ailing in the face of short production lines, inefficient plants, competition from Japanese and European compacts, and a heavy reliance on imported American parts. The Auto Pact, which created a qualified free trade arrangement for automobiles and automobile parts, addressed these problems by opening up the American market to Canadian plants and thereby allowing longer production lines, more specialization, and greater efficiency. The Pact greatly increased Canadian–American vehicle trade, although the larger volume of trade in automotive parts was less affected.

Tariff Protection

Trade between Canada and the United States has been the subject of ongoing and often intense political debate in Canada, debate which reached a crescendo in the 1988 federal election. Historically, the debate has turned on the degree to which tariffs should be imposed on imports from the United States, while the more contemporary debate has also embraced a variety of non-tariff barriers which impinge upon the Canadian–American trading relationship.

In 1879 the Government of Canada erected a 30 percent tariff wall between Canada and the United States in order to encourage the industrialization of the Canadian economy and, not incidentally, to increase federal revenues. Tariffs, the construction of a transcontinental railway system, and the settlement of the prairie West formed the interlocking pillars of Sir John A. Macdonald's *National Policy*. The tariff wall, it was hoped, would provide an east-west axis for the Canadian economy to counteract the north-south pull of continental forces, an axis which would sustain the transcontinental railway system then being put in place. In introducing the tariff legislation, the Minister of Finance declared that "the time has arrived when we are to decide whether we will simply be hewers of wood and drawers of water. . . . " With the National Policy, the choice was made; an industrialized economy was to be developed behind the protective tariff wall.

The tariff wall was designed to raise the price of American imports to the point where goods manufactured in Canada would be competitive. As a barrier to goods rather than to capital, it was not designed to keep out American investment. Indeed, the tariff actually encouraged foreign investment as American firms wishing to sell to the Canadian market found it more profitable to establish branch plants in Canada, and thus enjoy the protection of the tariff wall, than to try to export goods to Canada from American plants. (American investment was also promoted by proximity, by profitability, by the desire for a secure source of raw materials, and by the basic similarity of the two countries which reduced the anxieties attendant upon investing outside one's own country.) Thus the National Policy laid the foundations for an American dominated branch-plant economy and, as a consequence, for the extensive intrusion of American labour unions into Canada. The former outcome was by no means inadvertent; Canadian governments and private organizations actively courted American branch plants, not only through the tariff but also through vigorous promotional activities in the United States.[16] The goal was a healthy economy in Canada rather than a healthy Canadian economy. The question of who owned Canada's industrial plant was not to become a concern until much later.

The tariff structure put into place by the National Policy was to provide the basic framework for Canadian–American trade well into the twentieth century. Although there were abortive attempts in 1891 and 1911 to dismantle the tariff component of the National Policy, attempts discussed in Chapter 7, the framework remained essentially intact. Then, following the end of the Second World War, both Canada and the United States participated in a collective move by western industrialized countries to reduce tariff and non-tariff barriers to international trade. Both countries are signatories to the General Agreement on Tariffs and Trade (GATT) and, as a consequence, have reduced bilateral tariffs as part of more global tariff reductions negotiated through GATT. With the 1987 completion of the Tokyo round of GATT tariff reductions, approximately 80 percent of Canadian–American trade was tariff-free and the tariff rate on the remaining 20 percent had been significantly reduced; the average tariff on imports from the United States was approximately 10 percent, while the average American tariff on imports from Canada was approximately 5 percent. The remaining tariff-protected trade then became the target of the Canadian-American Free Trade Agreement which, when fully implemented in 1999, will virtually eliminate tariffs on Canadian–American trade. In this sense, then, the FTA has brought to a close a long and often very contentious political debate on Canadian tariff policy. It should be stressed, however, that changes in continental trade policy have been, in large part, a response to broader changes in the international trading environment. It should be stressed in addition that a multitude of non-tariff barriers to trade remain including quotas, technical standards, valuation and dumping procedures, and government procurement practices, many of which also pose significant barriers to interprovincial trade within Canada.[17]

Foreign Investment

At the turn of the century, British investment in Canada surpassed that from the United States by a margin of nearly six to one. Then, with the First World War, there was an acceleration of American investment abroad, particularly in Canada, coupled with a parallel decline in British investment abroad. By 1926, American investment in Canada surpassed British investment; by the early 1960s it accounted for more than 80 percent of all foreign investment in Canada; and by the mid-1980s it surpassed British foreign investment in Canada by a margin of more than eight to one. In 1985, 75.5 percent of all direct foreign investment in Canada originated in the United States, 9.3 percent in the United Kingdom, 2.9 percent in West Germany, 2.4 percent in the Netherlands, and 2.1 percent in Japan. American-controlled firms accounted for 71.5 percent of the assets, 75.6 percent of the sales, and 85.9 percent of the profits of all foreign-controlled corporations in Canada.[18]

Here it should be noted parenthetically that the decline in British investment reflected a general deterioration in the place of Britain and the British Empire in the international order. As a consequence of this decline, and of the ongoing continental pull of the United States, Canada's economic, cultural, and strategic focus shifted to the United States. That shift, and the altered international balance between Britain and the United States which lay behind it, had an important impact on English Canadian nationalism. In its formative stage, English Canadian nationalism had enthusiastically embraced imperial themes, drawing its confidence and expansionist thrust from Canada's tie to the British Empire.[19] Thus, Denis Smith argues, "as the Empire faded away in the fifties and sixties and as Britain turned inward to agonize over her own domestic problems, English Canada lost one—perhaps the most profound—of her spiritual props."[20]

The extent of foreign ownership in Canada, which far surpasses that in any comparable industrialized country, is highly variable across sectors of the economy. Foreign investment has been most prevalent in the manufacturing, mining, and energy sectors, and least prevalent in textiles, transportation, communications, and financial services. The extent of foreign ownership can also be quite variable over relatively short periods of time. For example, between 1985 and 1988, Canadian ownership of the oil and gas industry slipped from 48.2 percent to 42.5 percent, while Canadian control slipped from 42.7 percent to 34.0 percent.[21] Overall, foreign investors control approximately a third of the assets of the leading 500 economic enterprises in Canada and, among non-financial corporations, capture approximately 30 percent of Canadian sales and profits.[22]

As is the case with most things Canadian, foreign investment is not

Table 5.1
Contribution to Provincial Taxable Income
By Foreign-Controlled Corporations, 1985

Alberta	60.2%
Newfoundland	46.3
Ontario	43.5
British Columbia	41.1
Saskatchewan	40.6
Manitoba	35.1
Nova Scotia	32.9
Quebec	30.0
New Brunswick	18.2
Prince Edward Island	4.9
Canada	44.1

Source: Corporations and Labour Unions Returns Act, Report for 1985 (Ottawa: Supply and Services, 1988), chart 21, p. 35.

evenly distributed across the provinces. Table 5.1 shows that foreign investment has a greater impact on the provincial taxable income of Alberta than it does for other provinces. At the same time, seven of the ten provinces fall within a reasonably narrow band in which foreign-controlled corporations generate between 30 and 46 percent of the provincial taxable income.

Foreign control of the Canadian economy reached an historic high in 1971 when 37 percent of the non-financial corporations were foreign, and largely American, controlled. Not coincidentally, this period witnessed a virtual flood of publications championing economic nationalism. The forerunner was George Grant's *Lament for a Nation* (1965), in which Grant not only mourned the end of Canada as a sovereign nation, but elevated anti-Americanism to a conservative virtue in the face of an advancing continental and indeed global technological culture. In the early 1970s nationalists advanced the argument that foreign investment not only threatened Canada's political sovereignty and the survival of a distinctive national identity, but that it harmed the Canadian economy. Book after book hammered away at the belief that foreign investment was beneficial. Works such as D.W. Carr's *Recovering Canada's Nationhood* (1971), James Laxer's *The Energy Poker Game* (1970), Kari Levitt's *The Silent Surrender* (1970), Ian Lumsden's *Close the 49th Parallel Etc.* (1970), W.H. Pope's *The Elephant and the Mouse* (1971), Abraham Rotstein's *The Precarious Homestead* (1973), Rotstein and Gary Lax's *Independence: The Canadian Challenge* (1972), Philippe Sykes's *Sellout: The Giveaway of Canada's Resources* (1973), and John W. Warnock's *Partner to Behemoth* (1970) contributed to the nationalist cause. It is interesting to note that this nationalist outpouring, largely written by English Canadian academics, coincided with the Quiet Revolution in Quebec. *Maîtres chez nous*, the slogan of the Quiet Revolution, seems equally fitting for the economic nationalists of English Canada.

Who Is to Blame?

While nationalists lamented the American domination of the Canadian economy, they placed the blame squarely on Canadian rather than American shoulders:

- Donald Creighton (historian): "Canadians, themselves, half converted to the belief that economic development is the only sure road to happiness, have grown accustomed to selling out their birthright for a quick buck."
- Lester Pearson (while Leader of the Official Opposition in 1960): "The dependence of Canada on the United States market for trade and on U.S. capital for development is an increasing threat to our independence . . . But, if we lose our national purpose and identity, it will be by our own default, not by the design of anybody else."
- Mel Hurtig (publisher): "We are not victims of rape so much as witnesses to our own economic prostitution."
- Myrna Kostash (author and journalist) describes Canada as " . . . a nation whoring on the sidelines of the world's biggest dollar bonanza while plotting all the time a cultural get-away that will astound the Pharisees and renew the hope of the exploited everywhere."
- The late W.L. Morton (historian) argued that the present degree of American investment " . . . is solely the work and fault of Canadians, particularly of provinces and regions competing for foreign investment in any guise and at any cost. These Canadian harlots, having sold their bodies usually at a cheaper price than they could have got, will find they have also sold their souls."
- George Bain (*The Globe and Mail*): "If there is one thing that worries Canadians more than economic domination, it is that someone, sometime, will try to do something about it."
- Minutes after endorsing a United Auto Workers' resolution calling for Canadian content restrictions on foreign cars, the town council of Tilbury, Ontario, voted to buy a Japanese-made tractor because the dealer knocked $4,500 off the regular price.

Economic nationalists rejected the argument that freer trade with the United States would benefit the Canadian economy. While Canadian firms would have access to the American market, American firms with their longer production lines and lower per unit costs would gain access to the Canadian market. In the exchange, Canadian-owned firms could be swamped, while Canadian-based American subsidiaries would be unlikely to enter the American market. As Peter Newman argued,

It is Alice in Wonderland economics to expect branch plants in Canada to compete with their U.S. parent companies on their home ground. Indeed, the

reverse phenomenon is more likely: free trade will encourage the dismantling of Canadian branch plants . . . [23]

Of particular concern to economic nationalists was the fear that
foreign ownership would dilute Canada's *political* control over its economy. From the nationalist perspective, the economy is an instrument for
the attainment of not only individual consumptive goals but also collective social goals. Economic policy can be used to redistribute income
among individuals or across regions, to promote employment, or to
create nationally distinct social institutions and public services. However,
to the extent that the Canadian economy is integrated into a continental
scheme of things, the ability of Canadian governments to direct the
economy towards social ends may be weakened. It is in this sense, Kari
Levitt argued, that continentalism " . . . is fundamentally destructive of
Canadian unity because it rejects the maintenance of a national community as an end in itself."[24]

The fears of economic nationalists on this count were crystallized in
an often quoted passage by George Ball, the Undersecretary of State for
Presidents Lyndon Johnson and John Kennedy. Canada, Ball believed,
was fighting a "rearguard action against the inevitable":

> Sooner or later, commercial imperatives will bring about free movement of
> all goods back and forth across our long border; and when that occurs, or
> even before it does, it will become unmistakably clear that countries with
> economies so inextricably entwined must also have free movement of the
> other vital factors of production—capital, services and labor. The result will
> inevitably be substantial economic integration, which will require for its full
> realization a progressively expanding area of common political decision.[25]

For economic nationalists, it was the "expanding area of common political decision" that posed the threat. As Ian Wahn concluded in 1970:

> Oh sure, all our political paraphernalia would continue—the changing of the
> guard, the opening of Parliament—and it wouldn't be entirely form. There
> would be some substance to it. We could make all sorts of useful regulations,
> just as municipal governments do. We'd be doing all sorts of useful things in
> the Parliament of Canada, but they wouldn't be the vital, important, basic
> things. The decision on those things would be made south of the border.[26]

In the twenty years since Ball's prediction and Wahn's sardonic
observation, there has been little movement towards an expanding area of
common political decision, although the same fears played a central role
in the 1988 debates over the Free Trade Agreement. Indeed, the intervening years witnessed an overall decline in direct foreign investment, and
foreign ownership of the Canadian economy has steadily declined. The
intervening years also witnessed significant moves to assert greater
political control over the economy, and then to relax such control. Here

FIRA, the Foreign Investment Review Agency, has provided the symbolic centrepiece for an ongoing debate.

FIRA's creation had been recommended in the 1972 Gray Report[27] as an essential response to expanding foreign ownership of the Canadian economy. The agency was put into place in 1974 in response to growing nationalist pressure, and to growing political pressure on the Liberal minority government by the federal New Democrats. The intent of FIRA was to screen rather than to block foreign investment, to ensure that takeovers and, after 1975, new investment, were of "significant benefit" to Canada. As the Minister of Finance explained to a New York audience when FIRA was introduced, "it's not a dam, it's a filter."[28] Whether FIRA served as an effective gatekeeper was a matter of considerable debate. While some claimed that the only firm likely to be denied entry by FIRA would have been Murder Incorporated, FIRA's regulations did force foreign investors to address the issue of Canadian benefit. They also generated a good deal of red tape, a good deal of confusion as to what was and what was not of "significant benefit" to Canada, and delays of up to two years in the approval of investment proposals.

FIRA was not unique to Canada as most countries, including the United States, imposed analogous, if less formalized, restrictions on foreign investment.[29] Nevertheless, for Canadian nationalists, FIRA served as an important symbol of political control over the Canadian economy. For those with a more continentalist orientation, it served as an equally important symbol of misguided nationalism and excessive state intervention in the economy. In the early 1980s, as the Canadian economy worsened and unemployment rose, FIRA's nationalist mandate was subordinated to the overarching goal of maintaining a healthy economy. The welcome mat was thrown out to any foreign investment that might generate jobs; in the face of growing unemployment, the fear was not that foreign investors would flood into Canada but rather that they might not come at all. After the 1984 election, FIRA was renamed Investment Canada by the new Progressive Conservative government, and its primary mandate became to attract rather than to screen foreign investment. With the passage of the FTA, restrictions on American investment and the legacy of FIRA have been all but abolished. American investors are assured of "national treatment": they will receive treatment no less favourable than that extended to Canadian investors in Canada. Apart from some exceptions for cultural industries, there will be no screening of most new investment, no screening of direct acquisitions valued at less than $50 million, and no new policies on minimum levels of Canadian equity holdings.

A second important nationalist initiative came with the creation of Petro-Canada in 1974 and the introduction of the National Energy Program in 1980. Petro-Canada, a Crown corporation, became a major presence in all aspects of the oil industry from service stations to exploration in the Arctic and off the East Coast. The NEP was introduced to increase Canadian ownership of the oil industry from approximately 10 percent in 1980 to a target of 50 percent in 1990, to protect Canadians from rapidly rising world oil prices, and to promote energy self-sufficiency. While FIRA had sought to regulate foreign investment, the NEP constituted a more dramatic assertion of Canadian sovereignty in an important sector of the economy. The NEP was introduced at a time when the new Reagan administration in the United States was attempting to reduce state intervention in the economy. As a consequence, it ruffled ideological feathers in the United States and contributed to a general deterioration in Canadian-American relations.[30] American oil interests were upset at the NEP "back-in" provisions which allowed Petro-Canada to acquire up to 25 percent ownership in frontier and offshore oil leases held by multinational corporations. These provisions were seen as confiscatory and were attacked because they were a post facto change in the rules of the game governing foreign investment in Canada. The companies argued that if they came into Canada under one set of rules, the rules should not be changed once the investment was in place, a guarantee that has now been provided by the FTA. The NEP was also criticized within Canada, in part for parallel ideological reasons and, more vociferously, by western Canadians as a federal raid on provincial resource revenues.

In drawing this discussion to a close, note should be made of the association between economic nationalism and the political left. Just as the case for continentalism is, in essence, a case for a market-driven economic order in which the flow of capital, resources, and labour would be unimpaired by political constraints, the case for economic nationalism is a case for harnessing the economy to broader national and social goals. The association was central to George Grant's argument in *Lament for a Nation*:

> After 1940, nationalism [in Canada] had to go hand in hand with some measure of socialism. Only nationalism could provide the political incentive for planning; only planning could restrain the victory of continentalism.[31]

Or again, later in the same work:

> No small country can depend for its existence on the loyalty of its capitalists. International interests may require the sacrifice of the lesser loyalty of patriotism. Only in dominant nations is the loyalty of capitalists ensured.[32]

At the extreme, economic nationalism can be seen as a means of creating a more socialist economic order.[33] In its more moderate forms, economic nationalism prompts extensive government intervention in the economy in order to regulate foreign investment and to ensure that such investment serves the national interest. Thus the debate over economic nationalism becomes entangled in a broader ideological debate over the appropriate role of the state in the economy, and in a broader political debate over how and by whom the national interest is to be defined.

The political tension between continentalism and economic nationalism will likely endure even in the wake of the FTA. With the trade agreement in place, the terms of debate will shift to an examination of the free trade balance sheet: has American investment increased or decreased as a consequence, has employment risen or fallen, has the economy prospered or not? When, in 1968, Prime Minister Trudeau was asked if he was worried about the influx of American capital, he replied: "Well, I am not worried in the sense that I don't worry over something which is somewhat inevitable, and I think the problem of economic domination is somewhat inevitable ... these are the facts of life, and they don't worry me." In this respect at least, Trudeau did not reflect an important strand of Canadian political thought; economic nationalists have worried about, and will continue to debate, the inevitability of economic domination.

CULTURAL NATIONALISM

In the nineteenth century, Canada's nascent culture was shielded from American influence by the primitive state of communications technology. The political barrier between the two countries also served as a reasonably effective cultural barrier; the main cultural influences on Canadian life flowed from Great Britain, and not from the United States. However, with the introduction of mass circulation magazines, wire services, motion pictures, records, radio, and television, the greater proximity of the United States was brought to bear on increasingly permeable cultural barriers. Cultural influences flowed from south to north, but *not* from north to south, through a multitude of channels. The air waves in particular, which were at first envisaged as "highways of national cultural integration" in Canada, became "agents of denationalization by serving as roadways for foreign, largely American, cultural values."[34]

The response to American influence in the cultural realm was patterned after the response in the economic realm. Barriers were erected to shelter the Canadian culture and, more specifically, Canadian cultural artisans including authors, publishers, film and television producers, recording artists, and directors of dance and theatre. The intent was to create a protected domestic market for the producers of Canadian cultural artifacts, although in this case there was no anticipation that American artisans would leap the "tariff wall" and relocate in Canada, as American manufacturing firms had done by establishing Canadian branch plants. Thus, Canadian content regulations for radio and television broadcasts created a protected market for Canadian performers, a market in which "unfair" foreign competition has been legislatively restricted, although by no means excluded. It was hoped that a healthy Canadian cultural "industry" would flourish behind the protective wall of cultural tariffs, and that as a consequence a distinctive Canadian culture would survive and even flourish.

For Canadian nationalists, the cultural threat from the United States has been no less important than the economic threat, as the following quote from John Holmes illustrates:

> We are in danger of becoming a zombie nation, our physical structure intact but our souls and minds gone abroad. Having gloriously resisted with our loyal muskets the Yankee invader on the slopes of Quebec and Queenston, Canada may well be conquered by American television.[35]

While it can be argued that foreign investment brings in its wake employment and economic growth, the benefits of the American mass culture are more elusive and contentious. As a consequence, nationalists have contested the American presence on the cultural front with greater moral conviction than they have possessed on the economic front.

In a series of Royal Commissions conducted during the 1950s and early 1960s, two principal themes of Canadian cultural nationalism were established: "... that Canada's capacity for meaningful nationhood is somehow being thwarted and undermined by the proximity and potency of the cultural output of the United States" and that state intervention was essential "to create and support a countervailing cultural force to the unrelenting flow of Americana across the border."[36] Such intervention took the form of sticks and carrots. The "sticks" entailed regulations restricting the influx of American culture into Canada, regulations facilitated by the 1932 Supreme Court decision in the *Radio Case* giving jurisdiction over the airwaves to the federal government. Examples of such restrictions include the 1968 establishment of the Canadian Radio-Television Commission; the Canadian content regulations that the CRTC (now the Canadian Radio-Television and Telecommunications Commission) spawned; the elimination of tax deductions for firms advertising in the Canadian edition of *Time* (now defunct as a consequence) or on American border television stations transmitting into Canada; the "Baie Comeau" policy to promote Canadian ownership in the publishing industry;[37] and immigration restrictions which require artistic companies and universities seeking to hire outside Canada to demonstrate first that no suitable Canadian candidates are available. The "carrots" entailed public financial support for Canadian cultural artisans. Examples here would include the 1957 creation of the Canada Council, public funding for the CBC, and current requirements that cable television firms plough some of their revenue back into the production of Canadian programming. There is little doubt that the CBC has been the flagship for all such endeavours, which explains in part why any attempt by the federal

" ... To comply with government regulations this picture will be displayed for 7 minutes and 32 seconds to bring our Canadian content to the required 60 percent. Please do not adjust your set. To comply with ... "

Len Norris, *19th Annual*. Originally published in *The Vancouver Sun*, February 14, 1970.

government to reduce the CBC's funding sets off such a strong nationalist response.

During the late 1960s and early 1970s, Canadian universities provided a major battleground for cultural nationalists. Faced with rapid enrollment growth and limited production of Canadian PhDs, universities had little choice but to hire abroad. As a consequence, many universities came to have a high proportion of non-Canadian faculty members, mostly Americans, and an even higher proportion who had received their graduate training outside Canada. This raised fears about the Canadian content of university education and about the capacity of universities to help build, or at the very least transmit, a distinctive national culture.[38] In more recent years the concern has diminished, though not evaporated, as Canadians have come to make up a larger and larger proportion of university faculties, as more Canadian PhDs have come on the market,[39] and as many of the landed immigrants who staffed Canadian universities in the past have taken out Canadian citizenship. Whereas, in 1969-70, only 57 percent of faculty positions were held by Canadian citizens, this had increased to 77 percent by 1980.[40] If the shortage of PhDs and university professors projected for the 1990s indeed materializes, fears about the Canadian character of universities may well re-emerge.

Policies to shelter Canadian culture face serious technological constraints. For decades, Canadians living in major metropolitan centres close to the American border have been able to receive American radio and television signals. Now, for a modest fee, most Canadians have access to unimpaired American programming through cable television. While the content of cable television can be regulated to a degree by restricting the number of channels carrying American programming, recent advances in cable capacity and satellite delivery threaten the survival of any form of Canadian content regulation. In the future, as in the past, technological innovation is likely to progressively erode cultural barriers between Canada and the United States.

At this point it is difficult to determine what impact, if any, the FTA will have on Canadian culture and on the politics of cultural nationalism. Article 2005, paragraph 1, of the Agreement states that "cultural industries are exempt from the provisions of this Agreement," but paragraph 2 goes on to state that, "notwithstanding any other provision of this agreement, a Party may take measure of equivalent commercial effect in response to actions that would have been inconsistent with this Agreement but for paragraph 1." In short, American economic retaliation is not precluded. The supporters of the FTA argue that the Agreement addresses only goods and services, not culture, and therefore that the protection of Canadian culture is not threatened. Opponents argue that the exemption of cultural industries does not mean that the Agreement will be without cultural impact. For their part, Americans insist that "goods and services" includes culture, and that cultural industries cannot be distinguished analytically from other forms of commercial enterprise.

In concluding this discussion, it should be stressed that American cultural influences flow entirely from private sources. The American *government* has not been involved, except when its help has been enlisted by private American interests affected by Canadian regulations. Here, Henry Luce of *Time* magazine and border television broadcasters provide two prominent examples. It should also be stressed that restrictions on the inflow of American culture necessarily restrict the freedom of Canadians to watch, read, and listen to whatever they like, just as public support for cultural industries necessarily entails government interven-

Globe and Mail, June 25, 1988, p. D6.

tion in the marketplace. Cultural nationalism thus protects collective values—the survival of a distinctive national culture—through the curtailment of individual freedom, much as Quebec language policy protects a collective value—the survival of the French language—through similarly modest restrictions on individual freedom. The limited tolerance of Canadians for such curtailment in turn limits the potential height of cultural barriers between Canada and the United States. Cultural barriers are analogous to economic tariffs; we all pay a modest price while a few—recording artists, film and television producers, and so forth—reap substantial benefits. This creates both a vigorous lobby for cultural nationalism and countervailing consumer pressure for freer trade in cultural artifacts.

It is one of the ironies of Canadian life that more effective cultural barriers exist between the linguistic communities within Canada than between Canada and the United States. While technological change has eroded cultural barriers between Canada and the United States, it has done little to erode the language barriers within Canada. Even the CBC, with its mandate to foster national unity, operates through linguistically differentiated organizations (Radio Canada is the francophone voice) which have little in common. Arthur Siegel concludes that "the structural arrangement within CBC encourages the 'two solitudes' of Canada, reinforcing differences in outlook by such creative elements as journalists and entertainment producers rather than bridging them," and that, more generally, "television has played an almost insignificant role in explaining the French and English societies to each other."[41] Thus modern technology may erode cultural differences between Canada and the United States while strengthening cultural differences within Canada. In either case, government intervention is a minor factor, at best, in the tendency of a common language to unite and different languages to divide.

BORDER DISPUTES

John Holmes has written that "the great epic of North America is not the sharing of a continent; we only share a border."[42] It should come as no surprise, however, that sharing a border has given rise to numerous disputes. Given the simple length of the border, and given that it crosses the Great Lakes and is crossed in turn by rivers and winds, the potential for environmental conflict alone is staggering. As Arthur Meighen, former leader of the national Conservative party, stated in a 1937 address on Canadian–American relations, "we are not in the same boat but we are pretty much in the same waters." Border disputes, then, are bound to provide a source of ongoing irritation between the two national communities. And yet, perhaps because they are inevitable, border disputes rarely disrupt the broader Canadian–American relationship. The border exists primarily as a state of mind, and only secondarily as a physical demarcation with its own unique set of problems.

It should also come as no surprise that the national impact of border disputes is asymmetrical. Although 90 percent of Canadians live within 300 kilometres of the border, the American population is broadly dispersed well south of the border region. Few even moderately large American cities are close to the border, whereas Montreal, Kingston, Toronto, Hamilton, Windsor, and Vancouver are almost within a proverbial stone's throw of the United States. Thus, border disputes such as that over acid rain may potentially touch most Canadians, while *relatively* few Americans are affected. For most Americans, the Canadian–American border and the disputes it generates have about as much relevance to their immediate lives as does the border separating Portugal and Spain.

Over the years border disputes have taken a variety of forms, with those relating to water predominating. Disputes over off-shore fisheries have been present since the Convention of 1818 set limits on the right of Americans to fish in British North American waters. With the extension of national control over coastal waters from 5 to 20 kilometres in 1970, and to 320 kilometres in 1977, disputes concerning overlapping fishing claims and the need to manage a diminishing resource were further compounded. On the Pacific coast, for example, the inability of the two countries to reach an agreement on salmon fisheries stems, in large part, from a dispute on whether or not fish stocks should be conserved. The Canadian government has spent millions on salmon propagation and habitat enhancement, and favours reduced fishing quotas to protect both salmon stocks and the survival of the salmon industry in Canada. According to Stephen Clarkson, "American fishermen have retained a free market approach to fisheries, claiming that an exhaustion of the stocks will automatically reduce the number of vessels in the fishery and so allow the fish population to regenerate itself."[43] It should also be noted, however, that contemporary fishing disputes with the United States pale in importance when compared to those between Canada and the European Community.

Disagreements over the precise location of the international border still persist. A seven-year dispute over the maritime boundary through the Gulf of Maine was finally taken to the International Court of Justice in the Hague. At issue was fishing access to Georges Bank, an area rich in scallops, cod, and halibut, upon which some 3,500 Canadian fishing jobs depend. Canada had claimed about a third of Georges Bank, while the United States had claimed it all. On October 12, 1984, the International Court fixed a boundary giving Canada about one-sixth of Georges Bank. By prior agreement between Canada and the United States, the new boundary is binding on both sides and cannot be appealed. Other boundary disputes are still outstanding. There is disagreement, for example, on where to set the maritime boundary in the Arctic's Beaufort Sea, a boundary that could affect national ownership of offshore oil resources associated with the Prudhoe Bay oil field in Alaska. Maritime disputes of a more environmental character have arisen over the passage of American oil tankers among the Arctic Islands and down the Strait of Juan de Fuca between Vancouver Island and the British Columbia mainland.

On the continent, the management of shared river basins has been contentious at times. Hydro-electric development of the Columbia River Basin in Washington State touched off a 42-year argument over the potential flooding of the Skagit River Valley, running northwards into

British Columbia. The dispute was finally settled in 1984 when the Canadian and American governments signed an 80-year treaty prohibiting the flooding of Canadian land in exchange for a Canadian guarantee of extra electrical power to Seattle. For Manitobans, the planned Garrison Diversion irrigation project, which would irrigate 1.5 million acres in North Dakota, has been a source of conflict since it was first proposed in 1965. The Garrison diversion would introduce water from the Missouri River into Canada's Hudson Bay river basin, and thus transfer foreign fish, micro-organisms, and pollutants that could damage Manitoba's fishing industry. Looking ahead, a growing water shortage in the American Southwest is likely to reactivate American interest in massive water-diversion projects to move "unused" Canadian water south across the border. The supporters of one such project, the 1963 North American Water and Power Alliance, proposed spending $150 billion to send Canadian water south through the Rocky Mountain Trench.

In recent decades, environmental border disputes have become more common in the wake of greater environmental degradation and stronger environmental lobbies on both sides of the border. Disputes have ranged from efforts to clean up the Great Lakes to the construction of the world's largest garbage incinerator in Detroit. In the latter case, Ontario has protested that the incinerator, which will burn 2,000 tonnes of garbage a day to provide heat and electricity for the Detroit area, does not contain adequate air pollution control devices. The overriding environmental issue, however, has been the damage to Canadian lakes and rivers stemming from acid rain. Although Canadian industrial emissions of sulphur dioxide contribute substantially to the acid rain problem in Canada, industries and utility plants in the Ohio Valley states (Indiana, Illinois, Ohio, and Pennsylvania) also play a substantial role through emissions carried hundreds of kilometres north into Canada by prevailing winds. Canadian emissions contribute to the acid rain problem in the New England states, and Americans have expressed concern about environmental damage arising from the Inco smelter in Sudbury, and from Canadian thermal-power plants at Poplar River, Saskatchewan, and Atikokan, Ontario. Yet on balance, and due in large part to the pattern of prevailing winds, the northward drift of acid rain across the international border appears to exceed the southward drift by a margin of three or four to one.

Acid rain proved to be a particularly troublesome issue during the presidency of Ronald Reagan. Repeated Canadian calls for joint action on acid rain were met with indifference by the American administration, or at most with the response that the issue warranted further scientific study before an appropriate policy response could be formulated. While Canadian research teams repeatedly stressed the environmental hazards of acid rain, American research teams tended to produce more equivocal results. In short, little headway was made throughout most of the 1980s despite concerted efforts by the Canadian government. Then, in June 1989, President George Bush unveiled a major acid rain initiative that went a long way towards meeting Canadian environmental concerns and standards. The Bush initiative was part of a more comprehensive clean-air package which, at the time of writing, had yet to receive Congressional approval. If the initiative survives its passage through Congress, something which cannot be guaranteed, then a major irritant in the Canadian–American relationship will have been assuaged.

American reluctance to address the problem of acid rain helped convince many Canadians that American environmental standards were lower than those in Canada, and were less rigorously enforced. This in turn led to some apprehension concerning the Free Trade Agreement which, with the passage of time, can be expected to harmonize environmental standards north and south of the border. To the extent that this occurs, Canadians can expect to do the harmonizing. However, the assumption that American environmental standards are lower is just that— an assumption. There is little evidence that Americans are less conscious of environmental degradation than are Canadians, or that they are less supportive of environmental standards. In the 1989 *Maclean's* survey mentioned earlier in this chapter, respondents were asked the following question: "Would you favor or oppose shutting down a major company that provided many jobs in your community if it was polluting the environment?" Sixty-four percent of the American respondents would favor shutting down the company, an option favored by 60 percent of the Canadian respondents.[45]

Other forms of border disputes are not uncommon: a rock star is denied entry into Canada for drug-related reasons, a union official is denied entry to the United States because of a criminal record, a tourist is subjected to apparently unnecessary harassment by customs officials. Yet such incidents, when placed against the millions of uneventful border crossings that occur every month, constitute an extremely minor source of irritation.

In 1909 Canada and the United States established the International Joint Commission (IJC) to deal with border-related issues arising from the Boundary Waters Treaty, signed in the same year. Canada and the United States are equally represented on the IJC, which is actually composed of a three member commission in each capital. The IJC is empowered to make recommendations to the respective national governments, rather than to *impose* solutions, but it can act as a judicial body if the two governments so decide. Although the IJC has been the principal institutional mechanism for handling border disputes, it has by no means supplanted more conventional diplomatic and political relations between Canada and the United States.

TRANSNATIONAL AND INTERGOVERNMENTAL RELATIONS

Canada and the United States are not unique in sharing an international border, but the border they share has some interesting and perhaps even unique features. It is an "international" border only in the most formal sense, as there is little perception that one's neighbours are "foreign" to any significant degree. The Canadian–American relationship is more familial than international; the international environment begins off-shore, somewhere beyond the North American continent. This feeling stems in part from the ease with which the border can be crossed and, in most cases, from the absence of geographical features which might reinforce the political boundary. It also stems from the multitude of linkages which span the border, tying together families, friends, business associates, corporations, trade unions, professional associations, fraternal societies, voluntary organizations, and sports leagues. Even in its physical characteristics, the Canadian–American border is not like the international borders North Americans are likely to encounter in films, news reports, and spy novels. If it is not quite a domestic border, it is certainly domesticated.

Canadian–American relations are primarily *transnational* rather than *international* in character, transnational being defined as "contacts, coalitions, and interactions across state boundaries that are not controlled by the central foreign policy organs of government."[46] Transnational relations encompass interactions among a vast array of private actors, which by their sheer volume overwhelm intergovernmental relations. The American penetration of Canada, around which so much of the Canadian-American relationship revolves, has been almost entirely non-governmental in character, which may account for the lack of more acute Canadian concern.[47]

The dominance of transnational interaction is reflected in the lack, and indeed the impossibility, of any coherent "American policy" in Ottawa or "Canadian policy" in Washington. Even though Canadian–American relations are Canada's most important foreign policy concern, they are simply too vast and involve too many issues and actors to be neatly packaged within a single policy perspective. Thus when Ottawa published a major review of foreign policy options in 1970, Canadian policy towards the United States was only obliquely addressed.[48] Nor is any greater coherence readily apparent in American policy towards Canada. As Robert Keohane and Joseph Nye point out:

> Neither country has found it possible to list formally, with meaningful consensus, its priorities toward the other in any specific form. It could not be done without simultaneously applying corresponding priorities to aspects of domestic policy, and consequently to constituent groups. . . . [49]

Canada and the United States are more affected by each other's domestic policies than by their respective foreign policies. The American deregulation of natural gas prices, for example, has had a marked impact on Canadian gas exports, just as American air pollution standards have an impact upon Canadian problems with acid rain. American events entirely within the private domain ripple through Canadian life as American cultural patterns, entertainment trends, and consumer developments wash ashore in Canada. Particularly on the Canadian side of the fence, Canadian–American relations touch upon so many aspects of Canadian life, and are therefore so entangled with both national and provincial governments, that they can often be seen as an extension of Canadian domestic politics rather than as a form of international relations.

Nonetheless, it is important not to lose sight of the international dimension. While in many respects the two countries have a "special relationship" that falls outside the boundaries of conventional international relations, they also interact with one another as they interact with other states. *Intergovernmental* relations remain important, and there is no evidence, even in the most embryonic form, of an emerging continental state that would supplant the international relationship. Even with the Free Trade Agreement in place, there are no institutions which imply, to use Ball's phrase, "a progressively expanding area of common political decision." As John Redekop concludes, " . . . North American integration, such as it is, remains a low-level, uncoordinated, almost haphazard phenomenon. . . . "[50] Here John Holmes argues that the rules, commitments, and institutions which govern the bilateral relationship are not intended to bring the two countries closer together. On the contrary, their purpose " . . . is to regulate forces which, unless a Canadian place is staked out, would inevitably erode our sovereignty and our identity."[51]

Before the appointment of Vincent Massey as the first Canadian minister to Washington, Canadian affairs were handled by the British embassy. Since that appointment, Canada has maintained a vigorous diplomatic presence in the American capital, a presence recently expanded through a new embassy building and a $650,000 lobbying campaign. The use of Congressional lobbyists—paid professionals who keep their fingers on the pulse of the American Congress, alerting Canadian officials to both threats and opportunities and presenting Canadian views to Washington politicians—is a diplomatic response to both the complexity of American government and the impact that congressional legislation can have on Canadian interests. The point to be stressed is that intergovernmental contact alone between the Canadian Department of External Affairs and the American State Department cannot sufficiently protect Canadian interests. Increasingly, some direct penetration of the congressional arena is being sought.

Apart from the lobbying efforts of the Canadian embassy, there are over fifty "foreign agents" representing Canadian interests in the United States.[52] This rather melodramatic term for what are generally law firms, public relations agencies, or specialists in governmental affairs comes from the need for such lobbyists to register with the U.S. Department of Justice under the Foreign Agents Registration Act. The agents represent a variety of interests: private firms; industry organizations such as the Canadian Softwood Lumber Committee, the Canadian Manufacturers' Association, and the Independent Petroleum Association of Canada; public interest groups such as the Canadian Coalition on Acid Rain; provincial trade offices in the United States; provincial departments such as Ontario's Ministry of the Environment; and federal agencies such as the National Film Board of Canada. In all cases their tasks are essentially the same: warning clients about potentially harmful congressional legislation—legislation that often arises in response to private American interests and not to policy initiatives from the President or from the State Department—and presenting their clients' case within the American legislative process.

This lobbying activity reflects a fact of American political life: the U.S. State Department cannot guarantee congressional support for bilateral deals struck with Canada. The American Senate, unlike the Senate in Canada, must approve any treaties negotiated by the executive branch. Senators can thus use the threat of veto to force modifications in the terms of treaties brought before them. Therefore, if Canadian interests are to be protected, Canadians must be prepared to wade into congressional combat on their own behalf and not rely on the State Department alone to carry the Canadian flag. In a somewhat analogous development, provincial governments are increasingly active participants in Canadian–American relations. They too are unwilling to let External Affairs carry the flags of provincial interest. Thus, premiers engage in frequent political sorties to Washington, New York, and the capitals of border states, while provincial trade offices in the United States continue to expand in number and scope.

The American embassy in Ottawa, like its Canadian counterpart in Washington, is not involved in the great bulk of Canadian–American transnational interactions. Only rarely do American multinationals seek backing from the United States government in disputes with Canadian governments.[53] In the early 1980s, admittedly, American ambassadors were more prone to publicly criticize Canadian domestic policies, a change in diplomatic style that was also evident for Canadian ambassadors in the United States. In more recent years, ambassadorial commentary has once again become more subdued.

In many ways Canadian–American relations resemble a vast seamless web. For this reason, it is easy for issues and disputes to become entangled with one another. Somewhat paradoxically, this very interdependence of issues traditionally led to a mutual avoidance of "linkage politics"—a situation in which the settlement of one issue is tied to, or is dependent upon, the settlement of other, often substantively unrelated issues. As John Holmes has pointed out, not only have Canadians sensed that "linkage was a game that would inevitably be won by the stronger power," but that "the American government machine was too incoherent to formulate a coordinated Canadian policy in which fish or pork would be bargained for gas or relations with Cuba."[54] However, Stephen Clarkson argues that, in the early 1980s, Congress embraced linkage politics, retaliating in one sector of the bilateral relationship when American interests were hurt in another.[55] Canada, Clarkson suggests, should also embrace linkage politics in order to knit together a more coherent stance towards the bilateral relationship.

PLAYING WITH FIRE
Jeffrey Simpson,
The Globe and Mail, February 17, 1988

Linkage, which sometimes exists in the real world, is a strategy both Canada and the United States have tried hard to avoid in their bilateral dealings. The explanation for this avoidance is simple: relations are so extensive, complicated and close that linking issues would soon become a nightmare. If we don't like their farm policy, we decide to be ornery about energy. If they don't like that, they get nasty about our defence spending. And so on.

It is also in the interests of the smaller country in a bilateral relationship to avoid linkage, since linkage is essentially a power play—if you don't do what we want on this issue, we'll make life difficult for you on other issues. Unfortunately, Canada's capacity to make life difficult for the Americans is considerably less than their ability to do us harm. So linkage is a perilous game for Canada.

It is also a difficult game to play with the United States, given that country's division of powers. Even if we can turn the administration to our way of thinking, there is no guarantee that the Congress will agree. If we threaten the administration, we are implicitly insisting that it deliver the Congress, something a president would love to do but sometimes cannot.

Despite the ten-to-one difference in population and economic power, Canada has not fared badly in the bilateral relationship. Canadians have not won on all issues, but certainly win more frequently than the odds might predict. This success has encouraged a strategy of "quiet diplomacy," through which Canadians protect their "special relationship" with the United States by refraining from public criticism of American world leadership. And yet American activities in the international arena impact directly upon long-term Canadian interests, including the avoidance of nuclear war. As a consequence, the norms of quiet diplomacy can be strained when Canada is drawn into international disputes in which Canadian and American interests, or world views, do not coincide.

INTERNATIONAL RELATIONS AND MILITARY DEFENCE

Although Canada is not a major international power, she has been an active international player since the Second World War. Through participation in the United Nations, including its peace-keeping forces and specialized agencies such as the UN World Food Program and UNESCO, and through multilateral organizations such as GATT, the North Atlantic Treaty Organization (NATO), the British Commonwealth and the International Emergency Food Reserve, Canada has made and continues to make important contributions to the international order.

International involvement beyond the North American continent can take many forms, all of which may heighten the sense of belonging to a distinctive national community. It may be as personal as travelling abroad, wearing the maple leaf on the back of one's jeans, and taking pride that strangers recognize the symbol and are able to distinguish Canadians from Americans. It may come through international hockey competition as Canadian teams challenge and, alas, too often fail to beat the world's best. It may involve governmental participation in international organizations, participation that provides a valuable counterweight in our bilateral relationship with the United States. As John Holmes explains, "Canadian governments, if not always the Canadian people, have recognized that international institutions . . . are essential for a country our size to act effectively vis-à-vis a great power."[56] The assertion of Canadian sovereignty in the international arena thus protects Canadian sovereignty in the bilateral relationship with the United States. It is interesting to note, however, that the United States, like Canada, is willing to use international institutions such as GATT to provide leverage on the bilateral relationship.

While international activity may strengthen Canada's continental position, such activity is also heavily encumbered by the Canadian–American relationship. The two countries share many important characteristics which propel them, willy-nilly, into the same international camp: both are western, northern, non-socialist and industrialized states, linked together in a continental trading system. Where they differ dramatically is that the United States is a superpower with a global set of strategic interests, obligations, and entanglements that Canada shares only to a limited degree. Thus, in the eyes of other nations, Canada may be seen primarily as a supporting actor to the United States and as a smaller and weaker younger brother in the international schoolyard.

Canada is firmly and unavoidably in the American military camp, for in any nuclear exchange the two countries would be a common continental target. In the Ogdensburg Declaration of June, 1940, Canada and the United States declared that the "defence of the two countries constituted a single problem," a declaration backed by the establishment of the Permanent Joint Board of Defence to provide a common forum for the discussion and coordination of continental defence. In 1941 the two countries signed the Hyde Park Agreement, which all but erased the border as far as defence production was concerned.[57] The 1959 Defence Production Sharing Agreements updated and expanded the Hyde Park Agreement by allowing Canadian firms to compete without handicap for American defence contracts. Given that Canada requires modern weapons of war, that these have become too costly to produce for Canada's use alone, and that success as an international arms dealer may be both economically difficult and morally repugnant, the arrangement with the United States allows Canada to at least share in the economic benefits of defence production. Over the first twenty years of the DPS agreements, American military procurements in Canada totalled $5,195 million while Canadian procurements in the United States totalled $5,535 million.[58]

Canada, with the United States, is a member of NATO, and since 1958 has been a partner with the United States in the North American Air Defence Command (NORAD), rechristened the North American *Aerospace* Defence Command in March 1981. Over the years NORAD's importance has declined with the diminished threat of a Soviet bomber attack. NORAD's atrophy has shifted the focus of Canadian defence strategy from the bilateral Canadian–American relationship, in which the United States was overwhelmingly dominant, to the multilateral forum of NATO.

Canada's military alliance with the United States reflects not only her continental location but also a basic agreement between Canadians and Americans on the desired shape of the international order. Yet, even if that agreement did not exist, Canada would still lie across the northern flank of the United States. If Canadians were not prepared to defend that flank, the United States would have no choice but to do so itself. Thus, the Canadian military not only defends Canada against potential foreign aggression, but also defends Canadian political sovereignty from the United States. In this "defence against help," we encounter what has been termed the "sovereignty paradox." To protect its sovereignty, Canada must participate in bilateral defence arrangements with the United States, arrangements which in turn restrict Canadian sovereignty, given that Canada will be a junior, not equal, partner.[59] Fortunately, the diminished bomber threat and technological advances in satellite surveillance, over-the-horizon radar systems, and airborne warning-and-control systems (AWACS) have all but eliminated the need for an American military presence on Canadian soil. At the same time and for the same reasons, Canadians have even less leverage on American defence policy than they had in the past.

A Common Defence Policy?

In the 1989 *Maclean's* survey of 1,000 Canadians and 1,000 American respondents, Canadians showed little enthusiasm for a common defence policy (*Maclean's*, July 3, 1989, p. 49). Respondents were asked the following question: "Would you strongly support, support, oppose or strongly oppose Canada and the United States adopting common and identical policy on all matters relating to defence and foreign affairs?"

	Canada	United States
Strongly oppose	24%	4%
Oppose	36	19
Support	33	58
Strongly support	5	15
No opinion	2	3

Despite the basic complementarity of national views, conflicts between Canada and the United States over military policy are not uncommon. At times Canada is accused of spending too little on defence or, more specifically, of making an insufficient military contribution to NATO. In proportionate terms, Canada's contribution to NATO ranks above only those of Luxembourg and Iceland, and only Luxembourg spends a smaller proportion of its gross domestic product on defence. In 1988, the size of Canada's armed forces, as a proportion of the national labour force, reached its lowest level (0.9 percent) in fifty years. Here it is useful to note that the gulf between Canadian and American defence expenditures is immense. In early 1984, for example, President Ronald Reagan asked Congress to approve $313.4 billion in defence spending, an increase of $48.1 billion from the previous year. The *increase alone* was approximately six times the *entire* Canadian defence budget! In rough terms, American military expenditures are forty times those of Canada.

In the late 1950s and early 1960s, disagreement arose between the two countries and within Canada over the acquisition of nuclear weapons for Canadian interceptor aircraft and anti-aircraft missiles (the Bomarc) based in Canada and with Canadian forces in Europe. Progressive Conservative Prime Minister John Diefenbaker came to symbolize nationalist resistance to American military policy, a resistance that extended to Canada's delay in putting her forces on alert during the 1962 Cuban missile crisis. The nuclear weapons issue played a significant role in the 1963 general election, in which the pro-warhead Liberals defeated the Conservatives to form a minority government. The warheads were subsequently installed, although they remained under American control. In the early 1970s the warheads were withdrawn, leaving the Canadian forces without nuclear weapons of any sort.

American military intervention abroad has often provoked public and, more rarely, government criticism in Canada. American involvement in the Vietnam war received a generally negative press in Canada, although official opposition to the war was both muted and, if expressed, resented in the United States. When Prime Minister Pearson criticized the American bombing of North Vietnam in a 1965 speech at Temple University, President Lyndon Johnson bluntly rebuked Pearson, saying "you peed on my carpet."[60] More recently, the 1983 American invasion of Grenada, an island in the Caribbean, was widely criticized in Canada. Incidents like the Grenada invasion demonstrate some significant national differences in perceptions of the communist threat and in preferred strategies for coping with that threat. In comparison to the United States, Canada has attached less importance to the global threat of communism than has the United States, and has generally opposed military intervention as a response to communist threats in the Third World. Such incidents also provide the Canadian government with the opportunity to put some distance between Canada and the United States on the international stage without undermining the broader strategic principles of American foreign policy.

During 1983 and 1984 there was considerable protest in Canada over the testing of the cruise missile guidance system in northern Alberta. To some, the cruise testing implicated Canada in the international arms race and impaired the prospects for arms reduction, a nuclear freeze, and world peace. For others, the testing was seen as a modest contribution to a strengthened nuclear deterrent, and therefore to nuclear stability and world peace. Perhaps more importantly, it was also seen as a necessary fulfillment of Canadian alliance commitments under NATO. In a open letter to Canadians published in newspapers across the country on May 10, 1983, Prime Minister Trudeau stressed the alliance commitment:

> It is hardly fair to rely on the Americans to protect the West, but to refuse to lend them a hand when the going gets rough. In that sense, the anti-Americanism of some Canadians verges on hypocrisy. They're eager to take refuge under the American umbrella, but don't want to help hold it.

Foreign policy conflict between Canada and the United States has been primarily over the appropriate means to common ends, rather than over those ends per se. The question remains, however, as to just how much independence Canada enjoys on the international stage. A firm answer would require a situation in which Canada and the United States had clearly conflicting international interests, and in which Canada's pursuit of her own interests would be actively opposed by the United States. To date, such conflicts have not emerged and, given that the two countries have so much in common, they are unlikely to emerge in the years to come. In the absence of such a test, Canadians may be too quick to assume that Canadian sovereignty is tightly constrained.

Canada's history has been intimately tied to the two great English-speaking countries of the world, and two of the world's great imperial states. When British influence waned in Canada and around the world during the twentieth century, that of the United States waxed. It is not surprising, then, that Canada's colonial past has been used to model Canada's relationship with the United States. Harold Innis, Canada's most famous economic historian, first described Canada's progression from a British colony, to a brief period of national independence bounded by the two world wars, and then to a new colonial relationship with the United States. Historian Donald Creighton has written that, as Canada was growing apart from Great Britain, her " . . . links with the United States became so numerous and so powerful that they threatened to convert the nation into a political vassal, an economic tributary, and a cultural colony of the American Empire."[61] Walter Gordon, then President of the Privy Council, developed the colonial theme in a 1967 interview:

> During the last fifty years we have freed ourselves of traces of colonial status insofar as Britain is concerned. But having achieved our independence from Britain, we seem to have slipped, almost without knowing it into a semi-dependent position in relation to the United States.[62]

The colonial model is meant to be more than descriptive; it also embodies a sense of anger and despair. To quote again from Gordon's 1967 interview, " . . . it is sadly ironic that in a world torn asunder by countries who are demanding and winning their independence, our free, independent and highly developed country should be haunted by the spectre of a colonial or semi-colonial future."[63] It should be stressed, however, that the colonial model understates Canada's political independence. It fails to recognize the lack of continental political institutions, while at the same time directing insufficient attention to non-governmental relations. It may also understate the common values that work to integrate the Canadian and American societies, and which lead many Canadians to embrace the continental relationship. To the extent that a colonial relationship does exist, it has been largely self-imposed. As John Redekop points out, " . . . if the Canadian–American relationship constitutes colonialism, it must surely be the strangest colonial relationship extant."[64]

Redekop goes on to offer a comprehensive survey of concepts that have been used to model the Canadian–American relationship, concepts which include domination, dependency, partnership, interdependence, hegemony, continentalism, satellite, client state, neo-colonialism, and "continental subsystemic dominance," his own preference. Canada has also been described as an American hinterland, a term that suggests interesting parallels between Canadian–American relations and regionalism within Canada. Clearly the relationship can be modelled in many different ways, each of which directs our attention to different aspects of

Prime Minister Brian Mulroney leads the chorus in singing an Irish song on stage with his wife and U.S. President Ronald Reagan and First Lady Nancy Reagan at the conclusion of a 1985 gala performance in Quebec City.

The Canadian Press.

the relationship, and each of which distorts the reality of the relationship in different ways. Perhaps the most ubiquitous term, at least in American usage, has been "neighbors." Here it is worth citing at length a passage by James Eayrs that has retained its relevance through the years:

> If the Canadian–American relationship is to flourish to the mutual benefit of its partners, it will be because statesmen of both countries resist the temptation . . . of believing their politics to be neighbourly rather than international. They must realize that the two nations of North America are of the states-system, not beyond and above it, and shape their policies accordingly. President Johnson, with the best intentions in the world, observed . . . that "Canada is such a close neighbor and such a good neighbor that we always have plenty of problems there. They are kind of like problems in the

hometown." They are kind of not like that at all. They are the problems not of neighbours but of friendly foreign powers.[65]

CANADIAN NATIONALISM AND THE UNITED STATES

One of the best summaries of the Canadian–American relationship came in a speech to the House of Commons (February 4, 1963) by Robert Thompson, leader of the Social Credit Party. "The Americans," Thompson declared, "are our best friends whether we like it or not." Of course, if Canadians were able to choose their continental neighbour, most would choose the United States. It is ironic, then, that no country poses a greater threat to Canada's survival as a distinct and independent national community. It is because the United States is Canada's best friend that it is also Canada's "worst enemy."

Support for Political Union

In the 1989 Maclean's survey, respondents were asked if they would favour or oppose "Canada becoming the 51st state of the United States with full congressional representation and rights of American citizenship." As the following results show, there was little support for political union among the 1,000 Canadian respondents.

	Canada	United States
Strongly oppose	54%	10%
Oppose	31	22
Favour	12	54
Strongly favour	2	12
No opinion	1	3

It is interesting to note that support for union was highest (23 percent) in Quebec. It is also interesting to speculate on how respondents might have reacted to the prospect of Canada forming not the 51st state, but the 51st through 60th states; would Canadians be more enthusiastic and Americans less?

Nationalism has two components that are generally accepted as both core and universal elements: in-group loyalty, or patriotism, and out-group hostility towards other nationalities. Hans Kohn, in what has become a classic work on nationalism, stressed the "doublefaced" nature of nationalism: "intranationally, it leads to a lively sympathy with all fellow members within the nationality; internationally, it finds expression in indifference to or distrust and hate of fellow men outside the national orbit."[66] Although this conceptualization is not without its limitations,[67] it does identify the important role played by anti-Americanism in Canadian nationalism.

Survival vis-à-vis the United States has been a central theme of English Canadian nationalism,[68] just as *la survivance* has been a central theme of French Canadian nationalism. Not surprisingly, that quest for survival has often found expression in anti-Americanism. What is perhaps more surprising is that there is no American counterpart to the anti-Americanism one finds in Canada, no "anti-Canadianism" that can be tapped by political actors. For their part, Canadians are aggravated by the American indifference to things Canadian, by the too-ready assumption that Canadians and Americans are essentially the same under their different national skins. Northrop Frye links this reaction to Canadian fears about annexation, arguing that what is resented

> ... is not annexation itself, but the feeling that Canada would disappear into a larger entity without having anything of any real distinctiveness to contribute to that entity: that, in short, if the United States did annex Canada it would notice nothing except an increase in its natural resources.[69]

To be disliked is one thing; to be ignored is something else entirely.

As Canada's closest neighbour, the United States necessarily becomes the mirror in which Canadians see themselves. As a consequence, Canadian nationalism waxes and wanes in response to conditions in the United States as much as in response to conditions in Canada. In the distant past, the strength of Canadian nationalism was sapped by the national comparison. When Canadians looked at their own country they saw a poorer, colder, less developed, and less vibrant United States. They saw Americans with overshoes and colds, a country whose national symbol was not the soaring eagle but rather a large rodent noted for its ability to run for cover. Canadian nationalism thus seemed an irrational emotion that flew in the face of any objective national comparison. It was not coincidental, then, that Canadian nationalism bloomed during the 1960s when the American society was experiencing deep distress. Looking south at racial conflict, a spiralling crime rate, deteriorating cities, student unrest, and the horror of the Vietnam war as well as drawing upon radical American critiques of the American society, Canadians could objectively and somewhat smugly conclude that life was better in Canada than it was in the United States.

WITH A LITTLE HELP FROM OUR FRIENDS...
The Globe and Mail, April 10, 1984, p. 6

The annual strawberry festival with which Portage La Prairie, Man., reinforces its claim to be the "Strawberry Capital of Canada" will be held in June—just far enough ahead of the season that organizers will be relying on strawberries imported from the United States.

Meanwhile, the Nova Scotian Government's $300,000 television special to promote tourism will be counting on footage shot in Bermuda to give it that summery look.

Will this rampant nationalism never subside?

"I do hope Americans don't think of us as ugly Canadians... stuffy, dull, slow, mundane, colorless, bland, self-righteous hypocrites... but not ugly."

Len Norris, *The Vancouver Sun*

Canada looked good and Canadian nationalism was strong because things looked so much worse in the United States. As Canadian Senator John Nicol somewhat unkindly observed, just as Americans "... have seen their sense of destiny falter, we have picked up the torch of plastic nationalism and are dashing off at a dead run."[70] This dependency means, however, that any improvement in American conditions can have a corrosive impact on Canadian nationalism. The price of a healthy America is self-doubt among Canadians as to the worth of an independent country on the northern tier of the continent. Furthermore, to the extent that Canadian nationalism feeds off blemishes on the American society, Canadians may be too tolerant of blemishes on their own society and remain too unaware of the excellence Canada has attained. It is here that Canada suffers from having but a single point of national comparison, and that being perhaps the wealthiest and most powerful country in the world. As Margaret Atwood points out:

> One of Canada's problems is that it's always comparing itself to the wrong thing. If you stand beside a giant, of course you tend to feel a little stunted.[71]

An ironic feature of Canadian nationalism comes from the patriotic pride Canadians take in the very *weakness* of their nationalism. The more fervent displays of American nationalism, such as one encounters during halftime shows in college football games, are often denigrated by Canadians who refuse to sing their own national anthem in public, or who would like to sing but are no longer sure of the words. Moving beyond the American comparison per se, John Meisel has discussed the absence of a vigorous and active nationalism in Canada, "an absence, incidentally, which in the eyes of many who have elsewhere experienced the parochialism and inhumanity of chauvinism, bestows on Canada one of its most attractive characteristics."[72] While this point is well taken, the question remains whether Canadian nationalism is sufficiently strong to counterbalance the centrifugal forces inherent in a regionally diverse national community.

The United States has been the source of new and at times disruptive political ideas since the arrival of the United Empire Loyalists. Prior to the 1837 rebellions, radical reformers in both Upper Canada—the Clear Grits—and Lower Canada—the supporters of Louis-Joseph Papineau—drew much of their political inspiration from the United States, just as the later agrarian radical reformers in the Canadian West drew upon American populist thought. As James Mallory points out, "Canada has been nourished by the same stream of constitutional ideas, and in many respects, the same constitutional atmosphere, as the United States."[73] At the same time, there has been a countervailing reluctance to imitate American political institutions. Wise and Brown argue that "the real puzzle in the history of Canadian ideas about the United States is why the bulk of Canadians, standing on the very threshold of liberty, were so little susceptible to American institutions, a seeming contradiction of nature, environment, and proximity."[74] It was a contradiction, they claim, with an unfortunate impact on Canada:

> the urgent necessity for a small people, in the overwhelming presence of a supremely confident neighbour, to insist not merely upon their separateness and distinctiveness, but even upon their intrinsic political and moral superiority, had a paralytic effect upon the Canadian mind and upon the quality of Canadian thought. The rigidities established by the compulsion to maintain identity narrowed the range of political debate, channeled political thought along familiar paths, and discouraged the venturesome, the daring, and the

"Your problem of course is that you're too nationalistic . . . "

Roy Peterson, *The Vancouver Sun.*

rash. There is an imprecision and superficiality, a lack of progression and proliferation, about Canadian thought with respect to the United States that mirrors the general state of Canadian political thought in this era.[75]

Although one would have to be cautious in projecting this assessment of late nineteenth century Canada onto the contemporary political scene, one might argue that we have not been sufficiently attentive to the American experience in coping with political conflict in a vast, transcontinental society more like Canada than any other in the world.[76]

Canadian–American relations have often intensified regional and intergovernmental conflict in Canada. The tariffs of Macdonald's National Policy, designed to promote industrial development, soon became an enduring symbol of regional discontent, one associated with exacerbated provincialism and regional conflict:

The alleged "unfairness" of the tariff has always served as a potent argument for spokesmen, mainly provincial politicians, from the non-manufacturing regions of Canada when they have been seeking measures to promote their own self-interest. The resulting rampant regionalism has been antithetical to Confederation.... [77]

Canadian–American relations have also been entangled with the relationship between the English- and French-speaking communities. Lacking an effective language barrier with the United States, English Canadian nationalists have sought to erect economic and cultural barriers. Such endeavours, because they necessitate a relatively strong and activist federal government, have been viewed with suspicion by Quebec. Although English Canadian attempts to fend off assimilationist pressures from the United States parallel Québécois attempts to fend off assimilationist pressures from English-speaking North America, the two goals have at times come into conflict. When English Canadian nationalists promote a Canadian identity that obscures the French fact, such as occurred with John Diefenbaker's vision of "one Canada," they intensify the assimilationist threat to French Canada. Thus, while both Quebec and Ottawa have tried to build effective cultural walls, they have done so along quite different borders.

On the more positive side, French Canada makes a valuable contribution to English Canadian nationalism, as it is Canada's bilingual and bicultural character which, more than anything else, sets her apart from the United States. The question that arises is what English Canada has to offer French Canada in return. As Kari Levitt wrote in 1970, why should French Canadians

...remain within Confederation when the dominant English-Canadian majority appear to put such a low value on Canada's national independence? What is being offered? To wander hand-in-hand, biculturally and bilingually, into the gravitational orbit of the American empire?[78]

The catch is that a more vibrant Canadian nationality could itself pose a threat to French Canada if it does not fully embrace French Canadian culture and tradition.

In summary, Canadian–American relations are not only of intrinsic importance but they are also entangled with the other major strands of Canadian political life. Moreover, while conflict between Canada and the United States will wax and wane over time, and will shift in focus from one set of issues to another, it will never disappear. Nor will the debate within Canada between nationalist and continentalist options disappear. Canada's location on the North American continent ensures continued American penetration, and continued Canadian efforts both to embrace and resist that penetration.

Here it is useful to refer to a characterization of Canada advanced by

Mason Wade. Writing in 1964, Wade asserted that "Canada has always been a willed nation, existing despite the conscious and unconscious forces which have sought to absorb it into its much more populous and powerful neighbour."[79] The notion of a "willed nation" seems particularly powerful, even if it is by no means unique to the Canadian case. It points to the importance of nationalism in Canadian life, for it is by the strength of nationalism that we can measure the will of Canadians to resist a continental future. It also suggests that if the strength of Canadian nationalism is unduly sapped by regional conflict, if a national vision cannot be found that embraces the bilingual and bicultural realities of Canadian life, if political institutions fail to articulate a national interest that is truly national, then Canada's continued independence on the North American continent may be imperilled.

SUGGESTED READINGS

Charles F. Doran, *Forgotten Partnership: U.S.-Canada Relations Today* (Baltimore: John Hopkins University Press, 1984).

Terence J. Fay, "Canadian Studies on the American Relationship, 1945-1980," *The American Review of Canadian Studies*, XIII, 3 (Autumn 1983), p. 179-200. The appendix to this article contains a bibliography of 326 articles, books, and professional papers, grouped by historical period.

D.H. Flanerty and W.R. McKercher, eds., *Southern Exposure: Canadian Perspectives on the United States* (Toronto: McGraw-Hill Ryerson, 1986).

Marc Gold and David Leyton-Brown, eds., *Trade-Offs on Free Trade: The Canada-U.S. Free Trade Agreement* (Agincourt, Ontario: Carswell, 1988).

Alfred Olivier Hero, Jr. and Louis Balthazar, *Contemporary Quebec and the United States, 1960-1985* (Boston: University Press of America, 1988).

For an excellent overview of Canadian-American relations, see John W. Holmes, *Life with Uncle: The Canadian-American Relationship* (Toronto: University of Toronto Press, 1981); for a more extended treatment, see Graeme S. Mount and Edelgard Mahant, *An Introduction to Canadian-American Relations* (Toronto: Methuen, 1984).

For an analysis of the Auto Pact, see James F. Keeley, "Cast in Concrete for All Time? The Negotiation of the Auto Pact," *Canadian Journal of Political Science*, XVI: 2 (June, 1983), pp. 281-98.

For a classic and still insightful look at the American economic presence in Canada, see Kari Levitt, *Silent Surrender: The Multinational Corporation in Canada* (Toronto: Macmillan, 1970).

Although now twenty-five years old, George Grant's *Lament for a Nation: The Defeat of Canadian Nationalism* (Toronto: McClelland and Stewart, 1965) still provides a provocative ideological analysis of the Canadian-American relationship.

Glen Williams, *Not for Export: Toward a Political Economy of Canada's Arrested Industrialization* (Toronto: McClelland and Stewart, 1983).

STUDY QUESTIONS

1. In the early 1980s Francis Fox, at that time the federal minister responsible for Canadian communication policy, warned that by 1985 the spread of U.S. television channels through satellite delivery could make Canada "an occupied land, culturally." To what extent has this come to pass? To what extent can and should the Government of Canada impose controls on satellite reception by Canadian citizens? What risks do we run if such controls are not or cannot be imposed?
2. Where do you stand on the question of "free trade"? What are the political arguments that you would amass in defence of your position, and what are the political counter-arguments that you might expect?
3. To what extent, if any, might you expect residents of your own province to have a different perspective on Canadian–American relations than that held by the residents of other provinces? How would you explain such differences, should they exist?

NOTES

1. J. Barlet Brebner, *Canada: A Modern History* (Ann Arbor: University of Michigan Press, 1960), p. ix.
2. F.O. Matthiessen, *The Oxford Book of American Verse* (New York: Oxford University Press, 1950), pp. 547-48.
3. Dale Posgate and Kenneth McRoberts, *Quebec: Social Change and Political Crisis* (Toronto: McClelland & Stewart, 1976), p. 19.
4. A.R.M. Lower, *Colony to Nation* (London: 1953), p. 109.
5. J.M.S. Careless, *Canada: A Story of Challenge*, Revised Edition (Toronto: Macmillan, 1963), p. 113.
6. Cited in Joseph Barber, *Good Fences Make Good Neighbours* (Toronto: McClelland & Stewart, 1958), p. 31.
7. *Ibid.*, p. 31.
8. *The Globe*, June 1, 1871. Cited in S.F. Wise and Robert Craig Brown, *Canada Views the United States: Nineteenth-Century Political Attitudes* (Toronto: Macmillan, 1967), p. 109.

9. Olivar Asselin, *A Quebec View of Canadian Nationalism* (Montreal: 1909), p. 19.

10. Henri Bourassa, *Great Britain and Canada* (Montreal: 1901), p. 7.

11. Cited in Jonathon Green, compiler, *The Book of Political Quotes* (New York: McGraw-Hill, 1982), p. 59.

12. James Eayrs, "Sharing a Continent: The Hard Issues," in James Sloan Dickey, ed., *The United States and Canada* (Englewood Cliffs, N.J.: Prentice-Hall, 1964), p. 60.

13. Goldwin Smith, *Canada and the Canadian Question,* reprinted with an introduction by Carl Berger (Toronto: University of Toronto Press, 1971), pp. 223-24.

14. John W. Holmes, "In praise of national boundaries," *Saturday Night,* July 1974, p. 14.

15. Eayrs, "Sharing a Continent," p. 81.

16. Herbert Marshall, Frank Southard Jr., and Kenneth W. Taylor, *Canadian-American Industry* (Toronto: McClelland and Stewart, 1936, reprinted 1976), pp. 274-77.

17. H.G. Thorburn, *Planning and the Economy: Building Federal-Provincial Consensus* (Toronto: James Lorimer, 1984), pp. 11 and 119.

18. *Corporations and Labour Unions Returns Act, Report for 1985* (Ottawa: Supply and Services, 1988), p. 19.

19. Carl Berger, *The Sense of Power: Studies in the Ideas of Canadian Imperialism, 1867-1914* (Toronto: University of Toronto Press, 1970).

20. Denis Smith, "Political Parties and the Survival of Canada," in R. Kenneth Carty and W. Peter Ward, eds., *Entering the Eighties: Canada in Crisis* (Toronto: Oxford University Press, 1980), p. 139.

21. *Report of the Federal Petroleum Monitoring Agency,* August 1988.

22. For extensive graphic illustrations of the extent and character of foreign investment in Canada, see Nydia McCool, *Canadian Facts and Figures* (Edmonton: Hurtig, 1982), pp. 85ff.

23. Peter C. Newman, "The high cost of free trade," *Maclean's,* January 16, 1984, p. 38.

24. Kari Levitt, *Silent Surrender: The Multinational Corporation in Canada* (Toronto: Macmillan, 1970), p. 149.

25. George Ball, *Discipline of Power* (Boston: Little Brown & Company, 1968), p. 113.

26. *Eleventh Report of the Standing Committee on External Affairs and National Defence Respecting Canada-U.S. Relations* (Ottawa: Queen's Printer, 1970).

27. *Foreign Direct Investment in Canada* (Ottawa: Information Canada, 1972).

28. John W. Holmes, "Impact of Domestic Political Factors on Canadian-American Relations: Canada," in Annette Baker Fox, Alfred O. Hero, Jr., and Joseph S. Nye, Jr., eds., *Canada and the United States:*

Transnational and Transgovernmental Relations (New York: Columbia University Press, 1976), p. 25.

29. For a cross-national comparison, see Nicholas J. Patterson, "Canada–U.S. Foreign Investment Regulation: Transparency Versus Diffusion," in Earl H. Fry and Lee H. Radebaugh, eds., *Regulation of Foreign Direct Investment in Canada and the United States* (Salt Lake City: Brigham Young University, David M. Kennedy International Center, 1983), pp. 47-62.

30. Stephen Clarkson, *Canada and the Reagan Challenge: Crisis in the Canadian-American Relationship* (Toronto: James Lorimer, 1982), pp. 87ff.

31. George Grant, *Lament for a Nation: The Defeat of Canadian Nationalism* (Toronto: McClelland and Stewart, 1965), p. 15.

32. *Ibid.*, pp. 69-70.

33. See "The NDP 'Waffle' Manifesto: For an Independent Socialist Canada," in Paul Fox, ed., *Politics: Canada*, Third Edition (Toronto: McGraw-Hill, 1970), pp. 242-45.

34. Arthur Siegel, *Politics and the Media in Canada* (Toronto: McGraw-Hill Ryerson, 1983), p. 1.

35. Holmes, "In praise of national boundaries," p. 14.

36. Eayrs, "Sharing a Continent," p. 89.

37. Proclaimed in the summer of 1985, the Baie Comeau policy requires that Canadian-based and foreign-owned subsidiaries in the publishing industry must, if sold, divest 51 percent control to Canadian investors within two years of the takeover. The policy has not been enforced with a great deal of rigour or enthusiasm on the part of the federal government.

38. For a discussion of this debate as it relates to Canadian political science, see Alan C. Cairns, "Political Science in Canada and the Americanization Issue," *Canadian Journal of Political Science*, VIII, 2 (June 1975); and David P. Shugarman, "The Problems of the Reluctant Nationalist: A Comment on Alan Cairns," *CJPS*, IX, 1 (March 1976).

39. In 1980 Canadian universities awarded 403 PhDs in the social sciences (19 in political science) compared to 166 (7 in political science) in 1969/70. Thomas H.B. Symons and James E. Page, *Some Questions of Balance: Human Resources, Higher Education and Canadian Studies*, Vol. III of To Know Ourselves: The Report of the Commission on Canadian Studies, Association of Universities and Colleges of Canada, Ottawa, 1984, p. 114.

40. *Ibid.*, p. 58.

41. Siegel, *Politics and the Media*, p. 183. Siegel also shows (pp. 180-81) that the French-language broadcast media is much more Canadian in content than is the English-language media.

42. Holmes, "In Praise of National Boundaries," p. 16.
43. Cited in Patrick Nagle, "Border disputes still pending," *Calgary Herald*, October 20, 1984, p. A4.
44. Clarkson, *Canada and the Reagan Challenge*, p. 185.
45. *Maclean's*, July 3, 1989, p. 49.
46. Joseph S. Nye, Jr., and Robert O. Keohane, "Transnational Relations and World Politics: An Introduction," in Robert O. Keohane and Joseph S. Nye, Jr., eds., *Transnational Relations and World Politics* (Cambridge: Harvard University Press, 1972), p. ix.
47. John D. Redekop, "A Reinterpretation of Canadian-American Relations," *Canadian Journal of Political Science* IX:2 (June 1976), p. 237.
48. Government of Canada, *Foreign Policy for Canadians* (Ottawa: 1970). This was remedied somewhat by a special issue of *International Perspectives*, "Canada–U.S. Relations: Options for the Future," published in 1972.
49. Robert O. Keohane and Joseph S. Nye, Jr., *Power and Interdependence: World Politics in Transition* (Boston: Little Brown & Company, 1977), p. 170.
50. Redekop, "A Reinterpretation," p. 233.
51. Holmes, *Life with Uncle*, p. 43.
52. Peter Moon, "Agents look out for Canada's interests," *The Globe and Mail*, National Edition, August 15, 1983, p. 5.
53. David Leyton-Brown, "Canada and Multinational Enterprise," in Norman Hillmer and Garth Stevenson, eds., *A Foremost Nation: Canadian Foreign Policy and a Changing World* (Toronto: McClelland and Stewart, 1977), p. 81.
54. Holmes, *Life With Uncle*, p. 54.
55. Clarkson, *Canada and the Reagan Challenge*, p. 289.
56. Holmes, *Life With Uncle*, p. 7.
57. Eayrs, "Sharing a Continent," p. 66.
58. Clarkson, *Canada and the Reagan Challenge*, p. 261.
59. Michael Tucker, *Canadian Foreign Policy: Contemporary Issues and Themes* (Toronto: McGraw-Hill Ryerson, 1980), pp. 149-50.
60. Clarkson, *Canada and the Reagan Challenge*, p. 8.
61. Donald Creighton, *The Passionate Observer: Selected Writings* (Toronto: McClelland and Stewart, 1980), p. 23.
62. Cited in Levitt, *The Silent Surrender*, pp. 1-2.
63. *Ibid.*, p. 2.
64. Redekop, "A Reinterpretation," p. 230.
65. Eayrs, "Sharing a Continent," p. 93.
66. Hans Kohn, *The Idea of Nationalism* (New York: Macmillan, 1944), p. 20.
67. See Gibbins, "Models of Nationalism: A Case Study of Political

Ideologies in the Canadian West," *Canadian Journal of Political Science* (June 1977), pp. 341-73.

68. For a discussion of this theme's expression in Canadian literature, see Margaret Atwood, *Survival* (Toronto: Anansi, 1972).
69. Northrop Frye, *The Bush Garden* (Toronto: Anansi, 1971), p. iv.
70. *Vancouver Sun*, January 27, 1972, p. 6.
71. Margaret Atwood, *Second Words: Selected Critical Prose* (Toronto: Anansi, 1982), p. 380.
72. John Meisel, *Working Papers on Canadian Politics* (Montreal: McGill-Queen's University Press, 1973), p. 208.
73. J. R. Mallory, *The Structure of Canadian Government* (Toronto: Macmillan, 1971), p. 1.
74. Wise and Brown, *Canada Views the United States*, p. 94.
75. *Ibid.*, p. 96.
76. For an expansion of this point, see Gibbins, *Regionalism: Territorial Politics in Canada and the United States* (Toronto: Butterworths, 1982), p. 196.
77. J.H. Dales, " "National Policy" Myths, Past and Present," *Journal of Canadian Studies*, 14:3 (Fall 1979), p. 93.
78. Levitt, *Silent Surrender*, p. 148.
79. Mason Wade, "The Roots of the Relationship," in Dickey, *The United States and Canada*, p. 53.

6

Intergovernmental and Constitutional Politics

One of the most important features of the Canadian political system is the parliamentary *concentration* of power within cabinets, both in Ottawa and the provinces. As a consequence of the conventions of responsible government and the party discipline that those conventions foster, cabinets dominate not only the executive arm of government but also the legislative process. (See Appendix B for an expanded discussion of executive dominance.) Of equal importance, however, is the federal *dispersion* of power among the federal or national government, ten provincial governments, and, to an increasing degree, two territorial governments in the Canadian North. (Although the Yukon and Northwest Territories lack provincial status and are thus not constitutional components of the Canadian federal system, evolving political practice is rapidly blurring the formal distinctions between provincial and territorial governments.) The products of these two characteristics are unique patterns of intergovernmental relations and constitutional politics that set Canadian federal politics apart from the experience of other federal states.

For many readers the term "intergovernmental relations" may conjure up images of federal-provincial conflict, for indeed it is difficult to pick up a newspaper or watch the evening news without encountering disputes between Ottawa and the provinces. Federal-provincial conflict is so pervasive it seems to flow into virtually every crack and crevice of the political system. Unfortunately, its very pervasiveness obscures the fact that Canadian governments collaborate more than they fight, that a complex web of programs, agreements, committees, and conferences draws the governments together in a common cooperative enterprise. For example, between April 1, 1987, and March 31, 1988, the Alberta government signed more than sixty agreements with the federal government and/or other provincial governments, agreements ranging across such diverse issues as waterfowl crop damage compensation, improvements to the Yellowhead highway, compensation in the event of death or injury of civil defence workers, the "improved use of new binders in waterboard and oriented standboard production," and the Meech Lake Accord.[1] No matter where Canadians might live, many if not most of the government services they receive are the product of intergovernmental collaboration.

Universities or colleges, for instance, draw financial support from both federal and provincial governments. Although Ottawa's support for

Table 6.1
Federal Contributions to Provinces for Post-Secondary Education

1986/87 Fiscal Year
($000)

Newfoundland	109,278
Prince Edward Island	24,106
Nova Scotia	166,579
New Brunswick	135,811
Quebec	1,247,048
Ontario	1,728,062
Manitoba	202,804
Saskatchewan	192,228
Alberta	449,474
British Columbia	546,614
Yukon	4,291
NWT	9,597
Total	4,815,892

Source: *Federal-Provincial Programs and Activities, 1987-87* (Ottawa: Federal-Provincial Relations Office, 1987), pp. 219-20.

post-secondary education is less direct and hence less visible than that coming from provincial governments, Table 6.1 shows that it is substantial indeed. In addition, numerous federal departments and agencies, from National Defence to the Social Sciences and Humanities Research Council, are thoroughly entangled in post-secondary education, and even in primary and secondary education.[2]

In large part, the scale of contemporary intergovernmental relations reflects the general growth of government that has occurred since the end of the Second World War. As the "nightwatchman state," in which government was responsible primarily for little more than the protection of borders and the maintenance of public order, gave way to the welfare state and extensive government intervention in the economy, the sphere of government expanded further and further. As Richard Rose points out, the growth of government was a phenomenon that was in no way restricted to Canada or to federal political systems:

> Government is big in itself, big in its claims upon society's resources and big in its impact upon society. By every conventional measure, government looms large in the life of every Western nation today; governments differ from nation to nation only in their degree of bigness.[3]

In federal states, however, the growth of government takes on added dimensions because growth is seldom even across the various levels of government, and because it has such a marked impact on intergovern-

Nineteenth-Century Federalism

Contemporary Federalism

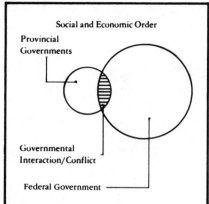
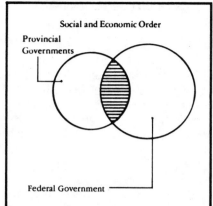

FIGURE 6.1

Growth of Government and Governmental Conflict/Interaction

mental relations. As Figure 6.1 illustrates, governmental growth is accompanied by an increase in intergovernmental contact and interaction, which in turn has resulted in " ... a large network of cooperative federal-provincial programs, most of which operate unobtrusively and cooperatively and together form a network of government which enables the country to function through the maze of elaborate jurisdictional overlaps that have emerged as government activities have expanded in recent years."[4]

Although cooperation is one product of increased intergovernmental interaction, conflict is another. Almost in a parody of the old western cliché, "this town ain't big enough for both of us," governments within federal states jostle against one another as they grow and necessarily interact. Intergovernmental friction can also stem from a number of other sources. In some fields, such as agriculture, the constitution assigns *concurrent jurisdiction* to both levels of government, although in this case federal legislation is given paramountcy should conflict arise. Quite apart from the constitutional provision for concurrent jurisdiction, the two levels of government are both active in a multitude of additional policy domains including such things as environmental protection, public health, aboriginal affairs, transportation, and consumer protection. Thus, intergovernmental conflict can arise if the two levels of government pursue different legislative intentions or regulatory procedures within the same policy domain. In policy areas not explicitly addressed in the formal constitutional division of powers, such as regulatory control over cable television, intergovernmental conflict can arise as the federal and provincial governments jockey for constitutional control.

As will be discussed in greater detail below, the federal government may use its spending powers to invade provincial areas of jurisdiction. We also find that the actions of one level of government, even when taken exclusively within its own domain, can have a major impact on programs at the other level. National taxation policies, locational decisions with respect to the siting of federal agencies and military bases, procurement decisions, and regulatory decisions with respect to foreign investment can all have a substantial impact on provincial governments and economies. Here the debate over the Goods and Services Tax provides a striking example. Conversely, provincial budgets may reinforce or counteract the fiscal policies of the federal government, and thus affect Ottawa's management of the national economy. All of these entanglements necessitate governmental interaction and provide potential ground for intergovernmental conflict.

Environmental protection provides particularly fertile soil for intergovernmental cooperation and conflict. Many environmental concerns, including but by no means limited to water and air pollution, are impervious by their very nature to the federal–provincial division of powers, and indeed to the division of the globe into sovereign nation states. Yet the fact that effective environmental protection necessitates intergovernmental cooperation does little to ensure that such cooperation will be easy or inevitable. At times conflict may even arise as governments, in the search for votes, try to outdo one another as environmental champions.

Although extensive intergovernmental relations are characteristic of all modern federal states, the nature of such relations can vary considerably. In Canada, they have taken on a higher public profile and a more acrimonious tone than has been the case elsewhere.[5] To understand why, we must place intergovernmental relations against the broader backdrop of a volatile federal system.

EVOLUTION OF THE CANADIAN FEDERAL STATE

Confederation created a highly centralized federal system in which the principal legislative responsibilities of the day were assigned to the federal government, and in which the powers of reservation and disallowance placed Ottawa in a quasi-imperial relationship with the provinces. If we imagine a continuum of hypothetical federal systems, anchored at one end by highly centralized federal systems and at the other by very decentralized systems in which provincial or state governments were preeminent, we would see that the Constitution Act of 1867 would lodge Canada at the centralized end. However, the *evolution* of Canadian federalism has been characterized neither by entrenchment at the centralized end of the continuum nor by a steady progression towards the decentralized end. Instead, the federal system has oscillated across this continuum. Within the bounds of a constitutional division of powers largely untouched by formal amendment, Canadians have experienced a variety of quite different federal arrangements.

Centralizing Factors

In the early years after Confederation, the centralized federal system put into place by the Constitution Act of 1867 was reinforced by a massive migration of political talent to Ottawa. With the exception of Ontario's Oliver Mowat, who went on to become the province's premier, all the politicians voting for Confederation opted for elected or appointed *national* office.[6] For the political movers and shakers, the action was in Ottawa and not in the provinces. The new provincial governments were all but denuded of political talent and, as a consequence, were not in a position to challenge Ottawa's dominance. It was not long, however, before the provincial governments, led by Ontario's Premier Mowat, began to develop as political centres of gravity and to emerge as increasingly effective counterweights to Ottawa. Federal–provincial conflicts emerged over language and education issues in Ontario and Manitoba, over the search for "better terms" in the Maritimes, and over boundary extensions for Ontario and Quebec. Nevertheless, the scope of intergovernmental conflict was contained by the small size and limited scope of the governments of the day. Given that neither level of government penetrated very extensively into the lives of citizens, there was little need for governmental interaction with respect to programs and services, and thus little opportunity for intergovernmental conflict. Both the federal and provincial governments had not yet had time to fully occupy their own legislative domains, much less encroach upon the domain of the other level of government.

As the nineteenth century drew to a close, Ottawa's stature within the federal system was eroded by Canada's sluggish economic growth. Caught in the midst of a prolonged world-wide depression, the federal government failed to deliver on the economic promise of Confederation. The West remained largely unsettled, and Canadians by the tens of thousands emigrated to seek their fortunes in the United States. Relief finally came in the mid-1890s. Coincident with the victory of Sir Wilfrid Laurier and the national Liberal party in the election of 1896 came a lifting of the depression, the depletion of free land in the American West, and a spectacular increase in immigration to the "last, best West." The consequence was an unprecedented economic boom which spurred the agricultural settlement of the West and the industrialization of central Canada. Both the federal and provincial governments shone in the reflected light of the economic boom. In the embryonic intergovernmental arena, the Laurier years were " . . . characterized by a more constructive and harmonious pattern of relations between the federal and provincial governments than prevailed in the previous decades or was ever established again."[7]

The First World War brought English Canadians together in a collective national endeavour and, not coincidentally, ushered in a sustained period of national dominance within the federal system. (The quite different response of French Canadians to the war is discussed in the next chapter.) The war experience and the economic growth it generated, the concentration of political power in Ottawa under the terms of the **War Measures Act**, and the recognition of Canadian independence that came with the 1926 Balfour Declaration and the 1931 Statute of Westminster all contributed to the growth of both Canadian nationalism and the federal government.

During the 1930s, provincial and local governments buckled under the massive economic and social dislocation of the Great Depression. Only the federal government appeared to have the fiscal and administrative resources to provide band-aids, though not always solutions. Yet Ottawa's response was limited by an ideological disinclination to intervene, and by a series of decisions made by the Judicial Committee of the Privy Council, which narrowly defined Parliament's jurisdictional domain. In short, the federal system was not up to the admittedly extraordinary demands of the day. As a consequence, a major overhaul of the federal system was recommended by the Rowell-Sirois Royal Commission on Dominion-Provincial Relations. In its 1940 report the Commission called for a restructured federal system in which the federal government would have a greater role in social policy and economic management, and in which federal-provincial fiscal arrangements would be reformed to provide a more uniform national tax structure and greater federal assistance to the provinces.

Although the distraction of the Second World War pre-empted any formal governmental response to the Rowell-Sirois recommendations, the war effort itself and the national economic recovery that it engendered moved the Canadian federal system along the path outlined by the Commission. As a general rule, federal systems tend to centralize during times of military crisis,[8] and Canada was no exception. Provincial government opposition to increased centralization was quickly quelled as federal politicians campaigned provincially in Ontario and Quebec to defeat what they depicted as opponents of the nation's war effort. Just as the new federal government had done in 1867, Ottawa attracted "the best and the brightest" to staff the huge bureaucratic machine that regulated, and regulated surprisingly well, virtually every aspect of Canadian life during the war years. At the war's end, Garth Stevenson writes,

> the federal government appeared to stand at the height of its power and prestige in relation to the provincial governments. Canada had operated in wartime practically as a unitary state, and the provincial governments had been reduced to insignificance.[9]

During the war years, Stevenson argues, Canadians had come to expect a predominant federal role in social legislation and economic management, a role that the enlarged federal bureaucracy was ready and eager to play in postwar Canada. Between 1945 and 1960 the federal government greatly expanded its legislative reach by encroaching on provincial fields of jurisdiction. It did so principally through the spending power which allowed Ottawa to spend, and thus indirectly to legislate, in provincial fields of jurisdiction. As Donald Smiley explains, "according to the constitutional doctrine that came to prevail, the central government might legally spend revenues as it chose, even on matters within the jurisdiction of the provinces, and could at its discretion fix the circumstances under which a potential recipient ... might receive the federal largesse."[10] Fuelled by tax money from a rapidly growing postwar economy, Ottawa established a series of *conditional grant programs* in the fields of health care, advanced education, and social welfare.

Conditional grant programs shared a number of characteristics, the most important being that they fell within the jurisdictional domain of the provinces. Program delivery was thus left to the provinces; the federal government's role was largely confined to providing financial support, with Ottawa matching provincial expenditures in return for the imposition of national standards such as universal accessibility. Conditional grant programs, and the national standards that they embodied, enjoyed broad public support in the postwar Canadian society. Although the provinces could choose not to participate, as Quebec did in some cases, the political and financial costs of non-participation were high. In fact, federal funds were generally welcomed, at least outside Quebec, as the provincial governments faced growing fiscal pressures from postwar electorates demanding enhanced programs in education, health care, and the social services. Caught between rising demand and limited fiscal resources—only Ottawa had the power to raise money "by any Mode or System of Taxation"—the provincial governments had little option but to accept conditional grants from the federal government.

Conditional grant programs were by no means cost-free to the provinces. They distorted provincial spending priorities by forcing provincial governments to give highest priority to those programs where matching federal funds were available. Provincial governments raised concerns about the long-term cost of the programs, the long-term commitment of the federal government to its share of the cost, and the inflexibility that conditional grant programs imposed on provincial budgets and spending priorities. There was also growing provincial resistance, led by Quebec, to the federal encroachment onto provincial constitutional turf that such programs represented. It is also worth noting that the programs significantly altered the nature of federal–provincial relations by requiring extensive intergovernmental collaboration and coordination.[11] The name given to this new pattern of intergovernmental relations was "cooperative federalism," a term that often belied the fact that cooperation was largely a one-way street, and that the government paying the piper called the tune.

To observers at the end of the 1950s, Ottawa's dominance in the Canadian federal system was an established fact. Bora Laskin, who was later to become Chief Justice of the Supreme Court, wrote in 1960 that "never since Confederation have the ideas so cherished by Macdonald for a strong and powerful central government, subordinating the provincial legislatures like so many larger municipal institutions, been so close to realization as they have been in the past ten years."[12] Also writing of the 1950s, J.A. Corry painted a similar scene:

> The most [a province] can hope to hold is its freedom for minor adventure, for embroidering its own particular patterns in harmony with the national design, for playing variant melodies within the general theme ... it is everywhere limited in the distance it can go by having become part of a larger, although not necessarily a better, scheme of things.[13]

And yet, by the early 1960s, the federal government was in retreat across a broad front in the face of resurgent provincial governments. What had appeared to be evolutionary movement towards an Ottawa-centred federal system had not only been stopped but suddenly reversed. What, then, had changed in order to produce such a dramatic realignment of the Canadian federal system?

Decentralizing Factor

Even during the heyday of the Macdonald governments, the provincial governments had begun to resist what they saw as an excessively centralized federal system. The principal resistance came from the two central Canadian provinces, with Liberal-dominated Ontario being by far the most militant.[14] Although in the early decades after Confederation the provincial governments were unable to muster political and bureaucratic resources comparable to those possessed by Ottawa, their command over such resources would only increase with the passage of time. In this respect they were greatly assisted by a series of judicial interpretations of

Canadian federalism which significantly augmented the powers of the provincial governments and eroded those of the federal government.

Until 1949 the umpire for the Canadian federal system was the Judicial Committee of the Privy Council, a circumstance that reflected not only Canada's colonial past but also the fact that the Constitution Act of 1867 was an act of the British rather than of the Canadian Parliament. Thus its adjudication ultimately rested in British rather than Canadian judicial hands. As James Mallory explains, the JCPL

> ... originated with the constitutional notion that British subjects in overseas colonies which owed their constitutions to prerogative grants had the right to bring grievances from the local courts to the foot of the throne for satisfaction.[15]

It is not surprising, then, that in the majority of cases in which the Judicial Committee was asked to rule on the federal division of powers, the Canadian governments themselves were not the protagonists and intergovernmental conflict per se was not the source of the litigation. Most cases were brought forward by private interests trying to stem the growth of government, be it federal or provincial.[16] Canadian governments were nonetheless greatly affected by a series of Judicial Committee decisions over sixty years which eroded the constitutional position of the federal government. Without formally altering sections 91 and 92 of the Constitution Act, the Committee expanded provincial powers, curtailed those of the federal government, largely transferred residual powers to the provinces (at least in peacetime), reduced the strength of the trade and commerce clause, and cut down federal attempts to regulate natural resource trade with the United States. The Peace, Order, and Good Government clause was restricted to the enumerated headings of Section 91, to emergency situations, and to matters of national concern or having a "national dimension."[17] During the Depression a "judicial massacre" struck down Prime Minister R.B. Bennett's attempt to impose a Canadian version of President Franklin Roosevelt's "New Deal."[18]

The long-term impact of the JCPC on the evolution of Canadian federalism is a matter of considerable debate. On the one hand, Donald Smiley describes a consensus among English-speaking scholars that the Committee's decisions were "nothing short of calamitous" in their erosion of the federal government's constitutional position.[19] Martha Fletcher concurs, arguing that the JCPL established a legal framework which "... operated as a centrifugal force in the federation, dividing jurisdiction and thwarting attempts to centralize control in important areas of economic and social concern."[20] Alan Cairns, on the other hand, argues that while the Committee's decisions unquestionably affected the nature of Canadian federalism and did depart from the 1867 formula, they

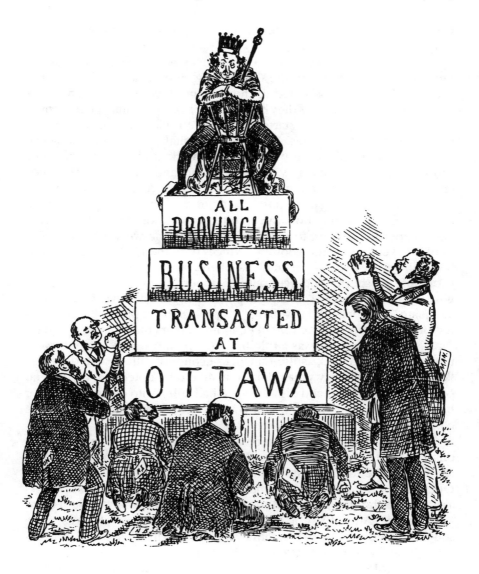

"Centralization;" or, "Provincial autonomy abolished." Is this what Sir John is aiming at?

In J.W. Bengough, *A Caricature History of Canadian Politics*, Vol. 2 (Toronto: Grip Printing and Publishing, 1886), p. 273.

were not out of line with other changes which were also promoting a more decentralized federalism.[21]

The legislative domain of the provinces had become increasingly important with changes in the Canadian society. Whereas in the 1860s many of the matters assigned to the provinces were in fact left to the private sector, by the 1950s they had not only become primary concerns of government but had also started to involved massive consumption of public funds and programs. Education, hospitals, highways, and social services all fell within the provincial bailiwick, and as a consequence provincial governments grew in both absolute and relative terms as they embraced these new and costly responsibilities. As provincial governments grew, they began to attract a degree of bureaucratic expertise comparable to that traditionally recruited by Ottawa. While this bureaucratic expertise was not to reach full flower in the wealthier provinces until the 1960s and in the poorer provinces until the 1970s, its impact was beginning to be felt by the late 1950s when a reversal in Canada's postwar economic prosperity undercut public support for an expanding federal government. The failure of national policies to provide what were seen as adequate levels of material welfare " . . . projected the provincial administrations into a more active role in economic affairs than they had heretofore assumed,"[22] and it was a role that the provincial governments were unwilling to surrender as the Canadian economy roller-coasted its way through the next thirty years. Finally, it should be noted that the federal powers of reservation and disallowance had fallen into disuse. The latter had last been used in 1943, and by the late 1950s both had become constitutional dead letters.

This stew of change in the federal system was brought to a boil by the onset of the Quiet Revolution in Quebec. Before 1960, Quebec had not challenged the fundamental character of the Confederation agreement; Quebec governments had concentrated more on protecting those powers assigned to the provinces and in warding off incursions by the federal government. After 1960, a number of interdependent changes were sought, including Ottawa's withdrawal from provincial areas of jurisdiction; the expansion of provincial jurisdiction to provide more autonomous control over cultural and social policy; the conversion of conditional to unconditional grants in order to provide greater fiscal autonomy for provincial governments; larger equalization payments; more formalized intergovernmental relations analogous to those between sovereign states; and the right to participate in international relations with respect to matters falling within provincial jurisdiction. At the very least, such changes entailed a fundamental restructuring of the federal system. To many observers both inside and outside Quebec, their realization implied a degree of political autonomy indistinguishable from independence.

Taken alone, the Quebec demands were a major shock to the federal system. The shock then spread as other provincial governments used Quebec as the pointman for their own assault on the federal status quo. In a 1977 speech to the Alberta Progressive Conservative party, Premier Peter Lougheed drew an explicit parallel between the Alberta and Quebec positions on Confederation:

> Just as Albertans want more control over their destiny—primarily for economic reasons—Quebecers, I sense, want also more control over their destiny, essentially for cultural and linguistic reasons. Hence, just as Albertans want more government decisions made in Edmonton than in Ottawa, I think Quebecers, for different reasons, but somewhat similar motives, want more government decisions made in Quebec City, and fewer in Ottawa.[23]

To be sure, no other provincial government went as far as Quebec, or came close to endorsing the extremes of independence or sovereignty association. There was also considerable variability among the English Canadian provinces, with Ontario and the Maritime provinces being more supportive of a strong national economic union refereed by a strong federal government than were provincial governments in the West and Newfoundland. Nevertheless, Quebec's pursuit of expanded provincial jurisdiction, the rollback of federal incursions, and greater fiscal autonomy for the provinces enjoyed generally enthusiastic governmental support outside Quebec. Across the board, provincial governments became more sensitive to jurisdictional issues and more alert to federal encroachments onto their constitutional turf than they had been during the 1950s.

To the extent that there was a broadly shared provincial constitutional strategy, it contained the following elements: (1) the rollback of federal intrusions into provincial fields of jurisdiction but the retention of the federal funds that had accompanied such intrusions; (2) the erection of more watertight barriers around provincial fields of jurisdiction; (3) the creation of more permeable barriers around federal fields of jurisdiction in order to facilitate greater provincial input into federal policy-making, particularly with respect to economic management; (4) more formalized intergovernmental relations; and (5) expanded provincial jurisdiction in selected fields. In the West, the search for a greater national role for provincial governments was intensified when the elections of 1963, 1965, 1972, 1974, and 1980 produced federal governments with meagre elected representation from the West. In Quebec, however, the emphasis continued to be placed on greater provincial autonomy rather than on greater provincial input into national policy.

INTERGOVERNMENTAL RELATIONS

The only intergovernmental mechanism built into the 1867 Constitution Act was the Lieutenant-Governor, who "... was originally envisaged as being a federal officer entrusted with the responsibility of communicating the views of the national government to provincial authorities and, if necessary, making certain that the provincial governments did not step too far off the path deemed correct for them by the national government."[24] It was assumed at the time that the federal and provincial governments would operate within their own constitutional domains and would rarely come into contact. Federal–provincial interaction would occur mainly through informal party mechanisms; governmental interaction per se was not institutionally accommodated apart from whatever federal intervention in provincial affairs might occur through the Lieutenant-Governor and through Ottawa's powers of disallowance and reservation. As a consequence, the very complex intergovernmental infrastructure, which we have today and which has shaped the process and products of constitutional change over the last two decades, evolved independently of the formal constitution and did not achieve even parenthetical constitutional recognition until the 1980s. However, its constitutional informality in no way negates its importance. In Canada, as in other federal states, intergovernmental relations are central to the operation of modern government.

The Evolution of Intergovernmental Relations

The early years saw little need for extensive or formalized intergovernmental relations. The governments of the day were largely inactive even within their own legislative domains, and encroachments upon each other's turf were rare. The initial conference of "first ministers"—the Prime Minister of Canada and the provincial premiers—was not held until 1906 when Wilfrid Laurier met with the premiers in Ottawa. Subsequent Dominion-Provincial Conferences, as they were then called, were characterized by a short agenda, poor staff work, and the dominance of the federal government. The major topic of discussion was the perennial bugbear of Canadian federalism: fiscal transfers. The initial Premiers' Conference was held in 1887, followed by meetings in 1902, 1910, 1913, and 1926. The 1887 conference, which was a meeting of predominantly Liberal premiers called to orchestrate a partisan attack on the Conservative government in Ottawa,[25] set the tone for the meetings to follow. Then as now, the premiers dealt less with the coordination of provincial programs and administrative practices than with complaints against the federal government.[26]

The near collapse of provincial governments during the Depression increased the tempo of federal–provincial, although not interprovincial, interaction. The first ministers met four times during the 1930s and began to consider greater institutionalization of federal–provincial relations. Speaking at the 1935 Dominion–Provincial Conference, Prime Minister Mackenzie King stated that "cooperation between the Dominion and the provinces is too vital a matter to be left entirely for intermittent conferences and to correspondence between governments."[27] King's stand was endorsed by the Rowell-Sirois Royal Commission, which recommended that a permanent intergovernmental relations secretariat be established. However, the outbreak of the Second World War pre-empted any such action. The War Measures Act sliced away federal–provincial entanglements, enabling Ottawa to act as if Canada were a unitary rather than a federal state. Moreover, after the initial electoral confrontations between Ottawa and the provincial governments of Quebec and Ontario, the war itself pushed federal–provincial issues from the nation's political agenda and reduced the public's tolerance for intergovernmental conflict.

By 1945 eighteen federal–provincial committees had been established to orchestrate Ottawa's wartime involvement in provincial fields of jurisdiction. This network formed the nucleus of what was to become a huge intergovernmental infrastructure. By the mid-fifties, when cooperative federalism was coming into full flower, more than sixty federal–provincial committees were in place, including a Coordinating Agency on Disease of the Beaver. The most important was the Continuing Committee on Fiscal and Economic Matters, a committee of senior finance officials which Donald Smiley has described as a major breakthrough in the institutionalization of federal–provincial fiscal relations.[28] By 1968 the number of federal–provincial committees, boards and agencies had risen to 190.[29] In 1972 there were more than 400[30] and by 1975 the total reached almost 800.[31] With the growth in this infrastructure came an increase in the number of federal–provincial conferences, with the first ministers alone meeting approximately twice a year during the 1970s.

This was the heyday of what Smiley has termed "executive federalism," a time when intergovernmental affairs overshadowed what seemed to be the more prosaic activities of the federal and provincial governments operating within their own jurisdictional domains. The importance of executive federalism stemmed not only from the frequency with which first ministers, ministers, and senior officials interacted, but also from the fact that such interaction played a critical role in shaping the multitude of programs and services which the governments of Canada provided for the Canadian people. Its importance was further reinforced by the Canadian pattern of executive dominance vis-à-vis legislative assemblies, be they provincial or national. Thus the participants in executive federalism could be confident that whatever agreements they hammered out would be endorsed by their respective legislative assemblies.

Table 6.2
Frequency and Size of First Ministers' Conferences*

Period	# of FMCs	Average # of First Ministers and Advisors
1906–16	1	23
1917–26	1	40
1927–36	6	62(a)
1937–46	3	165
1947–56	6	103
1957–66	11	136(a)
1967–76	16	132
1977–87	17	218(a)

(a) Data unavailable for one or more FMCs; averages based on available data.
*Data do not include informal meetings, bilateral and regional meetings of First Ministers, or meetings of the Premiers alone.
Data compiled by Scott McAlpine.

Extensive as they may be, federal–provincial relations encompass only part of the intergovernmental activity that takes place in Canada. They co-exist with, and to a degree engender, an imposing network of interprovincial relations. Federal–provincial conferences themselves and the interprovincial meetings held in preparation for such conferences provide provincial officials with the opportunity to discuss common interests and to promote interprovincial cooperation, often through the vehicle of federal–provincial programs. Interprovincial conferences quite apart from those linked to federal–provincial conferences are also commonplace; to provide but one example at the ministerial level, the Council of Ministers of Education brings the provincial education ministers together on an annual basis. The Premiers' Conference, initiated as an annual affair in 1960 by Quebec's Premier Jean Lesage, brings together the ten premiers and approximately 150 aides, federal observers, spouses, and children for three days of socializing, informal discussions, and rhetorical broadsides at the federal government. The Council of Maritime Premiers brings together the premiers of New Brunswick, Nova Scotia, and Prince Edward Island, while the annual Western Premiers' Conference brings together the four western premiers.

Premier's Conference

In late August 1989, the ten provincial premiers met in Quebec City for their 30th annual meeting. The conference was chaired by the host premier, Robert Bourassa, who was in the midst of a provincial election campaign at the time. As a consequence, the premiers agreed to avoid any formal discussion of the constitutional issue of the day, the ratification of the Meech Lake Accord. (Three years earlier, a declaration signed by the ten premiers in

Edmonton laid the political foundations for the Accord.) Instead, the premiers launched an attack on Ottawa's proposed Goods and Services Tax, while also addressing interprovincial barriers to trade and environmental protection. On the final day of the conference, the premiers were joined by two U.S. representatives of the National Association of Governors for discussions on the Free Trade Agreement and industrial pollution.

There is also extensive interaction between provincial governments and the local governments falling under their jurisdiction. However, at the present time there is little direct interaction between Ottawa and local governments, a situation unlike that in the United States where the large cities are vigorous congressional lobbyists and where federal programs frequently bypass the state governments to provide direct federal aid to local governments. Although Ottawa established a Ministry of State for Urban Affairs in the early 1970s, the experiment was quickly abandoned.

Table 6.3 provides some indication of the sheer volume of contemporary intergovernmental relations. While the Alberta case may not be typical of all Canadian provinces, the fact that most federal–provincial conferences are multilateral—involving all or most of the provincial governments—suggests that it is not abnormal. Table 6.3 shows that during the 1980s the Alberta government participated in approximately two federal–provincial conferences a week, every week of the year! On top of this, interprovincial conferences and meetings were occurring at an average of once a week.

The extensive Canadian network of intergovernmental relations attests to the fact that most matters of public policy have an intergovernmental dimension. For example, when legislation was first introduced in 1983 to transfer responsibility for national security matters from the RCMP to a new civilian agency, it ran afoul of provincial governments who charged that the proposed legislation would encroach upon the provincial responsibility for the administration of justice. We need only wait for the definitive Canadian spy novel in which lawyers from eleven governments lead the reader in an exciting chase through the Constitution Act in order to determine if the foreign agent is a matter of federal or provincial jurisdiction.

Institutionalization

In a detailed study of the evolution of Canadian intergovernmental relations, Timothy Woolstencroft notes that, during the 1950s and early 1960s, when cooperative federalism was in its prime and federal–provincial interaction centred upon shared-cost programs, "a community of interest, cutting across jurisdictional borders, developed among officials which facilitated harmony and cordial relations between the two levels of

Table 6.3

Intergovernmental Relations: The Case of Alberta

Since 1974, the Alberta Department of Federal and Intergovernmental Affairs has maintained a detailed record of the province's participation in federal-provincial and interprovincial conferences. While this record may not reflect that of other provincial governments, it does illustrate the scope of intergovernmental relations in the Canadian federal system.

	1980	1981	1982	1983	1984	1985	1986	1987
Frequency of Federal-Provincial Meetings and Conferences								
• Bilateral (Alberta and federal governments only)	12	26	17	27	22	17	23	9
• Regional (Alberta, one or more of the other western provinces, and the federal government)	9	3	8	2	4	5	3	3
• Multilateral (all or most of the provinces and the federal government)	41	55	68	55	49	103	112	106
Total	62	84	93	84	75	125	138	118
Frequency by Level of Participation								
• First Ministerial	3	2	3	3	2	5	4	9
• Ministerial	32	47	42	47	54	61	72	64
• Deputy Ministerial	27	35	48	39	19	59	62	45
Total	62	84	93	89	75	125	138	118
Frequency of Interprovincial Meetings and Conferences	58	89	67	47	61	39	32	54

Source: Annual Reports of the Alberta Department of Federal and Intergovernmental Affairs.

government."[32] By the late 1960s this community of interest, knit together by federal and provincial program officials who shared similar educational backgrounds, professional norms, and program commitments, came under growing suspicion. Provincial politicians in particular became concerned that bureaucrats were not sufficiently sensitive to jurisdictional issues, and that their commitment to program objectives might lead to the surrender of provincial jurisdiction in exchange for federal funds.[33] Thus, both governments began to create new central agencies through which they could exercise greater *political* control over the conduct of federal-provincial relations. These central agencies were established to protect the jurisdictional domain of their government from intrusions by other governments, and from jurisdictional compromises which might be entertained by program specialists within their own bureaucratic apparatus. They were also a response to the growing scope of intergovernmental relations, to the organizational demands imposed by the constant round of federal–provincial meetings, and to the need for greater intergovernmental expertise in order to protect governments in, and extract maximum advantage from, the intergovernmental arena.

In Ottawa, the first steps towards institutionalization were taken by creating separate federal–provincial divisions within the line departments such as Health and Welfare, Transport, and Agriculture. Here the cornerstone was laid by the 1954 establishment of a federal–provincial relations division in the Department of Finance. In 1968 a special Federal–Provincial Affairs division of the Privy Council Office was established to deal with federal–provincial relations, and by 1975 this had evolved into the Federal–Provincial Relations Office. In 1977 a Federal–Provincial Relations portfolio was established in the federal cabinet, but this was discontinued after the 1980 election; the FPRO then operated under the umbrella of the Prime Minister's Office and reported to the prime minister through the Secretary to the Cabinet for Federal–Provincial Relations. Following the 1984 election, FPRO was once again granted ministerial representation in the federal cabinet. Quite apart from FPRO there is an Intergovernmental Conference Secretariat in Ottawa staffed by officials seconded from the federal and provincial governments. The secretariat provides liaison for the steady stream of federal–provincial conferences, many of which are held in Ottawa's old Union Station, which has been renovated as the National Conference Centre.

Given that federal–provincial relations touch most activities of the federal government, the conduct of federal–provincial relations can be centralized to only a limited degree. While FPRO deals with high profile issues that have important symbolic or constitutional components— during the late 1970s and early 1980s, for example, it spearheaded Ottawa's counterattack on the Quebec independence movement, and more recently served as the federal government's pilot for the Meech

Lake Accord—the line departments must also maintain a capacity for extensive federal–provincial liaison and policy interaction. With a staff of approximately sixty officials, FPRO cannot *direct* the conduct of federal–provincial relations across the massive federal bureaucracy.

At the provincial level, where federal–provincial relations have also been institutionalized, the central control of intergovernmental relations has been more complete. The provincial trend-setter was Quebec, which established a *Ministère des Affaires federales-provinciales* in 1961. As the Quebec government expanded its international contacts, the mandate of the new ministry was also expanded and its name was changed in 1967 to the *Ministère des Affaires intergouvernementales*. The *Ministère* was divided into two sections covering international and Canadian affairs. In 1984 the two sections were elevated to independent departments, *Affaires internationales* (discussed below) and *Affaires canadiennes*. The latter department maintains offices in Edmonton, Moncton, and Toronto, and contains a special branch to handle liaison with franco-phone communities outside Quebec.

Other provinces soon followed the Quebec example, with the larger provinces going faster and further than the smaller ones. Ontario created a Federal–Provincial and Intergovernmental Affairs Secretariat in 1965. The Secretariat was upgraded to a ministry in 1978 and, until 1981, also had responsibility for municipal affairs. In 1971 the Alberta government created the Department of Federal and Intergovernmental Affairs, while in 1973 Newfoundland created an intergovernmental affairs secretariat attached to the premier's office. Saskatchewan created an Office of Intergovernmental Affairs within the Executive Council Office in 1977, and upgraded it to a ministry in 1978. British Columbia created an Office of Intergovernmental Affairs attached to the premier's office in 1976, upgrading it to a full ministry in 1979. While intergovernmental affairs are still handled by the premier's office in some provinces, the trend has been towards greater institutionalization with independent ministries.[34] Bucking this trend was Grant Devine's Progressive Conservative government in Saskatchewan, which in 1983 closed its Department of Intergovernmental Affairs and transferred the department's responsibility back to the premier's office.

There has been considerable controversy among Canadian political scientists as to the impact of institutionalization. Donald Smiley, one of Canada's foremost federal scholars, has argued that institutionalization intensifies intergovernmental conflict by shifting federal–provincial relations from line departments to more politicized central agencies where the symbolic, jurisdictional, and electoral stakes are considerably higher. Of particular concern to Smiley is the intergovernmental specialist whose "single-minded devotion to the power of his jurisdiction" makes him or her an agent of jurisdictional aggrandizement rather than a conflict conciliator.[35] Timothy Woolstencroft, on the other hand, argues that Smiley overstates the impact of and damage from intergovernmental relations specialists. He maintains that their dominance over program officials is far from complete, that when they do influence policy they are not always single-minded province builders, and that in any event, more profound forces than the specialists underlie intergovernmental conflict.[36]

Woolstencroft is supported by a recent study of intergovernmental affairs in Saskatchewan, a study in which Howard Leeson rejects the assertions that "... separate departments of intergovernmental affairs result from an expansion of contacts and the consequent need to manage these new relationships."[37] Leeson argues that specific entrepreneurial interests of the provincial state, rather than the simple volume of intergovernmental activity or the abstract need to protect provincial jurisdiction, determine the course of institutionalization. The Saskatchewan study also supports Woolstencroft's assertion that "... the impact of intergovernmental specialists in government is not nearly as decisive as other observers have concluded."[38]

For better or for worse, the institutionalization of intergovernmental relations has created what Hugh Thorburn describes as "a large and efficient machine" in each province to ward off intrusions from other governments, and "to sustain a status quo situation of watchful defence of individual provincial interests."[39] In this setting, even Woolstencroft describes the intergovernmental relations specialists as "the sentinels of the federal principle."[40]

In recent years provincial governments have also become increasingly active internationally. Quite apart from 140 offices staffed by External Affairs, there are now over 40 provincial offices abroad, mostly representing the governments of Quebec, Ontario, Alberta, and British Columbia. These offices are used to attract foreign investment and tourism, to search for new markets, and to provide political intelligence on both foreign governments and the international activities of the Canadian government. There is no question that provincial governments are pursuing legitimate interests through their international offices.[41] However, there is some concern, particularly when premiers foray abroad to promote trade and foreign investment, about the duplication of, and even conflict with, the representation of Canadian interests by the Department of External Affairs. This concern is most acute in the case of Quebec, where the provincial government has made a major effort to stake out an international presence. Quebec's *Affaires internationales* maintains posts in Abidjan, Atlanta, Boston, Brussels, Buenos Aires, Caracas, Chicago, Dallas, Dusseldorf, Hong Kong, Lafayette, Lisbon, London, Los Angeles, Mexico City, Milan, New York, Paris, Port-au-Prince, Rome, Tokyo, and Washington, posts which are staffed by over 300 men and women.[42] Internally, the department contains seven branches covering France, Europe, Asia, the United States, South America, cultural and educational affairs, and economic affairs.

Factors Affecting Canadian Intergovernmental Relations

Intergovernmental relations in Canada, at least as they are perceived by the man in the street, often take on a very acrimonious tone. Indeed, it can be argued that the pervasiveness of "Ottawa-bashing" and "province-baiting" sours public life. Federal–provincial conflict may also squeeze more important issues off the nation's political agenda. This is not to imply, however, that the tone of intergovernmental relations is in some way aberrant, that it distorts the true nature of Canadian political life, or that it is the fault of particular personalities. While personality clashes are not without consequence, they contribute to rather than explain the tone of intergovernmental conflict. The more important roots are to be found within the institutional fabric of the Canadian state.

Some of these roots have already come to light in Chapter 4's discussion of intrastate and interstate federalism. An impotent Senate, party cohesion within the House, the secrecy that envelops both cabinet and caucus, and an electoral system that distorts the regional composition of parliamentary parties, all impair the representation of territorial interests *within* the national government. As a consequence, such interests at times may find their primary expression through provincial governments; they are represented *to* rather than *within* national institutions. Regional conflict and intergovernmental conflict thus blend into and reinforce one another; regional conflict within national institutions becomes supplanted by conflict between powerful governments and their supporting bureaucracies.

Another root can be traced to the concentration of political power that occurs in parliamentary systems. In 1972, Richard Simeon introduced the notion of federal–provincial "diplomacy."[43] The term is an insightful one, acknowledging as it does that federal–provincial relations have taken on many of the trappings of international relations: the importance attached to the symbols of sovereignty; a stress on the formal equality of all actors regardless of the size of the province or the level of government; the conduct of federal–provincial "summit meetings" in an atmosphere laden with pomp and ceremony; the treatment of governments as unitary actors rather than as complex packages of conflicting bureaucratic, partisan, and personal interests; and the use by governments of diplomatic "listening posts" on one another's turf. This diplomatic mode of intergovernmental relations and the broader phenomenon of executive federalism of which it is a part are made possible by the parliamentary concentration of power. Agreements reached by ministers, and particularly first ministers, are assured of governmental and legislative support. This means, however, that the participation of the House of Commons and provincial legislatures in federal–provincial relations is reduced to little more than a discussion of actions that have already been taken and the rubberstamping of deals that have already been made. Given the scope of intergovernmental relations, this can entail a substantial constraint on legislative assemblies.

The limited number of provincial governments also facilitates a diplomatic mode of interaction. With only eleven principal participants at most federal–provincial conferences, albeit principals supported by numerous officials and advisors, everyone gets a chance to be seen and be heard, to know one another, and to garner maximum media coverage from conference events. The norm of formal equality can thus be maintained, whereas in the United States fifty states and the enormous gulf between the positions of President and Governor preclude anything analogous to the Canadian FMC. Incidentally, an implication of the role played by numbers is that the creation of new provinces in the North would seriously disrupt the intergovernmental status quo. Additional northern premiers, some of whom would represent populations equivalent to those found in small southern Canadian towns, would erode the diplomatic fiction of provincial equality, reduce the attention paid to any given premier, and, as a result, enhance the stature of the Prime Minister.

There is no question that intergovernmental conflict is at times exploited and exacerbated in election campaigns. Ottawa-bashing is employed by provincial governments who prefer to campaign against the distant federal government rather than against provincial opponents. (Because it is easier to campaign against the federal government when it is of an opposing partisan stripe, provincial governments may offer only lukewarm campaign support for the national wing of their party.) While the opportunities are less frequent, national parties have also featured intergovernmental conflict in their campaigns, with the government party presenting itself as the one party able to stand up against avaricious and fractious provincial governments, and the opposition parties pledging that they will return a spirit of harmony and cooperation to intergovernmental relations. Thus, to a modest degree, intergovernmental conflict can be seen as a campaign artifact. The more important roots, however, draw their nourishment from institutional features of the Canadian federal state.

The First Ministers' Conference

The intergovernmental centrepiece in Canada has been the First Ministers' Conference, which brings together the prime minister and the ten premiers. (Prior to 1974, formal meetings between the Prime Minister and his provincial counterparts were referred to as Dominion–Provincial or Federal–Provincial Conferences.) The importance of the FMC comes from the parliamentary concentration of power in the hands of the political executive and the further concentration of that power in the hands of the respective first ministers. If consensus reigns, the FMC can be a very powerful policy instrument as the participants can ensure the cooperation of both their cabinet colleagues and legislative assemblies. The First Ministers can even shuffle jurisdictional responsibilities without formal constitutional amendment, as long as all participants agree. However, consensus is essential, for there is no decision-making rule apart from unanimous consent. If one of the participants disagrees with the rest, no mechanism exists through which the majority will can be imposed.[44] Decisions are binding only to the extent that participants wish to be bound and only to the extent that they are legislatively enacted.

Although the FMC receives passing mention in sections 37 and 49 of the Constitution Act of 1982 and in the Meech Lake Accord, it has no constitutionally derived source of power or authority; it is not a government but rather a meeting of governments. When the First Ministers do not agree, as will likely be the case when serious matters are on the agenda, the FMC can become little more than a means of dodging responsibility or pointing the finger of blame at other governments. It is political theatre, not government, a theatre in which first ministers posture for their electorates back home, exchange information, provide impetus for subsequent ministerial negotiations, and at times ratify agreements reached before the meeting began. It is also a theatre with a rather large supporting cast; FMCs held over the 1980s averaged more than 200 formal participants over and above the First Ministers themselves.

Here it is useful to point out two important features of the FMC. The first is that the participants must play several conflicting roles. The prime minister is not only by norm the conference chairman but also one of the active players, representing his government and party. He is also expected to articulate the *national interest,* as opposed to the more narrow *provincial interests* articulated by the premiers, although in another sense the national interest is expected to emerge from the joint deliberations of all eleven first ministers. For their part, the premiers are expected to represent their provinces while at the same time compromising those interests in order to reach an intergovernmental consensus. The second and related feature is that the most productive sessions tend to be those held in private, frequently over dinner and drinks, and away from the television cameras and the glare of publicity. Negotiation and compromise are difficult in a public arena where the forceful defence of one's governmental interests is likely to be of greater electoral value.

It should not be surprising that intergovernmental consensus, either between the federal and provincial governments or among the provincial governments themselves, is difficult to achieve. Few of the issues that confront contemporary governments are easily resolved, and the participants at the FMC represent a wide variety of regional, governmental, and partisan interests. Neither should it be surprising that the FMC has come in for a good deal of critical comment. Premier Lévesque and Prime Minister Trudeau both assailed the 1982 First Ministers' Conference on the economy, Lévesque calling it a "dialogue of the deaf" and Trudeau accusing the premiers of using the conference " . . . to make ten speeches on television blaming the federal government for all the evils of the nation."[45] Garth Stevenson concludes that "despite all the advance preparation, expense and ballyhoo, the record of First Ministers' Conferences in reaching agreements or solving problems is exceedingly poor."[46] The FMC, Stevenson charges, resembles "a meeting of a medieval king with his feudal barons more than it does the government of a modern state."[47]

There is some concern that the symbolic output of the FMC may damage the fabric of Canadian federal politics. More often than not, the FMC has been a showcase for conflict and disunity, particularly in the public sessions. Related to this is a fear that the FMC may erode the legitimacy and authority of national parliamentary institutions. This general argument was advanced by Prime Minister Trudeau in a 1981 address:

> Executive federalism is characterized by the idea that the role of Parliament in governing the country should diminish while premiers should acquire more influence over national public policy. In effect, this theory means that Canada's national government would be a council of first ministers. . . . [48]

The FMC and executive federalism more generally undercut the importance of cabinet ministers, MPs, and Senators as channels of regional representation in the national political system; their role is pre-empted by provincial premiers and governments. Of equal importance, executive federalism undercuts the role of the parliamentary opposition. Opposition parties are not represented around the conference table; if they attend it is as observers only, and any agreements that might result are subjected to the most perfunctory parliamentary scrutiny. Yet, while the perspectives of parliamentary opposition parties may be excluded from the intergovernmental arena, other perspectives are ushered in. As Keith Banting notes,

> A central role for federal-provincial negotiations diversifies that range of ideologies and interests that are brought to bear on major issues. While regional interests are stoutly defended by provincial champions, partisan and ideological differences also flow into federal-provincial channels.[49]

Simplifying the World through the FMC

When countries participate in international affairs, they generally do so as unitary actors, speaking with one voice. Thus we hear that "France protested Y," "the United States backed X," and "Canada argued that Z warranted further study before any action is taken." Yet we know in fact that nation states are seldom unitary actors, that they encompass a vast array of conflicting views and competing groups. Treating states as unitary actors admittedly simplifies the world, but simplification may also distort our perception of important political realities.

In Canadian politics, some of the same effects may be attributed to the FMC. As governments participate in the quasi-diplomatic environment of the FMC, they take on the attributes of unitary actors. Divisions within a provincial government or governing caucus, divisions that may be readily apparent to provincial residents in other settings, tend to fade as New Brunswick or Manitoba "speaks," "is listened to," or "stalks away from" the FMC. Complex political reality becomes simplified political theatre with a cast of eleven, not thousands.

Although the FMC may be a flawed institution, there is little doubt that it will continue to play an important role in Canadian federal politics. (The Meech Lake Accord mandates annual FMCs on the economy and on the Constitution.) Provincial governments will continue to have an important stake in federal economic management, and will demand a stage upon which provincial opinions can be heard. For its part, the federal government will continue to need to bring the provincial governments on its side if it is to effectively pursue its management of both the economy and social programs. While unilateral action is not ruled out, its effectiveness is circumscribed by the importance of provincial governments in the economy and in the administration of basic national programs. Thus, some institutional forum in which the governments of Canada can be brought together is essential. However, it is not in the routine realms of social and economic management that the FMC has truly come into its own. The FMC has achieved its highest profile, and has had by far its greatest impact, in the more ratified realm of constitutional politics, to which we now turn.

CONSTITUTIONAL POLITICS IN THE 1980s

As noted above, throughout the late 1960s and 1970s provincial governments had moved towards a consensual constitutional vision in which both the formal powers and fiscal resources of provincial governments would be substantially increased. While provinces differed somewhat on their ultimate destination, they were all on the same road towards a more decentralized federal state. By and large, Ottawa's response to the provinces was one of accommodation. "Opting out" provisions initiated in

1964 opened the door for provinces to withdraw from joint federal–provincial programs without incurring any financial penalty if analogous provincial programs were established, although it was hoped that only Quebec would walk through. (With respect to the Canada Pension Plan, Quebec exercised its constitutional prerogative under Section 94A of the Constitution Act and did not opt in, establishing instead its own separate but fully compatible Quebec Pension Plan.) Fiscal ground rules were changed as conditional grants gave way to unconditional grants. Although federal funding of shared-cost programs continued under the terms of the Federal–Provincial Fiscal Arrangements and Established Programs Financing Act of 1977, the provinces were not obliged to spend the federal funds in any specific way, nor was the level of federal funding tied to the level of provincial expenditure. In an extended round of constitutional discussions during the 1970s, Ottawa also appeared willing to discuss the devolution of some federal powers to the provinces. Thus, despite Pierre Trudeau's image in parts of the country as an unrelenting centralist, his first eleven years in office were marked by an appreciable decentralization of the Canadian political system, a trend clearly at odds with that in other western countries.[50]

When the Trudeau Liberals returned to power in 1980, the accommodative stance disappeared as Ottawa began to reassert the constitutional and fiscal presence of the federal government. Cooperative federalism was devalued and Ottawa became increasingly resistant to provincial encroachments upon its own domain. Federal–provincial conferences, which had provided a highly publicized stage for provincial attacks on the federal government, were de-emphasized as Ottawa tried to recapture the power of unilateral action. (Federal–provincial constitutional conferences were an exception.) Extensive media campaigns were launched to explain what the Government of Canada was doing for, rather than to, Canadians. More subtly, these campaigns were designed to strengthen the bond between individual Canadians and their *national* government.

Ottawa also began to pull back from shared-cost programs, which were consuming a large part of the federal budget and contributing to a growing national debt. The federal government was growing uneasy about a situation in which it was accountable to Parliament for funds spent on such programs even though it had little control over how those funds were spent by the provinces. Of particular importance, however, was the matter of political credit or "visibility." If Ottawa, for example, was to continue to pick up half the cost of advanced education, federal politicians wanted taxpayers to realize that advanced education was not being provided exclusively by the provincial governments. Ottawa did not want to be seen as the government that taxed heavily and did little in return for the average Canadian, while the provincial governments enjoyed the

Andy Donato, Toronto Sun

In a 1982 news conference, Prime Minister Trudeau declared the death of cooperative federalism: "the old type of federalism where we give money to the provinces, where they kick us in the teeth because they didn't get enough . . . is finished."

Cited in Sheilagh M. Dunn, *The Year in Review 1982: Intergovernmental Relations in Canada* (Kingston: Institute of Intergovernmental Relations, Queen's University, 1982), p. 6.

enviable position of supplying popular programs invisibly financed in large part by federal transfer payments.

In short, it was "no more Mr. Nice Guy" as a reassertive federal government and unrelentingly assertive provincial governments met in the wake of the 1980 Quebec referendum on sovereignty association to hammer out a new constitutional framework for the Canadian federal state.

The Constitution Act, 1982

The seventeen months following the Quebec referendum witnessed intensive constitutional negotiations between the federal and provincial governments, and extensive constitutional discussions across the land. While the leading actors throughout were the federal and provincial governments, important supporting roles were played by the courts, the Progressive Conservative and New Democratic opposition parties in the House of Commons, the British Parliament, public opinion polls, journalists, academics, innumerable private Canadians participating in countless public debates, and a plethora of special interest groups among which women and native peoples were the most active. Yet despite all the activity, little progress was made until November 1981 when Ottawa and nine of the ten provincial governments, *excluding Quebec*, signed a Constitutional Accord. Five months later, on April 17, 1982, the Constitution Act was proclaimed by Queen Elizabeth II at a rain-swept ceremony in Ottawa, attended by all of the First Ministers except Quebec's René Lévesque. After a prolonged, tortuous and at times bitter process, Canadians had a new constitution, or what ex-Senator Eugene Forsey has more accurately described as the old constitution "with knobs on." Let us look first at the knobs.

CONSTITUTIONAL CHANGE

The Constitution Act of 1982 entailed a number of important changes. First, the Canadian constitution was patriated; the assent of the British Parliament is no longer needed for constitutional amendment. Patriation was achieved through the adoption of a Canadian formula for constitutional amendment, built into Part V, Sections 38 through 49, of the Constitution Act. The basic amendment procedure is defined in Section 38(1):

> An amendment to the Constitution of Canada may be made by proclamation issued by the Governor General under the Great Seal of Canada where so authorized by (a) resolutions of the Senate and House of Commons; and (b) resolutions of the legislative assemblies of at least two-thirds of the provinces that have, in the aggregate, according to the then latest general census, at least fifty per cent of the population of all the provinces.

However, any amendment "that derogates from the legislative powers, the proprietary rights or any other rights or privileges of the legislature or government of a province" requires the consent of each province affected. Any amendment to the amending formula itself, to the office of the Queen, Governor General or Lieutenant Governor, to the composition of the Supreme Court, to the right of a province to have at least the same number of MPs as it has Senators, and to most language guarantees requires the *unanimous* consent of Parliament and all ten provinces. Finally, the Senate's power in the amendment procedure has been limited to a suspensive veto; under Section 47(1), an amendment can proceed without the need for Senate approval if, after the passage of 180 days from approval by the House of Commons, the House again adopts a resolution in support of the amendment.

The long-term significance of the amending formula remains to be seen. As a general rule, formal procedures of constitutional amendment are rarely used in federal states; the tortuous and ultimately unsuccessful efforts to pass the Equal Rights Amendment in the United States illustrate the very cumbersome nature of formal methods of constitutional amendment. Other means such as judicial reinterpretation in the United States and ad hoc federal-provincial agreements in Canada's past provide more flexible means of keeping some rough congruence between constitutional rules and political realities. To the extent that formal amendment procedures inhibit more informal means of constitutional amendment, the significance of the amending procedure may come less from the constitutional flexibility that it engenders than from the flexibility it impairs.

By far the most important change in the 1982 Act was the constitutional entrenchment of the Charter of Rights and Freedoms. Prior to 1982, Canadian constitutional documents primarily addressed the structure of Canadian governments and the division of powers among governments. The Constitution Act of 1982 expands the reach of the written constitution to embrace the relationship between *citizens* and governments. This is not to suggest that Canadians lacked rights and freedoms in the past, for they did not, nor that such rights and freedoms were devoid of protection in the past, for they were not. However, the Charter enumerates those rights and freedoms, entrenches them within the written constitution, and transfers the power to determine the practical limits of their application from a political process that is federally divided to a judicial process which is not.[51] The courts have now been placed in a position where they can judge acts of either Parliament or provincial legislatures to be unconstitutional on grounds other than contravention of the federal division of powers.

Admittedly, there are a number of important formal limits on the extent to which the Charter constrains Canadian governments. (There may also be important informal limits if courts and judges prove unwilling to embrace an activist stance towards the Charter and judicial intervention.) Section 1 of the 1982 Act states that the Charter "guarantees the rights and freedoms set out in it *subject only to such reasonable limits prescribed by law as can be demonstrably justified in a free and demo-*

cratic society" (emphasis added). How this clause will be interpreted over the long run by the courts remains to be seen. Legislatures can also use the "notwithstanding" clause to override some sections of the Charter for a renewable five-year period. Section 33 reads that "Parliament or the legislature of a province may expressly declare in an Act of Parliament or of the legislature, as the case may be, that the Act or a provision thereof shall operate notwithstanding a provision included in section 2 or section 7 to 15 of this Charter." These sections include the fundamental freedoms of conscience, religion, thought, expression, peaceful assembly, and association; legal rights; and the equality rights set forth in Section 15. They do *not* include basic democratic rights, mobility rights, language rights, minority language educational rights and gender equality (Section 28 reads "notwithstanding anything in this Charter, the rights and freedoms referred to in it are guaranteed equally to male and female persons"), all of which have been placed beyond Section 33.

The notwithstanding clause provides a constitutional mechanism of non-compliance with Supreme Court decisions,[52] a mechanism that is available to both levels of government but which to date has only been employed by the legislative assemblies of Quebec and Saskatchewan. In May 1982, only weeks after the Constitution Act was proclaimed, the Quebec National Assembly passed Bill 62 which applied the notwithstanding provision to *all* Quebec legislation passed up to that point in time. Subsequent Quebec legislation incorporated the notwithstanding clause until, in 1986, Quebec discontinued its blanket use of the clause in order to help set the stage for the Meech Lake Accord. As discussed in Chapter 3, the notwithstanding clause was again invoked in December 1988 when the National Assembly responded to the Supreme Court's ruling on Quebec's sign laws. In Saskatchewan, the notwithstanding clause was used in the legislature's response to a threatened strike by provincial public employees.

The Supreme Court of Canada

The Supreme Court of Canada was created in 1875. In order to diminish French Canadian fears that the Court would pose a threat to provincial rights and powers, the Supreme Court Act guaranteed Quebec representation on the Court. At the same time, Parliament rejected a proposal that at least one of the judges come from British Columbia "because of the feeling on both sides of the House that the representative principle was not of the same importance to the other provinces as it was to Quebec."[53] The composition of the contemporary Supreme Court, which now encompasses nine justices including three from Quebec, is entrenched in Section 41.(d) of the Constitution Act and can only be changed with the *unanimous* consent of Parliament and the ten provincial legislative assemblies.

The Supreme Court Act did not abolish the right of appeal to the Judicial Committee of the Privy Council, and thus the Court became only a link in the chain of appeal rather than the final arbiter. Only in 1949 was the right of appeal to the JCPC abolished and the Court made supreme in fact as well as in name. The 1949 change opened the door for the Court's more active participation in Canadian political life.

The Supreme Court provides an interesting combination of the rule of law and the principle of representation. In theory, the rule of law is incompatible with the more political notion of representation. Nevertheless, while it is expected that the decisions of the Court will be guided by law, its structure, like that of other central government institutions, is based on representational principles. Thus the six non-Quebec justices are selected so as to ensure Atlantic and western Canadian "representation."

An important structural feature of the Supreme Court is that appointments have been made by the federal government alone. This feature had some important consequences. As James Mallory explains, "the Supreme Court of Canada—like that of the United States—is capable of playing a role of a 'nationalizing' institution, which interprets and imposes the sense of the whole community even when that consensus is openly rejected by part of the community."[54] At the same time, provincial governments have been wary of that very nationalizing potential. There has been a corresponding reluctance to have federal-provincial disputes settled in a judicial arena where the umpires have been appointed by one of the parties in the dispute. While, to date, the Supreme Court has not been overly centralist in its interpretation of constitutional disputes, provincial fears on that account have not evaporated.[55] Those fears have been addressed by the Meech Lake Accord, which, if ratified, will require that the federal government appoint future Supreme Court justices from lists submitted by the provinces.

Historically, the Court's role in the Canadian political process was limited not only by the right of appeal to the JCPC but also by the general subordination of Canadian courts to legislative assemblies. Apart from interpretations of the federal division of powers, the doctrine of parliamentary supremacy limited the Court's ability to strike out in different directions from those established by Parliament or the provincial legislative assemblies. Now, with the Charter in place, the Court has the constitutional authority and the political legitimacy to play a more central role in Canadian political life.

The notwithstanding clause is one of the most innovative features of the Constitution Act. In principle, it allows both federal and provincial legislatures to override court decisions when such decisions are at odds with public preferences, as reflected by elected politicians, and when such decisions rest upon section 2 or sections 7 to 15 of the Charter. Thus the clause provides a parliamentary check, and in some sense a democratic check, on judicial activism that departs too radically from the political mainstream; "its existence removes much of the anti-democratic sting from judicial decisions vetoing the acts of the democratically accountable branches of government."[56] For example, if the Supreme Court were to take an overly restrictive, or not sufficiently restrictive, approach to an issue such as abortion or pornography, legislative assemblies could step in to modify the policy parameters outlined by the Court and to "immunize" their legislative response from further court action. The notwithstanding clause also reflects the federal character of Canada in that it enables provincial governments to circumvent the universal application of the Charter. In 1988, for example, the Quebec National Assembly was able to use the notwithstanding clause to reinstate unilingual sign provisions in the province's language law after those provisions had been struck down by the Supreme Court.

As the sign debate also illustrates, any use of the notwithstanding clause is likely to be very contentious. Indeed, the sign debate brought the clause itself under political attack from those who wanted Charter-based rights placed beyond the reach of legislative assemblies. In a speech to the House of Commons on April 6, 1989, Prime Minister Mulroney went so far as to declare that "a constitution that does not protect the inalienable and imprescriptable individual rights of individual Canadians is not worth the paper it is written on." Mr. Mulroney called on MPs and premiers to amend the constitution so as to remove the notwithstanding clause: "All members ... will want to work together over the next few years as best we can to make sure that the Constitution is improved and that that major flaw [the notwithstanding clause] which reduces your individual rights and mine, which holds them hostage, is dealt with collectively by the premiers so that all Canadians have their fundamental rights and know they exist together." This suggestion was not met with any enthusiasm by Quebec Premier Robert Bourassa, who pointed out that Section 38.3 of the amending formula would make it impossible for the notwithstanding clause to be removed without Quebec's consent, and that Quebec's consent was not to be expected.

Putting aside the continuing debate over the notwithstanding clause, there is no question that the Charter has had a major impact on Canadian political life, and that its impact is likely to increase in the years ahead. The Supreme Court will ultimately determine what the rights embedded in the Charter mean in practice, and this role in turn will draw the Court into the centre of the political arena. More generally, and as the abortion debate has emphatically demonstrated, the Charter will politicize the judicial system. With the Charter in place, the courts now provide an important political resource for groups and individuals who feel their interests have not been adequately taken into account by Parliament and provincial legislatures, or who have lost in the legislative arena. Here again the ongoing controversy over abortion provides a stark illustration of the growing entanglement of the courts and political protest. It also shows how the Charter weakens the ability of government to control the political agenda; court action propelled abortion back onto the legislative agenda of Parliament despite the best efforts of the government to keep it off.

In the short run, the increased involvement of the courts in the political process may work to the detriment of more conventional political actors and institutions. As Leslie Pal and David Taras point out, Canadians have a somewhat unrealistic view of the courts, combined with a pervasive cynicism towards things political:

> We see judges and courts as above mundane politics. They are lordly, pristine, and they set precedents for our common welfare, unlike the lowly rascals who are elected to political office. This mistake is dangerous because it fails to recognize that when courts get into the rights game, they are no better equipped to decide matters of public policy than are legislatures.[57]

In the longer run, public perceptions of judges and the courts are likely to be corroded as both are drawn further and further into the political fray. However, there should be no expectation that perceptions of elected politicians will improve as a consequence.

For better or for worse, we can expect a greater "judicialization" of political life,[58] a greater pursuit of political ends through judicial means, and within a judicial arena that is national in design and intent.[59] For somewhat related reasons, the Charter may also affect the federal system itself. If Charter-related decisions by the courts continue to have a greater impact on provincial legislation than on legislation passed by Parliament,[60] and if the thrust of such decisions is to strike down provincial departures from national norms and standards, then the Charter could tilt the federal balance by nationalizing Canadian political life. It is for this reason that provincial governments have become increasingly concerned about appointments to the Supreme Court, and that the Meech Lake Accord brings provincial governments into the appointment process. (If the Accord is ratified, the federal government will continue to make appointments to the Supreme Court, but from lists of nominees submitted by provincial governments.) More generally, the Charter will force Canadians to grapple with the complex problems posed by the combination of judicial review and federalism, problems not addressed by the country's founding constitutional document despite a good deal of American precedent.[61]

A more abstract but potentially even greater change may come from the Charter's impact on the Canadian political culture, on the norms and values which bond the political community. Despite the notwithstanding clause, the Charter focuses our attention on rights shared by all Canadians, and on rights that will receive their definitive form through a national institution, the Supreme Court of Canada. In this sense, the Charter may tend to obscure the nation's federal character, and to blunt territorial cleavages, by reorienting the political culture to rights shared by all Canadians regardless of where they might happen to live. In Pierre Trudeau's words, "the Charter defines the common thread which pulls us together." It can be argued, however, that while a rights-based political culture may blur regional distinctions within Canada, it may also blur the distinction between Canada and the United States. In the words of Leslie Pal and David Taras, "Canada is moving toward an American-style system in which individual rights are the primal scream of political consciousness."[62]

Here it should also be noted that the Charter has had a marked impact on the nature of political discourse and debate, an impact which goes well beyond a diminished emphasis on the territorial and regional dimensions of Canadian political life. Our political language has become infused with, and perhaps overburdened by, the terminology of rights. Conflicts over matters of public policy are increasingly framed in terms of "rights"; where people used to speak of "interests" or "claims," they now speak in the more absolutist language of rights. Unfortunately, rights provide more barren ground for pragmatic political compromises and tradeoffs; they are not easily digested by the political process. As a consequence, the stakes in relatively routine political decisions are increased as the protagonists are unwilling to accept any decision which might compromise their rights.

Thus while the 1982 Constitution Act did not fundamentally recast the constitutional and institutional foundations of the Canadian federal state, the Charter of Rights has had and will continue to have a marked impact on Canadian political life. The Charter provides the foundation for a new rights-based and nationally oriented political culture, one that does not sit easily with the federally-based constitution represented by the Constitution Act of 1867.

THE EQUALITY INDUSTRY
Jeffrey Simpson
The Globe and Mail, April 7, 1989

The cry for equality, however defined, has been and remains an imperative in Canadian public discourse.

Governments everywhere are pressed daily to render justice to individuals, groups and regions feeling aggrieved. Such cries have been heard often before; nowadays they form the background music for everything that happens in government.

Naturally enough, governments have responded in a variety of ways, including a proliferation of bodies and laws attempting to define equality... there are now 11 provincial and territorial human rights commissions [plus the Canadian Human Rights Commission], nine provincial ombudsmen, four specialized federal ombudsmen or quasi-ombudsmen, plus a body of statutes governing equal employment. And, of course, there is the Charter of Rights and Freedoms.

We may, therefore, describe these institutions and laws as the bricks and mortar of the equality industry, whose clientele theoretically includes all citizens, though in practice it is made up of minority groups. In the evolution of this industry, persuasion is yielding to regulation and reaction to positive action.

Equality Rights

It is likely that the Charter's most wide-ranging impact on Canadian life will come from the equality provisions set forth in Section 15:

15.(1) Every individual is equal before and under the law and has the right to equal protection and equal benefit of the law without discrimination and, in particular, without discrimination based on race, national or ethnic origin, colour, religion, sex, age or mental or physical disability.

15.(2) Subsection (1) does not preclude any law, program or activity that has as its object the amelioration of conditions of disadvantaged individuals or groups including those that are disadvantaged because of race, national or ethnic origin, colour, religion, sex, age or mental or physical disability.

Section 15(2) thus gives constitutional sanction to what are termed "affirmative action programs". For example, a program designed to increase the employment of aboriginal persons within the federal government could not be overturned because it violated the equal rights provisions of Section 15 (1) by discriminating against those of non-aboriginal descent.

Before leaving this discussion, we should note four additional sections of the 1982 Constitution Act. Section 36 builds in a constitutional commitment to equalization payments, although it is unlikely that this section will have any immediate impact on public policy, as the principles that it enshrines are not new to the Canadian political community. Section 6 guarantees mobility rights that include the right of every citizen of Canada to enter, remain in, and leave Canada and the right of every citizen to take up residence in, and pursue a livelihood in, any province of his or her choice. Section 6(4), however, states that these latter provisions "do not preclude any law, program or activity that has as its object the amelioration in a province of conditions of individuals in that province who are socially or economically disadvantaged if the rate of employment in that province is below the rate of employment in Canada." Thus provincial legislation designed to give employment preference to residents of a particular province could be struck down by the courts if passed in Ontario, but not if passed in Newfoundland. Section 92A, which addresses the 1867 division of powers, shores up provincial ownership of and control over non-renewable natural resources, forestry resources, and electrical energy. Finally, s.35 defines the aboriginal peoples of Canada to include the Indian, Inuit, and Metis peoples and states that "the existing aboriginal and treaty rights of the aboriginal peoples of Canada are hereby recognized and affirmed." As neither these rights nor the constituent groups are defined in the Constitution Act, the practical significance of this provision remains to be determined.

CONSTITUTIONAL CONTINUITY

The 1982 Constitution Act undeniably altered Canada's constitutional underpinnings, for some of the "knobs" referred to by Senator Forsey are very big knobs indeed. However, the outstanding *federal* characteristic of the Act lies in its continuity with the past. Apart from s.92(A), there was no formal amendment to the federal-provincial division of powers, even though that division was an ongoing source of intergovernmental friction throughout most of the 1960s and 1970s. While the Charter may eventually alter the division of powers, such effects are likely to be subtle and indirect. The Act did not address the institutional constraints on regional representation discussed in Chapter 4. Although both the amending formula and s.92(A) closely match the stance adopted by the western premiers in the constitutional negotiations, the larger issues of Senate reform and electoral reform were not addressed. By making any future constitutional amendment the prerogative of legislative assemblies and not the people, by *not* appealing to popular sovereignty, the Act did nothing to strengthen the identification of individual Canadians with the constitutional apparatus of the federal state. As Reginald Whitaker has argued,

> a functioning federal state must strike some stable balance between regional, provincial or subcultural identities, and an identity *qua* citizens with their national state. The recognition of the principle of the sovereignty of the people is a way of encouraging such attachment over more limited identities.[63]

Although, over the long run, the Charter and a more activist Supreme Court may strengthen the bond between individual Canadians and national institutions, in the short run the Constitution Act did not address the major structural problems that had launched the search for a new constitution in the first place.

Most importantly, the 1982 Constitution Act did not address, except by its silence, the place of Quebec within the Canadian federal state and within the national political community. Although the federal government had pledged itself to a "renewed federalism" should Quebecers reject the 1980 referendum on sovereignty association, the end product of the constitutional negotiations set in motion by that defeat did not alter Quebec's role. Nothing was changed with respect to the jurisdictional authority of the National Assembly or with respect to Quebec's representation in federal institutions. Nor did the Act include a preamble within which Quebec's unique contribution to the national community could be acknowledged. For these reasons and more, Donald Smiley denounced the Constitution Act as a betrayal of Quebec:

The pressures of both government and opposition parties in Quebec provincial politics from 1960 onward has been for an enhanced range of autonomy for the authorities of that province and corresponding restrictions on the power of the federal government over Quebecers. The Constitution Act, 1982 *restricts* the powers of the Legislature and government of Quebec and was brought into being by a procedure which *was opposed* by that Legislature and government. Furthermore, the constitutional reform which was effected in the spring of 1982 was an integral part of a general initiative from Ottawa towards a more highly centralized federal system. The pledges of constitutional reform made to the Quebec electorate by the federal Liberal leaders have *not* been honoured, and it is not too much to say that this electorate has been betrayed.[64]

The proclamation of the Constitution Act on April 17, 1982, temporarily brought to a close a constitutional process which stretched back in time to the early 1970s. However, because the Act left so many loose ends, because it had not addressed fundamental questions relating to Quebec and institutional reform, the pause in constitutional negotiations was bound to be brief. As Alan Cairns observed in 1983:

In French-English relations, Quebec-Ottawa relations, and federal-provincial relations more generally, there is no resting place, no end to tensions and frustrations. There are no constitutional utopias. We have to be satisfied with the stumbling efforts of imperfect men to keep our problems at bay. From that perspective a restrained half cheer may be suggested as the appropriate response to the new Canadian constitution. It is the only constitution we have.[65]

In the spring of 1987, a very different group of imperfect men met at Meech Lake to address the loose ends of the Constitution Act, 1982.

THE MEECH LAKE ACCORD

In the first few years following the ratification of the 1982 Constitution Act, little could be done to overcome Quebec's exclusion from the constitutional agreement; constructive movement required, at the very least, a change in players. As it turned out, there was a relatively rapid turnout among the key first ministers. In the late winter of 1984, Pierre Trudeau announced his retirement and, in September 1984, a new Progressive Conservative government led by Brian Mulroney swept to power in Ottawa. In Quebec, René Lévesque also retired, and in the 1985 Quebec provincial election the Parti Québécois government went down to defeat to the provincial Liberals, led by Robert Bourassa. Thus Canada had a new prime minister determined to solidify his party's still tenuous hold on the Quebec electorate, and Quebec had a new premier determined to prove to nationalist forces in the province that a federalist premier could deliver, that he could secure a place for Quebec within Canada while at the same time protecting and enhancing the political autonomy of Quebec. Thus the stage was set for another round of constitutional negotiations.

The lead was taken by the government of Quebec which, in 1986, announced five conditions that would have to be met if Quebec were to return to the constitutional fold. The five conditions were: (1) constitutional recognition of Quebec as a distinct society; (2) the right to opt out, with full financial compensation, from new federal programs in fields of exclusive provincial jurisdiction; (3) an expanded provincial veto for constitutional amendments; (4) a provincial role in appointments to the Supreme Court of Canada; and (5) constitutional entrenchment of Quebec's role in immigration, a role which had been expanded over the years through agreements between the Quebec and federal governments. At the August 1986 Premiers' Conference in Edmonton, these five conditions were endorsed by the ten premiers as the foundation for a resumption of constitutional negotiations. Then, at a meeting at Meech Lake on April 30, 1987, a tentative constitutional accord was unanimously endorsed by the first ministers. After fine tuning the following month at a meeting at the Langevin Block in Ottawa, the Meech Lake Accord emerged on the 3rd of June. (See Appendix E for the text of the Accord.) The Accord was not only endorsed by all eleven first ministers, but also received enthusiastic support from the leaders of the two opposition parties in the House of Commons.

The Accord met the five conditions laid down by Quebec, but it did so in such a way as to overcome some of the traditional opposition, expressed by other provincial governments, to any special constitutional status for Quebec. The Accord expanded Quebec's veto on constitutional change by expanding the unanimous consent provisions of the 1982 amending formula to include the powers of the Senate; the method of selecting Senators; the number of Senators by which a province is entitled to be represented; the principle of proportionate representation of the provinces in the House of Commons; the Supreme Court of Canada; the extension of existing provinces into the territories; and the creation of new provinces. Thus while Quebec's role in the amending formula would be enhanced by the Accord, it would be no greater than that of any other province. The Accord gave all provinces the right to opt out, with full financial compensation, from new federal programs in areas of exclusive provincial jurisdiction, provided that the opting-out provinces initiated their own programs to meet the national objectives of the federal program. The Accord stated that future appointments to the Supreme Court and to the Senate would be made by the federal government from lists submitted by the provinces, although only in the case of Quebec were three positions on the Supreme Court tied specifically to one province.

Prime Minister Brian Mulroney shakes hands with
Quebec Premier Robert Bourassa following the
signing of an agreement that brought Quebec into
the Constitution.

The Canadian Press.

The Accord also gave expanded constitutional recognition to Quebec's
role in immigration, recognition that could be extended to other provinces in the future, should they request it. In these instances, then,
Quebec's conditions were universalized to include all ten provinces.
Quebec received special, albeit somewhat ambiguous, constitutional
status only in the Accord's recognition that "Quebec constitutes within
Canada a distinct society."

As noted above, the initial reaction to the Accord was generally positive. Although vigorous concerns were expressed by Pierre Trudeau, and although northerners, francophone minorities outside Quebec, Senate reformers, and some feminist organizations were uneasy with parts of the Accord, it appeared to be a constitutional *fait accompli*. However, the first ministers had allowed three years for the Accord's formal ratification by Parliament and the ten provincial legislative assemblies, and it was this decision that allowed opposition to the Accord to build. For an extended period the Accord was exposed as a target for increasingly critical public inspection as one group after another began to assess the potential impact of the Accord on their own interests and future. More importantly, the prolonged ratification period meant that some of the first ministers and provincial governments which had initially supported the Accord were bound to fall by the wayside in the wake of provincial elections. Just as the cast of players in 1987 was quite different from that in 1982, so too was it quite different again in 1989/90 from what it had been when the Accord first appeared.

Ratification proceeded quickly in some of the provinces, including Quebec, but it proceeded at a more leisurely pace in others. As a consequence, the Accord had not yet been ratified in New Brunswick when the incumbent Progressive Conservative government went down to defeat in a provincial election. The incoming Liberal government, led by Frank McKenna, stated that it was opposed to the Accord on a variety of grounds, and would not proceed with ratification until a public hearing had been held. Whether by design or not, Premier McKenna then became the national spokesperson for those who opposed the Accord, but who, to that point, had lacked a governmental spokesperson. In Manitoba, the incumbent NDP government also went down to defeat before the Accord's ratification. The new leader of the minority Progressive Conservative government, Gary Filmon, initially supported the Accord, but the opposition parties were opposed. Then in December 1988, when the Quebec government overrode the Supreme Court's decision on Bill 101, Filmon also came out against the Accord. In the spring of 1989, the Progressive Conservative government in Newfoundland, which had secured legislative ratification for the Accord, went down to defeat, and the new Liberal premier, Clyde Wells, announced that he would withdraw the province's support for the Accord unless changes were made. Thus, by the fall of 1989, unanimous support for the Accord had dissolved and ratification was in doubt.

With regard to the Accord, there are a number of important points to stress. The first is that the primary purpose of the Accord was to secure Quebec's support for the Constitution, to overcome Quebec's exclusion

Roy Peterson, *Swamped* (Vancouver/Toronto: Douglas & McIntyre, 1987), p. 12.

from the 1982 constitutional agreement. As Brian Mulroney somewhat prematurely said at the time that the Accord was first signed, "Tonight Canada is whole again, the Canadian family is together again, and the nation is one again." In an editorial calling for ratification of the Accord by

Manitoba and New Brunswick, *The Globe and Mail* (June 6, 1989) was even more emphatic:

> Meech Lake is intended almost solely to bring Quebec willingly under the authority of the 1982 Constitution Act. Meech Lake should be *immune to criticism* for failing to achieve other ends; it was not intended to do so. (emphasis added)

The second point, however, is that the impact of the Accord is by no means restricted to Quebec. The Accord, if ratified, would have a very broad impact on the Canadian federal system for it touches upon the power and role of all provincial governments; the nature of federal institutions including the Supreme Court, the Senate, and First Ministers' Conferences; the creation of new provinces; future social programs; and possibly judicial interpretation of the Charter. As Keith Banting notes:

> ... the dynamics that would be set in motion by the Accord point to a more regionally diverse pattern of social service initiatives in the future.... Canadians crossing provincial boundaries would notice greater variation in program design than they would otherwise have done.[66]

The Accord, in other words, is not a narrow document tailored to the specific constitutional interests and aspirations of Quebec; it is a much more sweeping constitutional agreement. Indeed, much of the opposition to the Accord has focused on those aspects, such as the Accord's potential impact on Senate reform, which are tangential at best to the initial concerns of Quebec.

The third point is that supporters and opponents of the Accord disagree on the Accord's potential impact on further constitutional change. Supporters argue that, although there are other constitutional matters which should be addressed, negotiations on such matters cannot proceed until the Accord has been ratified and Quebec has been brought back to the constitutional table. Certainly Quebec has been very adamant on this point. Opponents argue that once the Accord has been ratified, further constitutional change will be very difficult if not impossible to achieve, in part because of the expanded provisions for unanimous consent and in part because Quebec may be indifferent to and even hostile to further constitutional change once its own constitutional aspirations have been met. Opponents of the Accord therefore argue that other constitutional changes should be tied to the Accord's ratification. On this matter, both sides may well be correct.

The fourth and perhaps most important point is that a good deal of the opposition to the Accord has been directed as much to the constitutional process that produced the Accord as to the content of the Accord per se. More specifically, concern has been expressed about the way in which eleven men, meeting in private, could rewrite the basic constitutional parameters of the Canadian federal state. Admittedly, the process which produced the Accord was not significantly different from that which produced the Constitution Act of 1982, and in the case of the Constitution Act there was little procedural criticism. Since the introduction of the Charter, however, Canadians have been more prone to see the Constitution as a contractual agreement between citizens and their governments, and not solely as an agreement among governments. As a further consequence, there has been increased interest in some form of public participation in the process of constitutional change, although the extent and parameters of that participation are hazy at best.

Here it is interesting to note Alan Cairns's insightful analysis of opposition rhetoric to the Accord. Professor Cairns examined testimony to both Senate and House committees examining the Accord, and came to the following conclusion:

> The bitterness and passion that inform the presentations of the numerous groups objecting to the Accord are not based on a narrow instrumental calculation of its effects on the future flow of material benefits. Their anger is not driven by the fear of tangible gains foregone, but by a more complex battery of emotions. The representatives of women's groups, of aboriginals, of visible minorities, of supporters of multiculturalism, along with northerners and basic defenders of the Charter employ the vocabulary of personal and group identity, of being included or excluded, of being accepted or being treated as an outsider, of being treated with respect as a worthy participant or being cast into the audience as a spectator as one's fate is being decided by others. They employ the language of status—they are insulted, wounded, hurt, offended, bypassed, not invited, ignored, left out, and shunted aside. They evaluate their treatment through the lens of pride, dignity, honour, propriety, legitimacy, and recognition—or their reverse. Their discourse is a minority, outsider discourse. They clearly distrust established governing elites. They are in, but not of the constitution.[67]

The ongoing debate over the Accord demonstrates the symbolic and emotional importance of constitutional politics. Discussions of constitutional change necessarily entail a discussion of the underlying nature of the political community, and of the direction that community should take in generations to come. Thus, such discussions can touch very deep emotional roots and, in some circumstances, they can expose deeply ingrained divisions within the political community. Constitution-making is an important form of community expression, and it should be expected that the community will speak through discordant voices. As Howard Aster observes:

> The Canadian soul is indeed a conundrum. Through political actions we give it a face and a character. Making a constitution is not simply making a deal. It

" ...WELL THEN... IF NOT A RATIFIED CONSTITUTIONAL ACCORD WHAT DO YOU FEEL FORMS THE HEART AND SOUL OF THE CANADIAN PSYCHE?... "

Brian Gable, *Gable: The Editorial Cartoons of Brian Gable* (Saskatoon, Sask.: Western Producer Prairie Books, 1987), p.20.

is defining, slowly, carefully, and painfully, the fate of our next generation. Open debate, not foreclosing discussion, is desperately needed.[68]

Since 1982 and the arrival of the Charter, Canadians have been less willing to speak through their first ministers on constitutional issues. The Charter has changed the Canadian political culture so as to open up the process of constitutional change to more broadly cast citizen participation.

THE CANADIAN FEDERAL COMMUNITY

In the confederation agreement a collective decision was reached that Canadians would be served by a federal system, and that the powers of the state would be divided between the federal and provincial governments. The latter in turn have delegated some of their powers to local governments, giving Canadians a three-tiered political system. Over time, this decision has resulted in an extensive network of intergovernmental relations, the federal-provincial component of which has been the focus of this chapter. As governments at all levels expanded in size and extended their regulatory reach further into the economy and society, this network became not only more complex but also more vital to the provision of government programs and services. To borrow an analogy used by the American political scientist Karl Deutsch, intergovernmental relations can be seen as the nervous system of the modern federal state. Just as the nervous system of an athlete coordinates the various parts of his or her body to produce fluid motion, intergovernmental relations coordinate the governments of the federal state. And, to extend the analogy further, just as the athlete occasionally stumbles or performs below potential, intergovernmental relations also fail us from time to time.

While a great deal of the interaction between governments occurs in a cooperative and productive atmosphere, some intergovernmental friction and conflict is inevitable. Both federal and provincial governments have become large, complex, and ponderous entities, and the task of coordination is inherently difficult. The federal system represents a precarious balance of fiscal resources, jurisdictional responsibilities, and citizen demands. Maintaining this balance in the face of changing economic and social conditions requires no small degree of political skill. Friction is generated by competition among political elites,[69] by conflicting partisan interests, by conflicting bureaucratic ambitions, and by substantive disagreements over the direction of public policy. Such friction is the price we pay for the size and complexity of modern government and for the adoption of a federal system. While the system can always be fine-tuned and lubricated, intergovernmental friction will never entirely disappear.

Intergovernmental conflict becomes a more serious matter when it serves as an outlet for major cleavages within the Canadian society. Conflict between Ottawa and the government of Quebec, for example, may go well beyond the intrinsic problems of governmental coordination to a fundamental debate over the place of Quebec within the Canadian political community. At issue is which government best speaks for Quebec when the two governments pursue quite different political visions. Conflict between Ottawa and the western provinces may go beyond the intergovernmental friction inherent in any modern federal state to regional dissatisfaction with the representational character of national political institutions. Intergovernmental conflict in the energy sector may reflect opposing views on Canada's economic relationship with the United States, and the competing interests of energy-producing and energy-consuming provinces. Intergovernmental conflict over medicare engages basic redistributive principles, as did conflict between Newfoundland and Ottawa over the ownership and control of offshore resources. Not infrequently, then, intergovernmental relations provide the stage upon which we act out the dominant themes in Canadian political life.

It is at this point that intergovernmental conflict becomes more than the inevitable price of federalism. Intergovernmental conflict can seriously disrupt the provision of government services and programs. As Hugh Thorburn observes, " . . . our economy has become balkanized and our politics confrontational, leading us to dissipate our top decision-making resources on struggles of allocation between regions, provinces, industries and so on instead of building a consensus around an agreed-upon program of development."[70] Both Thorburn and Garth Stevenson agree that intergovernmental conflict weakens Canada's international trading position, with Stevenson going on to argue that it distorts the Canadian political agenda: " . . . a lessening of the Canadian obsession with provincial interests and jurisdictional controversies might direct our attention to more significant issues, such as the unequal distribution of wealth, power and opportunity across the population."[71] There is a danger that our political imagination has become too blinkered, too narrowly confined to the intergovernmental arena. By restricting our gaze to visions of which government should do what, we may ignore important ideological questions concerning the role of the state in the Canadian society and economy, the maintenance or dismemberment of the postwar welfare state, and the nature of our relationship with the United States.

Given the general importance of intergovernmental relations and their more specific entanglement with the basic cleavages of Canadian political life, it is not surprising that the call for reform is frequently heard. Suggestions for reform include replacing the Senate with a provincially appointed upper house, redistributing legislative powers so as to provide a more watertight compartmentalization and thereby reduce the need for intergovernmental relations, annual meetings of the First Ministers (as called for in the Meech Lake Accord), and creating an elected Senate to strengthen the political authority of the federal government. Richard Simeon, one of Canada's foremost experts on intergovernmental relations, has recommended the establishment of a permanent intergovernmental forum, a Council of Federation that would not have legislative powers and would not serve as a revised Senate, but which would enhance coordination and cooperation among governments. At the same time, however, Simeon argues that . . .

to rely almost entirely on the intergovernmental mechanism to reconcile centre and periphery, French and English, is to place an intolerable burden on this fragile structure. Thus, while strengthening this mechanism, we must at the same time look elsewhere: and in particular to political parties.[72]

Just as we cannot untangle the "big" issues of Canadian political life from intergovernmental relations, we should not expect an intergovernmental solution to those issues.

SUGGESTED READINGS

For an insightful collection of essays on the 1982 Constitution Act, see Keith Banting and Richard Simeon, eds., *And No One Cheered: Federalism, Democracy & The Constitution Act* (Toronto: Methuen, 1983). For a lively account of the process leading up to the Constitution Act, see Robert Sheppard and Michael Valpy, *The National Deal: The Fight for a Canadian Constitution* (Toronto: Fleet Books, 1982).

For a conceptual discussion of Canadian federalism, see Edwin R. Black, *Divided Loyalties: Canadian Concepts of Federalism* (Montreal: McGill-Queen's Press, 1975).

For a discussion of fiscal transfers in the Canadian federal system, see Dan Butler and Bruce D. Macnaughton, "More of Less for Whom? Debating Directions for the Public Sector," in Michael S. Whittington and Glen Williams, eds., *Canadian Politics in the 1980s*, Second Edition (Toronto: Methuen, 1984), pp. 1-32.

Alan C. Cairns, "The Governments and Societies of Canadian Federalism," *Canadian Journal of Political Science*, Vol. 10, 1977, pp. 695-726.

For a discussion of the impact of intergovernmental relations on legislative authority, see John Meisel, "New Challenges to Parliament: Arguing Over Wine Lists on the Titanic?", *Journal of Canadian Studies*, Vol. 14, 1979, p. 23; and Donald V. Smiley, "Federalism and the Legislative Process in Canada," in William A. W. Neilson and James C. MacPherson, eds., *The Legislative Process in Canada: The Need for Reform* (Montreal: Institute for Research on Public Policy, 1978), p. 73.

Patrick Monahan, *Politics and the Constitution: Federalism and the Supreme Court of Canada* (Toronto: Carswell-Methuen, 1987).

Larry Pratt, "The state and province-building: Alberta's development strategy," in Leo Panitch, ed., *The Canadian State: Political Economy and Political Power* (Toronto: University of Toronto Press, 1977), pp. 133-62. For an examination of province-building in Ontario and Quebec, see the special issue of the *Journal of Canadian Studies*, Vol. 18, No. 1 (Spring 1983).

Roy Romanow, John Whyte, and Howard Leeson, *Canada... Notwithstanding: The Making of the Constitution 1976-1982* (Toronto: Methuen, 1984).

Peter H. Russell, *The Judiciary in Canada: The Third Branch of Government* (Toronto: McGraw-Hill Ryerson, 1987).

Donald V. Smiley, *Canada in Question: Federalism in the Eighties*, Third Edition (Toronto: McGraw-Hill Ryerson, 1980).

Garth Stevenson, "Federalism and Intergovernmental Relations," in Michael S. Whittington and Glen Williams, eds., *Canadian Politics in the 1990s*, Third Edition (Toronto: Methuen, 1984), pp. 371-90.

H.G. Thorburn, *Planning and the Economy: Building Federal-Provincial Consensus* (Toronto: James Lorimer, 1984).

Timothy B. Woolstencroft, *Organizing Intergovernmental Relations* (Kingston: Institute for Intergovernmental Relations, Queen's University, 1982).

STUDY QUESTIONS

1. Over the course of this term, what federal–provincial conference activity has been reported in the press? What meetings have been held, and who attended—were the participants first ministers, cabinet ministers, or deputy ministers? What coverage were the meetings given in the press, what issues did they deal with, and what were the results?
2. This chapter has suggested that the growth of government has been a major factor in the growth of intergovernmental relations, and in the increase in intergovernmental conflict. To what extent do you think this relationship might work in reverse? If the growth of government is brought to a halt or if the size of government is actually decreased, should we expect any corresponding change in intergovernmental relations? What factors might promote or inhibit such change?
3. Make a note of all government programs and services to which you and your family have had access over the past few years. Try to be as inclusive as possible, keeping in mind local services and programs such as Medicare and Youth Allowances. What proportion of these programs and services has been provided by the federal government? By your provincial government? By your local government? What proportion has involved more than one level of government?
4. How does your own province handle federal–provincial relations? Is there a provincial ministry charged with this responsibility, or are they handled through the premier's office? If there is a ministry or department, does your library have its annual report? Can you document the

scope of your province's involvement in federal–provincial interaction?

5. Carefully read through the Constitution Act, 1982 and the Meech Lake Accord. What sections strike you as most important? Which are likely to have the greatest impact on your own life in the years ahead?

NOTES

1. Alberta Federal and Intergovernmental Affairs, *Fifteenth Annual Report*, Edmonton, July 7, 1989.
2. For a comprehensive survey, see Ernest D. Hodgson, *Federal Involvement in Public Education* (Toronto: Canadian Education Association, 1988).
3. Richard Rose, *Understanding Big Government: The Programme Approach* (London: Sage, 1981), p. 1.
4. H.G. Thorburn, *Planning and the Economy: Building Federal-Provincial Consensus* (Toronto: James Lorimer, 1984), p. 160.
5. See Gibbins, *Regionalism: Territorial Politics in Canada and the United States* (Toronto: Butterworths, 1982), Chapter 4.
6. W.L. Morton, "Confederation 1870 to 1896," *Journal of Canadian Studies*, Vol. 1, 1966, p. 23.
7. Donald V. Smiley, *The Canadian Political Nationality* (Toronto: Methuen, 1967), p. 21.
8. Ivo D. Duchacek, *Comparative Federalism: The Territorial Dimension of Politics* (New York: Holt, Rinehart and Winston, 1970), p. 324.
9. Garth Stevenson, *Unfulfilled Union: Canadian Federalism and National Unity* (Toronto: Macmillan, 1979), p. 138.
10. Smiley, *The Canadian Political Nationality*, p. 41.
11. Donald V. Smiley, *Constitutional Adaptation and Canadian Federalism Since 1945*, Documents of the Royal Commission on Bilingualism and Biculturalism (Ottawa: Information Canada, 1970), p. 28.
12. Bora Laskin, *Canadian Constitutional Law*, Second Edition (Toronto: Carswell, 1960), p. 19.
13. A. Corry, "Constitutional Trends and Federalism," in J. Peter Meekison, ed., *Canadian Federalism: Myth or Reality* (Toronto: Methuen, 1968), p. 57.
14. Garth Stevenson, "Federalism and the Political Economy of the Canadian State," in Leo Panitch, ed., *The Canadian State: Political Economy and Political Power* (Toronto: University of Toronto Press, 1977), p. 75.
15. J.R. Mallory, *The Structure of Canadian Government*, Revised Edition (Toronto: Gage, 1984), p. 377.
16. *Ibid.*, p. 385.
17. The "national dimension" criterion was established in 1882 by the

JCPC ruling in *Russell v. the Queen*. It has since been used to uphold federal legislation relating to aeronautics, broadcasting, the regulation of the National Capital District, and the production of uranium. For a detailed discussion of the judicial interpretation of the Peace, Order, and Good Government clause, see Donald V. Smiley, *Canada in Question: Federalism in the Eighties*, Third Edition (Toronto: McGraw-Hill Ryerson, 1980), pp. 24-25.

18. Frank R. Scott, "Our Changing Constitution," in W.R. Lederman, ed., *The Courts and the Canadian Constitution* (Toronto: McClelland and Stewart, 1967), p. 21.

19. Smiley, *The Canadian Political Nationality*, p. 20.

20. Martha Fletcher, "Judicial Review and the Division of Powers in Canada," in Meekison, *Canadian Federalism*, p. 157.

21. Alan C. Cairns, "The Living Canadian Constitution," in Meekison, *Canadian Federalism*, pp. 86-99.

22. Smiley, *The Canadian Political Nationality*, p. 54.

23. *Calgary Herald*, April 12, 1977, p. 7.

24. R.I. Cheffins, *The Constitutional Process in Canada* (Toronto: McGraw-Hill, 1969), p. 140.

25. Stevenson, *Unfulfilled Union*, p. 188.

26. Edwin R. Black, *Divided Loyalties: Canadian Concepts of Federalism* (Montreal: McGill-Queen's University Press, 1975), p. 101.

27. Government of Canada, "Dominion-Provincial Conference 1935," in *Dominion-Provincial Conferences 1927, 1935, 1941* (Ottawa: King's Printer, 1946).

28. Donald V. Smiley, *Canada in Question: Federalism in the Seventies*, Second Edition (Toronto: McGraw-Hill Ryerson, 1976), p. 58.

29. Institute of Intergovernmental Relations, *Report: Intergovernmental Relations on Fiscal and Economic Matters* (Ottawa: Queen's Printer, 1969), p. 103.

30. Richard J. Van Loon and Michael S. Whittington, *The Canadian Political System: Environment, Structure, and Process*, Second Edition (Toronto: McGraw-Hill Ryerson, 1976), pp. 366-67.

31. V. Seymour Wilson, "Federal-Provincial Relations and the Federal Policy Process," in G. Bruce Doern and Peter Aucoin, eds., *Public Policy in Canada* (Toronto: Macmillan, 1979), p. 198.

32. Timothy B. Woolstencroft, *Organizing Intergovernmental Relations* (Kingston: Institute of Intergovernmental Relations, Queen's University, 1982), p. 9.

33. *Ibid.*, p. 2.

34. Woolstencroft argues that the degree of institutionalization is related directly to the degree of discontent with the federal status quo. Certainly this relationship appears to be borne out in the cases of Quebec and Alberta. *Ibid.*, p. 5.

35. Donald Smiley, "An Outsider's Observations of Federal-Provincial Relations Among Consenting Adults," in Richard Simeon, ed., *Confrontation and Collaboration: Intergovernmental Relations in Canada Today* (Toronto: Institute of Public Administration of Canada, 1979), p. 110.
36. Woolstencroft, *Organizing Intergovernmental Relations*, pp. 79-80.
37. Howard Leeson, "The Intergovernmental Affairs Function in Saskatchewan, 1960-1983," *Canadian Public Administration*, Vol. 30, No. 3 (Fall 1987), p. 419.
38. *Ibid.*
39. Thorburn, *Planning and the Economy*, p. 190.
40. Woolstencroft, *Organizing Intergovernmental Relations*, p. 15.
41. Provincial governments have an ambiguous position in international affairs. Any treaties signed by Canada which concern matters of provincial jurisdiction can only be implemented through provincial legislation. At the same time, the provinces are not recognized as states in international law, and therefore can only negotiate treaties or other state-to-state agreements through the Government of Canada, even though such agreements may cover matters falling exclusively within provincial jurisdiction. See Mallory, *The Structure of Canadian Government*, p. 386-87.
42. Michael McDowell, "Quebec's quest for world identity still provokes rows," *The Globe and Mail*, National Edition, January 7, 1984, pp. 1 and 5.
43. Richard Simeon, *Federal-Provincial Diplomacy: The Making of Recent Policy in Canada* (Toronto: University of Toronto Press), 1972.
44. A major but nonetheless isolated exception occurred in the constitutional negotiations when patriation proceeded without the consent of Quebec. In this case the Supreme Court had ruled that a federal-provincial consensus *but not unanimous consent* was required to amend the constitution. Constitutional amendment will now be handled through the amending formula contained within the Constitution Act, 1982, a formula which has no general applicability to the FMC.
45. House of Commons, *Debates*, December 14, 1982, p. 21569.
46. Garth Stevenson, "Federalism and Intergovernmental Relations," in Michael S. Whittington and Glen Williams, eds., *Canadian Politics in the 1980s* (Toronto: Methuen, 1981), p. 288.
47. *Ibid.*, p. 289.
48. Speech at the Liberal Party of Canada fund raising dinner, Vancouver, November 12, 1981.
49. Keith Banting, "Political Meaning and Social Reform," in K.E. Swing-

ton and C.J. Rogerson, eds., *Competing Constitutional Visions: The Meech Lake Accord* (Toronto: Carswell, 1988), p. 172.

50. Gibbins, *Regionalism*, pp. 1-3.
51. Peter H. Russell, "The Political Purposes of the Canadian Charter of Rights and Freedoms," *Canadian Bar Review*, 1983, pp. 43-46.
52. Rainer Knopff and F.L. Morton, *Nation-Building and the Charter*, Research Report prepared for the Royal Commission on the Economic Union and Development Prospects for Canada, 1984, p. 90.
53. Frank MacKinnon, "The Establishment of the Supreme Court of Canada," in W.R. Lederman, ed., *The Courts and the Canadian Constitution* (Toronto: McClelland and Stewart, 1964), p. 112.
54. J. R. Mallory, *The Structure of Canadian Government* (Toronto: Macmillan, 1971), p. 331.
55. For a review of the Supreme Court's record on federal-provincial disputes, see Peter W. Hogg, "Is the Supreme Court of Canada Biased on Constitutional Cases?," *Canadian Bar Review*, 1979.
56. Peter H. Russell, Rainer Knopff, and Ted Morton, *Federalism and the Charter: Leading Constitutional Decisions* (Ottawa: Carleton University Press, 1989), p. 5.
57. Leslie Pal and David Taras, "Better to Tolerate a Practice Than Establish Too Many 'Rights,' " *The Financial Post*, 12-14, January 1989.
58. F.L. Morton, "The Political Impact of the Canadian Charter of Rights and Freedoms," *Canadian Journal of Political Science* XX:1 (March 1987), pp. 31-56.
59. Knopff and Morton, *Nation-Building and the Charter*, pp. 31-34.
60. F.L. Morton, G. Solomon, I. McNish, and D.W. Poulton, "Judicial Nullification of Statutes Under the Charter of Rights and Freedoms, 1982-1988," Occasional Papers Series 4.3, Research Unit for Socio-Legal Studies, University of Calgary, June 1989.
61. Russell et al., *Federalism and the Charter*, p. 3. As pointed out, s.52 of the 1982 Constitution Act establishes an explicit basis for judicial review and veto by declaring that the Constitution is "the supreme law of Canada" and that "any law that is inconsistent with the provisions of the Constitution is, to the extent of the inconsistency, of no force or effect."
62. Pal and Taras, "Better to Tolerate a Practice."
63. Reginald Whitaker, "Democracy and the Canadian Constitution," in Keith Banting and Richard Simeon, eds., *And No One Cheered: Federalism, Democracy and the Constitution Act* (Toronto: Methuen, 1983), p. 250.
64. Donald V. Smiley, "A Dangerous Deed: The Constitution Act, 1982," in Banting and Simeon, *And No One Cheered*, pp. 75-76.

65. *Ibid.*, p. 55.
66. Banting, "Political Meaning and Social Reform," p. 170.
67. Alan C. Cairns, "Citizens (Outsiders) and Governments (Insiders) in Constitution-Making: The Case of Meech Lake," *Canadian Public Policy*, XIV Supplement (September 1988), pp. 139-40.
68. Howard Aster, "Meech Lake and the Long Shadow of Pierre Trudeau," *The New Federation* (August/September 1989), p. 17.
69. Richard Simeon, "Regionalism and Canadian Political Institutions," in Meekison, *Canadian Federalism*, pp. 301-2.
70. Thorburn, *Planning and the Economy*, p. 242.
71. Stevenson, "Federalism and Intergovernmental Relations," p. 291.
72. Richard Simeon, "Some Suggestions for Improving Inter-governmental Relations," in Paul W. Fox, ed., *Politics: Canada*, Fifth Edition (Toronto: McGraw-Hill Ryerson, 1982), p. 102.

7

The Canadian Party System

Political parties play a starring role in democratic politics. Much, if not most, of what we think of as "politics" entails political parties, their leaders, and the competition among parties and leaders in federal and provincial election campaigns. Yet, while there is little dispute as to the centrality of the party role, there is considerable disagreement as to the nature of that role. At the heart of the disagreement lie conflicting expectations about the policy role parties should play in democratic elections.

Elections provide one instrument through which the policy preferences of citizens can be conveyed to governments. Admittedly, the ballot is a very simple, if not crude, instrument, allowing us only to print a single "X" on a piece of paper. As a consequence, elections can convey policy preferences unambiguously only if the election campaign features a single, dominant issue, and only if there are reasonably clear differences among the parties with respect to that issue. Then, and only then, can elections provide a "policy mandate." Parties which differ only as Tweedledum and Tweedledee differ deny citizens the opportunity to direct their governments, or to use the electoral process to deliver not only a judgment on the past performance of government but also a mandate for the future.

The normative vision of electoral politics underlying this stance is largely discounted by political scientists, who see parties primarily as *brokerage* organizations bound together more by the pursuit of power than by any consistent or even distinctive set of ideas, policies, or principles. As Harold Clarke et al. explain,

> Rather than dividing the electorate among themselves along clear and stable lines of social cleavage, [brokerage parties] constantly compete for the same policy space and the same votes. . . . They organize around leaders rather than around political principles and ideologies, and expect the leader to work out the multitude of compromises required. . . . [1]

From this perspective, an election is seen primarily as an instrument through which voters can cast a retrospective judgment on the performance of governments, and through which they can choose *representatives but not policies* for the future. Election campaigns feature the clash of leaders, not ideologies, and are fought on the plains of policy consensus rather than from the heights of competing principles.

Brokerage parties, and the electoral competition among such par-

"Of course our party recognizes the fundamental nature of the crisis we find our nation facing.... We have to get elected again."

Len Norris, *27th Annual.* Originally published in *The Vancouver Sun*, March 15, 1978.

ties, can provide important means for bridging cleavages within the political community. As Richard Van Loon and Michael Whittington explain, the brokerage party " ... must aggregate a wide range of interests into a voting coalition, and in so doing it performs an integrative function for the political system as a whole."[2] Yet, while Canadian parties have generally tried to build electoral coalitions spanning the linguistic, regional, and class cleavages within the Canadian society, their success in so doing has been less than complete. As vehicles for national political integration, both the party system and its constituent elements have at times encountered considerable difficulty. Brokerage aspirations have not ensured brokerage results.

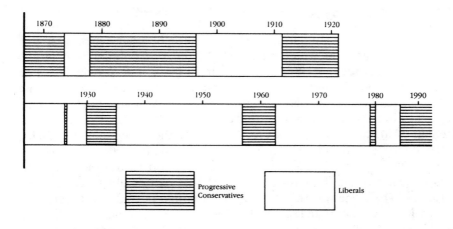

FIGURE 7.1

Party Forming Federal Government, 1867-1990

THE EVOLUTION OF THE CANADIAN PARTY SYSTEM

> Although they are in part shaped by a series of specific election outcomes, party systems reflect and respond to a broad spectrum of influences which transcend elections and go to the very roots of society.[3]

Only a handful of Canada's thirty-four general elections have had a major impact on the party system, or for that matter on Canadian political life. Only twelve elections resulted in a change in government,[4] and in some of these cases the change represented little more than a minor ripple in the established pattern of Canadian politics. Between June 1979 and February 1980, for example, the government changed hands twice, but the nine-month Progressive Conservative government headed by Joe Clark was little more than a temporary deviation from Liberal rule. As Figure 7.1 illustrates, Canada's political history has been marked by long periods of one-party dominance more than it has by frequent turnover in party control of the federal government.

National political life has been dominated by two parties. The first to emerge was the Conservative Party—it did not become the *Progressive* Conservative party until 1942—which began to take shape in 1854 as the Liberal-Conservative legislative coalition in the Province of Canada. Led by John A. Macdonald and George Etienne Cartier, the early Conservative legislative coalition brought together the business interests of Montreal and Toronto with the hierarchy of the Catholic Church in Quebec. In the 1867 general election, which was a post-mortem on Confederation fought out among a wide array of candidates in four separate provincial campaigns, the loosely knit Conservatives won 60 percent of the seats and Macdonald became Canada's first prime minister. Although the Conservatives lost in 1874, they were returned to power in 1878. The Conservatives remained in office through the election of 1891, the last election fought by Macdonald. Shortly after the 1891 election, the party's strength began to unravel with the death of Macdonald, a series of short-lived and generally ineffectual leaders, and the erosion of the party's electoral base in Quebec. The stage was set for the first sustained period of Liberal rule.

Under the uncertain leadership of Alexander Mackenzie, the Liberals had first come to power in 1874 when the **Pacific Scandal** led to the defeat of Macdonald's Conservative government.[5] The Liberal party provided an umbrella for a variety of groups: agrarian populist reformers from Ontario, the "Clear Grits"; anticlerical francophones from Quebec; anti-confederates from Quebec, New Brunswick, and Nova Scotia; and, more generally, those who supported provincial rights and opposed the centralist and nation-building thrust of the Macdonald Conservatives. It was a "disparate and ineffectual alliance,"[6] easily routed by the Conservatives in 1878. Only after their defeat did the Liberals begin to pull together as a truly national party, and only under the direction of a new leader, Quebec's Wilfrid Laurier, did they emerge as a serious threat to the dominant Conservatives.

The Liberal rise to national power came with a reversal of the two parties' fortunes in Quebec. The Liberals, whose association with anticlerical elements in Quebec brought on the political wrath of the Catholic church, won only 16 Quebec seats in the 1884 general election, compared to 49 won by the Conservatives. In 1887, following the hanging of Louis Riel and the death of Etienne Cartier, Macdonald's powerful Quebec lieutenant, the Liberals captured 32 Quebec seats to the Conservatives' 33. In the 1891 election, with Wilfrid Laurier now at the Liberal helm, the Liberals won 37 Quebec seats compared to 28 for the Conservatives. This was the first in a string of Liberal majorities in Quebec that was not to be broken until 1958. Five years later, in 1896, the Laurier Liberals came to power, winning 49 of the 65 Quebec seats in the process.

The Liberals were to remain in power until 1911, during which time their earlier support for provincial rights gave way to enthusiastic leadership of nation-building activities in the Canadian West. In 1911 the Liberals went down to defeat after a campaign featuring two issues: a Liberal proposal for greater free trade with the United States (discussed below) and, as war clouds gathered in Europe, Canada's participation in the naval defence of the British Empire. The new Conservative government was led by Robert Laird Borden, who was to steer Canada's passage through the First World War.

The elections of 1917 and 1921 were of critical importance in the evolution of the national party system. The 1917 election was fought on the single issue of military conscription, which was strongly opposed in Quebec and by the Liberals, but generally supported elsewhere in Canada and by the Conservatives. The election had at least three major consequences. First, the Liberals were all but purged in western Canada, winning only 2 of the 56 seats. Second, Quebec was turned into a Conservative wasteland: Conservative candidates won only 3 of Quebec's 65 seats, down from 27 in 1911. (The Liberals, conversely, won 62 of their 82 seats in Quebec.) In combination, the election results in Quebec and the West meant that the two national parties were no longer national in terms of electoral support or representation in the House. Third, the election blurred existing party lines as both the Conservatives and a significant number of pro-conscription Liberals ran under the banner of the Union Government. This in turn set the stage for a new political movement which held non-partisanship as one of its leading principles.

At Last, Women Get the Vote!

From the late 1800s, suffragettes in Britain, the United States, and Canada had been campaigning for the extension of the voting franchise to women. Success, however, was not to come until the First World War.

The war years fundamentally changed the place of women within the Canadian economy and society. The domestic war effort, coupled with the manpower demands of the military, produced a dramatic surge in female participation in the labour force. In turn, this surge brought women's exclusion from the franchise into greater and greater question. The war years were also marked by widespread interest in social reform. Through their leadership of reform organizations such as the Women's Christian Temperance Union, women were able to place the extension of the franchise near the top of the reform agenda. If the war was being fought to protect democracy, women argued, then surely women were entitled to the vote at home.

The specific impetus for the extension of the franchise came from the Wartime Elections Act. This notorious piece of legislation inflated support for conscription by, among other things, enfranchising the close female relatives of men on active overseas service. The assumption going into the 1917 campaign was that such women would endorse conscription. The public rationale for extending the vote was that servicemen, who were predominantly English rather than French Canadians, would have trouble finding the time to vote; their female relatives could thus vote in their place. In fact, however, servicemen were given twenty-seven days and every opportunity in which to vote, and few if any were disenfranchised.

Nellie McClung was born in Chatsworth, Ontario, in 1873 and moved to Manitoba when she was seven. Trained as a teacher, McClung became a leader in the Women's Suffrage Movement. In 1921 she was elected to the Alberta Legislature, becoming the first woman in the British Empire to be elected to a Legislative Assembly.

Public Archives of Canada/C27674.

In 1921 the federal franchise was extended to all women on the same terms as were applied to men.

The events set in motion by the 1917 election, including the crippling of both the Conservative and Liberal parties as national organizations, led in 1921 to a fundamental transformation of the Canadian party system. The incumbent Conservatives, having discarded the wartime umbrella of the Union Government, failed to win a single seat in Quebec or on the prairies. Overall, the Conservatives captured only 50 seats, down from 153 seats for the Union Government in 1917. The Liberals won 116 seats in 1921, including every seat in Quebec. However, with only 5 seats in the West, the Liberals formed Canada's first minority government. The most dramatic outcome came with the emergence of the Progressive Party of Canada, which swept out of the prairie West to capture 64 seats including

Women's political organizations have a long history in Canada. The above photo shows an 1898 meeting of the National Council of Women with the Governor General of Canada, Lord Aberdeen.

Public Archives of Canada/PA28033.

37 of the 39 prairie seats, 24 seats in Ontario, 3 in British Columbia, and 1 in New Brunswick.

Although the core support of the Progressive Party came from agrarian unrest in western Canada and rural Ontario, the new party was also the vehicle for a more widespread interest in social reform, stemming from the war years. The Progressives' non-partisan approach to politics appealed to those who had supported the wartime Union Government, while support for the Progressives provided a means by which western Canadians could register their growing regional discontent with the partisan and parliamentary organization of Canadian political life, discontent that transcended agrarian concerns alone. Yet, despite these numerous albeit overlapping sources of support, the Progressives faded quickly. In 1925 they won only 24 seats, including 22 from the prairie provinces. In 1926 the Progressives won only 20 seats, including 18 from the prairies, and in 1930 only 12, including 11 from the prairies. In less than a decade the Progressives were driven back to a prairie enclave, and then driven from the political stage.

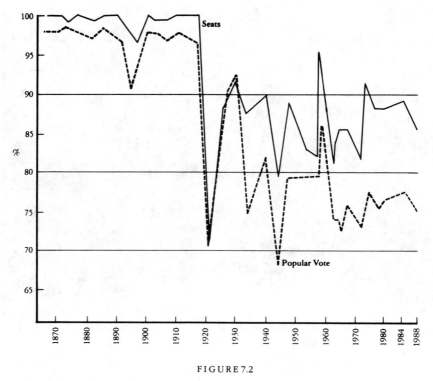

FIGURE 7.2

Percentage of Seats and Popular Vote Won by the Conservative and Liberal Parties Combined

As Figure 7.2 illustrates, the major parties rebounded quickly after the 1921 debacle. By 1930, when together they captured 94 percent of the votes cast and 93 percent of the seats, it appeared that the 1921 election had been but a temporary deviation from an enduring pattern of two-party dominance. That pattern, however, was conclusively broken in the 1935 election, an election fought in the middle of the Great Depression. Voters turned out R.B. Bennett's Conservative government, which had come into power in 1930 just as the Depression was beginning, and returned the Liberals to power. At the same time, they elected thirty-two candidates from a variety of third parties, two of which were to leave a permanent mark on the Canadian party system.

The **Cooperative Commonwealth Federation**, a left of centre party that brought together the remnants of the Progressive party, agrarian organizations from western Canada, elements of the nascent labour movement, and central Canadian left-wing intellectuals grouped under the banner of the League for Social Reconstruction, captured 8.8 percent of the popular vote and seven seats in the House of Commons. Over the next five federal elections the CCF was to average 11.9 percent of the popular vote and over 19 seats in the House; in 1944, the CCF formed the provincial government in Saskatchewan. The Social Credit party, also running candidates for the first time in 1935, captured only 4.1 percent of the popular vote but, because its support was more concentrated, the party won three more seats than the CCF. Across the next five general elections the Social Credit party averaged 4.2 percent of the popular vote and over 13 seats in the House.[7] The other significant entry in the 1935 election was the Reconstruction Party, a splinter group of Conservative candidates running under the leadership of H.H. Stevens, the Minister of Trade and Commerce in R.B. Bennett's government. Although Reconstruction candidates captured 8.7 percent of the popular vote, only Stevens was elected. Shortly after the election, the party vanished without a trace.

The 1921 and 1935 elections not only marked the end of an uncomplicated two-party system: they also put into place a Liberal dominance of national politics that was to last through to 1984. Re-elected in 1935, the Liberals remained in office until their defeat at the hands of John Diefenbaker in 1957, and then returned to power in 1963. From 1963 to 1984 they dominated the federal scene, apart from the brief Conservative interlude in 1979/80. A quip by Jack Pickersgill, Liberal cabinet minister and party stalwart, took on the appearance of an iron law: "living under a Conservative government is like having a childhood disease—everyone has to experience it once, but never wants to do it again."[8]

The major departure from Liberal dominance came with the "Diefenbaker interlude," which stretched from 1957 to 1963. John Diefenbaker, a prairie populist with a dramatic platform style, transformed the Conservative party by shifting its centre of gravity westward. The Conservatives had earlier sought western Canadian support when, in 1942, they enticed John Bracken, the Progressive premier of Manitoba, to lead the national party. Part of that enticement was a change in the party's name to the *Progressive* Conservative Party of Canada. As Table 7.1 shows, however, neither Bracken's leadership nor the change in name greatly improved the party's position in the West. When Bracken was replaced in 1948 by the Conservative premier of Ontario, George Drew, little improvement in the West was to be expected, and none was forthcoming.

John Diefenbaker was chosen as the Conservative leader in 1956 after George Drew resigned for reasons of health. In the 1957 campaign, Diefenbaker led his party to a minority government, with strong support in Atlantic Canada (21 seats, up from 5 in 1953) and Ontario (61 seats, up from 33 in 1953), and more modest gains in the West and Quebec. Then,

Table 7.1
Conservative Support in Western Canada

	% of Popular Vote			Western Canadian Seats	
	All 4 provs.	Prairies only	B.C. only	#	%
1940	21.2%	17.7%	30.5%	7	9.9
1945	23.5	20.7	30.0	10	14.1
1949	20.8	17.6	27.9	7	9.9
1953	16.0	17.0	14.1	9	12.9
1957	30.0	28.6	32.6	21	30.4
1958	53.9	56.2	49.4	65	92.9
1962	38.8	44.9	27.3	48	68.6
1963	38.8	47.0	23.4	45	64.3
1965	36.0	45.3	19.2	45	64.3
1968	33.0	40.8	19.4	25	36.8
1972	42.1	47.5	33.0	42	61.8
1974	47.2	50.6	41.9	49	72.1
1979	49.6	53.0	44.4	57	74.0
1980	46.8	50.6	41.5	49	63.6
1984	51.7	55.3	46.6	58	75.3
1988	40.8	44.5	35.3	78	55.8

in 1958, the Conservatives rolled up the largest majority ever recorded in a federal election,[9] taking 208 of the 265 seats in the House, including 70 of 75 seats in western Canada and 50 of the 75 seats in Quebec. The Liberals won only 49 seats and were shut out in six provinces; CCF seats were cut from 25 to 8, and no Social Credit candidates were elected. Although Diefenbaker himself was closely associated with the West, Conservative candidates did well throughout the country, collecting 55 percent of the popular vote in Atlantic Canada, 50 percent in Quebec, 56 percent in Ontario, and 54 percent across the West.

Despite their landslide victory in 1958, the Conservatives retained only a minority government after the 1962 election; in 1963, they lost power to the Liberals, who formed a minority government under the leadership of Lester Pearson. The 1958 Conservative gains in Quebec quickly evaporated: 36 of the 50 seats won in 1958 were lost in 1962, with another 6 lost in 1963. Ontario support also faded with the Conservative seat total falling from 67 in 1958 to 35 in 1962, and 27 in 1963. What did *not* evaporate was the Conservative resurgence in western Canada. As Table 7.1 demonstrates, Diefenbaker not only led the West, and particularly the prairie West, into the Conservative camp, but he kept it there throughout the early sixties. Although western support for the Conservatives fell in

1968, it quickly rebounded. Thus, Diefenbaker's transformation of western Canada from a Conservative wasteland to the Conservative heartland was a lasting gift to the party he had led.

The Diefenbaker years touched off a number of other important changes in the party system. The 1958 Conservative rout of the CCF led to that party's collapse and, in 1961, to its reincarnation as the New Democratic Party. The NDP brought together what was left of the CCF's agrarian support in western Canada with the growing labour movement, led by the Canadian Labour Congress. The new party also reached out more effectively than its predecessor to white-collar, urban constituencies, although NDP support, like CCF support before it, all but stopped at the Quebec–Ontario border. Since its first campaign in 1962 the NDP has been a major player in Canadian national politics, though not a prime contender for national office.

The 1962 election also marked the rebirth of the Social Credit party, this time in Quebec under the leadership of Réal Caouette. Although the *Créditistes* were restricted almost exclusively to Quebec, they had a significant impact on the politics of the time, winning 26 federal seats in 1962, 20 in 1963, and 9 in 1965. They continued to survive as a political force in Quebec even during the Liberal hegemony of the Trudeau years, winning 14 seats in 1968, 15 in 1972, 11 in 1974, and 6 in 1979 before being driven from the political stage in 1980.

In many respects, the most dramatic transformation of the party system to date came in 1984 when the Progressive Conservatives, led by Brian Mulroney, captured 211 of the 282 seats in the House of Commons. The Conservative sweep occurred across the country, with Tory candidates taking 25 of the 32 seats in Atlantic Canada, 58 of 75 in Quebec, 67 of 95 in Ontario, 58 of 77 in the West, and all 3 in the North. After more than two decades in which neither the Conservatives nor the Liberals had been able to build a truly *national* electoral coalition, the country once again had a federal government which enjoyed strong support across the land. In Quebec, the magnitude of the electoral change was staggering. The Conservatives, campaigning for the first time with a Quebec leader, increased their share of the Quebec popular vote from 12.6 percent in 1980 to 50.2 percent in 1984. Conversely, the Liberal share of the Quebec popular vote fell from 68.2 percent in 1980 to only 35.4 percent in 1984. Fifty-seven Tory candidates were elected in 1984, compared to a single candidate in 1980. One of the most important constants in Canadian political life—the Liberal fortress of Quebec—had been shattered.

The Liberal party had *never* done as badly in a federal election as it did in 1984; even in the 1958 Diefenbaker rout, the Liberals retained 49 seats and almost 34 percent of the vote. The party that had come to be known as "the government party" was now out of office, not only in Ottawa but also across the ten provinces.[10] The NDP withstood the Tory tide more successfully, actually gaining eight seats in Ontario to help offset the nine NDP seats lost in the West.

The 1988 election largely replicated the 1984 results, albeit with some modifications. Brian Mulroney's Progressive Conservative government retained office despite the net loss of 42 seats and a drop in the party's share of the popular vote to 43.0 percent, down from 50.0 percent in 1984. The Liberals more than doubled their number of seats in the House, while the NDP reached a historic high by winning 43 seats. Quebec support for the Conservatives, which seemed like an aberration in 1984, actually increased in 1988: the Conservatives won 63 seats in Quebec, compared to 58 in 1984, and received almost 53 percent of the Quebec popular vote, compared to just over 50 percent in 1984. Overall, 32.5 percent of Conservative votes and 37.2 percent of Conservative seats came from Quebec in 1988, up 5 percent and 10 percent respectively.

Table 7.2 shows that a host of candidates ran in 1988 under banners other than those of the Conservatives, Liberals, or NDP. Minor parties ranged from the Communist party of the far left to the Party for the Commonwealth of Canada on the far right. Overall, however, minor parties had little impact on the campaign, although in specific constituencies they did have an effect. There is no doubt, for example, that Reform Party candidates contributed to Conservative losses in western Canada. Still, when all the smoke had settled after the 1988 campaign, minor party candidates and independents in total picked up only 4.3 percent and 0.4 percent of the popular vote respectively.

ELECTORAL PATTERNS IN THE CANADIAN PARTY SYSTEM

At this point it is useful to step back from the details of the Canadian party system and look at the general patterns which tie those details together.

Major Party Dominance

The national dominance of the Progressive Conservative and Liberal parties has already been noted in Figure 7.2. Although that dominance was shaken in 1921 and substantially reduced from 1935 onward, the two major parties continue to capture the support of three Canadian voters in four. Figure 7.3 shows that, among "third parties," the dominance of the NDP is equally apparent. With the disappearance of the *Créditistes*, the NDP's domination of the third party field is even more complete than the Conservative and Liberal parties' dominance of the national party system. Other parties continue to exist (and indeed may even be increasing in number), but the party *system* is no more complex; other parties may be in the electoral arena, but they are not yet in the game.

Table 7.2
1988 National Election Results

Party	Number of Candidates	Candidates Elected	Number of Votes	% Total Popular Vote	Average Vote per Candidate
Progressive Conservative	295	169	5,667,563	43.0	19,212
Liberal	295	83	4,205,072	31.9	14,254
New Democratic	295	43	2,685,308	20.4	9,103
Reform	72		275,767	2.1	3,830
Christian Heritage	63		102,533	0.8	1,628
Rhinoceros	74		52,173	0.4	705
None/Independent	136		47,406	0.4	349
Green	68		47,228	0.4	695
Confederation of Regions	52		41,342	0.3	795
Libertarian	88		33,135	0.2	377
Party for Commonwealth	60		7,497	0.1	125
Communist	52		7,168	0.1	138
Social Credit	9		3,407	0.0	379
Total	1,577	295	13,175,599	100.0%	835

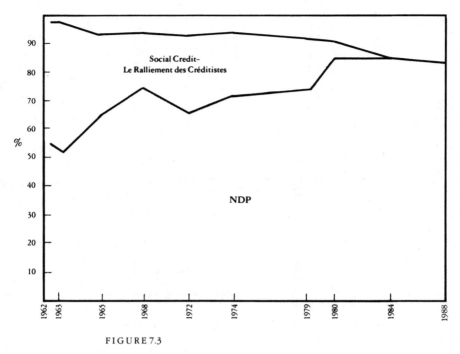

FIGURE 7.3

Distribution of the Third-Party Popular Vote

Provincial Variations on the National Theme

One of the most important features of the Canadian party system is that the national cast of party actors is not faithfully replicated across the ten provinces; substantial variation exists with respect to both federal voting behaviour and provincial party systems.

In Atlantic Canada, the Liberal and Conservative parties have dominated both federal and provincial elections, to the virtual exclusion of
other parties. In the ten general elections held between 1962 and 1988,
Liberal and Conservative candidates captured 26 percent of the national
popular vote while capturing 88 percent across the four Atlantic provinces. Across those same ten elections, Liberal and Conservative candidates won 318 of the 323 Atlantic seats (98 percent), losing just four seats
to the New Democrats and one to an independent. In provincial elections
held during the 1960s and early 1970s, the two major parties were even
more dominant. In Prince Edward Island and New Brunswick their
candidates captured 100 percent of the seats with 98 percent of the
popular vote; in Newfoundland and Nova Scotia, they captured 97 percent
of the seats with 94 percent and 92 percent of the popular vote respectively.[11] Thus Atlantic Canada departs from the national pattern in its
relative weakness of third-party support.

The national party system is best replicated in Ontario, where the Conservatives, Liberals, and New Democrats have all been significant players in federal elections, and where provincial politics have also been dominated by the same three parties. Yet, while the party players are the same, their relative strength differs across the federal and provincial arenas. While the Conservatives formed the provincial government from 1941 to 1985, the Liberals enjoyed a slight edge federally, winning 443 seats in the ten elections held between 1962 and 1988, compared to 376 Ontario seats won by the Conservatives. In the 1988 federal election, Conservative candidates won 46 Ontario seats with 38.2 percent of the popular vote, and Liberal candidates won 43 seats with 38.9 percent of the vote. The NDP has enjoyed greater provincial than federal success within Ontario, although it remains competitive at both levels. In 1988, NDP candidates won 10 seats with 20 percent of the popular vote.

In Quebec, strong provincial parties lacking any federal counterpart have often dominated the provincial stage. The Union Nationale, which controlled the Quebec provincial government for twenty-four years between 1936 and 1970, did not run federal candidates. The Parti Québécois, in power from 1976 to 1985, did not run federal candidates, although in 1984 it did endorse the *Parti Nationaliste*. Conversely, the federal Conservative party has not had a provincial counterpart in Quebec since 1936. Thus, federal and provincial campaigns in Quebec are fought along quite different party lines.

In western Canada, the relationship between federal and provincial party systems defies any simple description. The most "deviant" province has been British Columbia, where, since 1952, provincial elections have been fought out between the Social Credit party and the CCF/NDP, with the provincial Liberal and Conservative parties being all but moribund. Yet, on the federal scene the Liberals and Conservatives have been both active and successful. Only the New Democrats have been competitive at both levels, while the Social Credit party, in power provincially for all but three years since 1952, has not been active federally since three Socred MPs were elected in 1965.

Alberta provincial politics have been dominated in turn by the Liberals (1905-1921), the United Farmers of Alberta (1921-1935), the Social Credit party (1935-1971) and, from 1971 on, the Progressive Conservatives. Opposition parties of whatever stripe have been chronically weak, with government control of over 90 percent of the legislative seats being the rule, not the exception. Since Social Credit's defeat in 1971 and its subsequent departure from the provincial stage, Alberta has deviated from the national pattern more in terms of the relative strength of the party players than in the players themselves.[12] It is interesting to note, however, that recent developments appear to be bringing the province more into step with the national party configuration. In the March 1989 provincial election, the Progressive Conservatives retained power, but did so in the face of stiff competition from both the provincial New Democrats and the Liberals.

Saskatchewan voters elected North America's first socialist government in 1944, when the CCF broke the Liberals' virtual monopoly in the provincial arena. The CCF remained in office until 1964, when the Liberals were returned to power. The Liberals were then defeated in 1971 by the New Democrats, who were defeated in turn by Grant Devine's Progressive Conservatives in 1982. Since Devine's victory in 1982, partisan competition within Saskatchewan, both federal and provincial, has been dominated by the Conservatives and New Democrats. In the 1988 federal election, for example, the New Democrats elected ten MPs with 44 percent of the popular vote, the Conservatives elected four MPs with 36 percent and the Liberals failed to elect any candidates with its 18 percent of the popular vote.

Manitoba presents a different picture again. In the midst of the Depression the provincial Liberals and Progressives merged to form the nucleus of a non-partisan and initially all-party administration, which was to govern Manitoba until 1958. Over time, the government became more Liberal and less non-partisan, as first the CCF and then the Conservatives left, in 1942 and 1952 respectively. In the 1958 provincial election, the Conservatives came to power and remained in power until 1969, when they were defeated by the New Democrats. The Conservatives returned to power in 1977 and then lost again to the New Democrats in 1982. The 1987 election returned the Conservatives to office, but with only a minority government; the official opposition was formed by the provincial Liberals, led by Sharon Carstairs.

The Canadian party system is asymmetrical not only across provinces but also, in many cases, across the two levels of government within specific provinces.[13] This latter asymmetry is reflected in the growing organizational independence of federal and provincial parties sharing the same party label. Thus Van Loon and Whittington conclude that " . . . while the Canadian political system can be described as federal, its political parties are at best only confederal."[14]

Party Tenure

The Canadian political system is marked by the longevity of its governments. As Figure 7.1 has shown, it is an unusual federal election in which the government changes hands. This stability is further reflected in Figure 7.4, which plots the proportion of the popular vote received by the Conservative and Liberal parties. What can be seen in this figure is not any regular oscillation in party fortunes, but rather sustained periods of dominance.

If anything, Canadian voters have been even *more* steadfast in their

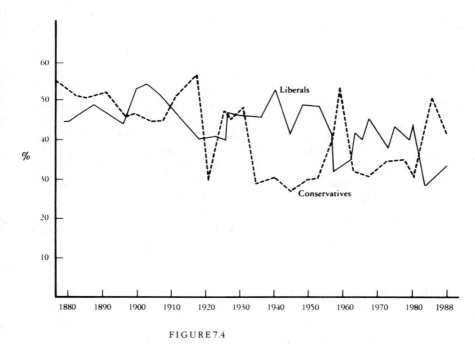

FIGURE 7.4

Percentage of the Popular Vote in General Elections, 1878–1988

support of provincial governments; the tenure of many provincial governments has been nothing short of remarkable. The Ontario government
remained in Conservative hands for 42 years, from 1943 to 1985. The
Social Credit party was in power from 1935 to 1971 in Alberta, and in
British Columbia from 1952 to the present, with the exception of a brief
NDP interregnum from 1972 to 1975. Joey Smallwood's Liberal party
controlled the government of Newfoundland from 1949 to 1971.

To illustrate the lengthy tenure of Canadian governments, it is useful
to draw upon an American comparison. During the time that Pierre
Trudeau was prime minister of Canada, Americans experienced five
different presidential administrations: those of Lyndon Johnson, Richard
Nixon, Gerald Ford, Jimmy Carter, and Ronald Reagan. Each administration, with the possible exception of Ford's, is commonly seen as a unique
and distinctive episode in American political life. In Canada, the tempo of
change is much slower, as voters retain incumbent governments and as
leaders enjoy lengthy terms of office unknown in the United States.

Electoral "Distortions"

In the 1988 general election, over 13,000,000 votes were cast to determine the occupants of 295 seats in the House of Commons. It is the *electoral system* which translates votes into seats, and thereby determines the partisan composition of the government. That system is based on single-member constituencies, the winner in each constituency being the candidate receiving a *plurality* of the votes cast within the constituency. Thus to win in what is called a "first-past-the-post" system, one needs only more votes than any other candidate, and not a majority of the votes cast. Given that the three major parties run candidates in every riding, pluralities well short of majorities are common. The party winner of the election is determined by aggregating the results of the 295 constituency contests; the party with the most seats wins the right to form the next government. While party leaders play a critical role in the national campaign, they do not run as national candidates but rather seek election as MPs in specific constituencies.

This electoral system is only one of many possible mechanisms that could be used to translate votes into seats. Many countries use *proportional representation* systems designed to ensure that a party's share of seats is roughly proportionate to its share of the popular vote. Such outcomes are not characteristic of the electoral translation that takes place in Canada, as the Canadian system tends to over-reward the party capturing a plurality of the national vote. In Figure 7.5 we can see that the winning party in national elections consistently receives a much higher percentage of the seats in the House of Commons than its percentage of the popular vote. Indeed, since 1921 the winning party has received a majority of the popular vote on only three occasions. On four occasions—1957, 1962, 1972, and 1979—minority governments were formed by parties receiving less than 40 percent of the popular vote. This tendency of the electoral system to over-reward the leading party is often seen as a positive distortion, one that increases the probability of stable majority government despite the lack of a majority preference among Canadian voters.

There is an important caveat to note here. Although it is generally true that the party winning a plurality of the national popular vote also receives a plurality of seats in the House of Commons, this is not always the case. In 1979, for example, the Liberals received 39.8 percent of the popular vote compared to only 35.6 percent for the Conservatives, yet the Conservatives won 136 seats compared to only 114 for the Liberals. Thus, it is not the number of votes alone that counts but also the distribution of those votes. In 1979 Liberal candidates ran up huge wins in Quebec, outpolling the Conservatives by a margin of over five to one. Yet in a sense such massive majorities are wasted; a party is no further ahead in winning

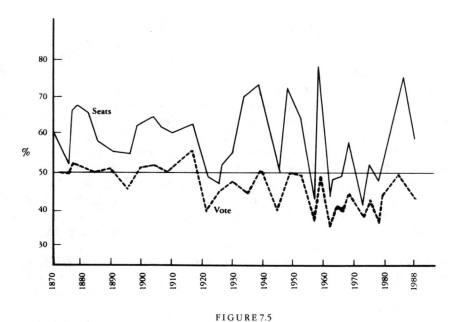

FIGURE 7.5

Percentage of Seats and Popular Vote Received by Winning Party in General Elections, 1867-1988

a constituency by 20,000 votes than it is in winning by a single vote. While the Conservative share of the 1979 national popular vote was depressed by the massive Liberal victories in Quebec, Conservative candidates won seats in the much closer Ontario contests.

If winning parties tend to be over-compensated, other parties must be disadvantaged by an electoral system based on simple pluralities. In general terms, the second-place finisher receives a smaller proportion of seats than its share of the popular vote. Here again, however, the electoral effects depend upon the distribution of the vote. Parties with a broadly dispersed popular vote tend to fare more poorly than do parties whose vote is regionally concentrated. In the abstract, one can see that a party could win 10 percent or 20 percent of the vote in every constituency across the land, without winning a single seat. The NDP, which runs candidates in every federal constituency no matter what the odds are of success, received 70 percent of the votes cast by Canadians between 1962 and 1988, but won only 9.4 percent of the seats in the House of Commons. Conversely, the Social Credit party received only 4.3 percent of the votes cast in the six general elections held between 1935 and 1957 and yet, because those votes were concentrated in Alberta, managed to capture 5.5 percent of the seats in the House of Commons.

In most elections, the majority of votes goes to the parties and candidates which ultimately lose those elections. For example, in the twelve consecutive provincial elections won by the Ontario Conservatives between 1943 and 1981, the party averaged only 43.3 percent of the popular vote. In the ten federal elections held between 1962 and 1988, 58.0 percent of Canadians voted for parties which ultimately lost. In the West, the losers averaged 64.6 percent of the electorate compared to 57.2 percent in Ontario, 55.2 percent in Atlantic Canada, and 53.8 percent in Quebec. The high average in the West may not only have reflected western alienation but may also have been a contributing factor to that alienation. It is interesting to speculate on whether the relative proportion of winners and losers is related to citizen support for political institutions, and on whether a system like the one used in American presidential elections, which produces more winners than losers, might also generate higher levels of citizen support and satisfaction. In any event, the fact that more people usually vote against, rather than for, the winning party should make us wary of election assessments that begin with statements like *"Newfoundlanders* renew the government's mandate." What most people want is not what they get. In the 1988 federal election, the Progressive Conservatives, who both championed the Free Trade Agreement and won the election, received 43 percent of the popular vote; 52 percent of the electorate supported the Liberals and New Democrats in their opposition to the Agreement.

As Figure 7.5 illustrates, minority governments are not uncommon in Canada; five of the last ten federal governments have been minority governments. They are the consequence, but not the only possible consequence, of a multiparty system. In other countries with multiparty systems, coalition governments are common, governments in which legislators from two or more parties hold cabinet portfolios. In Canada, however, coalition governments have not emerged at the federal level,[15] and have been rare in provincial politics.[16] Minority governments behave in essentially the same manner as majority governments, although they may be more cautious and can expect a shorter life. All cabinet ministers come from the party with the plurality of seats.

One of the most frequently raised concerns about the Canadian electoral system stems from the fact that the regional composition of parliamentary parties often fails to reflect the regional composition of their popular vote. As a consequence, the party system may exacerbate rather than moderate cleavages within the electorate, driving the country apart rather than pulling it together. This problem was first addressed in a landmark article by Alan Cairns,[17] and can be illustrated by a brief look at party fortunes during the Trudeau years.

The Trudeau years started well for the Liberal party in western Canada. After a severe electoral drought under the leadership of Lester Pearson, the Liberals rebounded in 1968 to win 27 seats and 37 percent of the popular vote across the region. In the ensuing four elections, Liberal fortunes waned again as the party's share of the regional popular vote fell to 28 percent in 1972, rose slightly to 30 percent in 1974, and then fell to only 23 percent in 1979 and 1980. The Liberal Party, however, did even worse with respect to seats: 30.7 percent of the regional popular vote across the five Trudeau elections yielded only 14.5 percent of the seats. In the 1980 election, 23 percent of the regional vote produced only two Liberal seats. As a direct consequence, the essential two-way flow of communication between citizens and the government was twice disrupted; there was an insufficient number of Liberal MPs from the West to carry effective regional input into the federal government, and an insufficient number of elected spokesmen for the government to communicate effectively with the West. Western Canadians perceived the national government almost exclusively through the understandably jaundiced viewpoint of opposition MPs. In this respect, then, the electoral system contributed to western alienation.

The Conservatives faced a similar problem in Quebec. Although the Trudeau years were not fruitful ones for the Conservatives in Quebec, the party did average 16.6 percent of the vote across the five elections. Yet this vote yielded only 3.2 percent of the Quebec seats, including just a single seat in 1980. If the Conservatives had won seats in proportion to their share of the popular vote, there is little question that the party would have been more sensitive to the concerns of Quebec, and that the Liberals would not have been able to claim that they alone were the party of national unity. More Conservative seats would probably have produced more Conservative votes, just as a more proportionate share of western seats would have enhanced the Liberal's appeal in the West.

Such regional distortions weakened the national parties as vehicles of political integration. In observing the House of Commons in the late 1970s and early 1980s, it was easy to forget that there were Liberal supporters by the hundreds of thousands in the West, just as there were Conservative supporters by the hundreds of thousands in Quebec. In response to this situation, considerable interest in electoral reform developed within the political science community; the challenge was to find an electoral system which would generate parliamentary contingents that more faithfully reflected party shares of the regional popular vote.[18] Given the more national character of the governments elected in 1984 and 1988, this interest has subsided.

ORGANIZATIONAL CHARACTERISTICS OF
CANADIAN POLITICAL PARTIES

Both the Progressive Conservative and Liberal parties find their roots in the organizational imperatives of parliamentary government. The conventions of responsible government require that a group of MPs coalesce under the leadership of a single individual—the prime minister or premier—and that the group assume collective responsibility for the conduct of government. The adversarial format of the House of Commons has the same effect among those left out of the government coalition; power on both sides of the House can be wielded more effectively by groups than by individuals. While there is nothing to say that this legislative orchestration of MPs will produce party organizations that are stable over time, this has invariably occurred across western political systems.

In the decades after Confederation, the parliamentary caucuses—the MPs and Senators—*were* the national parties; they chose the party leaders and organized legislative activity in Ottawa. The "extra-parliamentary" parties consisted of little more than a loose assortment of financial backers, fund raisers, backroom advisors, and journalistic supporters unbound by any formal organizational structure. Away from Parliament Hill, the parties were phantom organizations which came briefly to life during election campaigns, and then quickly faded away. Although partisanship was often pervasive and intense in local communities across Canada, there was no organizational infrastructure through which the local parts were knit into a coherent national whole.

As time progressed, the extra-parliamentary wings of the two parties came to acquire greater organizational coherence and stability. In 1919 in the case of the Liberals, and 1927 in the case of the Conservatives, the selection of the national party leader passed from the exclusive control of the parliamentary caucus to a national leadership convention in which MPs and Senators formed a small, albeit very influential, minority. The national parties began to maintain an organizational presence between election campaigns. In 1932, for example, the National Liberal Federation was formed to provide some organizational coherence independent of the provincial Liberal parties. Constituency organizations became more stable, more formal in their organizational structure, and more extensive in their membership. If we consider today only those individuals who occupy a formal executive position somewhere within the extra-parliamentary organizations of the three major federal parties, be it at the constituency, provincial, or national level, we are looking at close to 10,000 men and women. Thus, while the primary role of extra-parliamentary parties is still to provide campaign support, the extra-parliamentary wings have become significant political players in their own right. This is particularly true for opposition parties.

Most of the third parties that have played on the Canadian political stage have originated outside Parliament or the provincial legislative assemblies. Parties such as the CCF and NDP, the Parti Québécois, the Alberta and British Columbia Social Credit, and the *Créditistes* emerged from strains in the broader social fabric and were, at least initially, characterized by relatively strong extra-parliamentary organizations. Even so, there have been no ready Canadian equivalents for some of the mass parties that have existed in western Europe, parties which have formal memberships running into the millions and which provide a wide array of not only political but also recreational, educational, and social activities for their members. With the exception of small ideological organizations such as the Communist Party, Canadian parties are, first and foremost, electoral organizations. Their memberships swell when election campaigns or leadership conventions are to be held, and shrink as such activities wind down. Relatively few members are required to keep the national, provincial, and constituency organizations ticking over until their services are called upon again for electoral combat, and thus we find that less than 5 percent of Canadian adults are active party members.[19]

On average, about 75 percent of Canadians vote in federal elections, a turnout that is relatively modest by international standards.[20] Other forms of political participation[21] are engaged in much less frequently. The 1979 Election Study found that, with respect to federal politics, 43 percent of the respondents said that they often read about politics in the newspapers, 25 percent that they often discussed politics with friends, 8 percent that they often tried to convince friends to vote as they did, 4 percent that they often attended political meetings or rallies, 3 percent that they actively campaigned on behalf of candidates, and 3 percent that they often tried to contact public officials or politicians.[22] (Provincial findings were virtually identical.) In a parallel study of the 1974 campaign, the same authors note that "the range of participation is wide—from the mere act of voting, which only five percent and ten percent report *never* doing in federal and provincial elections respectively, to working in a campaign, which only seventeen percent report *ever* doing at either level."[23] Overall, high rates of political participation tend to be associated with relatively high levels of income, formal education, and occupational prestige.

Who Is to Blame?

William Mishler argues that more could be done by the political parties to draw citizens into active participation:

Part of the reason that citizens do not participate more extensively in political parties and campaigns may be that many are unaware of the opportunities that exist. Surveys indicate that greater numbers are willing to contribute both time and money, but have never been contacted by parties and candidates and asked to contribute. In Canada, as in the United States, political

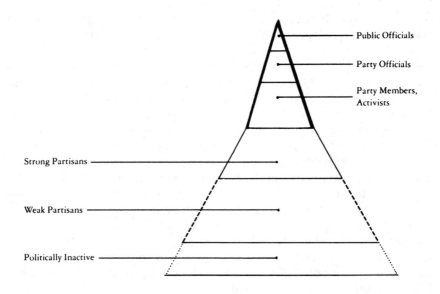

FIGURE 7.6

The Party Hierarchy

parties are poorly organized and highly inefficient in recruiting volunteer political activists.[24] Mishler nonetheless concludes that "the structure of citizen participation in Canada is surprisingly wide and deep."[25]

Against this participatory backdrop we can sketch in a rough model of Canadian political parties. The apex is formed by the small handful of party members who hold elected *public* office. Such individuals make up a minute percentage of the total party membership, a percentage that is necessarily exaggerated in Figure 7.6. Below them comes a wider but still narrow band of individuals who hold elected *party* office in the national party association, in provincial wings of the national party, or in constituency associations. Next comes a broader band of party members who do not at the time hold any formal party position but who attend party meetings, rallies, and conventions, and who participate in election campaigns by knocking on doors, giving or raising money, distributing literature, stuffing envelopes, and answering phones. The level of participation within this band, which embraces less than ten percent of the electorate, can vary from those for whom politics is a major part of their lives to those who are formal but generally inactive party members.

Below those who are formal party members we encounter citizens who, while not formal members, nevertheless have a strong partisan identification with one of the parties. Such individuals think of themselves as Conservatives, Liberals, or New Democrats. They view political life through distinctly partisan spectacles, cheering on "their team" and suffering with it in defeat, and they generally, although not always, vote for their party whenever the opportunity arises. In the 1984 National Election Study, 23 percent of the respondents reported a very strong federal party identification.[26] Another 43 percent reported a "fairly strong" party identification, and 19 percent reported a party identification that was "not very strong." Only 14 percent reported no partisan attachment whatsoever at the federal level.[27] It is among individuals with strong party identifications but without formal party memberships that we find the greatest overlap between federal and provincial parties sharing the same label.

Political parties reach much further into the electorate than their limited formal memberships would suggest. Large numbers of Canadians have a very real emotional stake in the party system even though they may not be card-carrying Conservatives, Liberals, or New Democrats. However, as we move "down" through the levels of Figure 7.6, the parties become increasingly wraithlike. As partisanship weakens, so too does the general level of citizen involvement in political life. Thus, towards the bottom of Figure 7.6 we find those individuals who not only have a tenuous connection to the party system, but who are also characterized by low levels of political participation and unstable electoral preferences.

The concept of partisanship is an important one in political science; it provides the bridge between formal party organizations on the one hand, and the electoral behavior of the majority of citizens, on the other hand, citizens who do not have formal party ties.[28] Partisan identifications tend to be acquired early in life, to be relatively stable over time, and to have a significant impact on a wide range of political perceptions.[29] Partisanship, it should be stressed, is not the same as voting intention or voting behaviour; in any given election many voters will, for a multitude of reasons, abandon "their" party to vote for another party's candidate. Party identification is nonetheless the best predictor of voting behaviour. Strong partisans will stick by their party "through hell or high water," believing that nothing could be worse than having the other team win. Weaker partisans are more likely to be swayed by the host of short-term factors at work in any election campaign.[30]

Partisanship enables us to make sense out of what can be a very complex and confusing political world; it narrows the range of political opinions to which we are exposed, and to which we attribute some credibility. Partisanship simplifies and thus admittedly distorts a complex reality. And yet that very act of simplification may be essential for most voters, given that the great bulk of their time and energy will be quite properly devoted to non-political activities. In short, partisanship provides a chart and compass with which we can sail our own private ship through the turbulent waters of political life.

Political parties, like most other private organizations, have an important social dimension. Although many people join parties in pursuit of policy objectives, many more are drawn in through friends, relations, and business associates, and for a variety of reasons that are more social than political. Brokerage parties, in particular, are held together less by a common set of principles than by the social bonds formed through the intense interpersonal relations characteristic of political activity. Political activity, in other words, can be socially rewarding in and of itself, quite apart from its instrumental value.

During his 1984 bid for the leadership of the federal Liberal party, Jean Chrétien was asked why he entered political life. His reply goes to the roots of party politics:

> My dad got me the taste of politics as a game, as a sport. In some ways it was kind of a hobby for him. He had strong convictions but he enjoyed politics as an activity, a social activity.[31]

Political parties differ from other private organizations, however, in that their overriding objective, their raison d'être, is to capture *public office*. Because they seek to do so through the ballot, which is a public rather than a private instrument, parties come under much closer public scrutiny than do most other private organizations. Scrutiny has become particularly intense with respect to the raising and expenditure of party funds.

The financing of political parties in general, and of campaign expenditures in particular, has been a matter of long-standing public concern. The basic fear has been that elections might be "bought" by those with the financial wherewithal to do so, and the electoral process thus distorted to the advantage of monied interests. Public concern has been made more acute by the rising costs of modern election campaigns; extensive reliance on media advertising, prolonged travel by party leaders, exhaustive public opinion polls all cost dearly.

The major federal legislative response to such concerns came with the 1974 Election Expenses Act, for which legislative counterparts now exist in most provinces.[32] The Act and its subsequent amendments regulate the campaign activities of registered political parties and their candidates. (To be registered through the office of the Chief Electoral Officer, parties must present candidates in at least fifty ridings.) A 1983 amendment—Bill C-169—forbids unregistered parties or other groups from advertising to promote or oppose a particular candidate or party without the permission of a registered party or candidate. If such advertising takes place, its cost must be included under the campaign expenditures of the candidate or party sanctioning the advertising.

Brian Gable, *Gable: The Editorial Cartoons of Brian Gable* (Saskatoon, Sask.: Western Producer Prairie Books, 1987), p. 5.

The Election Expenses Act imposes campaign spending limits on both national party organizations and local candidates. For the national party organizations during the 1984 campaign, these limits amounted to approximately 40 cents for each voter in each constituency in which the party was running candidates, or approximately $6.5 million for the three major parties running full slates. An individual candidate was allowed to spend up to $1.30 for each of the first 15,000 names on the electoral list in his or her riding, plus $0.65 each for the next 10,000 voters and $0.33 for each voter thereafter. In 1984, the average candidate faced an expenditure ceiling of approximately $35,000. The Act controls advertising expenditures by prohibiting party advertising during the first twenty-two days of the campaign. It also requires each broadcast outlet to allocate six and half hours for party advertising during the last four weeks of the campaign. This time is allocated to the parties by the Canadian Radio and Telecommunications Commission on the basis of the parties' shares of the popular vote during the last election. Finally, the Act requires public disclosure of the total funds raised by the parties and candidates, and the identification of all sources contributing more than $100. Registered parties must file an annual financial statement and a post-election financial statement with the Chief Electoral Officer. The statements reveal how much money was raised during the year, who it was raised from, and how much was spent.

Party Finance

In 1988 the national Progressive Conservative party raised $24.5 in corporate ($14.4 million) and individual ($10.2 million) donations. Party expenditures during the year totalled $26.6 million, of which $17.8 million went towards the federal campaign.

During the same year the Liberals raised $13.2 million, and spent $6.95 million on the 1988 campaign. Corporate donations to the Liberals outpaced individual donations by a margin of two to one. The NDP, on the other hand, raised only 2.2 percent of its $11.7 million from the corporate sector. The NDP spent $12.1 million on the 1988 campaign.

Of the nine parties submitting returns to the Chief Electoral Officer, the Rhinoceros Party trailed the field with $1,826 from ten individuals.

Chief Electoral Officer,
1988 Annual Report.

The Election Expenses Act goes beyond the financial regulation of parties to put in place three forms of public subsidy. First, the federal government now reimburses the parties for one half of the advertising bill charged by private broadcasters. Second, candidates who receive 15 percent or more of the popular vote are entitled to a federal rebate on campaign expenses, a rebate of more than forty cents per voter in the candidate's constituency. In total, rebates to candidates and parties amount to approximately 50 percent of direct campaign costs. Third, the Act encourages financial contributions to the parties by providing tax credits. Seventy-five percent of donations, up to $100, can be claimed as a tax credit when the donor computes his or her federal income tax the following year. Donations ranging from $100 to $500 qualify on a sliding scale, with a refund of 55 percent being paid for a donation of $500.

The Costs of Democracy

The 1984 election was expected to cost Elections Canada approximately $95 million, up from $63 million in 1980 and $64 million in 1979. This amounts to $5.60 a voter in 1984.

The 1984 expenditures covered a variety of costs including the hiring of about 110,000 enumerators at approximately $200 each, $90 each for polling clerks in the country's 68,000 polling stations, salaries for returning officers (approximately $9,000 each) and deputy returning officers, between $5 and $6 million to mail out cards informing voters where to vote, and an estimated $15-18 million rebate to the registered parties and their candidates to cover the federal contribution to campaign expenditures.

To get some handle on the total price tag, it is useful to consider the per capita cost. Given that federal elections occur about once every three years, the annual cost per voter works out to $1.85, or about the price of a beer or a package of cigarettes. From this perspective, the cost of democracy seems less than onerous.

"Electoral machinery shifts into high gear," *The Globe and Mail*, National Edition, July 10, 1984, p. 5.

Although the Election Expenses Act and similar provincial legislation have opened up party financing to public scrutiny and have broadened the financial base of the parties, they have not reduced the cost of elections. Indeed, by making both public and private funds more readily available, they have enabled the parties to spend more rather than less. Spending limits have generally been set well above anticipated expenditures, and thus rarely do the major parties approach their spending limits.

Now that the parties' financial affairs have been brought under public regulation, increased attention is being paid to the gender composition of candidate slates. Although women have been active in party organizations for most of this century, their participation was traditionally channelled through separate women's organizations, parallel to and yet apart from the main party organization. The National Liberal Federation, for example, had three affiliated organizations—the Women's Liberal Federation of Canada (formed in 1928), the Young Liberal Federation, and the Canadian University Liberal Federation—which hived off their constituent groups from the main party.[33] Few women were chosen as candidates, except in ridings where a party was given no chance of winning and thus where male candidates were hard to find, and only a minuscule number were elected either to the House of Commons or to provincial legislatures. To date, no Canadian prime minister, national party leader, or premier has been a woman. Women, however, have assumed the leadership of a number of provincial parties, parties which in some cases are also serious contenders for provincial office.

In recent years, women have been playing a more active role within the main party organizations. In 1973 the WLFC was disbanded and replaced by the Women's Liberal Commission; the latter was responsible to the women's caucus *within* the national party, and was not an affiliated organization. In 1983 Iona Campagnolo was elected president of the Liberal Party of Canada. At the 1983 Conservative and 1984 Liberal leadership conventions, women delegates were present in great numbers although there were no female candidates. In the 1984 election, women's issues played a major role in the campaigns of all major parties, and more women than ever before ran for election to the House of Commons. Of the 846 candidates from the three major parties, 131 were women, up from 70 in the 1980 campaign. In 1988, 174 women sought office as mainstream party candidates—84 as New Democrats, 53 as Liberals, and 37 as Tories. Thus, slightly less than 20 percent of the mainstream party candidates were women. Of the 282 MPs elected in September 1984, 10 percent were women. In the 1988 federal election, the proportion of women MPs rose to 13.2 percent as 39 women were elected.

Political parties are unlike other private organizations in a number of important ways. They extend more broadly and more deeply into the Canadian society, if not through their formal memberships, then at least through the partisan identifications held by most members of the electorate. Their financial affairs are subjected to extensive public regulation, and their expenditures are heavily subsidized by the public treasury. Their composition, be it in terms of gender, ethnicity, or regional residence, is seen as a legitimate matter of public concern and inquiry. Because they compete through a public ballot for the control of public office, parties are hybrid organizations, both quasi-private and quasi-public.

PARTIES, INTEREST GROUPS, AND PUBLIC OPINION POLLS

In a Canadian general election, more than thirteen million voters go to the polls, carrying with them multitudinous concerns and interests, policy preferences and principles, inbred prejudices, and partisan loyalties. Yet an election makes sense to us only when the thirteen million individual voting decisions are aggregated into a *collective* decision. In part, this aggregation is achieved through the electoral system, which reduces the individual decisions to 282 constituency decisions, and then from the latter extracts a national government. But because elections are so central to democratic political life, we cannot help but look for some meaning in election outcomes beyond the composition of the next government. We cannot help but look for the *policy mandate* lying behind individual voting decisions.

In the mythology of democratic politics, elections provide an opportunity for citizens to not only *choose* their government also *instruct* it. In practice, elections rarely provide citizens with a meaningful vehicle through which to convey policy preferences to those who govern. If elections are to provide a policy mandate, there must first be meaningful policy differences among the parties with respect to those issues of concern to voters. However, policy-oriented elections are rare in Canada;

the 1988 Free Trade election was very much the exception rather than the rule.[34] To the degree that parties do differ, they are likely to do so across an array of issues, thereby raising a second difficulty in determining the policy mandate. I may vote for Party A because I support its policies on abortion even though I do not support its policy on Canadian–American relations. If successful, Party A may, however, interpret its victory as a mandate for its policy on Canadian–American relations, and not abortion.

Consider, for example, what may be some of the policy concerns of a typical voter going into the next federal election. She may be particularly concerned about her own employment situation and that of her spouse, along with the employment prospects for her children. Interest rates may well be a concern, with the mortgage coming up for renewal. She may see the election as the opportunity to advance a range of feminist concerns. She may be concerned about the growing national debt without fully understanding (if anyone could), what should and could be done. She may have a nagging irritation with policies already in place—bilingualism, the abolition of capital punishment—and a marginal interest in a range of new policy issues—pornography, acid rain, and aboriginal self-government. Behind all of these concerns may lurk a growing fear of nuclear war and a growing mistrust of those who seek to preserve peace by building weapons of mass destruction. All of these concerns, however, have to be reduced to a single "X" printed on a ballot, to a choice among parties which may not address her concerns or may not differ in any meaningful way. Moreover, her policy message must be conveyed through the endorsation of a local candidate, about whose views on these issues she knows nothing at all.

The authors of *The Absent Mandate* conclude that "the persistent failure of major political parties to present voters with distinctive, well-defined policy platforms turns the electoral process into more of a spectator sport for those who enjoy political 'horseraces' than an exercise in informed citizen participation."[35] Elections do, however, produce a clear policy mandate in one very important sense. They give to the winner the right to articulate a mandate, to state what the people meant to say when they elected their government. A new or returning prime minister has the electoral authority to give shape to the election mandate through words and legislation. Admittedly, we have no way of knowing if the mandate that emerges corresponds with what the voters were trying to say, but if the two diverge too markedly the government can be expected to pay the price in the next election.

While parties may be primarily instruments of governance rather than transmission belts for the flow of policy preferences from the electorate to the government, other transmission belts are by no means absent. To begin with, there are a number of steps that individuals can take on their own. They can write or phone their MP, their MLA, or the cabinet minister(s) responsible for the policy at issue. They can write letters to the editor and phone in to radio talk shows. They can write to the various departments of the federal and provincial governments that may be involved. However, there are very real limits on the ability of any one individual to move the policy process. What is generally called for is some form of collective action, and it is here that organized interest groups come into play.

To illustrate the role of organized groups, let us look briefly at the interest many people have in protecting whales. As an individual, I may be very concerned about the fate of the whales, having watched them off the Pacific coast and listened to stereo recordings of their songs. But, again as an individual, there is little *direct* action that I can take on their behalf. I could refuse to buy products containing whale components, but only if I knew what such products were and only if they were for sale in Canada. I could not set forth from Calgary to try to stop foreign whaling fleets, nor could I expect individual letters sent to the governments of whaling nations to have much effect. In short, as an individual I would be powerless were it not for the existence of organized groups such as Greenpeace. On my behalf, Greenpeace can lobby internationally for the protection of whales, sail small boats in front of the whaling fleets, organize consumer boycotts, and raise concern for whales in newspapers and magazines around the world. Greenpeace becomes my "hired gun" in the fight against the whalers, and yet no more is demanded of me than the thirty seconds it takes to write a small cheque. This very minimal form of individual participation, when aggregated across thousands of individuals, provides the foundation for an effective political organization.

Interest groups, of which Greenpeace is but one example, are private organizations which attempt to influence public officials, and through them, public policy. Unlike political parties, they do not run candidates for public office under their own label. While interest groups may try to influence election outcomes by throwing their weight behind candidates sympathetic to their causes, their primary activity takes place between elections. Their efforts are directed towards cabinet, and towards the government's bureaucratic arm, not towards the political parties. With the growing judicialization of politics noted in the last chapter, interest groups are increasingly using the courts to pursue political objectives. Given the strictures of party discipline and the cabinet's dominance of the legislative process, interest groups expend relatively little energy lobbying common garden MPs and MLAs.

Most interest groups are stable organizations representing long-standing group interests within the society. Groups such as the Canadian Medical Association, the Canadian Manufacturers' Association, the Sierra Club, the Canadian Association of University Teachers, the Canadian Broadcasters' Association, the Consumers' Association of Canada, the

Canadian Federation of Agriculture, and the Canadian Hospital Association will remain in place no matter who wins a given election. These "institutionalized" groups are interested in protecting their access to government, and are thus unlikely to become embroiled in election campaigns that might fragment their membership base and disrupt that access.[36] Because they are as interested in the implementation of public policy as they are in its formulation, contacts with the federal and provincial bureaucrats are carefully nurtured. However, there are also other "issue-oriented" interest groups which may pursue a more active electoral role, and which are less concerned with, although not indifferent to, their own organizational survival. At least in theory, their issues are capable of resolution and could potentially be removed from the nation's political agenda. Such issues might include the reinstatement of capital punishment and the legislative prohibition of abortion.

While institutionalized groups generally pursue interests which are negotiable—one can have, for example, somewhat more or somewhat less consumer protection or environmental regulation—single-interest groups in particular often pursue non-negotiable interests. Right to life groups, for instance, will not settle for *fewer* abortions. In general, non-negotiable interests are much more difficult for the political system to handle than are issues for which compromises and trade-offs can be struck. Here it should also be noted that we cannot assume that all "interests" within society will find adequate expression through organized groups. Effective organization requires money, leadership skills, and organizational resources, none of which are evenly distributed throughout the population or across the multitude of interests potentially open to political mobilization. Thus, interest group politics may extend the political influence of already powerful interests as much as they open up the political arena to a wider array of competing interests.

Although interest groups are important political actors, they are not exclusively or even primarily concerned with political activity. An organization like the Canadian Medical Association engages in a wide range of non-political activities including medical conferences, research support, group life insurance, travel assistance, legal advice, informational seminars, and professional education. As Paul Pross points out, for many groups political activity " . . . is a minor and unwelcome addition to more general concerns."[37] Individuals may also join interest groups for a variety of non-political reasons including social functions, access to charter airfares, and an interest in publications put out by the groups. Yet at some point interest groups will be involved in the political process; they will represent shared group interests through contact with federal and provincial bureaucrats, cabinet presentations, briefs to task forces and royal commissions, letters of concern or support to cabinet ministers, and even media advertisements designed to increase public support for policies in line with the group's interests. Interest groups thus play an essential role in the communication of citizen policy preferences. If I wish to communicate with the government as an academic or as a supporter of whales, the Canadian Association of University Teachers and Greenpeace provide far more effective channels than does the ballot.

Interest groups keep governments informed about the opinion of *specific sectors* of the electorate. If, however, governments want to know the opinion of the public *at large* rather than the specific opinions of cattlemen, oilmen, academics, physicians, or manufacturers, they have at their disposal sophisticated public opinion polls. Such polls provide a more precise and less biased reading of the public mood than can be obtained through election results or party organizations. Thus polls provide another, albeit passive, instrument through which citizens can communicate their concerns to governments.

Polling itself can assume many forms. Governments follow the routine polling by commercial firms, much of which we encounter in the daily press. They also commission a great deal of polling research, often "piggy-backing" their questions onto omnibus commercial surveys. Government departments routinely track trends in investor confidence, anticipated consumer spending, and political priorities. In whatever form, polls have become an indispensable tool for keeping governments abreast of the shifting currents of public opinion. Polls provide a powerful tool with which governments can dissect the public mood. Thus, the ambiguous policy mandate which can be discerned by reading the entrails of election results is supplemented, and to a large degree replaced by, an ongoing diagnosis of the citizen predispositions carried out through public opinion polls.

Public opinion polls have been subjected to a great deal of critical commentary. Even if we put aside questions about their accuracy, neutrality and cost, serious concerns remain. Polls have been accused of having a pernicious impact on campaigning, leading parties and candidates to do little more than echo what the public wants to hear. To argue that polls report but do not shape opinion seems less tenable after the experience of the 1984 election campaign. The 1984 polls, which from early in the campaign indicated a Conservative landslide, arguably had at least three important although not necessarily decisive effects. First, they undercut morale within the Liberal campaign organization, making it difficult to attract financial support and volunteer assistance. Second, they undercut the Liberal campaign strategy in the West; if western Canada wanted an effective voice in Ottawa, there was little sense in voting for the Liberals, as the Conservatives were expected to win. Third, they assured Quebec voters that a shift to the Conservative party would not isolate Quebec from the federal government.

Gable, *Regina Leader Post*. Reprinted in *Calgary Herald*, August 4, 1984.

Ever Wonder Why No One Interviews You?

In a typical Gallup poll, approximately 1,000 respondents are interviewed. Given an adult Canadian population of some 17,000,000 persons, the odds of any one individual being interviewed are remote. If a Gallup survey were conducted every month and an entirely different set of respondents used each time, any given individual could expect to be interviewed once in every 1,417 *years!*

The odds of being picked as a respondent in any one survey are approximately one in 17,000. The odds of being picked *in your lifetime*, should you live to be eighty, are approximately one in 23.

Given the role played by interest groups and opinion polls, it is clear that the parties have been relegated to a secondary role in conveying citizen policy preferences to governments. Nevertheless, parties continue to perform a number of other essential roles. They continue to structure the legislative process, providing reasonably stable governments and a focused legislative opposition. They continue to recruit political leaders. Most importantly, parties enable voters to hold governments responsible for their actions. As Richard Van Loon and Michael Whittington point out, "we can vote to 'throw the rascals out' because we can draw a line between 'rascals' and 'non-rascals'; the party labels provide us with this line."[38] Thus, the electoral process enables citizens to cast a retrospective judgment on government performance. The fact that it does not enable citizens to direct or handcuff the course of public policy seems to be of little consequence, given that a profusion of alternative policy instruments exists. If the party system is to be judged, it should be judged on its success or failure in holding the country together, in moderating rather than exacerbating those conflicts which strain the national fabric.

POLITICAL PARTIES AND POLITICAL CONFLICT

The preceding chapters have identified four principal axes of Canadian political life, axes which provide a useful framework for assessing parties and the party system. Here, then, we turn to a brief discussion of how the four axes have shaped and have been shaped by party politics.

Language Politics

In the early decades after Confederation, Macdonald's Conservative party formed the political bridge between Canada's two linguistic communities. Indeed, the Conservatives' initial dominance of national political life reflected the party's electoral success in both communities, just as the rise to power of the Laurier Liberals reflected the collapse of Macdonald's linguistic coalition. Speaking in 1904, Henri Bourassa described the vision of Canada that underlay the success of both the Macdonald Conservatives and the Laurier Liberals:

> We work for the development of a Canadian patriotism which is in our eyes the best guaranty of the existence of the two races and of the mutual respect they owe each other ... The nation that we wish to see develop is the Canadian nation, composed of French Canadians and English Canadians, that is of two elements separated by language and religion ... but united in a feeling of brotherhood, in a common attachment to a common fatherland.[39]

The mutual respect and brotherhood of which Bourassa spoke were to be severely tested, and found wanting, in the conscription crisis of World War I, a crisis in which, for the first time, one of the linguistic communities was excluded from the federal government.

Canada had gone into the First World War with a volunteer army and, prior to 1917, Robert Borden's Conservative government steadfastly maintained that conscription would not be introduced. By 1917, however, the unexpected carnage of trench warfare had created a desperate manpower shortage. Efforts in the first part of that year to recruit additional volunteers were largely futile; in English Canada the manpower pool was all but exhausted, and in Quebec, where the recruiting drive produced only 92 volunteers, an earlier enthusiasm for a short European war had evaporated. As Armstrong explains:

> ... there could not have been any more striking illustration of the indifference and hostility of French Canada to the Dominion's war effort. The wholehearted enthusiasm of 1914 had turned to bitter mistrust and open opposition by the summer of 1917.[40]

The attempt to recruit French Canadian volunteers turned into a shambles as anglophone recruiters were sent into Quebec to urge French Canadians to fight, not for Canada, but for England and France. Their appeal fell on deaf ears. Finally, the government introduced the Military Service Bill on June 11, 1917. The Bill's introduction was greeted by massive anti-conscription rallies across Quebec, and its proclamation on August 29 met with violence and riots in Montreal.

French Canadian opposition to conscription can be traced in part to the isolation of a small linguistic community, cut off from its European roots for 150 years and further isolated on a predominantly anglophone continent. It also reflected French Canadian anger over the limits placed on Ontario bilingual schools in 1915. Perhaps of greatest importance were the different forms of Canadian nationalism that emerged during the war. While involvement in the British war effort was an expression of Canadian nationalism for most English Canadians, the nationalist horizon of French Canadians stopped at Canadian shores. In the parliamentary debate on the Military Service Bill, "hardly a French Canadian spoke ... who did not insist that his compatriots felt deeply that the only country to which they owed loyalty and service was Canada and that to ask them to rush to the aid of France and England was asking a great deal too much."[41]

Conscription had a profound impact on both the Conservative and Liberal parties. In an attempt to broaden the political base of support for conscription, Borden formed a Union Government in October 1917. The new cabinet comprised thirteen Conservative ministers and ten pro-conscription Liberal ministers. The Union Government unquestionably served its intended purpose in English Canada, but it also isolated Quebec. Borden's cabinet included only two weak French Canadian ministers. In the December 1917 general election, only three Unionist candidates were elected in Quebec. Those Liberals who remained under the leadership of Wilfrid Laurier fought conscription and, in so doing, greatly strengthened what was already a strong electoral position for the Liberal party in Quebec. Figure 7.7 illustrates the wedge that the 1917 election drove between the two major parties in Quebec. At the same time, Laurier's opposition to conscription caused a deep division within

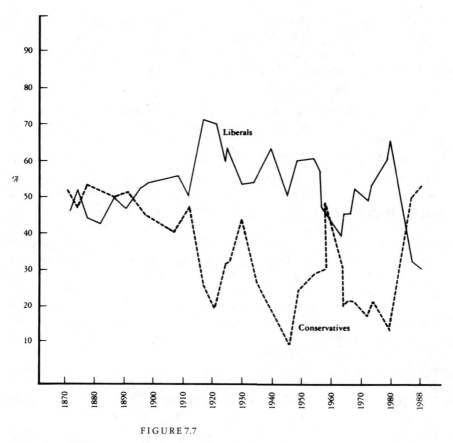

FIGURE 7.7

Party Shares of the Quebec Popular Vote in Federal Elections

the Liberal party itself. Many English Canadian Liberal MPs crossed the floor of the House to support the Union government, and the party's electoral base in English Canada was severely damaged. *Thus the 1917 conscription crisis caused the party system to collapse as a vehicle of political integration across the linguistic divide.*

In the Second World War the conscription crisis was played out again. This time Mackenzie King was prime minister. King, who had become leader of the Liberal party in 1919, was acutely aware how badly both his party and the national fabric had been damaged by the conscription crisis of the First World War. Thus, in a speech to the House of Commons shortly after the Second World War broke out, King promised that Canada's war effort would not entail conscription:

I wish to repeat the undertaking I gave in Parliament on behalf of the Government on March 30th last. The present Government believes that conscription of men for overseas service will not be a necessary or effective step. No such measure will be introduced by the present Administration.[42]

This was the bargain King presented to Quebec in the 1940 general election; Canada would pursue the war at Britain's side, but not at the cost of conscription. In that election, the Liberals captured 61 of Quebec's 65 seats, with 3 seats going to independent Liberals and only 1 to a Conservative candidate.

As the war dragged on, King's promise proved more and more difficult to keep, and the Liberal government began a series of incremental steps towards conscription. In a rare national plebiscite, held in April 1942, King asked voters to release the government from its pledge not to impose conscription. The plebiscite, it should be stressed, was held on the government's pledge and not on conscription per se. The government's policy, King maintained, was "conscription if necessary but not necessarily conscription." The plebiscite quantified the sharp linguistic cleavage that existed on the conscription issue: 72 percent of Quebecers voted not to release King's government from its pledge, while 80 percent of those outside Quebec, and a national majority overall, voted yes.[43] Conscription was subsequently introduced, but only for home defence; conscripted soldiers, or "Zombies," as they came to be called, could not yet be sent overseas. By late 1944, however, the attrition of Canadian forces overseas and the government's inability to raise sufficient replacements through voluntary enlistment forced King to send conscripted men overseas. After five years of war and despite strenuous opposition from Quebec, conscription for overseas service had again been imposed.

This time the impact on the party system was less pronounced. In the 1945 general election, the Liberals lost only eight Quebec seats while the nationalistic and anti-conscriptionist Bloc Populaire elected ten members. As Figure 7.7 shows, the Progressive Conservatives were devastated in Quebec, electing only one member with a meagre 8.4 percent of the vote in their worst showing ever. Although the Liberal government had eventually imposed conscription, Mackenzie King had clearly resisted doing so as long as possible. French Canadians who were nonetheless dissatisfied could hardly throw their support to the Conservatives, who had been, after all, much more supportive of conscription than had the Liberals. To vote en mass for the Bloc Populaire was to risk Quebec's isolation from the federal government. Thus, the Liberals survived more or less intact in Quebec, while the poor showing by the Conservatives was an extension of, rather than a significant change in, the political status quo. Even though the Liberals lost 48 seats outside Quebec and the Progressive Conservatives gained 26, the Liberals retained both a 7-seat advantage over the Tories outside Quebec and a majority government. The country was not split along linguistic lines as it had been in 1917.

Following the war, the Conservatives found themselves trapped in a vicious circle, or what George Perlin has called the "Tory Syndrome," in Quebec.[44] Because so few Conservatives were elected from Quebec, the party's parliamentary caucus lacked sufficient sensitivity to Quebec's concerns. Because the party lacked such sensitivity, it tended to come down on the "wrong side" of whatever linguistic conflicts arose, further damaging its electoral prospects in Quebec. Because the party did so poorly in Quebec, it could not compete on equal terms with the Liberals in federal elections; the Liberals were able, with a reasonable degree of veracity, to portray themselves as the only truly *national* party. Successive national defeats led to self-perpetuating internal attacks on the party's leaders, attacks which undermined the party's credibility as an alternative government and thus further weakened its electoral support.

The trend was broken briefly in 1958 when Quebec voters climbed aboard the Diefenbaker bandwagon and elected fifty Progressive Conservative MPs. The Quebec MPs, however, felt ill at ease within the predominantly anglophone Tory caucus. Nor were they a particularly able lot, and the performance of Tory cabinet ministers from Quebec left a great deal to be desired. For his part, Diefenbaker was unable to exploit the Conservative opening in Quebec. As George Grant explains,

> the keystone of a Canadian nation is the French fact.... English-speaking Canadians who desire the survival of their nation have to co-operate with those who seek the continuance of Franco-American civilization. The failure of Diefenbaker to act on this maxim was his most tragic mistake.[45]

In 1962 only fourteen Quebec Tories were re-elected, and in 1963 only eight.

While the Conservatives were mired in Quebec, the Liberals were making the province their own. In 1948, Mackenzie King retired and was replaced by Louis St. Laurent, the Liberals' second French Canadian leader. St. Laurent was replaced by Lester Pearson in 1957, who was in turn replaced by Pierre Trudeau in 1968. Trudeau was very popular in Quebec, and his leadership came to be identified with the bilingualism policies of the federal government. Although initiated before Trudeau became prime minister and endorsed by the opposition parties, those policies, along with Trudeau, were the basis of a seemingly invincible Liberal fortress in Quebec. (When the Official Languages Act came to a vote, seventeen Conservative MPs, including John Diefenbaker, defied Robert Stanfield and voted against the legislation.) The party's strength in Quebec enabled the Liberals to argue in turn that they alone could form a truly national government spanning the country's two linguistic communities. At a time when English Canadians were nervous about a growing separatist movement in Quebec, the Liberals' argument was a telling one.

During Trudeau's leadership, 47 percent of the Liberal seats *came* from Quebec and 84 percent of Quebec's seats *went* to the Liberal party. The Liberal party's near monopoly in Quebec gave it a virtual armlock on national power. In the 1972 general election, the Conservatives elected more MPs than the Liberals in eight of the ten provinces, and tied with the Liberals in the ninth. Yet even this was not enough to overcome the Liberal edge in Quebec, where the Liberals won fifty-six seats to only two for the Conservatives. Without a breakthrough in Quebec, the most that the Conservatives could hope for was a minority government, and even that eluded Robert Stanfield by two seats in 1972.

The Conservative resurgence in Quebec began under Joe Clark's leadership. Clark devoted more time and effort to Quebec than any Conservative leader before him, and improved his own grasp of French to the point where he could campaign effectively in Quebec. Ironically, though, Clark's efforts bore no fruit whatsoever in the short run. In the 1979 general election, the Conservative share of the Quebec popular vote fell from 21.2 percent in 1974 to only 13.5 percent. In the 1980 election it fell again to 12.6 percent, and the Conservatives elected only one Quebec MP.[46] Yet Clark's efforts, in combination with the 1979 minority Conservative government and its 1980 defeat, drove home to Conservatives the necessity of a breakthrough in Quebec. The promise of that breakthrough was the major card played by Brian Mulroney in his successful 1983 bid for the leadership of the Conservative party.

Mulroney was the first Tory Leader to come from Quebec, and the first central Canadian Conservative leader in twenty-seven years. Fluent in both official languages, he proved to be the standard-bearer so badly needed by the Conservative party in Quebec. In the 1984 campaign, Mulroney's personal appeal, along with the retirement of Pierre Trudeau, John Turner's defeat of Jean Chrétien in the Liberal leadership convention, and a weariness in Quebec after a decade of confrontation between nationalists and federalists, produced the long-awaited breakthrough. Tory candidates captured 58 Quebec seats, a gain of 57 from 1980. In 1988 Mulroney strengthened the Conservatives' hold in Quebec by taking 63 seats and leaving only 12 seats to Liberal candidates. Back in 1980, only one Tory vote in ten (10.5 percent) came from Quebec. In the 1984 election, 27.5 percent of the total Conservative vote came from Quebec, a proportion that climbed even further to 32.5 percent in 1988.

The national fate of the Conservative and Liberal parties has been largely determined by their success or failure in Quebec. This has also been the case for the New Democrats, although here the party's Quebec record has been one of unmitigated failure. Since the formation of the

NDP in 1962, there has yet to be an NDP candidate elected in Quebec. In 1988, the NDP ran a very high profile campaign in Quebec, in part because public opinion polls taken in 1986 and 1987 had indicated a Quebec surge in NDP support. However, in the election itself, the New Democrats failed again to elect a candidate in Quebec, and finished with only 14 percent of the Quebec popular vote. Without at least an electoral toehold in Quebec, New Democrats will continue to have difficulty convincing Canadians that they have the potential to form a national government. The "Tory Syndrome" has passed to the NDP.

Overall, the parties have been more affected by language-related conflict than they have shaped the resolution of such conflict. As Smith points out, the parties per se made, at best, a modest contribution to resolving the constitutional crisis posed by Quebec in the 1970s and early 1980s; Ottawa's response was a governmental response rather than one emerging from the Liberal party.[47] Brian Mulroney must certainly be given much of the credit for the Meech Lake Accord, but here again the constitutional agreement was a creation of governments, not parties. Here it is important to note that, in the run-up to the 1988 federal election, the Conservatives, Liberals, and New Democrats all supported the Accord. In the wake of that election, an election in which Liberal and NDP aspirations were dashed in Quebec, both Liberal and New Democratic support for the Accord softened appreciably.

Regional Politics

Although the emergence of national political parties has been associated with the decline of territorial conflict in many western countries,[48] this association has been less apparent in Canada. The history of protest parties in western Canada and the more contemporary collapse of the Liberal party in the region suggest that the party system has been an imperfect vehicle of national political integration. Whether the parties have contributed to regional conflict, or have been impaled upon it, is more difficult to determine.

Figure 7.8 traces out the regional composition of the Liberal and Conservative electoral coalitions from the turn of the century, and that of the NDP coalition from 1962. As discussed in more detail above, the contribution of Quebec voters varies considerably across the three parties. While traditionally a core component of the Liberal coalition, they have constituted a more erratic component of the Conservative coalition, and a more negligible part of the NDP coalition.

If we turn to voters from Atlantic Canada, Figure 7.8 shows a modest but generally progressive decline in their contribution to the Conservative and Liberal coalitions. It is not, however, that Atlantic voters are turning away from the two parties, as the figure shows no migration to the

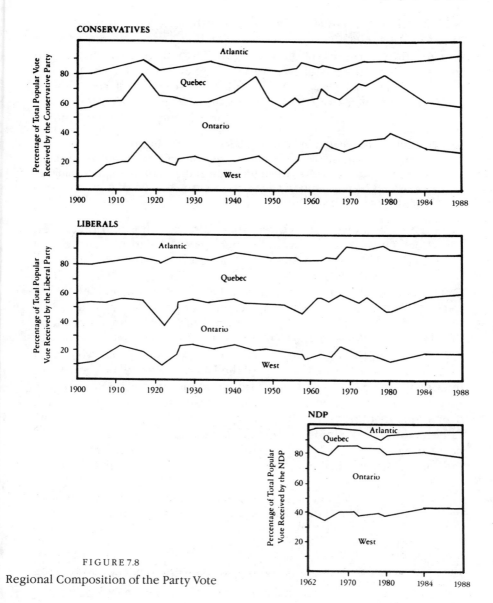

FIGURE 7.8

Regional Composition of the Party Vote

NDP. It is simply that Atlantic Canadians constitute a declining proportion of the national electorate, and hence a declining proportion of specific party coalitions. There is nothing in Figure 7.8 to suggest that the regional interests of Atlantic Canadians have found a clear champion or opponent within the national party system. With the exception of very modest regional support for the NDP, Rawlyk and Brown's discussion of the region in the 1870s applies with equal force to the subsequent century:

> Throughout the region the disintegration of any political movement which did not correspond to the sole Canadian cleavage of Liberal and Conservative signified the complete political integration of the Maritimes into Canada. . . . there would be no significant attempts to channel regional protest outside the traditional two-party system.[49]

Figure 7.8 shows that all three parties draw a major portion of their vote from Ontario, as we would expect given Ontario's share of the national population. It is nonetheless interesting to note that, until very recently, it was the NDP which drew the largest share of its vote from Ontario. Across the nine elections from 1962 to 1984, 43.0 percent of the total NDP vote, as opposed to 38.1 percent of the Conservative and 36.9 percent of the Liberal total vote, came from Ontario, a finding that reflects the electoral weakness of the NDP east of the Ontario–Quebec border. In 1988, however, the NDP drew only 35.0 percent of its total vote from Ontario, compared to 43.3 percent of the Liberal vote and 31.5 percent of the Conservative vote which came from Ontario. It is also interesting to note that Ontario's contribution to the Conservative vote has declined over time. In the twelve elections held between 1900 and 1945, the Conservatives drew almost 46 percent of their total vote from Ontario. In postwar elections, that proportion fell to just under 40 percent. In 1984, the Tory resurgence in Quebec reduced Ontario's contribution to only 33 percent.

The Diefenbaker elections of 1957 and 1958 initiated a pronounced westward shift in the Conservatives' centre of gravity, and an off-setting, although less pronounced, eastward shift for the Liberal party. The modest 1984 Liberal revival in the West suggested by Figure 7.8 is deceptive; the "revival" is simply an artifact of the Liberal collapse in Quebec. In the 1984 election, Liberal candidates in the West captured only 16.3 percent of the regional popular vote, *down* from 23.4 percent in 1980. In all four western provinces, the Liberal party finished third. It is thus somewhat ironic that the Liberals emerged from the 1984 election with a party leader, John Turner, representing a Vancouver riding.

Overall, Figure 7.8 suggests a party system that has been reasonably stable in its regional composition, although there are two important qualifications to any such conclusion. The first is that a more erratic picture would emerge if we looked at the regional distribution of party

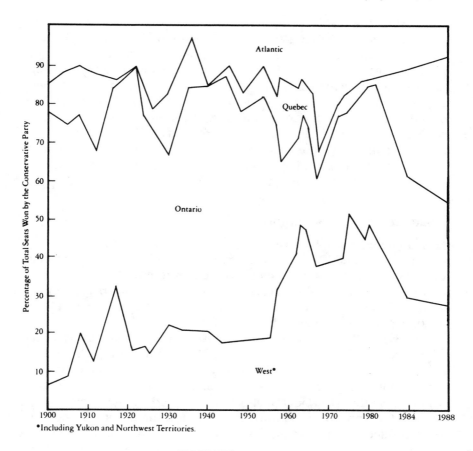

*Including Yukon and Northwest Territories.

FIGURE 7.9

Regional Distribution of Conservative Seats in the House of Commons

seats rather than *votes*. The difference can be illustrated by a comparison of the regional composition of the Conservative popular vote, shown in Figure 7.8, and the regional composition of Conservative seats in the House of Commons, shown in Figure 7.9. The latter figure brings Ontario's pre-Diefenbaker dominance of the party into bold relief. The patterns revealed in Figure 7.8 are amplified in Figure 7.9. The Conservatives' historical weakness in Quebec is more dramatic, as are the regional shifts that occurred in 1984 and following the Diefenbaker sweep in 1958.

The second qualification is that Figure 7.8 does not capture the host of protest parties that have arisen in western Canada since 1921. Certainly it can be argued that parties such as the Progressives, the United Farmers of Alberta, the CCF, the Social Credit party, and the Reform Party demonstrate the party system's inability to integrate the West into the Canadian political mainstream. As Denis Smith notes, such parties have been skeptical towards the national community since 1921.[50] It can also be argued that the western penchant for third parties does more than reflect western alienation; it may also have contributed to alienation by choking off western input into the only parties forming national governments. If western Canadians have elected MPs to protest rather than to govern, then to a degree they have been architects of their own misfortune.

Canadian-American Relations

Canada's economic relationship with the United States played a central role in the 1891 and 1911 general elections, and the Canada–U.S. military relationship played a significant if less central role in 1963. Throughout the 1970s and early 1980s, Canadian–American relations played a more peripheral role in federal elections, with primary attention being paid to the tone, rather than to the substance, of the relationship.

In 1891, Sir John A. Macdonald's Conservative government appeared to be on the brink of collapse. Macdonald himself was ailing, the country had been unable to shake a prolonged economic depression, and the government was plagued by scandal and the acrimonious Manitoba Schools dispute. The Liberal opposition moved to the attack with a proposal for *unrestricted reciprocity* with the United States,[51] and in so doing handed Macdonald the issue that was to save the Conservative government. Reciprocity, Macdonald argued, would reduce the national government's revenues and necessitate an annual per capita tax of $15 to make up for the loss. More importantly, Macdonald portrayed reciprocity as a threat to Canada's British ties and to the very survival of Canada. He accused the Liberals of "veiled treason which attempts by sordid means and mercenary proffers to lure our people from their allegiance."[52] There was, he concluded, " . . . a deliberate conspiracy by force, by fraud or by both to force Canada into the American union."[53] This was strong language indeed, and was reinforced by Macdonald's ringing statement that "a British subject I was born, and a British subject I shall die."

The campaign engaged the country's major economic interests. The farming community endorsed reciprocity, but the major transportation, financial, and manufacturing interests opposed it, and carried more weight in the campaign. Of greatest importance, however, were the emotional loyalties brought into play. In Quebec, the Conservative party argued that reciprocity would launch French Canadians down the slippery slope to absorption into American secular materialism. In the

Maritimes, the threat to the British connection was emphasized. The *Halifax Morning Herald*, planting the Red Ensign on its masthead for the duration of the campaign, proclaimed that the Canadian people were being brought to a parting of the ways: would they choose to be bound in vassalage to their foreign foes—the Americans—or to continue to prosper as part of the greatest empire the world had ever seen?[54] Under the emotional barrage of Macdonald's campaign, the Liberals and the reciprocity proposal went down to defeat.

In 1911 the Liberals, now in power, once again ventured into the reciprocity thicket. In January 1911, a reciprocity agreement had been reached between Canada and the United States, and had been approved by the American Congress. Prime Minister Wilfrid Laurier, however, decided to go to the Canadian people in a general election before introducing the reciprocity legislation in Parliament. Again, the farming community supported reciprocity, and again reciprocity was opposed by the major transportation, financial, and manufacturing interests. As in 1891, the purely economic debate was soon obscured by an emotional debate over the future of Canada. The Conservatives' campaign slogan was "No Truck Nor Trade with the Yankees," a slogan coined in the advertising department of a wholly American-owned subsidiary.[55] Premier McBride of British Columbia summed up the emotional stakes with a simple placard that superimposed "Which?" over pictures of the Union Jack, on the one side, and the Stars and Stripes on the other. As in 1911, the Liberals had the wrong emotional end of the issue, and went down to defeat. Taken together, the 1891 and 1911 campaigns demonstrated that the Canadian–American relationship could engage deeply felt emotions and national insecurities. Twice burned, the Liberals were never again to inject proposals for free trade into federal campaigns. When the issue of Canadian–American relations entered the 1963 campaign, the focus was upon Canada's military relationship with the United States.

During John Diefenbaker's term of office, the Conservative government had purchased a considerable stock of military hardware which, to be effective, required tactical nuclear warheads. By early 1963, however, warheads had yet to be acquired and the cabinet, badly split on the issue, vacillated on whether to proceed with their acquisition. The government's indecision was openly criticized by the American government, and was made a central issue by the Liberal opposition in the 1963 general election campaign. The Liberal leader, Lester Pearson, argued that Canada must acquire nuclear weapons to fulfill its alliance commitments to the United States and NATO. The Conservatives remained badly divided on the issue, and it is likely that the party's internal disarray hurt it as much at the polls as did Diefenbaker's opposition to nuclear weapons. George Grant argues that Diefenbaker faced the "full power of the Canadian ruling class, the American government and the military," and that in the unequal contest Canadian nationalism was dealt a lethal blow.[56] In any event, the minority Conservative government went down to defeat, to be replaced by a minority Liberal government.

Over the next twenty-five years, the substance of Canadian–American relations rarely intruded into federal election campaigns. In an extensive analysis of issue-voting in Canadian elections, the authors of *The Absent Mandate* concluded that debate over important Canadian–American issues in the 1970s " . . . occurred outside the electoral arena, as did any conflict resolution."[57] To the extent that Canadian–American relations played a significant role, the focus was on the tone rather than the substance of the relationship. Thus, in the 1984 campaign, for example, the Conservatives called for an improved and friendlier relationship without specifying what an altered relationship might entail. Admittedly, the federal parties differed among themselves with respect to the Canadian–American relationship. The NDP staked out a clear position on the nationalist end of the continuum, the Liberal party was the architect of the nationalist policies embedded in the Foreign Investment Review Agency and the National Energy Program, and the Conservatives favoured a more hospitable environment for American investment. However, neither the Liberals nor the Conservatives sought to move Canadian–American relations to the top of the electoral agenda.

This situation changed dramatically when the Mulroney government announced its intention to negotiate the Free Trade Agreement with the United States. When legislation to implement the Agreement was blocked in the Canadian Senate, the Conservatives went to the people in a general election. The historical irony of the fall 1988 campaign was that the Conservatives, who had traditionally opposed closer integration with the United States, supported the FTA, while the Liberals, who had traditionally been the free trade party, opposed the Agreement. In any event, the free trade issue dominated the 1988 campaign and, as had happened in the past, emotional argument played a central role. When it became difficult to sort out the hypothetical economic arguments, the potential impact of the Agreement on national unity, on the Canadian culture, and indeed on the very survival of Canada, provided ample grounds for impassioned political debate. When the election came, the Conservatives and the FTA carried the day. The FTA legislation was subsequently reintroduced into Parliament, passed by both the House and Senate, and the Agreement came into effect on January 1, 1989.

Intergovernmental Relations

In the complex world of federal–provincial relations, conflict among governments has often been overlaid with partisan conflict. The first meeting of provincial premiers, held in 1887, was called by the predom-

Globe and Mail, January 4, 1988, p. A6.

inantly Liberal premiers to orchestrate a partisan attack on the then-Conservative federal government. As the Depression descended in 1930, Prime Minister King declared in the House of Commons that his government would not give a nickel in federal relief to provincial governments controlled by Conservative administrations. During the latter part of the Trudeau era, when the Liberals controlled the federal government but all ten provincial governments were in non-Liberal hands, intergovernmental conflicts frequently took on a partisan air. Certainly the energy conflicts between the government of Canada, on one side, and the governments of Alberta and Newfoundland, on the other, appeared to be sharpened by the partisan conflict between the federal Liberals and the provincial Conservatives.

Despite such examples, however, there is a general consensus within the political science literature that partisanship plays, at most, a very modest role in the bargaining positions and outcomes of federal–provincial negotiations,[58] and that it affects the tone more than the substance of intergovernmental relations. This consensus has been pulled together by Donald Smiley, who notes that political parties "... appear to be of diminishing importance in the aggregation and articulation of citizen interests and the conversion of these into public policy."[59] While this diminished importance is a general phenomenon, it has been particularly evident in federal–provincial relations. In First Ministers' Conferences, Smiley argues, cleavages "... are on axes other than partisan ones: between 'have' and 'have-not' provinces; between governments which put an urgent priority on bilingual and bicultural matters and those which do not; between Quebec and other jurisdictions; between the heartland of Ontario and Quebec and the peripheral provinces."[60] The provinces have enduring characteristics including their size, wealth, resource base, and regional location, which persist no matter which party forms the provincial government, and which will tend to be of primary importance in shaping intergovernmental relations. Partisanship may shape the tone of and strategy employed in such relations, but provincial interests and concerns are relatively immutable.

Setting the Political Agenda

This *Canadian Press* story appeared in *The Globe and Mail* on August 17, 1984, during the final stages of the federal election campaign:

The federal Conservatives made a pact with the premiers and provincial energy ministers not to let energy policy become an issue in the election campaign, Tory energy critic Pat Carney says.

She told a group of businessmen yesterday in Toronto that the Tories consciously decided the topic was too hot to touch and wanted to keep it under wraps until after the Sept. 4 election.

"This is one of my few chances to talk on energy policy in this campaign," Miss Carney said to about 200 business executives at an economic seminar sponsored by the Conservatives.

"And that has been by very careful design because the producing provinces and the big consuming provinces and the premiers and energy ministers have a quiet little accord going that we did not want energy to be an issue in this campaign.

"The reason for it has been that energy in the past and energy policy has been a source of great bitterness in the country."

In federal states, political parties have a potentially important role to play in the operation of the federal system. Highly centralized party systems, in which the national parties dominate those in the states or provinces, may centralize the federal system far beyond what we might expect from the constitutional framework, by acting as a solvent on the constitutional division of powers.[61] In the Canadian case, however, the party system has, if anything, reinforced the division of powers. In part, this reinforcement stems from an asymmetrical party system, with quite different parties being dominant at the federal and provincial levels. This very asymmetry precludes political parties serving as effective bridges across the constitutional division of powers and among the governmental actors in executive federalism. It also contributes to the lack of mobility between the provincial and federal parties. The situation which arose after the 1984 election, in which a single party was in power both nationally and in seven of the ten provinces, has not been typical of the Canadian experience.

Career Paths

Relatively few politicians move from provincial to federal politics. Of the MPs elected in 1980, only 11.7 percent had ever run for provincial office, only 6.4 percent had done so successfully, and only 2.8 percent had served in a provincial cabinet before being elected to the House of Commons. No premier has become prime minister of Canada although a few, including Ontario's George Drew, Nova Scotia's Robert Stanfield, and Manitoba's John Bracken, have gone on to lead national parties. Recent prime ministers including Brian Mulroney, John Turner, Pierre Trudeau, Joe Clark, and Lester Pearson have had no background whatsoever in provincial legislative politics.

This lack of career mobility stems in part from the asymmetrical party system. Successful Social Credit members in British Columbia or Parti Québécois members in Quebec, for example, have no federal option. In the case of provincial premiers, mobility is impaired by the long and relatively secure tenure enjoyed by many premiers, by the limited turnover among federal party leaders, and by the fact that most premiers enjoy more clout, more opportunity to leave their mark on public life, and even a higher profile in *national* politics than do virtually all MPs, apart from party leaders.

The lack of mobility has important consequences for intergovernmental relations. Most federal MPs, cabinet ministers, and party leaders lack the sensitivity to provincial concerns that might have come from provincial legislative experience. There is a tendency for federal and provincial politicians to see one another as very different breeds of political animal, with MPs seeing their provincial counterparts as those who choose to restrict themselves to the narrow horizons of provincial life, while provincial legislators tend to see their federal counterparts as those who have lost touch with, if not abandoned, their provincial roots. Because most provincial cabinet ministers lack federal ambitions, they may be more receptive to the transfer of power from Ottawa to the provinces than they would be if their ultimate goal was to serve with the national government. Greater mobility, such as exists within the United States, could provide a useful lubricant to federal–provincial relations. Instead, as Smiley concludes, "so far as federal-provincial relations are concerned, cabinet ministers deal with one another in the absence of either personal experience or ambition at the other level of government."[62]

The impression should not be left that intergovernmental relations are completely divorced from party politics. The atmosphere within which intergovernmental relations are conducted can be affected by the partisan mix of governments and first ministers. "Ottawa-bashing" can often play an important role in provincial election campaigns, as government parties wage electoral combat with the federal government rather than with provincial opponents. Federal–provincial relations can enter federal campaigns, as they did in the 1979 and 1980 campaigns when Trudeau offered his leadership as the country's best defence against voracious provincial premiers, and in 1984 when both Brian Mulroney and John Turner pledged that their administrations would bring renewed harmony to federal–provincial relations. Nonetheless, party influences operate primarily at the margins of intergovernmental relations, acting more as either a lubricant or grit within intergovernmental machinery that is driven by an array of forces largely removed from the partisan arena. The reluctance of all three major parties to discuss the Meech Lake Accord during the 1988 election campaign underscores this conclusion.

POLITICAL PARTIES AND POLITICAL LEADERSHIP

Writing in 1975, John Meisel argued that "in the absence of national and nationalizing nonpolitical institutions . . . parties and the party system have become important factors in nation building and in the evolution and preservation of national unity."[63] Although the parties have not had an unblemished record as vehicles of national integration, there is little doubt that they have generally pursued brokerage strategies designed to knit together the often disparate elements of the Canadian political community. In such strategies, the party leaders have played a pivotal role.

One of the outstanding characteristics of Canadian party leaders has been their longevity. For example, both Premier Joey Smallwood of Newfoundland and Premier W.A.C. Bennett of British Columbia were in power for twenty years, and Premier Ernest Manning of Alberta remained in office for twenty-five years. In federal politics, longevity has been equally commonplace. Macdonald led his Conservative party into Confederation in 1867 and remained at its helm until his death in 1891; Laurier led his party for over thirty years and was prime minister for fifteen of those years; and Mackenzie King led his party for twenty-nine years, and was prime minister for twenty-one. Pierre Trudeau led his party from 1968 to 1984, during which time he was prime minister for all but nine months.

Leaders at both the provincial and federal level have done more than survive for long terms; they have left an indelible mark on the political life of their country. It is difficult to imagine, for example, Newfoundland politics without Joey Smallwood; Quebec politics without Maurice Duplessis and René Lévesque; Saskatchewan politics without Tommy Douglas; Alberta politics without Ernest Manning and Peter Lougheed; or

British Columbia politics without W.A.C. Bennett and William Bennett, his son. At the national level, leaders such as Macdonald, Laurier, Diefenbaker, and Trudeau did more than ride the political currents of their times; they shaped their political environment as much as they took shape from it.

Phrases like "the Macdonald era," "the Trudeau years," and the "Mulroney Conservatives" capture the central role that leaders have played in the life of both their party and nation. Given this importance, the constitutional framework of the Canadian state is somewhat at odds with political reality. Although voters in the 1984 campaign were urged to "vote for John Turner," only the voters in Vancouver–Quadra in fact had the opportunity to do so, just as only the voters in Manicouagan had the opportunity to vote directly for Brian Mulroney. Although party leaders tend to dominate both federal and provincial campaigns, the format of the ballot restricts voters to a choice among local candidates. Nor is the public at large involved in the selection of party leaders in the first place. While the national conventions that selected Brian Mulroney in 1983 and John Turner in 1984 were each attended by three to four thousand party members, those in attendance constituted a minuscule proportion of the national electorate. In a somewhat contradictory fashion, the constitutional framework fails to recognize the central role of party leaders, while at the same time the parliamentary concentration of power in the hands of the political executive contributes much to the power leaders wield, and to their ability to shape the political landscape.

Consensus as to the importance of leaders should not imply any consensus on what distinguishes good leadership from bad. Indeed, Canadians may hold quite contradictory leadership expectations, as Ron Graham illustrates in his 1983 comparison of the public's reaction to Joe Clark and Pierre Trudeau:

> For seven years Clark had suffered in comparison with Pierre Trudeau, although most agreed that Clark was a better human being, more sympathetic, more dedicated, more open-minded, perhaps more complex and courageous. But Trudeau was what Canadians really wanted to be—intellectual, suave, worldly, independent, and unpredictable—while Clark was what they feared they were—earnest, nice, competent, unimaginative, honest and rather dull. . . . Joe Clark wasn't good enough. They wanted to be something greater.[64]

In democratic countries, there is a special tension to leadership expectations. A leader is expected to lead and yet to follow the people, to rise above the narrow views of the electorate while remaining its servant.

Canada has certainly experienced leaders who have been charismatic in character, who have risen above the confines of party politics to capture, if only momentarily, a national vision that touched not only the minds but also the hearts of the electorate. There is little question, for example, that René Lévesque accomplished this in Quebec, just as John Diefenbaker and Pierre Trudeau were able to do in the 1958 and 1968 campaigns. Yet it should also be noted that some of Canada's most successful leaders have been marked by very different political styles. For example, although few political commentators have described Bill Davis, Ontario's premier from 1971 to 1985, as a charismatic leader, his low-keyed search for the middle ground was coupled with daunting electoral success.

Canada's most famous example of successful non-charismatic leadership is provided by William Lyon Mackenzie King. Although often defeated himself at the polls—as a consequence representing ridings in Ontario, Saskatchewan, and Atlantic Canada—King led his party to victory in 1921, narrowly lost to the Conservatives yet clung to power in 1925, won in 1926, lost in 1930, and then piled up impressive wins for the federal Liberals in 1935, 1940, and 1945. King was cautious in the extreme, arguing that " . . . in the course of human history far more has been accomplished for the welfare and progress of mankind in preventing bad actions than in doing good ones."[65] As Joseph Wearing notes, King was not devoid of principles, but he " . . . was not one to let his ideals lead him into precipitate action."[66] A poor speaker with a cool and aloof public presence, King has been widely and harshly criticized. F.R. Scott, who was closely associated with the CCF during King's leadership of the Liberal party, summed up King's style in a poem, "W.L.M.K.," written shortly after King's death:

> He blunted us.
> We had no shape
> Because he never took sides,
> And no sides
> Because he never allowed them to take shape.
> He skilfully avoided what was wrong
> Without saying what was right,
> And never let his on the one hand
> Know what his on the other hand was doing. . . .
> He seemed to be in the centre
> Because we had no centre,
> No vision
> To pierce the smokescreen of his politics.
> Truly he will be remembered
> Whenever men honour ingenuity,
> Ambiguity, inactivity, and political longevity.[67]

Whitaker describes King's government as "the defender of the people against the big interests and the defender of the big interests against the people."[68]

Nonetheless, King has a legitimate claim to being Canada's most successful prime minister. His party enjoyed significant electoral support across the country; in the seven national campaigns in which King was leader, the Liberals won 913 seats compared to only 541 for their Conservative opponents. He reinforced the Liberal base in Quebec, even though he himself was unilingual, while maintaining a substantial electoral base in western Canada. He steered Canada through the Second World War, during which Canada's impressive military contribution abroad was combined with economic growth and, more so than during the First World War, political tranquillity at home. His career stands as a monument to political craftsmanship. He may not have lifted the hearts and souls of Canadians, but the party he led commanded their electoral support.

In contemporary electoral politics, the party leader is so central to the campaign, so much the focus of media coverage and campaign advertising that the party and leader have almost fused into a single entity.[69] The importance of the leader, however, extends well beyond the electoral process. As the late Walter Young noted, the contemporary importance of leadership is a response to the growth of government:

> Instead of the vast and faceless bureaucracy, there is a prime minister who speaks for and to the nation. At a time when the engine of the state at both the federal and provincial levels is large and complicated, the existence of a single individual as the functioning head of the apparatus provides credibility and a much needed focus. The need for such a figure increases with the growth of the machine, and the power of such a figure increases accordingly.[70]

Leaders help personify the political system, and thus provide us with handles on a reality which might otherwise be overwhelming in its complexity.

SUGGESTED READINGS

Ivan Avakumovic, *The Communist Party in Canada: A History* (Toronto: McClelland & Stewart, 1975); and *Socialism in Canada: A Study of the CCF-NDP in Federal and Provincial Politics* (Toronto: McClelland & Stewart, 1978).

Sylvia B. Bashevkin, ed., *Canadian Political Behaviour* (Toronto: Methuen, 1985).

Janine Brodie and Jane Jenson, "The Party System," in Michael S. Whittington and Glen Williams, eds., *Canadian Politics in the 1990s*, Third Edition (Scarborough: Nelson, 1989), pp.249-67.

William Christian and Colin Campbell, *Political Parties and Ideologies in Canada*, Second Edition (Toronto: McGraw-Hill Ryerson, 1983).

Harold D. Clarke, Jane Jenson, Lawrence LeDuc, and Jon H. Pammett, *Political Choice in Canada* (Toronto: McGraw-Hill Ryerson, 1979); and *Absent Mandate: The Politics of Discontent in Canada* (Toronto: Gage, 1984).

Alain G. Gagnon and A. Brian Tanguay, eds., *Canadian Parties in Transition* (Scarborough: Nelson, 1989).

Patrick Martin, Alan Gregg, and George Perlin, *Contenders: The Tory Quest for Power* (Scarborough: Prentice-Hall, 1983).

Christina McCall-Newman, *Grits: An Intimate Portrait of the Liberal Party* (Toronto: Macmillan, 1982).

William Mishler, *Political Participation in Canada* (Toronto: Macmillan, 1979).

Leslie A. Pal and David Taras, eds., *Prime Ministers and Premiers: Political Leadership and Public Policy in Canada* (Scarborough: Prentice-Hall, 1988).

Paul Pross, "Pressure Groups: Talking Chameleons," in Whittington and Williams, *Canadian Politics*, pp. 295-312.

Jeffrey Simpson, *Discipline of Power: The Conservative Interlude and The Liberal Restoration* (Toronto: Personal Library Publishers, 1980).

Hugh G. Thorburn, ed., *Party Politics in Canada*, Fifth Edition (Scarborough: Prentice-Hall, 1985).

Conrad Winn and John McMenemy, *Political Parties in Canada* (Toronto: McGraw-Hill Ryerson, 1976).

Walter D. Young, *The Anatomy of a Party: The National CCF, 1932-1961* (Toronto: University of Toronto Press), 1969.

STUDY QUESTIONS

1. In order to explore the concepts of partnership and party identification, ask yourself the following questions. Do you have an emotional loyalty for one party rather than another and tend to identify with one particular partisan camp? If so, has your identification always been with one party, or has it changed over time? If it has changed, how would you account for the change? Do you identify with the same or different parties in federal and provincial politics? Which level of government commands the strongest partisan loyalties in your case? Can you identify the partisanship of your parents? How evident were

partisan affiliations in your environment when you were growing up? Is your own partisanship in line with, or at odds with, that of your parents?

2. Divide a piece of paper into three columns, labelling the first Conservative–Liberal, the second Conservative–NDP, and the third Liberal–NDP. Now jot down, in the appropriate column, those aspects of public policy for which you feel significant party differences exist. How many differences can you identify? Which two parties are the most clearly distinguishable from each other, and which two are the least so?

3. If the federal government were to change hands overnight, what difference would you expect for people like yourself? Jot down any significant differences on a piece of paper. Now pose the same question for your provincial government; what changes would you expect if the government were to change hands? In examining your answers, determine your perceptions of party differences, and the policy significance of election outcomes for people such as yourself.

NOTES

1. Harold D. Clarke, Jane Jenson, Lawrence Le Duc, and Jon H. Pammett, *Absent Mandate: The Politics of Discontent in Canada* (Toronto: Gage, 1984), p. 10.
2. Richard J. Van Loon and Michael S. Whittington, *The Canadian Political System: Environment, Structure and Process*, Third Edition (Toronto: McGraw-Hill Ryerson, 1981), p. 307.
3. John Meisel, "The Party System and the 1974 Election," in Howard R. Penniman, ed., *Canada at the Polls: The General Election of 1974* (Washington, D.C.: American Enterprise Institute for Public Policy Research, 1975), p. 1.
4. The 1925 and 1926 elections are not included in this total. On October 29, 1925, the incumbent Liberals elected only 99 MPs compared to 116 for the Conservatives. Yet, because neither party could form a majority government, the Liberal Prime Minister, William Lyon Mackenzie King, decided to stay in power until late June 1926, when King sought a dissolution of the House. The Governor General, Lord Byng, refused and instead asked the leader of the Conservative party, Arthur Meighen, to form a government. The Meighen government lasted only three days before it was defeated in the House. Meighen was then granted a dissolution, a general election was called for September 14, 1926, and the Liberals won a majority government with 128 seats, compared to 91 for the Conservatives.
5. The Pacific Scandal exposed financial entanglements among Mac-

donald, the Conservative party, and the builders of the new Canadian Pacific Railroad.

6. Meisel, "The Party System," p. 14.

7. Seventy-six of all eighty-four seats won by Social Credit candidates came from Alberta, where the party overwhelmingly dominated provincial politics from 1935 to 1971.

8. Cited in Joseph Wearing, *The L-Shaped Party: The Liberal Party of Canada 1958-1980* (Toronto: McGraw-Hill Ryerson, 1981), p. 1.

9. The Conservatives captured 78.5 percent of the House seats, whereas the 211 Conservative seats in 1984 constituted 74.8 percent of the seats in a slightly larger House of Commons.

10. The term "government party" comes from Reginald Whitaker's *The Government Party: Organizing and Financing the Liberal Party of Canada 1930-58* (Toronto: University of Toronto Press, 1977).

11. The election statistics come from Loren M. Simerl, "A Survey of Canadian Provincial Election Results, 1905–1976," in Paul W. Fox, ed., *Politics: Canada*, Fourth Edition (Toronto: McGraw-Hill Ryerson, 1977), pp. 602-13.

12. The pro-separatist Western Canada Concept party, which captured 11 percent of the vote but no seats in the 1982 provincial election, provides a notable exception.

13. For a detailed analysis of the relationship between federal and provincial party support, see Wearing, *The L-Shaped Party*, pp. 81-86.

14. Van Loon and Whittington, *The Canadian Political System*, p. 319. For an extended discussion of the confederal nature of Canadian parties, see Donald V. Smiley, *Canada in Question: Federalism in the Eighties*, Third Edition (Toronto: McGraw-Hill Ryerson, 1980), Chapter Five.

15. The Union Government is a unique case in that the Conservative Party had a clear parliamentary majority before embarking upon the Union coalition with pro-conscription Liberals.

16. Brian H. Coulter, *Coalition Governments in Canada: A Comparative Analysis of Four Case Studies* (University of Calgary: Unpublished M.A. Thesis, 1982).

17. Alan C. Cairns, "The Electoral System and the Party System in Canada, 1921-1965," *Canadian Journal of Political Science*, Volume 1 (1968), pp. 55-80.

18. For example, see William P. Irvine, *Does Canada Need a New Electoral System?* (Kingston: Institute of Intergovernmental Relations, Queen's University, 1979).

19. William Mishler, "Political Participation and Democracy," in Michael S. Whittington and Glen Williams, eds., *Canadian Politics in the 1980s*, Second Edition (Toronto: Methuen, 1984), p. 178.

20. Clarke et al., *Absent Mandate*, p. 35.

21. Mishler, "Political Participation," p. 175. He defines political participation as "voluntary activities by citizens which are intended to influence the selection of government leaders or the decisions they make."

22. Clarke et al., *Absent Mandate*, p. 37.

23. Harold D. Clarke, Lawrence LeDuc, Jane Jenson, and Jon H. Pammett, *Political Choice in Canada* (Toronto: McGraw-Hill Ryerson, 1979), p. 87.

24. Mishler, "Political Participation," pp. 179-80.

25. *Ibid.*, p. 190.

26. For the 1974 comparison, see Clark et al., *Political Choice*, p. 137.

27. Partisanship was measured by first asking: "Thinking of federal politics, do you usually think of yourself as a Liberal, Conservative, NDP, Social Credit or what?" Respondents who mentioned a party were then asked: "How strongly (Liberal, Conservative or whatever) do you feel—very strongly, fairly strongly, or not very strongly?"

28. For a useful discussion of partisanship, see Clarke et al., *Political Choice*, Chapter Five.

29. *Ibid.*, p. 136.

30. Considerable debate exists as to the general strength and stability of partisan identifications in Canada. In summarizing this debate, Jon Pammett concludes that the majority predisposition is towards *flexible partisanship*, that about 60 percent of voters " . . . develop party loyalties that are either weak, changeable over time or different at the two levels of the federal system." See "Elections" in Whittington and Williams, *Canadian Politics*, p. 276.

31. *The Globe and Mail*, National Edition, June 2, 1984, p. 1.

32. For an overview of both federal and provincial legislation, see Khayyam Z. Paltiel, "Canadian Election Expense Legislation: Recent Developments," in Hugh G. Thorburn, ed., *Party Politics in Canada*, Fourth Edition (Scarborough: Prentice-Hall, 1979), pp. 100-110.

33. Wearing, *op. cit.*, p. 216.

34. For a general and informative discussion of the policy mandates of Canadian elections, see Clarke et al., *Absent Mandate*.

35. Clarke et al., *Absent Mandate*, p. 34.

36. For a discussion of the distinction between institutionalized and issue-oriented interest groups, see Paul Pross, "Pressure Groups: Adaptive Instruments of Political Communication," in Pross, ed., *Pressure Group Behavior in Canadian Politics* (Toronto: McGraw-Hill Ryerson, 1975), pp. 8-18.

37. Pross, *Pressure Group Behavior*, p. 3.

38. Van Loon and Whittington, *op. cit.*, p. 313.

39. Cited in Mason Wade, *The French Canadians, 1860-1967*, Vol. II, pp. 524-25.

40. Elizabeth Armstrong, *The Crisis of Quebec, 1914-1918* (Toronto: McClelland and Stewart, 1937, reprinted 1974), p. 166.
41. *Ibid.*, p. 187.
42. *House of Commons Debates*, September 8, 1937, p. 36.
43. Although the voting returns did not distinguish between the two linguistic communities in Quebec, it is clear that the "no" vote among francophones alone was even higher.
44. George C. Perlin, *The Tory Syndrome: Leadership Politics in the Progressive Conservative Party* (Montreal: McGill-Queen's University Press, 1980).
45. George Grant, *Lament for a Nation: The Defeat of Canadian Nationalism* (Toronto: McClelland and Stewart, 1965), p. 20.
46. In the 1980 election, 102 ridings contained a francophone population of 10 percent or more. Of these, the Liberals won 100 and the Conservatives won two. As Mulroney argued in his 1983 leadership bid, "give the Liberals a 100 seat lead and they'll beat you ten times out of ten." Patrick Martin, Allan Gregg, and George Perlin, *Contenders: The Tory Quest for Power* (Scarborough: Prentice-Hall, 1983), p. 84.
47. Denis Smith, "Political Parties and the Survival of Canada," in R. Kenneth Carty and W. Peter Ward, eds., *Entering the Eighties: Canada in Crisis* (Toronto: Oxford University Press, 1980), pp. 142 ff.
48. Stein Rokkan, "Electoral Mobilization, Party Competition, and National Integration," in Joseph LaPalombara and Myron Weiner, eds., *Political Parties and Political Development* (Princeton: Princeton University Press, 1966), pp. 241-66; and Seymour Martin Lipset and Stein Rokkan, "Cleavage Structures, Party Systems, and Voter Alignments: An Introduction," in Lipset and Rokkan, eds., *Party Systems and Voter Alignments: Cross-National Perspectives* (New York: The Free Press, 1967), pp. 1-64.
49. G.A. Rawlyk and Doug Brown, "The Historical Framework of the Maritimes and Confederation," in G.A. Rawlyk, ed., *The Atlantic Provinces and the Problems of Confederation* (St. John's: Breakwater Press: 1979), p. 16.
50. Smith, "Political Parties," p. 140.
51. The term "unrestricted reciprocity" refers to the reciprocal removal of tariff barriers to trade. The more contemporary term would be "free trade."
52. For a discussion of the 1891 and 1911 campaigns, see J.M. Beck, *Pendulum of Power* (Scarborough: Prentice-Hall, 1968), pp. 57-68 and 120-33.
53. *Ibid.*, p. 64.
54. *Ibid.*, p. 68.

55. Ramsay Cook, *The Maple Leaf Forever* (Toronto: Macmillan, 1971), p. 212.
56. Grant, *Lament for a Nation*, p. 12 and Chapter Three.
57. Clarke et al., *Absent Mandate*, pp. 20-21.
58. *Ibid.*, p. 12.
59. Smiley, *Canada in Question*, p. 146.
60. *Ibid.*, p. 148.
61. This point is developed in a comparative context by Ivo D. Duchacek, *Comparative Federalism: The Territorial Dimension of Politics* (New York: Holt, Rinehart and Winston, 1970), p. 329); and William H. Riker, *Federalism: Origin, Operation, Significance* (Boston: Little Brown & Company, 1964), p. 129.
62. Smiley, *Canada in Question*, Second Edition, p. 98.
63. Meisel, "The Party System," p. 2.
64. Ron Graham, "The Legacy of Joe Clark," *Saturday Night*, September 1983, p. 30.
65. Cited in Peter C. Newman, *The Distemper of Our Times* (Toronto: McClelland and Stewart, 1968), p. 57.
66. Wearing, *The L-Shaped Party*, p. 4.
67. F.R. Scott, "W.L.M.K.," from *Selected Poems of F.R. Scott* (Toronto: Oxford University Press, 1966), pp. 60-61.
68. Whitaker, *The Government Party*, p. 141.
69. In the 1980 post-election study, the following rather difficult question was posed to respondents: "Take a moment to think over all the reasons why you decided to vote the way you did, and just briefly tell me the things that were most important to you." More respondents— 30 percent—named a party leader or leadership than identified any other single factor. Twenty-three percent named a party, while only 9 percent cited local candidates. Clarke et al., *Political Choice in Canada*, p. 273.
70. Walter D. Young, "Leadership and Canadian Politics," in John H. Redekop, ed., *Approaches to Canadian Politics*, Second Edition (Scarborough: Prentice-Hall, 1983), pp. 269-70.

8

Conclusions

The issues addressed in this text have been perennial features of the Canadian political landscape, and they are unlikely to fade from view in the foreseeable future. At the same time, it is essential to be alert for the emergence of new political cleavages which, over time, could come to rival although not supplant those discussed in the preceding chapters.

Some of these cleavages have already established themselves on the nation's political agenda. Gender politics have already come to the fore, and have become thoroughly entangled with the politics of abortion, pay-equity, and childcare support. As the demographic structure of the population changes over time and the proportion of Canadians who are elderly continues to grow, redistributive conflict across generations may emerge. The continuing quest by aboriginal Canadians for a fundamental redefinition of their relationship with the Canadian state will test the political system's capacity for institutional accommodation and innovation. Social concerns with pornography, immigration, racial discrimination, and the handicapped may move up the political agenda. The development of natural resources in the North, coupled with the evolution of new political institutions in the region, promises to provide daunting challenges for the political system. A growing list of environmental concerns, and indeed the threat of environmental collapse, will severely test the capacity of existing political institutions. And, as a country that has always been exposed to the international environment, Canada will continue to be buffeted by changes in international trade, by the problems of development in the Third World, and by the continuing threat of international conflict.

Here it is interesting to note the neo-conservative current that appears to be flowing through Canada's closest neighbours, the United States and Britain. The central ideological thrust of neo-conservatism—the emphasis on a reduced role for government in the economic and social orders—runs counter to the activist state that has been used to address many of the political issues discussed in this text. For example, nationalist attempts to restrict American intrusions into the Canadian economy have relied upon state intervention. The development of Quebec nationalism since the onset of the Quiet Revolution, and the language policies of both the Quebec and federal governments, have entailed an activist state. As Canadians grapple with deficit reduction and ideological

"I say, Roger . . . do we look to the new year in trepidation, or as a challenge to the enduring spirit of man, or simply let the universe unfold however the hell it likes?"

Len Norris, *26th Annual.* Originally published in *The Vancouver Sun,* December 31, 1976.

critiques of the welfare state, they will be forced to re-examine the basic institutional and constitutional features of the Canadian federal state.

Given that the political agenda is already so full and that perennial problems refuse to leave while a host of new problems looms on the horizon, it could be easy to slip into a state of apathy or cynicism. We might follow the acerbic advice of Toronto columnist Richard Needham, who sees little hope for the world "until voters are as cynical towards politicians as the politicians are towards them."[1] Yet the fact that there are no perfect or final solutions does not mean that solutions do not exist, or that some solutions are not better than others. Neither the search for perfection nor the rejection of the real world when perfection proves to be illusive, as it always will, are of great value in the political world. As an old aphorism observes, the best is the enemy of the good.

The study of political science offers a modest remedy for the frustration that can arise in trying to come to grips with a complex political reality. Courses in political theory provide a way of strengthening one's conceptual grasp of political issues, of appreciating how a variety of thinkers have grappled with common political problems across the ages. Courses in comparative politics provide an opportunity to examine how other political systems have handled the types of issues that have shaped Canadian political life. Hopefully, though, a wider exposure to the study of political science will not have the same disheartening impact as political exposure seemed to have on the Atlantic Canadian respondents surveyed by Rawlyk and Perlin in 1978. The 1939 respondents in the survey were asked the following question: "Comparing your opinions when you first began to think about politics and government with your opinions now, would you say you have more confidence or less confidence in the people in politics, and in government generally?" Across the region, only 17 percent had come away with more confidence while 58 percent had less, 10 percent felt there was no difference, and 15 percent did not know.

Political science in general, and perhaps the format of this text in particular, may emphasize the conflictual side of political life. In closing, then, it is appropriate to draw attention to what in many ways has been a remarkable success story. Canada has thus far succeeded, where many other countries have failed, in maintaining a relatively harmonious tension between two linguistic communities. The survival and contemporary vitality of the French fact in Canada provide evidence of political success, just as the dominance of one community would be a mark of political failure. Canadians have succeeded in maintaining a reasonable degree of independence from the United States, which has been no mean feat in itself given the economic and cultural pull exerted by our continental neighbour. Canadian governments have also provided citizens with a reasonable degree of economic security and material well-being, and have to a degree smoothed out regional variations in the standard of living.

If we measure the political system against the boundless potential of the country, it may be that we have fallen short. If, however, we measure the political system against the many serious problems that it has been forced to confront, there is reason for a considerable degree of satisfaction and even pride.

NOTE

1. Richard Needham, *You and All the Rest: The Wit & Wisdom of Richard Needham* (Toronto: M. Sutkiewicz Publishing, 1982), p. 35.

Appendix A

The Legislative Process

When Canadian think of Parliament, they think first and foremost of the House of Commons. Parliament, however, incorporates not only the House but also the Senate and the Queen as integral if unequal components of the legislative process. Any legislative proposal becomes an Act of Parliament only when it has been passed by both the House and the Senate, and has been given royal assent by the Queen's representative in Canada, the Governor General. The legislative process can thus be seen as a chain in which the House of Commons, the Senate, and the Governor General are the formal links. Figure A provides an expanded, albeit still somewhat simplified, illustration of this chain.

Legislative proposals emerge from a complex policy environment which includes departments within the federal bureaucracy, interest groups, task forces and **Royal Commissions**, other governments both domestic and foreign, the parliamentary caucus of the governing party, and party policy resolutions. It is Cabinet which forms the interface between that policy environment and the legislative process. Parliament itself is the recipient rather than the initiator of legislative proposals. Its primary legislative role is to debate *and then ratify* government legislation.

Cabinet ministers have the exclusive right to introduce tax legislation or legislation calling for the expenditure of public funds. Moreover, most legislation of any general application *and with any prospect of being enacted* is introduced to Parliament as a government "bill," the term applied to legislative proposals which have not yet been ratified as "Acts of Parliament." Although "private members' bills" can be introduced by any member of Parliament on any subject, as long as they do not call for the expenditure of public funds, their prospects of being passed are remote.[1] In the words of an old advertising cliché, private members' bills are used to "run an idea up the flagpole and see if anyone salutes." Very rarely does anyone do so, or at least very rarely does the government do so, which is all that really counts.

Both government bills and private members' bills are termed *public bills* in that they are intended to have some general impact on the population. *Private bills* apply only to specified individuals. They are used primarily for the federal incorporation of individuals, companies, and charitable foundations. Private bills are generally introduced in the Senate, where they are given detailed committee examination before

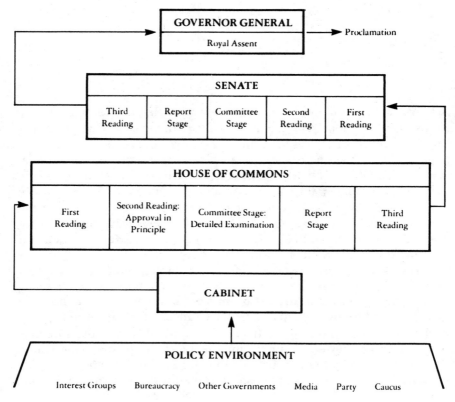

Figure A The Legislative Process

being sent to the House for more pro forma consideration, and to the Governor General for royal assent.

Most bills are first introduced in the House, where the minister responsible places the bill on the order paper, and asks "leave to introduce" the legislation. (While there is nothing to prevent legislation being first introduced in the Senate and then being sent to the House, this is rarely done with public bills.) The bill is then "read" for the first time. There is no debate on first reading, which is used solely to alert Parliament to the proposed legislation and to allow for its printing. With the bill's second reading, vigorous debate takes place across the floor of the House on the principles *but not the details* of the legislation. Amendments are not permitted at this stage, which concludes with a resolution to approve the legislation in principle. In virtually all cases, party discipline ensures that government bills will be approved in principle unless the government itself decides to withdraw the legislation.

Once the bill has passed second reading and been approved in principle, it moves to the committee stage for a detailed, clause-by-clause examination. Here a number of paths can be followed. The bill can be sent to the Committee of the Whole, in which case it is examined by the House sitting as a committee with more relaxed rules of procedure. It can also be sent to one of approximately twenty standing committees of the House, or to a special committee formed to consider that particular bill. In most cases the second route is followed.

Prior to 1968, the standing committees played a modest role at best in the legislative process, as most legislation was processed through the Committee of the Whole. From 1968 on, the principal legislative routing has been through the standing committees, which have between ten and fifteen members allocated in proportion to the parties' strength in the House of Commons. The government party has a majority on all committees, and all except the Public Accounts Committee are chaired by a government backbencher. Only the Joint Committee on Regulations and Other Statutory Instruments and the Public Accounts Committee have regular support staff. Party discipline prevails within the committee system just as it prevails on the floor of the House. While the strictures of party discipline may be somewhat looser at the committee stage, the cabinet is no more prepared to see its legislation lost or rewritten in committee than on the floor of the House. Committee latitude is further circumscribed by the fact that the legislation has already been approved in principle.

The committee stage concludes with a report to the full House where committee amendments are considered and new amendments may be proposed. When all amendments have been dealt with, the third reading is held. Debate at this point is brief, and party discipline virtually guarantees the passage of government legislation. Third reading concludes the legislative process in the House, and the bill is then sent to the Senate.

In a formal sense, the appointed Senate has nearly the same legislative powers as the elected House; legislation must be passed by *both* chambers to become law. (The Senate, however, cannot introduce money bills.) In practice, a bill's passage by the House virtually ensures its acceptance by the Senate. Debate in the Senate, which largely takes place in standing committees, focuses primarily on legislative craftsmanship and technicalities rather than on the broader principles embodied in the legislation. The Senate has not rejected a House bill for over forty years, and its amendments " . . . are almost always clarifying, simplifying, tidying-up amendments, and are almost always accepted by the House of Commons." However, when different parties control the Senate and House, the Senate can obstruct the government majority in the House by delaying legislative approval and by passing amendments which force reconsideration by the House. In 1988, the Senate took the extraordinary step of refusing to approve the government's free trade legislation until an election was called. When the Progressive Conservative government was returned to power in November, the Senate quickly approved the re-introduced Free Trade legislation.

If there is any consistent pattern to the input of the Senate apart from that of legislative craftsmanship, it comes in the form of corporate vigilance. As Jackson and Atkinson point out, "... a small portion of the Senate's membership is actively engaged in challenging, delaying, and amending any government legislation which may be detrimental to major business and financial concerns."[3]

The legislative stages within the Senate are essentially identical to those within the House. Once a bill has passed third reading in the Senate, and any Senate amendments have been approved by the House, it goes to the Queen's representative in Canada, the Governor General, for royal assent. This stage is a true formality as royal assent has never been refused in Canada. (It was last refused in Britain in 1707.) Once a bill has been signed by the Governor General it comes into immediate effect as an Act of Parliament unless the legislation contains a provision for proclamation at a later date.

This, in broad outline and stripped of its many interesting quirks and anomalies, is the national legislative process. The provincial process is similar except that committees tend to have less weight, there is no Senate stage as no province has an upper chamber, and royal assent is given by the Lieutenant-Governor rather than by the Governor General.

The Speech from the Throne

The Throne Speech, which is used to open each new session of Parliament, plays a special role in the legislative process. Written by the Prime Minister and the cabinet, the Throne speech is read by the Governor General to a joint meeting of the Senate and House of Commons held in the Senate Chamber. The Throne Speech does not introduce legislation directly, but rather sets forth the legislative priorities of the government for the forthcoming session of Parliament. While providing few legislative details, the speech does alert both the opposition parties and the public to the government's legislative agenda. The subsequent debate on the Throne Speech enables the opposition parties to set forth their own agenda, and to attack the government for interests neglected or opportunities lost in the Throne Speech.

Throughout the legislative process there is a good deal of tension between the government's desire to move bills quickly through the legislative process and the opposition's desire to maintain adequate opportunity for criticism and delay. This tension, and the procedural complexities that it engenders, are presided over by the Speaker of the House. While the Speaker is nominated by the Prime Minister and comes from the ranks of the governing party, he or she is elected by the House and is expected to preside over the affairs of the House in a non-partisan manner. Primary control over the flow of legislation through Parliament rests with the government House Leader, whose task is to enforce the government's legislative priorities and steer government bills through the legislative process. The opposition parties, however, can have a considerable impact on the flow of legislation, if not on its substance. The ability of the opposition to obstruct the legislative process can at times be bartered for changes in government bills.

As the only institution composed of elected politicians from across the land, the House of Commons provides the symbolic centrepiece for the Canadian political system. Its importance, however, goes well beyond the symbolic. The House provides the pool from which the prime minister draws the cabinet. The daily Question Period when the House is in session brings into focus the clash of parties, principles, and personalities that energizes political life. The House provides the national stage upon which the government can present and defend its policies, and upon which opposition parties can hold it accountable for such policies. The House dramatizes and to an important degree simplifies political life for the electorate, making it easier for citizens to throw bouquets and brickbats, to allocate credit and blame for the conditions of national life. If we adopt David Easton's now-famous definition of politics as the "authoritative allocation of values,"[4] it is the House which provides that authoritative allocation in federal politics.

SUGGESTED READINGS

For a discussion of the provincial legislative process, see Michael M. Atkinson and Graham White, "The Development of Provincial Legislatures," in Harold D. Clarke, Colin Campbell, F.Q. Quo, and Arthur Goddard, eds., *Parliament, Policy and Representation* (Toronto: Methuen, 1980), pp. 225–75; Allan Kornberg, William Mishler, and Harold D. Clarke, *Representative Democracy in the Canadian Provinces* (Scarborough: Prentice-Hall, 1982), pp. 171–83; and Philip Laundy, "Legislatures," in David Bellamy, Jon H. Pammett, and Donald C. Rowat, eds., *The Provincial Political Systems: Comparative Essays* (Toronto: Methuen, 1976), pp. 280–96.

For an overview of the national legislative process, see Michael M. Atkinson, "Parliamentary Government in Canada," in Michael S. Whittington and Glen Williams, eds., *Canadian Politics in the 1990s*, Third Edition (Scarborough: Nelson, 1989) pp. 336-58. For a more extended discussion, see J.R. Mallory, *The Structure of Canadian Government*, Revised Edition (Toronto: Gage, 1984), Chapters Six and Seven; and Robert J. Jackson and Michael M. Atkinson, *The Canadian Legislative System*, Second Edition (Toronto: Macmillan, 1980).

Appendix B

The Government of Canada

It is common for people to speak of "the Government of Canada" or "the Government of Saskatchewan" as if it were a simple, unitary actor. We speak, for instance, of "the government" doing this or that, of governments clashing like gladiators in the federal–provincial arena. Thus it is important to note that modern governments are in fact complex and elaborate organizations which embrace a vast number of loosely coordinated and at times competitive components.

The federal government encompasses close to five hundred departments and ministries, Crown corporations, regulatory agencies, boards, commissions, and councils. On the provincial side of the ledger the situation is no less complex. In Ontario, for example, there are almost seven hundred semi-independent agencies, boards, and commissions that fall under the purview of the Ontario legislature.[1] In the regulatory field alone there are some 117 federal and 1,253 provincial agencies, boards, commissions, and tribunals, including Atomic Energy of Canada, the British Columbia Grape Marketing Board, the Prince Edward Island Rentalsman, the Nova Scotia Horse Racing Commission, the Ontario Securities Commission, and the ten provincial liquor control boards.[2]

There is, however, a focal point to this picture, a more specific sense in which the term "government" is used. When one talks about the "Government of Canada," or the "Government of British Columbia" the specific reference is to the federal or provincial *cabinet*. The larger governmental apparatus radiates out from and is responsible to the cabinet. To risk what may be a contentious analogy, the cabinet rests at the centre of government like a spider at the centre of an immense and complex web.

If we restrict our gaze to the federal government, the executive authority exercised by the cabinet is formally vested in the *Privy Council*, which in turn consists of all those who are are ever have been in the cabinet and who have thus taken an oath as Privy Councillors.[3] Once admitted into the Privy Council, an individual retains the title "The Honourable" for life. The Council, however, has met in its entirety only three times: when it was first constituted in 1867, when Elizabeth II became Queen of Canada in 1952, and when the Constitution Act was proclaimed in 1982. In practice, the Privy Council's powers are exercised by the cabinet, *a committee of the Privy Council* whose members have

"They start messing about with the organization and it will end up in chaos."

Len Norris, *9th Annual.* Originally published in *The Vancouver Sun*, January 21, 1960.

seats in Parliament (either in the House or the Senate) and who have been invited into the cabinet by the current prime minister.[4]

It is difficult to overstate the importance of the federal cabinet in the Canadian political system. Cabinet ministers control the executive or administrative side of the federal government; all departments are headed by cabinet ministers who direct and are responsible for their operations. Because the cabinet is drawn from the majority party in the House and is able to rely upon firm party discipline, the cabinet also dominates the legislative process. Thus cabinet serves as a "buckle," tying together the executive and legislative branches of government.

The cabinet exercises what are called *prerogative powers*, or "those powers of the sovereign that have never been formally delegated to any other government organ and which are exercised by the cabinet on behalf of the the sovereign."[5] These include the right to introduce money bills, to recommend the dissolution of Parliament (this being exercised by the prime minister alone), to participate in international affairs, and to grant clemency. The cabinet also exercises *statutory powers* which have been delegated to it by Parliament. In many cases legislation passed by Parliament does not include the detailed rules and administrative details necessary to put it into effect. Parliament delegates the formulation of such subordinate legislation to cabinet or to the particular minister responsible for the Act, restricting itself to providing a " . . . framework for the rulemaking that will take place in the bureaucracy."[6] When cabinet exercises statutory or prerogative powers it does so through Orders-in-Council or minutes of council which are as legally binding as Acts of Parliament. There are literally thousands of Orders-in-Council and council minutes issued each year.

Cabinet meetings are governed by a number of important conventions. First, ministers are sworn to secrecy by their oath as Privy Councillors. Second, all members of cabinet are collectively responsible for each and every decision reached by cabinet. In public and in tendering its advice to the Crown, cabinet speaks with a single voice and individual ministers speak with the authority of the full cabinet behind them. Collective responsibility is made possible by the confidential nature of cabinet meetings; ministers can disagree among themselves while retaining a united front in public. Third, votes are not taken within cabinet. Voting would imply equality among the ministers when in fact they are not at all equal. Some head ministries that are more directly involved in the issue at hand, some may represent regional interests which are more directly at stake, some will be brighter and others more politically astute. Thus decisions are made by consensus, and the consensus is articulated by the prime minister. Ministers who disagree with that consensus must support it in public or resign from cabinet.

In recent decades the size of federal cabinets has increased considerably. At the end of the Second World War, the cabinet contained nineteen ministers. This increased to twenty-seven with Pierre Trudeau's first cabinet in 1968, and to thirty-seven by Trudeau's last cabinet. While John Turner's short-lived cabinet, appointed in June 1984, contained only twenty-nine ministers, the forty-member cabinet appointed by Brian Mulroney in September 1984 was the largest in Canadian history. Along with major portfolios such as National Defence, External Affairs, Finance, and Justice, the Mulroney cabinet included ministers responsible for youth, tourism, small business, fitness and amateur sport, and forestry.

The Size of Provincial Cabinets

Proportionate to the size of their legislative assemblies, provincial cabinets are considerably larger than the federal cabinet. In Nova Scotia, for example, the twenty-three members of the 1983 cabinet accounted for 61 percent of the government caucus and 44 percent of the entire legislative assembly. A federal cabinet of similar proportions would contain 124 members.

In 1983, columnist Don McGillivray (*Calgary Herald*, November 14, 1983, p. A8) compared the sizes of the federal and provincial cabinets. Alberta's cabinet at that time had thirty members, only six members less than the federal cabinet, while Ontario's had twenty-nine and Quebec's had twenty-seven. Saskatchewan (twenty-five), New Brunswick (twenty-three) and Nova Scotia (then twenty-one) were not far behind. Prince Edward Island (ten) and Newfoundland (eighteen) held down the low end of the scale.

In total, there were 257 federal and provincial cabinet ministers, an increase from 224 five years before, 200 ten years before, and only 155 twenty years before.

Cabinets have grown in size in part because of the increased scope of modern government, and in part because of the desire of prime ministers to represent a broader array of interests within the cabinet. As a consequence of both the increase in size and the increased complexity of government legislation, a great deal of the cabinet's workload is now handled through an elaborate cabinet committee system. The cabinet committees are backstopped by the Privy Council Office secretariat, which provides not only support services but also policy advice. The most important committee is the Committee on Planning and Priorities, chaired by the prime minister. This committee forms the de facto "inner cabinet."

The Canadian political system is characterized by executive dominance. The cabinet sits astride the legislative process like a jockey astride a horse, controlling the formulation of policy, its ratification by Parliament, and its administration by the federal public service. While in theory cabinet is responsible to Parliament, in fact Parliament has little control over a cabinet backed by a majority in the House. Parliament debates government legislation before passing it, rather than debating to determine whether it should pass.

Executive dominance has also come to characterize internal dynamics within cabinet. Traditionally, the prime minister's relationship with his cabinet colleagues was described by the phrase "primus inter pares," or "first among equals." If that phrase ever fit the reality of the relationship, it certainly does not today. The prime minister's dominance over his cabinet colleagues, both individually and collectively, stems from a number of sources:

- The prime minister decides not only who is appointed to the cabinet but also what portfolio they will hold and how long they will hold it.
- The prime minister alone has the authority to call for the dissolution of Parliament, and thus to cast his cabinet colleagues to the electoral wolves.

- The prime minister has been elected as party leader by a national convention of the extra-parliamentary party, not by his cabinet colleagues or by the parliamentary caucus, and the mantle of leadership can only be removed by that party.
- The prime minister controls much of the government patronage that may be of critical importance to ministers' constituents or to their long-term career plans.
- Because national election campaigns have become so leader-oriented, the prime minister can claim responsibility for the electoral success of his party. Cabinet ministers hold their positions because of the prime minister's electoral appeal, not the other way around.
- It is the prime minister who ultimately articulates the consensus of cabinet, and thus has the final say in the arbitration of policy disputes within cabinet.

The prime minister's mastery is further strengthened by his personal control of the Privy Council Office and the Prime Minister's Office. As noted above, the PCO not only acts as the secretariat to the cabinet but has also come to play a critical role in the governmental policy process. The PMO performs similar functions for the prime minister, providing secretarial support, policy information, and strategic advice. The PCO and the PMO, along with the Federal–Provincial Relations Office, strengthen the prime minister's hand in dealing not only with his cabinet colleagues, individually or as a group, but also with the larger governmental system.

Provincial Comparisons

Executive dominance is even more characteristic of provincial legislatures than it is of the House of Commons.[7] Within the Canadian political science literature there is " ... a rather firm consensus that all provinces have been characterized by a debilitating subservience of the legislature of the executive."[8] A number of factors may account for this subservience, including the shorter length of provincial sessions, the proportionately larger size of provincial cabinets, less firmly entrenched parliamentary norms, and less developed legislative committee systems.

With respect to his cabinet colleagues, the premier's position is very similar to that of the prime minister. His role in provincial election campaigns equals that of the prime minister in federal campaigns. The premier exercises the same control over cabinet appointments and dissolution, and he has the same control over central agencies, the organization of cabinet committees, and executive staff resources. Just as the prime minister can enhance his standing within the government and the country through international travel and participation in world affairs, so can the premier enhance his own standing through travel and high-profile participation in federal–provincial diplomacy. In short, as Kornberg et al. conclude, " ... he is the boss, and the other ministers, although colleagues, are his agents."[9]

While the prime minister is not on an equal plan with his cabinet colleagues, this should not imply that he can run roughshod over their views. A successful prime minister leads rather than imposing his will, or at least imposes his will only in carefully limited areas of concern and expertise. The prime minister must try to maintain unity within cabinet and within caucus, and in this endeavour a dictatorial style is of little use. Still, in a cabinet of forty ministers, the prime minister stands apart. Preoccupied with their own portfolios, ministers are not in a position to challenge the pre-eminence of the prime minister even should they wish to do so.

Appendix C

Constitution Act, 1982

Part I
Canadian Charter of Rights and
Freedoms

Whereas Canada is founded upon principles that recognize the supremacy of God and the rule of law:

GUARANTEE OF RIGHTS AND FREEDOMS

Rights and freedoms in Canada

1. *The Canadian Charter of Rights and Freedoms* guarantees the rights and freedoms set out in it subject only to such reasonable limits prescribed by law as can be demonstrably justified in a free and democratic society.

FUNDAMENTAL FREEDOMS

Fundamental freedoms

2. Everyone has the following fundamental freedoms:

(a) freedom of conscience and religion;
(b) freedom of thought, belief, opinion and expression, including freedom of the press and other media of communication;
(c) freedom of peaceful assembly; and
(d) freedom of association.

Democratic
rights of citizens

3. Every citizen of Canada has the right to vote in an election of members of the House of Commons or of a legislative assembly and to be qualified for membership therein.

Maximum
duration of
legislative bodies

4. (1) No House of Commons and no legislative assembly shall continue for longer than five years from the date fixed for the return of the writs at a general election of its members.

Continuation in
special
circumstances

(2) In time of real or apprehended war, invasion or insurrection, a House of Commons may be continued by Parliament and a legislative assembly may be continued by the legislature beyond five years if such continuation is not opposed by the votes of more than one-third of the members of the House of Commons or the legislative assembly, as the case may be.

Annual sitting of
legislative bodies

5. There shall be a sitting of Parliament and of each legislature at least once every twelve months.

MOBILITY RIGHTS

Mobility of
citizens

6. (1) Every citizen of Canada has the right to enter, remain in and leave Canada.

Rights to move
and gain
livelihood

(2) Every citizen of Canada and every person who has the status of a permanent resident of Canada has the right
(a) to move to and take up residence in any province; and
(b) to pursue the gaining of a livelihood in any province.

Limitation

(3) The rights specified in subsection (2) are subject to
(a) any laws or practices of general application in force in a province other than those that discriminate among persons primarily on the basis of province of present or previous residence; and

(b) any laws providing for reasonable residency requirements as a qualification for the receipt of publicly provided social services.

Affirmative action programs

(4) Subsections (2) and (3) do not preclude any law, program or activity that has as its object the amelioration in a province of conditions of individuals in that province who are socially or economically disadvantaged if the rate of employment in that province is below the rate of employment in Canada.

LEGAL RIGHTS

Life, liberty and security of person

7. Everyone has the right to life, liberty and security of the person and the right not to be deprived thereof except in accordance with the principles of fundamental justice.

Search or seizure

8. Everyone has the right to be secure against unreasonable search or seizure.

Detention or imprisonment

9. Everyone has the right not to be arbitrarily detained or imprisoned.

Arrest or detention

10. Everyone has the right on arrest or detention
(a) to be informed promptly of the reasons therefor;
(b) to retain and instruct counsel without delay and to be informed of that right; and
(c) to have the validity of the detention determined by way of *habeas corpus* and to be released if the detention is not lawful.

Proceedings in criminal and penal matters

11. Any person charged with an offence has the right
(a) to be informed without unreasonable delay of the specific offence;
(b) to be tried within a reasonable time;
(c) not to be compelled to be a witness in proceedings against that person in respect of the offence;
(d) to be presumed innocent until proven guilty according to law in a fair and public hearing by an independent and impartial tribunal;

(e) not to be denied reasonable bail without just cause;

(f) except in the case of an offence under military law tried before a military tribunal, to the benefit of trial by jury where the maximum punishment for the offence is imprisonment for five years or a more severe punishment;

(g) not to be found guilty on account of any act or omission unless, at the time of the act or omission, it constituted an offence under Canadian or international law or was criminal according to the general principles of law recognized by the community of nations;

(h) if finally acquitted of the offence, not to be tried for it again and, if finally found guilty and punished for the offence, not to be tried or punished for it again; and

(i) if found guilty of the offence and if the punishment for the offence has been varied between the time of commission and the time of sentencing, to the benefit of the lesser punishment.

Treatment or punishment

12. Everyone has the right not to be subjected to any cruel and unusual treatment or punishment.

Self-incrimination

13. A witness who testifies in any proceedings has the right not to have any incriminating evidence so given used to incriminate that witness in any other proceedings, except in a prosecution for perjury or for the giving of contradictory evidence.

Interpreter

14. A party or witness in any proceedings who does not understand or speak the language in which the proceedings are conducted or who is deaf has the right to the assistance of an interpreter.

EQUALITY RIGHTS

Equality before and under law and equal protection and benefit of law

15. (1) Every individual is equal before and under the law and has the right to the equal protection and equal benefit of the law without discrimination and, in particular, without discrimination based on race, national or ethnic origin, colour, religion, sex, age or mental or physical disability.

Affirmative
action programs

(2) Subsection (1) does not preclude any law, program or activity that has as its object the amelioration of conditions of disadvantaged individuals or groups including those that are disadvantaged because of race, national or ethnic origin, colour, religion, sex, age or mental or physical disability.

OFFICIAL LANGUAGES OF CANADA

Official
languages of
Canada

16. (1) English and French are the official languages of Canada and have equality of status and equal rights and privileges as to their use in all institutions of the Parliament and government of Canada.

Official
languages of
New Brunswick

(2) English and French are the official languages of New Brunswick and have equality of status and equal rights and privileges as to their use in all institutions of the legislature and government of New Brunswick.

Advancement of
status and use

(3) Nothing in this Charter limits the authority of Parliament or a legislature to advance the equality of status or use of English and French.

Proceedings of
Parliament

17. (1) Everyone has the right to use English or French in any debates and other proceedings of Parliament.

Proceedings of
New Brunswick
legislature

(2) Everyone has the right to use English or French in any debates and other proceedings of the legislature of New Brunswick.

Parliamentary
status and
records

18. (1) The statutes, records and journals of Parliament shall be printed and published in English and French and both language versions are equally authoritative.

New Brunswick
statutes and
records

(2) The statutes, records and journals of the legislature of New Brunswick shall be printed and published in English and French and both language versions are equally authoritative.

Proceedings in
courts
established by
Parliament

19. (1) Either English or French may be used by any person in, or in any pleading in or process issuing from, any court established by Parliament.

(2) Either English or French may be used by any person in, or in any pleading in or process issuing from, any court of New Brunswick.

Communications
by public with
federal
institutions

20. (1) Any member of the public in Canada has the right to communicate with, and to receive available services from, any head or central office of an institution of the Parliament or government of Canada in English or French, and has the same right with respect to any other office of any such institution where

(*a*) there is a significant demand for communications with and services from that office in such language; or

(*b*) due to the nature of the office, it is reasonable that communications with and services from that office be available in both English and French.

Communications
by public with
New Brunswick
institutions

(2) Any member of the public in New Brunswick has the right to communicate with, and to receive available services from, any office of an institution of the legislature or government of New Brunswick in English or French.

Continuation of
existing
constitutional
provisions

21. Nothing in sections 16 to 20 abrogates or derogates from any right, privilege or obligation with respect to the English and French languages, or either of them, that exists or is continued by virtue of any other provision of the Constitution of Canada.

Rights and
privileges
preserved

22. Nothing in sections 16 to 20 abrogates or derogates from any legal or customary right or privilege acquired or enjoyed either before or after the coming into force of this Charter with respect to any language that is not English or French.

MINORITY LANGUAGE EDUCATION RIGHTS

Language of
instruction

23. (1) Citizens of Canada

(a) whose first language learned and still understood is that of the English or French linguistic minority population of the province in which they reside; or

(b) who have received their primary school instruction in Canada in English or French and reside in a province where the language in which they received that instruction is the language of the English or French linguistic minority population of the province,

have the right to have their children receive primary and secondary school instruction in that language in that province.

Continuity of
language
instruction

(2) Citizens of Canada of whom any child has received or is receiving primary or secondary school instruction in English or French in Canada, have the right to have all their children receive primary and secondary school instruction in the same language.

Application
where numbers
warrant

(3) The right of citizens of Canada under subsections (1) and (2) to have their children receive primary and secondary school instruction in the language of the English or French linguistic minority population of a province

(a) applies wherever in the province the number of children of citizens who have such a right is sufficient to warrant the provision to them out of public funds of minority language instruction; and

(b) includes, where the number of those children so warrants, the right to have them receive that instruction in minority language educational facilities provided out of public funds.

ENFORCEMENT

Enforcement of
guaranteed rights
and freedoms

24. (1) Anyone whose rights or freedoms, as guaranteed by this Charter, have been infringed or denied may apply to a court of competent jurisdic-

tion to obtain such remedy as the court considers appropriate and just in the circumstances.

Exclusion of evidence bringing administration of justice into disrepute

(2) Where, in proceedings under subsection (1), a court concludes that evidence was obtained in a manner that infringed or denied any rights or freedoms guaranteed by this Charter, the evidence shall be excluded if it is established that, having regard to all the circumstances, the admission of it in the proceedings would bring the administration of justice into disrepute.

GENERAL

Aboriginal rights and freedoms not affected by Charter

25. The guarantee in this Charter of certain rights and freedoms shall not be construed so as to abrogate or derogate from any aboriginal, treaty or other rights or freedoms that pertain to the aboriginal peoples of Canada including

(a) any rights or freedoms that have been recognized by the Royal Proclamation of October 7, 1763, and

(b) any rights or freedoms that may be acquired by the aboriginal peoples of Canada by way of land claims settlement.

Other rights and freedoms not affected by Charter

26. The guarantee in this Charter of certain rights and freedoms shall not be construed as denying the existence of any other rights or freedoms that exist in Canada.

Multicultural heritage

27. This Charter shall be interpreted in a manner consistent with the preservation and enhancement of the multicultural heritage of Canadians.

Rights guaranteed equally to both sexes

28. Notwithstanding anything in this Charter, the rights and freedoms referred to in it are guaranteed equally to male and female persons.

Rights respecting certain schools

29. Nothing in this Charter abrogates or derogates from any rights or privileges guaranteed by or under the Constitution of Canada in respect of denominational, separate or dissentient schools.

Application to
territories and
territorial
authorities

30. A reference in this Charter to a province or to the legislative assembly or legislature of a province shall be deemed to include a reference to the Yukon Territory and the Northwest Territories, or to the appropriate legislative authority thereof, as the case may be.

Legislative
powers not
extended

31. Nothing in this Charter extends the legislative powers of any body or authority.

APPLICATION OF CHARTER

Application of
Charter

32. (1) This Charter applies
(*a*) to the Parliament and government of Canada in respect of all matters within the authority of Parliament including all matters relating to the Yukon Territory and Northwest Territories; and
(*b*) to the legislature and government of each province in respect of all matters within the authority of the legislature of each province.

Exception

(2) Notwithstanding section (1), section 15 shall not have effect until three years after this section comes into force.

Exception where
express
declaration

33. (1) Parliament or the legislature of a province may expressly declare in an Act of Parliament or of the legislature, as the case may be, that the Act or a provision thereof shall operate notwithstanding a provision included in section 2 or sections 7 to 15 of this Charter.

Operation of
exception

(2) An Act or a provision of an Act in respect of which a declaration made under this section is in effect shall have such operation as it would have but for the provision of this Charter referred to in the declaration.

Five year
limitation

(3) A declaration made under subsection (1) shall cease to have effect five years after it comes into force or on such earlier date as may be specified in the declaration.

Re-enactment

(4) Parliament or a legislature of a province may re-enact a declaration made under subsection (1).

Five year
limitation

(5) Subsection (3) applies in respect of a re-enactment made under subsection (4).

CITATION

Citation

34. This Part may be cited as the *Canadian Charter of Rights and Freedoms.*

Part II
Rights of the Aboriginal Peoples of Canada

Recognition of
existing
aboriginal and
treaty rights

35. (1) The existing aboriginal and treaty rights of the aboriginal peoples of Canada are hereby recognized and affirmed.

Definition of
"aboriginal
peoples of
Canada"

(2) In this Act, "aboriginal peoples of Canada" includes the Indian, Inuit and Métis people of Canada.

Part III
Equalization and Regional Disparities

Commitment to
promote equal
opportunities

36. (1) Without altering the legislative authority of Parliament or of the provincial legislatures, or the rights of any of them with respect to the exercise of their legislative authority, Parliament and the legislatures, together with the government of Canada and the provincial governments, are committed to
(*a*) promoting equal opportunities for the well-being of Canadians;
(*b*) furthering economic development to reduce disparity in opportunities; and
(*c*) providing essential public services of reasonable quality to all Canadians.

Commitment
respecting public
services

(2) Parliament and the government of Canada are committed to the principle of making equalization payments to ensure that provincial govern-

ments have sufficient revenues to provide reasonably comparable levels of public services at reasonably comparable levels of taxation.

Part IV
Constitutional Conference

Constitutional conference

37. (1) A constitutional conference composed of the Prime Minister of Canada and the first ministers of the provinces shall be convened by the Prime Minister of Canada within one year after this Part comes into force.

Participation of aboriginal peoples

(2) The conference convened under subsection (1) shall have included in its agenda an item respecting constitutional matters that directly affect the aboriginal peoples of Canada, including the identification and definition of the rights of those peoples to be included in the Constitution of Canada, and the Prime Minister of Canada shall invite representatives of those peoples to participate in the discussions on that item.

Participation of territories

(3) The Prime Minister of Canada shall invite elected representatives of the governments of the Yukon Territory and the Northwest Territories to participate in the discussions on any item on the agenda of the conference convened under subsection (1) that, in the opinion of the Prime Minister, directly affects the Yukon Territory and the Northwest Territories.

Part V
Procedure for Amending Constitution of Canada

General procedure for amending Constitution of Canada

38. (1) An amendment to the Constitution of Canada may be made by proclamation issued by the Governor General under the Great Seal of Canada where so authorized by

(*a*) resolutions of the Senate and House of Commons; and

(*b*) resolutions of the legislative assemblies of at least two-thirds of the provinces that have, in the aggregate, according to the then latest general census, at least fifty per cent of the population of all the provinces.

Majority of members

(2) An amendment made under subsection (1) that derogates from the legislative powers, the proprietary rights or any other rights or privileges of the legislature or government of a province shall require a resolution supported by a majority of the members of each of the Senate, the House of Commons and the legislative assemblies required under subsection (1).

Expression of dissent

(3) An amendment referred to in subsection (2) shall not have effect in a province the legislative assembly of which has expressed its dissent thereto by resolution supported by a majority of its members prior to the issue of the proclamation to which the amendment relates unless that legislative assembly, subsequently, by resolution supported by a majority of its members, revokes its dissent and authorizes the amendment.

Revocation of dissent

(4) A resolution of dissent made for the purposes of subsection (3) may be revoked at any time before or after the issue of the proclamation to which it relates.

Restriction on proclamation

39. (1) A proclamation shall not be issued under subsection 38(1) before the expiration of one year from the adoption of the resolution initiating the amendment procedure thereunder, unless the legislative assembly of each province has previously adopted a resolution of assent or dissent.

Idem

(2) A proclamation shall not be issued under subsection 38(1) after the expiration of three years from the adoption of the resolution initiating the amendment procedure thereunder.

Compensation

40. Where an amendment is made under subsection 38(1) that transfers provincial legislative powers relating to education or other cultural matters from provincial legislatures to Parliament,

Canada shall provide reasonable compensation to any province to which the amendment does not apply.

Amendment by unanimous consent

41. An amendment to the Constitution of Canada in relation to the following matters may be made by proclamation issued by the Governor General under the Great Seal of Canada only where authorized by resolutions of the Senate and House of Commons and of the legislative assembly of each province:

(a) the office of the Queen, the Governor General and the Lieutenant Governor of a province;

(b) the right of a province to a number of members in the House of Commons not less than the number of Senators by which the province is entitled to be represented at the time this Part comes into force;

(c) subject to section 43, the use of the English or the French language;

(d) the composition of the Supreme Court of Canada; and

(e) an amendment to this Part.

Amendment by general procedure

42. (1) An amendment to the Constitution of Canada in relation to the following matters may be made only in accordance with subsection 38(1):

(a) the principle of proportionate representation of the provinces in the House of Commons prescribed by the Constitution of Canada;

(b) the powers of the Senate and the method of selecting Senators;

(c) the number of members by which a province is entitled to be represented in the Senate and the residence qualifications of Senators;

(d) subject to paragraph 41(*d*), the Supreme Court of Canada;

(e) the extension of existing provinces into the territories; and

(f) notwithstanding any other law or practice, the establishment of new provinces.

Exception

(2) Subsections 38(2) to (4) do not apply in respect of amendments in relation to matters referred to in subsection (1).

Amendment of provisions relating to some but not all provinces

43. An amendment to the Constitution of Canada in relation to any provision that applies to one or more, but not all, provinces, including

(a) any alteration to boundaries between provinces, and

(b) any amendment to any provision that relates to the use of the English or the French language within a province, may be made by proclamation issued by the Governor General under the Great Seal of Canada only where so authorized by resolutions of the Senate and House of Commons and of the legislative assembly of each province to which the amendment applies.

Amendments by Parliament

44. Subject to sections 41 and 42, Parliament may exclusively make laws amending the Constitution of Canada in relation to the executive government of Canada or the Senate and House of Commons.

Amendments by provincial legislatures

45. Subject to section 41, the legislature of each province may exclusively make laws amending the constitution of the province.

Initiation of amendment procedures

46. (1) The procedures for amendment under sections 38, 41, 42 and 43 may be initiated either by the Senate or the House of Commons or by the legislative assembly of a province.

Revocation of authorization

(2) A resolution of assent made for the purposes of this Part may be revoked at any time before the issue of a proclamation authorized by it.

Amendments without Senate resolution

47. (1) An amendment to the Constitution of Canada made by proclamation under section 38, 41, 42 or 43 may be made without a resolution of the Senate authorizing the issue of the proclamation if, within one hundred and eighty days after the adoption by the House of Commons of a resolution authorizing its issue, the Senate has not adopted such a resolution and if, at any time after the expiration of that period, the House of Commons again adopts the resolution.

Computation of period

(2) Any period when Parliament is prorogued or dissolved shall not be counted in computing the

one hundred and eighty day period referred to in subsection (1).

Advice to issue
proclamation

48. The Queen's Privy Council for Canada shall advise the Governor General to issue a proclamation under this Part forthwith on the adoption of the resolutions required for an amendment made by proclamation under this Part.

Constitutional
conference

49. A constitutional conference composed of the Prime Minister of Canada and the first ministers of the provinces shall be convened by the Prime Minister of Canada within fifteen years after this Part comes into force to review the provisions of this Part.

Part VI
Amendment to the Constitution Act, 1867

Amendment to
*Constitution Act,
1867*

50. The *Constitution Act, 1867* (formerly named the *British North America Act, 1867*) is amended by adding thereto, immediately after section 92 thereof, the following heading and section:

"NON-RENEWABLE NATURAL RESOURCES, FORESTRY
RESOURCES AND ELECTRICAL ENERGY

Laws respecting
non-renewable
natural
resources,
forestry
resources and
electrical energy

92A. (1) In each province, the legislature may exclusively make laws in relation to
(*a*) exploration for non-renewable natural resources in the province;
(*b*) development, conservation and management of non-renewable natural resources and forestry resources in the province, including laws in relation to the rate of primary production therefrom; and
(*c*) development, conservation and management of sites and facilities in the province for the generation and production of electrical energy.

Export from
provinces of
resources

(2) In each province, the legislature may make laws in relation to the export from the province to another part of Canada of the primary production from non-renewable natural resources and forestry

resources in the province and the production from facilities in the province for the generation of electrical energy, but such laws may not authorize or provide for discrimination in prices or in supplies exported to another part of Canada.

Authority of Parliament

(3) Nothing in subsection (2) derogates from the authority of Parliament to enact laws in relation to the matters referred to in that subsection and, where such a law of Parliament and a law of a province conflict, the law of Parliament prevails to the extent of the conflict.

Taxation of resources

(4) In each province, the legislature may make laws in relation to the raising of money by any mode or system of taxation in respect of

(*a*) non-renewable natural resources and forestry resources in the province and the primary production therefrom, and

(*b*) sites and facilities in the province for the generation of electrical energy and the production therefrom,

whether or not such production is exported in whole or in part from the province, but such laws may not authorize or provide for taxation that differentiates between production exported to another part of Canada and production not exported from the province.

"Primary production"

(5) The expression "primary production" has the meaning assigned by the Sixth Schedule.

Existing powers or rights

(6) Nothing in subsections (1) to (5) derogates from any powers or rights that a legislature or government of a province had immediately before the coming into force of this section."

Idem

51. The said Act is further amended by adding thereto the following Schedule:

"The Sixth Schedule
PRIMARY PRODUCTION FROM NON-RENEWABLE NATURAL RESOURCES AND FORESTRY RESOURCES

1. For the purposes of section 92A of this Act,
(a) production from a non-renewable natural resource is primary production therefrom if
  (i) it is in the form in which it exists upon its recovery or severance from its natural state, or
  (ii) it is a product resulting from processing or refining the resource, and is not a manufactured product or a product resulting from refining crude oil, refining upgraded heavy crude oil, refining gases or liquids derived from coal or refining a synthetic equivalent of crude oil; and
(b) production from a forestry resource is primary production therefrom if it consists of sawlogs, poles, lumber, wood chips, sawdust or any other primary wood product, or wood pulp, and is not a product manufactured from wood."

Part VII
General

Primacy of Constitution of Canada

52. (1) The Constitution of Canada is the supreme law of Canada, and any law that is inconsistent with the provisions of the Constitution is, to the extent of the inconsistency, of no force or effect.

Constitution of Canada

(2) The Constitution of Canada includes
(a) the *Canada Act, 1982*, including this Act;
(b) the Acts and orders referred to in the schedule, and
(c) any amendments to any Act or order referred to in paragraph *(a)* or *(b)*.

Amendments to Constitution of Canada

(3) Amendments to the Constitution of Canada shall be made only in accordance with the authority contained in the Constitution of Canada.

Repeals and new names

53. (1) The enactments referred to in Column I of the schedule are hereby repealed or amended to the extent indicated in Column II thereof and, unless repealed, shall continue as law in Canada under the names set out in Column III thereof.

Consequential amendments

(2) Every enactment, except the *Canada Act, 1982*, that refers to an enactment referred to in the schedule by the name in Column I thereof is hereby amended by substituting for that name the corresponding name in Column III thereof, and any British North America Act not referred to in the schedule may be cited as the *Constitution Act* followed by the year and number, if any, of its enactment.

Repeal and consequential amendments

54. Part IV is repealed on the day that is one year after this Part comes into force and this section may be repealed and this Act renumbered, consequential upon the repeal of Part IV and this section, by proclamation issued by the Governor General under the Great Seal of Canada.

French version of Constitution of Canada

55. A French version of the portions of the Constitution of Canada referred to in the schedule shall be prepared by the Minister of Justice of Canada as expeditiously as possible and, when any portion thereof sufficient to warrant action being taken has been so prepared, it shall be put forward for enactment by proclamation issued by the Governor General under the Great Seal of Canada pursuant to the procedure then applicable to an amendment of the same provisions of the Constitution of Canada.

English and French versions of certain constitutional texts

56. Where any portion of the Constitution of Canada has been or is enacted in English and French or where a French version of any portion of the Constitution is enacted pursuant to section 55, the English and French versions of that portion of the Constitution are equally authoritative.

English and French versions of this Act

57. The English and French versions of this Act are equally authoritative.

58. Subject to section 59, this Act shall come into force on a day to be fixed by proclamation issued by the Queen or the Governor General under the Great Seal of Canada.

Commencement of paragraph 23(1)(*a*)

59. (1) Paragraph 23(1)(*a*) shall come into force in respect of Quebec on a day to be fixed by proclamation issued by the Queen or the Governor General under the Great Seal of Canada.

Authorization of Quebec

(2) A proclamation under subsection (1) shall be issued only where authorized by the legislative assembly or government of Quebec.

Repeal of this section

(3) This section may be repealed on the day paragraph 23(1)(*a*) comes into force in respect of Quebec and this Act amended and renumbered, consequential upon the repeal of this section, by proclamation issued by the Queen or the Governor General under the Great Seal of Canada.

Short title and citations

60. This Act may be cited as the *Constitution Act, 1982*, and the Constitution Acts 1867 to 1975 (No. 2) and this Act may be cited together as the *Constitution Acts, 1867 to 1982*.

Appendix D

Excerpts from the Constitution Act, 1867

The federal division of powers is set forth in a number of sections of the Constitution Act, 1867. The most general treatment is contained in Sections 91 and 92, while subsequent sections deal in more detail with particular powers.

VI. Distribution of Legislative Powers

POWERS OF PARLIAMENT

91. It shall be lawful for the Queen, by and with the advice and consent of the Senate and House of Commons, to make laws for the peace, order, and good government of Canada, in relation to all matters not coming within the classes of subjects by this Act assigned exclusively to the Legislatures of the Provinces; and for greater certainty, but not so as to restrict the generality of the foregoing terms of this section, it is hereby declared that (notwithstanding anything in this Act) the exclusive Legislative Authority of the Parliament of Canada extends to all matter coming within the classes of subjects next hereinafter enumerated, that is to say:—

1. The amendment from time to time of the Constitution of Canada, except as regards matters coming within the classes of subjects by this Act assigned exclusively to the Legislatures of the Provinces, or as regards rights or privileges by this or any other Constitutional Act granted or secured to the Legislature or the Government of a Province, or to any class of persons with respect to schools or as regards the use of the English or the French language or as regards the requirements that there shall be a session of the Parliament of Canada at least once each year, and that no House of Commons shall continue for more than five years from the day of the return of the Writs for choosing the House: provided, however, that a House of Commons may in time of real or apprehended war, invasion or insurrection be continued by the Parliament of Canada if such continuation is not opposed by the votes of more than one-third of the members of such House.(39)

1A. The Public Debt and Property.(40)

2. The regulation of Trade and Commerce.

2A. Unemployment insurance.(41)

3. The raising of money by any mode or system of Taxation.

4. The borrowing of money on the public credit.
5. Postal service.
6. The Census and Statistics.
7. Militia, Military and Naval Service, and Defence.
8. The fixing of and providing for the salaries and allowances of civil and other officers of the Government of Canada.
9. Beacons, Buoys, Lighthouses, and Sable Island.
10. Navigation and Shipping.
11. Quarantine and the establishment and maintenance of Marine Hospitals.
12. Sea Coast and Inland Fisheries.
13. Ferries between a Province and any British or Foreign country or between two Provinces.
14. Currency and Coinage.
15. Banking, incorporation of banks, and the issue of paper money.
16. Savings Banks.
17. Weights and Measures.
18. Bills of Exchange and Promissory Notes.
19. Interest.
20. Legal tender.
21. Bankruptcy and Insolvency.
22. Patents of Invention and Discovery.
23. Copyrights.
24. Indians and lands reserved for the Indians.
25. Naturalization and Aliens.
26. Marriage and Divorce.
27. The Criminal Law, except the Constitution of Courts of Criminal Jurisdiction, but including the Procedure in Criminal Matters.
28. The establishment, maintenance, and management of Penitentiaries.
29. Such classes of subjects as are expressly excepted in the enumeration of the classes of subjects by this Act assigned exclusively to the Legislatures of the Provinces:

And any matter coming within any of the classes of subjects enumerated in this section shall not be deemed to come within the class of matters of a local or private nature comprised in the enumeration of the classes of subjects by this Act assigned exclusively to the Legislatures of the Provinces.(42)

EXCLUSIVE POWERS OF PROVINCIAL LEGISLATURES

92. In each Province the Legislature may exclusively make laws in relation to matters coming within the classes of subjects next hereinafter enumerated, that is to say,

1. The amendment from time to time, notwithstanding anything in this Act, of the Constitution of the Province, except as regards the Office of Lieutenant-Governor.
2. Direct Taxation within the Province in order to the raising of a Revenue for Provincial purposes.
3. The borrowing of money on the sole credit of the Province.
4. The establishment and tenure of Provincial offices and the appointment and payment of Provincial officers.
5. The management and sales of the Public Lands belonging to the Province, and of the timber and wood thereon.
6. The establishment, maintenance, and management of public and reformatory prisons in and for the Province.
7. The establishment, maintenance, and management of hospitals, asylums, charities, and eleemosynary institutions in and for the Province, other than marine hospitals.
8. Municipal institutions in the Province.
9. Shop, saloon, tavern, auctioneer, and other licenses, in order to the raising of a revenue for Provincial, local, or municipal purposes.
10. Local works and undertakings other than such as are of the following classes,—
   a. Lines of steam or other ships, railways, canals, telegraphs, and other works and undertakings connecting the Province with any other or others of the Provinces, or extending beyond the limits of the Province;
   b. Lines of steam ships between the Province and any British or Foreign country;
   c. Such works as, although wholly situate within the Province, are before or after their execution declared by the Parliament of Canada to be for the general advantage of Canada or for the advantage of two or more of the Provinces.
11. The incorporation of companies with Provincial objects.
12. The solemnization of marriage in the Province.
13. Property and civil rights in the Province.
14. The administration of justice in the Province, including the constitution, maintenance, and organization of Provincial Courts, both of civil and of criminal jurisdiction, and including procedure in civil matters in those Courts.
15. The imposition of punishment by fine, penalty, or imprisonment for enforcing any law of the Province made in relation to any matter coming within any of the classes of subjects enumerated in this section.
16. Generally all matters of a merely local or private nature in the Province.

EDUCATION

93. In and for each Province the Legislature may exclusively make laws in relation to education, subject and according to the following provisions:—

1. Nothing in any such law shall prejudicially affect any right or privilege with respect to denominational schools which any class of persons have by law in the Province at the Union.

2. All the powers, privileges, and duties at the Union by law conferred and imposed in Upper Canada on the separate schools and school trustees of the Queen's Roman Catholic subjects shall be and the same are hereby extended to the dissentient schools of the Queen's Protestant and Roman Catholic subjects in Quebec.

3. Where in any Province a system of separate or dissentient schools exists by law at the Union or is thereafter established by the Legislature of the Province, an appeal shall lie to the Governor-General in Council from any Act or Decision of any Provincial authority affecting any right or privilege of the Protestant or Roman Catholic minority of the Queen's subjects in relation to education.

4. In case any such Provincial law as from time to time seems to the Governor-General in Council requisite for the due execution of the provisions of this section is not made, or in case any decision of the Governor-General in Council on any appeal under this section is not duly executed by the proper Provincial authority in that behalf, then and in every such case, and as far only as the circumstances of each case require, the Parliament of Canada may make remedial laws for the due execution of the provisions of this section and of any decision of the Governor-General in Council under this section.(43)

. . .

OLD AGE PENSIONS

94A. The Parliament of Canada may make laws in relation to old age pensions and supplementary benefits, including survivors' and disability benefits irrespective of age, but no such law shall affect the operation of any law present or future of a provincial legislature in relation to any such matter.(44)

AGRICULTURE AND IMMIGRATION

95. In each Province the Legislature may make laws in relation to Agriculture in the Province, and to Immigration into the Province; and it is hereby declared that the Parliament of Canada may from time to time make laws in relation to Agriculture in all or any of the Provinces, and to Immigration into all or any of the Provinces; and any law of the Legisla-

ture of a Province relative to Agriculture or to Immigration shall have effect in and for the Province as long and as far only as it is not repugnant to any Act of the Parliament of Canada.

. . .

VIII. Revenues; Debts; Assets; Taxation

. . .

109.   All lands, mines, minerals, and royalties belonging to the several provinces of Canada, Nova Scotia and New Brunswick at the Union, and all sums then due or payable for such lands, mines, minerals, or royalties, shall belong to the several Provinces of Ontario, Quebec, Nova Scotia and New Brunswick in which the same are situate or arise, subject to any trusts existing in respect thereof, and to any interest other than of the Province in the same.(48)

. . .

Appendix E

Constitution Amendment, 1987

Following is the text of the Constitutional Accord approved by the Prime Minister and all provincial Premiers on June 3, 1987, which provided the basis for submitting a resolution to Parliament and the provincial legislatures, seeking approval of the *Constitution Amendment, 1987*.

1987 CONSTITUTIONAL ACCORD

WHEREAS first ministers, assembled in Ottawa, have arrived at a unanimous accord on constitutional amendments that would bring about the full and active participation of Quebec in Canada's constitutional evolution, would recognize the principle of equality of all the provinces, would provide new arrangements to foster greater harmony and cooperation between the Government of Canada and the governments of the provinces and would require that annual first ministers' conferences on the state of the Canadian economy and such other matters as may be appropriate be convened and that annual constitutional conferences composed of first ministers be convened commencing not later than December 31, 1988;

AND WHEREAS first ministers have also reached unanimous agreement on certain additional commitments in relation to some of those amendments;

NOW THEREFORE the Prime Minister of Canada and the first ministers of the provinces commit themselves and the governments they represent to the following:

1. The Prime Minister of Canada will lay or cause to be laid before the Senate and House of Commons, and the first ministers of the provinces will lay or cause to be laid before their legislative assemblies, as soon as possible, a resolution, in the form appended hereto, to authorize a proclamation to be issued by the Governor General under the Great Seal of Canada to amend the Constitution of Canada.

2. The Government of Canada will, as soon as possible, conclude an agreement with the Government of Quebec that would

(a) incorporate the principles of the Cullen-Couture agreement on the selection abroad and in Canada of independent immigrants, visitors for medical treatment, students and temporary workers, and on the selection of refugees abroad and economic criteria for family reunification and assisted relatives,

(b) guarantee that Quebec will receive a number of immigrants, including refugees, within the annual total established by the federal government for all of Canada proportionate to its share of the population of Canada, with the right to exceed that figure by five per cent for demographic reasons, and

(c) provide an undertaking by Canada to withdraw services (except citizenship services) for the reception and integration (including linguistic and cultural) of all foreign nationals wishing to settle in Quebec where services are to be provided by Quebec, with such withdrawal to be accompanied by reasonable compensation,

and the Government of Canada and the Government of Quebec will take the necessary steps to give the agreement the force of law under the proposed amendment relating to such agreements.

3. Nothing in this Accord should be construed as preventing the negotiation of similar agreements with other provinces relating to immigration and the temporary admission of aliens.

4. Until the proposed amendment relating to appointments to the Senate comes into force, any person summoned to fill a vacancy in the Senate shall be chosen from among persons whose names have been submitted by the government of the province to which the vacancy relates and must be acceptable to the Queen's Privy Council for Canada.

MOTION FOR A RESOLUTION TO AUTHORIZE AN AMENDMENT TO THE CONSTITUTION OF CANADA

WHEREAS the *Constitution Act, 1982* came into force on April 17, 1982, following an agreement between Canada and all the provinces except Quebec;

AND WHEREAS the Government of Quebec has established a set of five proposals for constitutional change and has stated that amendments to give effect to those proposals would enable Quebec to resume a full role in the constitutional councils of Canada;

AND WHEREAS the amendment proposed in the schedule hereto sets out the basis on which Quebec's five constitutional proposals may be met;

AND WHEREAS the amendment proposed in the schedule hereto also recognizes the principle of the equality of all the provinces, provides new arrangements to foster greater harmony and cooperation between the Government of Canada and the governments of the provinces and requires that conferences be convened to consider important constitutional, economic and other issues;

AND WHEREAS certain portions of the amendment proposed in the schedule hereto relate to matters referred to in section 41 of the *Constitution Act, 1982*;

AND WHEREAS section 41 of the *Constitution Act, 1982* provides that an amendment to the Constitution of Canada may be made by proclamation issued by the Governor General under the Great Seal of Canada where so authorized by resolutions of the Senate and the House of Commons and of the legislative assembly of each province;

NOW THEREFORE the (Senate) (House of Commons) (legislative assembly) resolves that an amendment to the Constitution of Canada be authorized to be made by proclamation issued by Her Excellency the Governor General under the Great Seal of Canada in accordance with the schedule hereto.

SCHEDULE

CONSTITUTION AMENDMENT, 1987

CONSTITUTION ACT, 1867

1. The *Constitution Act, 1867* is amended by adding thereto, immediately after section 1 thereof, the following section:

Interpretation

2. (1) The Constitution of Canada shall be interpreted in a manner consistent with
(a) the recognition that the existence of French-speaking Canadians, centred in Quebec but also present elsewhere in Canada, and English-speaking Canadians, concentrated outside Quebec but also present in Quebec, constitutes a fundamental characteristic of Canada; and

(b) the recognition that Quebec constitutes within Canada a distinct society.

Role of
Parliament and
legislatures

(2) The role of the Parliament of Canada and the provincial legislatures to preserve the fundamental characteristic of Canada referred to in paragraph (1)(*a*) is affirmed.

Role of
legislature and
Government of
Quebec

(3) The role of the legislature and Government of Quebec to preserve and promote the distinct identity of Quebec referred to in paragraph (1)(*b*) is affirmed.

Rights of
legislatures and
governments
preserved

(4) Nothing in this section derogates from the powers, rights or privileges of Parliament or the Government of Canada, or of the legislatures or governments of the provinces, including any powers, rights or privileges relating to language.

2. The said Act is further amended by adding thereto, immediately after section 24 thereof, the following section:

Names to be
submitted

25. (1) Where a vacancy occurs in the Senate, the government of the province to which the vacancy relates may, in relation to that vacancy, submit to the Queen's Privy Council for Canada the names of persons who may be summoned to the Senate.

Choice of
Senators from
names submitted

(2) Until an amendment to the Constitution of Canada is made in relation to the Senate pursuant to section 41 of the *Constitution Act, 1982*, the person summoned to fill a vacancy in the Senate shall be chosen from among persons whose names have been submitted under subsection (1) by the government of the province to which the vacancy relates and must be acceptable to the Queen's Privy Council for Canada.

3. The said Act is further amended by adding thereto, immediately after section 94 thereof, the following heading and sections:

Agreements on Immigration and Aliens

Commitment to
negotiate

95A. The Government of Canada shall, at the request of the government of any province, negotiate with the government of that province for the purpose of concluding an agreement relating to immigration or the temporary admission of aliens into that province that is appropriate to the needs and circumstances of that province.

Agreements

95B. (1) Any agreement concluded between Canada and a province in relation to immigration or the temporary admission of aliens into that province has the force of law from the time it is declared to do so in accordance with subsection 95C(1) and shall from that time have effect notwithstanding class 25 of section 91 or section 95.

Limitation

(2) An agreement that has the force of law under subsection (1) shall have effect only so long and so far as it is not repugnant to any provision of an Act of the Parliament of Canada that sets national standards and objectives relating to immigration or aliens, including any provision that establishes general classes of immigrants or relates to levels of immigration for Canada or that prescribes classes of individuals who are inadmissible into Canada.

Application of
Charter

(3) The *Canadian Charter of Rights and Freedoms* applies in respect of any agreement that has the force of law under subsection (1) and in respect of anything done by the Parliament or Government of Canada, or the legislature or government of a province, pursuant to any such agreement.

Proclamation
relating to
agreements

95C. (1) A declaration that an agreement referred to in subsection 95B(1) has the force of law may be made by proclamation issued by the Governor General under the Great Seal of Canada only where so authorized by resolutions of the Senate and House of Commons and of the legislative assembly of the province that is a party to the agreement.

Amendment of agreements

(2) An amendment to an agreement referred to in subsection 95B(1) may be made by proclamation issued by the Governor General under the Great Seal of Canada only where so authorized
(a) by resolutions of the Senate and House of Commons and of the legislative assembly of the province that is a party to the agreement; or
(b) in such other manner as is set out in the agreement.

Application of sections 46 to 48 of *Constitution Act, 1982*

95D. Sections 46 to 48 of the *Constitution Act, 1982*, apply, with such modifications as the circumstances require, in respect of any declaration made pursuant to subsection 95C(1), any amendment to an agreement made pursuant to subsection 95C(2) or any amendment made pursuant to section 95E.

Amendments to sections 95A to 95D or this section

95E. An amendment to sections 95A to 95D or this section may be made in accordance with the procedure set out in subsection 38(1) of the *Constitution Act, 1982*, but only if the amendment is authorized by resolutions of the legislative assemblies of all the provinces that are, at the time of the amendment, parties to an agreement that has the force of law under subsection 95B(1).

4. The said Act is further amended by adding thereto, immediately preceding section 96 thereof, the following heading:

General

5. The said Act is further amended by adding thereto, immediately preceding section 101 thereof, the following heading:

Courts Established by the Parliament of Canada

6. The said Act is further amended by adding thereto, immediately after section 101 thereof, the

following heading and sections:

Supreme Court of Canada

Supreme Court continued

101A. (1) The court existing under the name of the Supreme Court of Canada is hereby continued as the general court of appeal for Canada, and as an additional court for the better administration of the laws of Canada, and shall continue to be a superior court of record.

Constitution of court

(2) The Supreme Court of Canada shall consist of a chief justice to be called the Chief Justice of Canada and eight other judges, who shall be appointed by the Governor General in Council by letters patent under the Great Seal.

Who may be appointed judges

101B. (1) Any person may be appointed a judge of the Supreme Court of Canada who, after having been admitted to the bar of any province or territory, has, for a total of at least ten years, been a judge of any court in Canada or a member of the bar of any province or territory.

Three judges from Quebec

(2) At least three judges of the Supreme Court of Canada shall be appointed from among persons who, after having been admitted to the bar of Quebec, have, for a total of at least ten years, been judges of any court of Quebec or of any court established by the Parliament of Canada, or members of the bar of Quebec.

Names may be submitted

101C. (1) Where a vacancy occurs in the Supreme Court of Canada, the government of each province may, in relation to that vacancy, submit to the Minister of Justice of Canada the names of any of the persons who have been admitted to the bar of that province and are qualified under section 101B for appointment to that court.

Appointment from names submitted

(2) Where an appointment is made to the Supreme Court of Canada, the Governor General in Council shall, except where the Chief Justice is appointed from among members of the Court,

appoint a person whose name has been submitted under subsection (1) and who is acceptable to the Queen's Privy Council for Canada.

Appointment from Quebec

(3) Where an appointment is made in accordance with subsection (2) of any of the three judges necessary to meet the requirement set out in subsection 101B(2), the Governor General in Council shall appoint a person whose name has been submitted by the Government of Quebec.

Appointment from other provinces

(4) Where an appointment is made in accordance with subsection (2) otherwise than as required under subsection (3), the Governor General in Council shall appoint a person whose name has been submitted by the government of a province other than Quebec.

Tenure, salaries, etc., of judges

101D. Sections 99 and 100 apply in respect of the judges of the Supreme Court of Canada.

Relationship to section 101

101E. (1) Sections 101A to 101D shall not be construed as abrogating or derogating from the powers of the Parliament of Canada to make laws under section 101 except to the extent that such laws are inconsistent with those sections.

References to the Supreme Court of Canada

(2) For greater certainty, section 101A shall not be construed as abrogating or derogating from the powers of the Parliament of Canada to make laws relating to the reference of questions of law or fact, or any other matters, to the Supreme Court of Canada.

7. The said Act is further amended by adding thereto, immediately after section 106 thereof, the following section:

Shared-cost program

106A. (1) The Government of Canada shall provide reasonable compensation to the government of a province that chooses not to participate in a national shared-cost program that is established by the Government of Canada after the coming into force of this section in an area of exclusive provincial jurisdiction, if the province carries on a program or initiative that is compatible with the national objectives.

Legislative power
not extended

(2) Nothing in this section extends the legislative powers of the Parliament of Canada or of the legislatures of the provinces.

8. The said Act is further amended by adding thereto the following heading and sections:

XII – CONFERENCES ON THE ECONOMY AND OTHER MATTERS

Conferences on
the economy and
other matters

148. A conference composed of the Prime Minister of Canada and the first ministers of the provinces shall be convened by the Prime Minister of Canada at least once each year to discuss the state of the Canadian economy and such other matters as may be appropriate.

XIII – REFERENCES

Reference
includes
amendments

149. A reference to this Act shall be deemed to include a reference to any amendments thereto.

CONSTITUTION ACT, 1982

9. Sections 40 to 42 of the Constitution Act, 1982 are repealed and the following substituted therefor:

Compensation

40. Where an amendment is made under subsection 38(1) that transfers legislative powers from provincial legislatures to Parliament, Canada shall provide reasonable compensation to any province to which the amendment does not apply.

Amendment by
unanimous
consent

41. An amendment to the Constitution of Canada in relation to the following matters may be made by proclamation issued by the Governor General under the Great Seal of Canada only where authorized by resolutions of the Senate and House of Commons and of the legislative assembly of each province:

(a) the office of the Queen, the Governor General and the Lieutenant Governor of a province;

(b) the powers of the Senate and the method of selecting Senators;

(c) the number of members by which a province is entitled to be represented in the Senate and the residence qualifications of Senators;

(d) the right of a province to a number of members in the House of Commons not less than the number of Senators by which the province was entitled to be represented on April 17, 1982;

(e) the principle of proportionate representation of the provinces in the House of Commons prescribed by the Constitution of Canada;

(f) subject to section 43, the use of the English or the French language;

(g) the Supreme Court of Canada;

(h) the extension of existing provinces into the territories;

(i) notwithstanding any other law or practice, the establishment of new provinces; and

(j) an amendment to this Part.

10. Section 44 of the said Act is repealed and the following substituted therefor:

Amendments by Parliament

44. Subject to section 41, Parliament may exclusively make laws amending the Constitution of Canada in relation to the executive government of Canada or the Senate and House of Commons.

11. Subsection 46(1) of the said Act is repealed and the following substituted therefor:

Initiation of amendment procedures

46. (1) The procedures for amendment under sections 38, 41 and 43 may be initiated either by the Senate or the House of Commons or by the legislative assembly of a province.

12. Subsection 47(1) of the said Act is repealed and the following substituted therefor:

Amendments without Senate resolution

47. (1) An amendment to the Constitution of Canada made by proclamation under section 38, 41 or 43 may be made without a resolution of the Senate authorizing the issue of the proclamation if, within one hundred and eighty days after the adoption by the House of Commons of a resolution authorizing its issue, the Senate has not adopted such a resolution and if, at any time after the expiration of that period, the House of Commons again adopts the resolution.

13. Part VI of the said Act is repealed and the following substituted therefor:

PART VI

CONSTITUTIONAL CONFERENCES

Constitutional conference

50. (1) A constitutional conference composed of the Prime Minister of Canada and the first ministers of the provinces shall be convened by the Prime Minister of Canada at least once a year, commencing in 1988.

Agenda

(2) The conferences convened under subsection (1) shall have included on their agenda the following matters:

(a) Senate reform, including the role and functions of the Senate, its powers, the method of selecting Senators and representation in the Senate;

(b) roles and responsibilities in relation to fisheries; and

(c) such other matters as are agreed upon.

14. Subsection 52(2) of the said Act is amended by striking out the word 'and' at the end of paragraph (b) thereof, by adding the word 'and' at the end of the paragraph (c) thereof and by adding thereto the following paragraph:

(d) any other amendment to the Constitution of Canada.

15. Section 61 of the said Act is repealed and the following substituted therefor:

References

61. A reference to the *Constitution Act, 1982*, or a reference to the *Constitution Acts 1867 to 1982*, shall be deemed to include a reference to any amendments thereto.

GENERAL

16. Nothing in section 2 of the *Constitution Act, 1867* affects section 25 or 27 of the *Canadian Charter of Rights and Freedoms*, section 35 of the *Constitution Act, 1982* or class 24 of section 91 of the *Constitution Act, 1867*.

CITATION

Citation

17. This amendment may be cited as the *Constitution Amendment, 1987*.

Appendix F

Writing a Term Paper

Instructors vary considerably in what they expect from student term papers. The following notes are therefore intended to provide guidelines which can be adapted to fit the requirements of your course and instructor.

1. PAY ATTENTION TO THE SPECIFIC ASSIGNMENT

All term paper assignments are *not* the same. The nature of the assignment will differ across departments within your university, and across courses and instructors within departments. Therefore it is essential to pay close attention to the *specific* assignment. Do not assume that a paper format that has worked well for you in the past will necessarily work this time around.

2. GET AN EARLY START

The sooner you start on the paper assignment, the more likely you are to find research material. Library resources will invariably be strained towards the end of the term. If you give yourself enought lead time, useful material is likely to emerge from newspaper and magazine articles, from other sources, from conversations with friends, and from random thoughts and observations that you might have.

3. SOURCES

There are a number of leads that can be pursued in trying to locate research material for your paper. Use the suggested readings in this and other recent texts, and work backward from the footnotes. Use the card catalogue in your library. Use the *Canadian Periodicals Index*, and go through the recent and as yet unindexed issues of journals such as the *Canadian Journal of Political Science, Canadian Public Policy*, and the *Journal of Canadian Studies*. Keep a close eye on the newspapers, and on magazines such as *Maclean's, Saturday Night*, and *Canadian Forum*. When you find one useful source, plunder its footnotes and bibliography from other leads.

4. DO NOT REINVENT THE WHEEL

Your paper should draw upon the existing social science literature, as a term paper in an introductory course can carry only a limited amount of original research. What counts is your ability to apply existing knowledge and theories to the particular subject under examination in your paper.

5. CREATE A MEMORY BANK

Set up a file folder or large envelope for each assignment you face during the term. Then, whenever you have a thought or insight into the assignment, whenever you encounter a possible source of research material, jot it down on a piece of paper and file it away in the folder or envelope. Whenever you encounter something that might be useful, be it in a text, journal article or newspaper, take notes (including the source of the information) and file them away. All the relevant material for each assignment will then be gathered together in one place, ready to be dumped out on your desk when the writing begins. Less material will be lost from a paper memory than from a mental one.

6. RESPECT DEADLINES AND PAGE LIMITS

Take deadlines seriously, and frame your assignment within the page limits set by your instructor. After all, in the "real world" projects have to be done on time and within specified limits. If you are asked for a fifteen-page synopsis by Friday, your employer will not expect a thirty-page synopsis by the following Thursday.

7. WRITE *AT LEAST* TWO DRAFTS

Do not expect to produce a good paper on the first draft. Allow enough time that you can write a rough draft and let it sit for a few days. Then go through the draft as dispassionately as possible, pretending, if you like, that someone else wrote it. Rewrite the sections that are rough, add in new material, and correct problems of style, substance, and interpretation. Remember that rewriting in the early stages often entails substantial reorganization of the material, not merely correcting spelling and grammatical errors. Writing is a cognitive process, a way of thinking about your material and discovering what you want to say. Thus do not be surprised if your paper changes considerably from one draft to the next.

8. A RESEARCH PAPER IS NOT AN ESSAY

A research paper must do more than present your own viewpoint. It should explore a particular theme or question through a marshalling of the available evidence. While it is acceptable to be argumentative, you should not stray beyond the bounds of the existing evidence. The argument should be derived from the evidence, or at least supported by it, rather than an expression of one's own beliefs.

9. THE THEMATIC STRUCTURE

A good paper pursues an explicit theme or thesis. This should be laid out as early as possible, perhaps in the introductory paragraph. The main body of the paper should then develop this thesis or theme, and the concluding paragraph should link back to the introductory paragraph. There is, then, a circular structure to the paper: you state what it is you intend to do, you go out and do it, and then you conclude by summarizing what you did, answering the questions posed in your introductory paragraph.

10. PAY ATTENTION TO STYLE AND ORGANIZATION

In the famous words of Marshall McLuhan, "the medium is the message." How you communicate your ideas will have a critical impact on their reception. Do not expect your instructor to sift through awkward sentences, indifferent organization, and a sloppy style searching for intellectual gold. Good ideas poorly presented are indistinguishable from poor ideas poorly presented.

11. DO NOT RUSH TO THE ATTACK

It is relatively easy and at times satisfying to attack, to condemn and deplore. However, while a moralistic stance *may* enrich a paper, your primary task is to *understand* the phenomenon, event, or personality under investigation. Why did something happen? What were the alternatives? Why were some options pursued and others avoided? Once you understand the complexities of the issue, then and only then are you in a position to render some judgment.

12. AVOID LOADED WORDS

Be careful in your use of words like genocide, lie, murder, deceive, catastrophic, and disaster. Strong words in a research paper are analogous to swear words in more common discourse; if overused, they lose their impact. If you call something a disaster, be sure that you really mean a *disaster* and not merely an unfortunate or unpleasant event. Readers are more impressed by firm but *reasonable* statements supported by evidence than by fervently held beliefs expressed in highly charged language.

13. DO NOT PLAGIARIZE

To plagiarize means to pass off the words *or ideas* of others as your own. In many schools, plagiarism can lead to automatic failure and even expulsion. If you use the words of other writers, enclose them within quotation marks and provide their source in a footnote. If you paraphrase other writers, you must still indicate the source of the material. There is no problem in using the work of other people, and indeed this is what much of the research enterprise is all about—building upon an existing body of knowledge and insights. However, where the work of others is used, *it must be acknowledged.*

14. PARAGRAPHING

A good paragraph has its own internal structure and coherency. It explores a single theme or issue, and the break between paragraphs is used to signify a shift in analysis or emphasis. (A good check on the coherence of a paragraph is to read the first and last sentences; they should make sense together and should contain the essence of the paragraph.) Be wary of very long paragraphs—I once received a paper with a paragraph that stretched over five and a half pages! Paragraphs of over a page in length suggest an indifference on the part of the writer to organization.

15. SUBHEADINGS

Subheadings can be used to impose an organizational structure upon your paper. They break up the paper into more easily digested chunks, and convey the impression that you have paid attention to the structural form and coherency of your argument. It is essential, however, to provide some transition between the sections of your paper. Subheadings emphasize points of transition; they do not provide a substitute for transitions in the body of your text.

16. DO NOT ASSUME SHARED KNOWLEDGE

Students are often unsure whether to include information that they feel will be "obvious" to the marker. Often when I have criticized students for failing to include certain information, they have replied "I just assumed you knew that." The problem is that it is difficult for a marker to assume that the writer indeed knows information that is not contained in the paper. You may well assume that I know that John A. Macdonald was the leader of the Conservative party, but I have less grounds for assuming that you know. Therefore it pays to err on the side of including what you may assume to be shared or common knowledge. Write less for your instructor than for some other, impartial audience that is not privy to what has gone on in your course.

17. AVOID LONG QUOTES

Excessively long quotes suggest an overreliance on the work of others, and a reluctance on the writer's part to come to grips with the ideas behind the quote. Your job, after all, goes well beyond *presenting* the works of others. When quotes of more than one sentence in length are used, they should be set off from the main body of the paragraph and they should be introduced. Phrases like "As Smith has observed..." and "Jones elaborates upon this point at some length" can be useful in introducing long quotes.

18. AVOID TERMINOLOGICAL CONFUSION

A good argument can be obscured by terminological confusion. Be careful, for example, not to confuse Parliament with the Government of Canada, or French Canadians with the Québécois, or Nova Scotia with the Government of Nova Scotia. Be sure to define the key terms and concepts in your paper. In doing so, do not rely on an English language dictionary. A dictionary of political science or an encyclopedia of social sciences provides a much better source.

19. FOOTNOTES

Footnotes provide the linkage between your text and the research material that you have employed. Whatever footnote style you adopt—and some institutions specify a particular format—apply it consistently. Footnotes are not peripheral to a good research paper; they are an intrinsic part of it and should not be passed over lightly. It should be possible for a reader to reconstruct the paper from the footnotes, and thus to verify your findings.

20. BIBLIOGRAPHY

A bibliography should be included to acknowledge the sources that you consulted, and in particular those sources that have been of general use but to which specific reference has not been made either in the text or in the footnotes. Do not pad your bibliography by throwing in material that you have *not* looked at.

21. END WITH AN EMPHATIC CONCLUSION

Avoid a paper that fizzles out at the end, that creates the impression that you ran out of things to say and just stopped. The conclusion should not simply review the main points in the paper. It should tie the paper together, looping back to the introduction in order to demonstrate that you have done what you set out to do. Admittedly, a conclusion is often not easy to write, but it is the conclusion that pulls the research enterprise together and answers the question, "so what?"

22. HAND-WRITTEN PAPERS

Most universities and colleges have regulations which state that students are not to penalized for hand-written papers. The fact remains, however, that poor handwriting will lessen the impact of your paper. If the reader has to struggle through, word by word and sentence by sentence, there is a good chance that at the end of the paper he or she will have little appreciation of the paper's broader theme and argument. Poor handwriting *will* hurt you, no mater how hard the marker tries to keep to the spirit of institutional regulations.

23. PROOFREAD

Always proofread your paper and, better still, have a friend do it also. Pay particular attention to grammar and spelling, and to the agreement between subjects and verbs. A paper that has not been proofread suggests sloppiness and indifference on the part of the author. A careful proofreading ensures that your paper is as good as it can be, that the marker will not be distracted from your argument and ideas by a progression of typos, spelling mistakes, and grammatical errors.

24. GOOD LUCK!

Glossary

Asbestos Strike. In 1949 a prolonged strike by Quebec asbestos miners in Asbestos and Thetford Mines provided a highly publicized stage for a confrontation between Quebec trade unions and reform-minded intellectuals (including P.E. Trudeau) on the one side and the Union Nationale provincial government on the other. Retrospectively, the Asbestos strike is seen as one of the first signs of the Quiet Revolution.

"Better Terms." Regional discontent in the Maritimes has been associated with the search for "better terms." The reference is to adjustments in the financial terms under which the Maritime provinces entered Confederation rather than to other constitutional parameters such as the federal division of powers.

Canada West Foundation. The Canada West Foundation was established in 1973 as a non-profit and non-partisan organization to pursue two objectives: (1) to conduct economic, social, and political research on western Canadian concerns, and (2) to conduct informational and educational programs encouraging an appreciation of the Canadian heritage, and of the role played by the West in Canada. Based in Calgary, the Foundation is supported by governments, corporations, and individuals in western Canada.

Conditional Grant Programs. Conditional grant programs came into use in the 1950s and early 1960s. Through such programs Ottawa provided matching funds to the provinces for health care, advanced education, and social assistance programs administered by the provincial governments. Although such programs fell within provincial jurisdiction, the federal government was able to impose national standards as a condition for the receipt of federal funding. In this sense conditional grant programs represented the fiscal intrusion of the national government into provincial fields of jurisdiction.

Co-operative Commonwealth Federation. The Co-operative Commonwealth Federation (Farmer, Labour, Socialist) was formed at the 1932 Calgary meeting of delegates from farm, labour, and socialist organizations in the West, and to a lesser extent from labour organizations and left-of-centre intellectuals in the East. The CCF's platform, set forth in the 1933 Regina Manifesto, was emphatically socialistic, calling for the public ownership of banks and trust companies, insurance companies, utilities, and "all other industries and services essential to social planning."

Crown Lands. All land in Canada which is not privately owned by individuals or corporations belongs to the Crown. Thus the term "Crown land" refers to land owned by the Government of Canada or by one of the ten provincial governments.

Disallowance. Under the terms of the Constitution Act, 1867, the federal government can "disallow" provincial legislation, or prevent it from coming into effect, up to one year after its passage. Disallowance can occur even if the legislation falls wholly within the province's jurisdictional domain. Last used in 1943, disallowance has now become a constitutional dead letter.

Equalization Payments. Equalization payments are unconditional grants from the national governments to those provinces whose yield from provincial tax sources is less than the average yield of all provinces. They are designed to ensure that Canadians, no matter where they live, will have access to approximately the same level of public services provided at roughly the same level of taxation.

Great Depression. The 1929 collapse of the American stock market signalled the onset of a prolonged economic depression that lasted until the start of the Second World War and afflicted all industrialized countries. Per capita income in Canada fell by 50 percent, export prices fell to a fraction of 1929 prices, and the number of unemployed rose from 107,000 in 1929 to 646,000 at the height of the Depression in 1933. In western Canada the Depression's impact was intensified by ruinous agricultural markets, drought, and crop infestation.

Judicial Committee of the Privy Council. Under the terms of Great Britain's Colonial Laws Validity Act, the Judicial Committee of the Privy Council served as Canada's court of final appeal. Canadian court decisions, including those of the Supreme Court, could thus be appealed to the JCPC in London. This right of appeal was finally abolished in 1949 by the Supreme Court Act which established the Supreme Court of Canada as the court of final appeal.

National Policy. The National Policy is most closely associated with the protective tariffs adopted by the Government of Canada in 1878, tariffs designed to protect an infant Canadian manufacturing base and to encourage foreign investment. The tariffs were also designed to raise public funds for the construction of a transcontinental railway system, and to ensure sufficient east–west trade on that railway system. More generally, the National Policy is associated with the industrialization of central Canada and the agricultural settlement of the West.

Neoconservatism. Neoconservatism encompasses a number of beliefs which arose in reaction to the postwar growth of government. These include the belief that the size of government should be reduced, that government regulation of the economy should be reduced, and that the private market should be restored as the primary vehicle for the distribution of wealth and economic opportunity.

North-West Rebellion, 1885. In the spring of 1885 several hundred Métis from settlements along the South Saskatchewan River, led by Louis Riel, took up arms against the Canadian government. The rebellion ended at Batoche, Saskatchewan, where the Métis and a small number of Indians faced roughly one thousand recently mobilized Canadian troops. Approximately one hundred men lost their lives, and Riel was subsequently executed.

October Crisis. The 1970 October Crisis was touched off by the kidnapping of James Cross, the British trade commissioner in Montreal, by a cell of the *Front de Libération du Québec* (FLQ). The crisis escalated with the kidnapping of Pierre Laporte, Quebec's Minister of Labour, the imposition of the War Measures Act by the federal government, and the murder of Laporte. The crisis ended with the release of Cross in early December.

Pacific Scandal. The financial entanglements of John A. MacDonald and his Conservative party with the backers of the proposed Canadian Pacific Railway came to light in the Pacific Scandal of 1873–74. The scandal led to the Conservatives' defeat in the 1874 general election.

Paramountcy. Section 95 of the Constitution Act, 1867, gives Parliament and the provincial legislatures concurrent powers with respect to agriculture and immigration. However, should provincial and federal legislation conflict, Parliament is held to be paramount and the federal law to prevail: "any law of the Legislature of a Province relative to Agriculture or to Immigration shall have effect . . . as long and as far only as it is not repugnant to any Act of the Parliament of Canada."

Remedial Legislation. Section 93.3 of the Constitution Act, 1867, gives Parliament the power to pass remedial legislation should a province make laws "affecting any Right or Privilege of the Protestant or Roman Catholic Minority of the Queen's Subjects in relation to Education." In this narrow sense, Parliament is permitted to legislate within a provincial field of jurisdiction.

Residual Powers. At the time that a constitution is written there will inevitably be powers that are not enumerated and responsibilities for which the constitution writer cannot be aware. For example, the allocation of powers in Sections 91 and 92 of the Constitution Act does not cover such contemporary concerns as cable television and nuclear wastes. Federal constitutions thus contain a provision which assigns residual powers, or the power to deal with unforeseen eventualities, to one level of government or the other. In the Canadian case, residual powers are covered in part by the Peace, Order and Good Government clause of Section 91.

Royal Commissions. Royal Commissions are appointed by the Government of Canada or by provincial governments to investigate specific problems or policy issues. They are not legislative bodies; their responsibility is to make appropriate recommendations for government action. Although in most cases Royal Commissions have quite restricted mandates, at times their scope can be very extensive, as the Royal Commission on the Economic Union and Development Prospects for Canada illustrates.

Social Gospel. The movement for social reform which arose within Protestant churches during the early part of this century came to be known as the Social Gospel. Its proponents argued that individuals trapped by destitution could not be expected to lead virtuous lives, and thus that social reform was a necessary precondition for saving souls. The Social Gospel was a particularly active force in western Canada, where it was closely associated with the agrarian revolt of the early 1920s.

War Measures Act. The War Measures Act gives the federal cabinet virtually unlimited powers in times of war or invasion, and in times of "real or apprehended insurrection." It served as a fundamental instrument of government during the First and Second World Wars, and was invoked in a more limited form during the 1970 October Crisis. The Act allows the national government to put aside temporarily the federal division of powers and permits widespread restrictions on individual freedoms.

Winnipeg General Strike, 1919. Canada's only general strike began in Winnipeg in May 1919, with a strike in the metal and building trades over wages and union recognition. The Winnipeg Trades and Labour Council then called for a general strike in support of the metal and building trades. The city was all but paralyzed in a six-week strike. The strike climaxed with, and was brought to a close by, a clash between parading strikers and police on "Bloody Sunday," June 21, in which two people were killed and scores injured.

Index